D0984480

HISTORICAL DICTIONARIES OF U.S. DIPLOMACY
Edited by Jon Woronoff

1. *U.S. Diplomacy from the Civil War to World War I*, by Kenneth J. Blume, 2005.
2. *United States–China Relations*, by Robert Sutter, 2006.
3. *United States–Latin American Relations*, by Joseph Smith, 2007.
4. *United States–Japan Relations*, by John Van Sant, Peter Mauch, and Yoneyuki Sugita, 2007.

Historical Dictionary of United States– Latin American Relations

Joseph Smith

Historical Dictionaries of U.S. Diplomacy, No. 3

The Scarecrow Press, Inc.
Lanham, Maryland • Toronto • Plymouth, UK
2007

SCARECROW PRESS, INC.

Published in the United States of America
by Scarecrow Press, Inc.
A wholly owned subsidiary of
The Rowman & Littlefield Publishing Group, Inc.
4501 Forbes Boulevard, Suite 200, Lanham, Maryland 20706
www.scarecrowpress.com

Estover Road
Plymouth PL6 7PY
United Kingdom

British Library Cataloguing in Publication Information Available

Library of Congress Cataloging-in-Publication Data

Smith, Joseph, 1945–
    Historical dictionary of United States–Latin American relations / Joseph Smith.
    p. cm. — (Historical dictionaries of U.S. diplomacy ; no. 3)
    Includes bibliographical references.
    ISBN-13: 978-0-8108-5529-8 (hardcover : alk. paper)
    ISBN-10: 0-8108-5529-1 (hardcover : alk. paper)
    1. Latin America—Foreign relations—United States—Dictionaries. 2. United
States—Foreign relations—Latin America—Dictionaries. I. Title.

F1418.S638 2007
327.7308—dc22

2006028403

∞™ The paper used in this publication meets the minimum requirements of
American National Standard for Information Sciences—Permanence of Paper
for Printed Library Materials, ANSI/NISO Z39.48-1992.
Manufactured in the United States of America.

Contents

Editor's Foreword   *Jon Woronoff*   vii

Acknowledgments   ix

Reader's Note   xi

Acronyms and Abbreviations   xiii

Map   xv

Chronology   xvii

Introduction   xxix

THE DICTIONARY   1

Appendixes

  A. U.S. Presidents and Secretaries of State, 1789–2006   237

  B. Extracts from Selected Presidential Statements on
  United States–Latin American Policy   243

Bibliography   251

About the Author   277

Editor's Foreword

Considering that Latin America is, in a sense, the "backyard" of the United States, one might expect this to be a region characterized by particularly intense relations. Yet Latin America is largely forgotten and usually considered of distinctly less interest in the whirl of diplomatic activity surrounding Europe, the Middle East, or Asia—that is, unless something goes wrong or is so perceived by policymakers in Washington. As for the Latin Americans themselves, while they periodically hanker after closer relations with their northern neighbor, they are often quite happy to be ignored because when they are not, they may face a scolding—or worse. Yet this is a potentially and sometimes actually rich region, with many natural resources and not yet overpopulated and with, in many ways, a similar background and culture. Moreover, the Latin American population of the United States keeps growing. Thus, even while studying the numerous initiatives that have occurred over the past decades, it is also necessary to ask just why U.S.–Latin American relations have been so limited and, on the whole, so inadequate and awkward.

The task of *Historical Dictionary of United States–Latin American Relations* is not explicitly to explain these contradictions, but it certainly does help toward a better understanding of the situation by providing a wealth of information. This it achieves, among other things, through a broad survey of relations in a general introduction covering the period from earliest times to the present. The salient events are followed from year to year in the chronology. But the bulk of the material is provided in several hundred entries on all the countries involved (those in Latin America) and many specific ones on the United States and even on the former colonial powers and other interlopers. Many other entries deal with significant events, major crises and the occasional rapprochement, the doctrines and policies that have evolved, the institutions that have been established, and especially the nagging issues that have preoccupied policymakers in the past and still do today. The bibliography then points to other relevant literature.

This volume is written by Joseph Smith, a specialist on American foreign relations, in particular with Latin America, although he is also an expert on the Cold War. At present, Dr. Smith is a member of the Department of History at Exeter University in England. He has written numerous articles and several books on Latin America and the United States and also authored, with Simon Davis, *Historical Dictionary of the Cold War*. This was all very good training for the most recent exercise and definitely helps us understand just why this potentially important relationship has so far failed to bear the hoped-for fruit.

Jon Woronoff
Series Editor

Acknowledgments

I wish to thank Jon Woronoff, the series editor, for asking me to write this book and for reviewing it in manuscript form. I am also grateful to Martin Hoare for providing the map. As always, my greatest debt is to Rachael for her patience and encouragement.

The list of U.S. presidents and secretaries of state in appendix A is used by permission of Eve Cary and originally appeared in *Historical Dictionary of United States–China Relations* by Robert Sutter.

Reader's Note

This volume concentrates on the history of diplomatic relations between the United States and the nations of Latin America from the creation of the independent United States in the late 18th century to the present. Another historical dictionary in this series is intended to deal with U.S. relations with the countries of the Caribbean. Consequently, this volume covers U.S. policy toward those specific countries forming the mainland of the Western Hemisphere. Reference is made to Cuba and the Dominican Republic insofar as events in and leading figures representing those nations affected inter-American relations more broadly.

In the dictionary section a word, term, or name in bold print indicates that there is an alphabetical entry for further reading. Names can be looked up under the last name. Cross-references for Spanish names—which might have two surnames, the father's name first, mother's second—will be listed under either the first or second surname.

Acronyms and Abbreviations

ABC	Argentina, Brazil, Chile
AID	Agency for International Development
ALCA	Área de Libre Comercio de las Américas
APRA	Alianza Popular Revolucionaria Americana (Popular Revolutionary Alliance Party)
CACM	Central American Common Market
CEPAL	Comisión Económica para América Latina
CIA	Central Intelligence Agency
DEA	Drug Enforcement Administration
EAI	Enterprise for the Americas Initiative
ECLA	Economic Commission for Latin America
ECLAC	Economic Commission for Latin America and the Caribbean
ERP	European Recovery Program (Marshall Plan)
EXIM	Export-Import Bank
FBI	Federal Bureau of Investigation
FEB	Força Expeditionária Brasileira (Brazilian Expeditionary Force)
FMLN	Frente Farabundo Martí para la Liberación Nacional (Farabundo Martí National Liberation Front)
FSLN	Frente Sandinista de Liberación Nacional (Sandinista National Liberation Front)
FTAA	Free Trade Area of the Americas
GATT	General Agreement on Tariffs and Trade
IADB	Inter-American Defense Board
IAPF	Inter-American Peace Force
IBRD	International Bank for Reconstruction and Development (also known as the World Bank)
IMF	International Monetary Fund

IPC	International Petroleum Company
LAFTA	Latin American Free Trade Association
MERCOSUR	Common Market of the South
MNR	Movimento Nacional Revolucionario (National Revolutionary Movement)
NAFTA	North American Free Trade Agreement
NATO	North Atlantic Treaty Organization
NSC	National Security Council
OAS	Organization of American States
OCIAA	Office of Coordinator of Inter-American Affairs
PAU	Pan-American Union
UFCO	United Fruit Company
UN	United Nations
U.S.	United States
USS	United States Ship

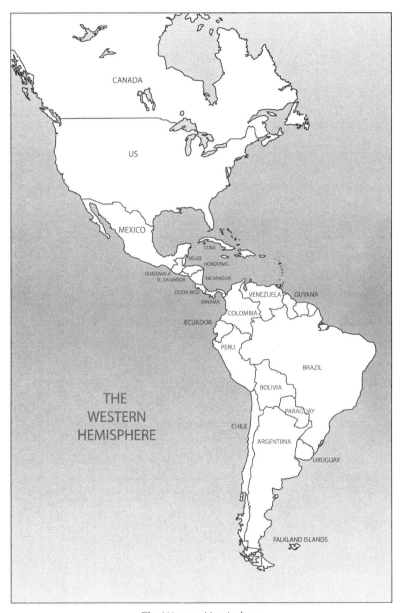

CANADA

US

MEXICO

CUBA

BELIZE

HONDURAS

GUATEMALA

EL SALVADOR

NICARAGUA

COSTA RICO

PANAMA

VENEZUELA

GUYANA

COLOMBIA

ECUADOR

PERU

BRAZIL

BOLIVIA

PARAGUAY

THE
WESTERN
HEMISPHERE

CHILE

ARGENTIINA

URUGUAY

FALKLAND ISLANDS

The Western Hemisphere

Chronology

1776 **July 4:** U.S. Declaration of Independence.

1783 **September 3:** Treaty of Paris between Great Britain and the United States recognizes the independence of the United States of America.

1787 **September 17:** U.S. Constitution is signed.

1789 **April 30:** George Washington inaugurated as first president of the U.S. **July 14:** French Revolution begins with the sacking of the Bastille.

1796 **September 18:** Publication of President George Washington's Farewell Address.

1803 **April 30:** U.S. government makes Louisiana Purchase from France.

1806 **June–August:** British naval expedition to Buenos Aires is defeated.

1808 **May 10:** Ferdinand VII, king of Spain, is forced to abdicate in favor of Napoleon Bonaparte's brother, Joseph Bonaparte. **September 25:** Anti-French junta formed in Spain.

1810 **May 25:** Formation of a revolutionary junta in Buenos Aires marks beginning of the wars for Latin American independence. Revolts also take place in Venezuela, Mexico, and Chile.

1811 **January 11:** U.S. Congress passes No-Transfer Resolution. **July 5:** Venezuela declares independence from Spain.

1814 Ferdinand VII restored as king of Spain.

1815 **September 26:** European monarchs form Holy Alliance.

1819 February 22: Signing of Adams-Onís Treaty between the United States and Spain. **August 19:** After leading his army across the Andes, Simón Bolívar defeats royalist forces at the Battle of Boyacá.

1821 February 14: Spain ratifies Adams-Onís Treaty.

1822 January: American settlers under Stephen Austin establish settlements in Texas. **June 19:** President James Monroe receives the Colombian chargé d'affaires and recognizes the independence of the Republic of Colombia. **October 12:** Brazil formally proclaims itself independent of Portugal.

1823 September: Bolívar enters Lima, Peru, and is recognized as dictator. **December 2:** In his Annual Message to Congress, President James Monroe enunciates a U.S. policy that later becomes known as the Monroe Doctrine.

1824 December 9: Spanish army defeated at Battle of Ayacucho, Peru.

1826 January 23: Surrender of royalist garrison in Callao, Peru, marks formal end of the wars for Latin American independence. **June 22–July 15:** Panama Congress meets at invitation of Bolívar.

1830 December 17: Death of Bolívar at Santa Marta, Venezuela.

1833 January 1: Great Britain takes possession of the Falkland Islands.

1836 March 2: Texas proclaims itself independent of Mexico. **April 21:** General Antonio López de Santa Anna is defeated and captured by Texans at Battle of San Jacinto.

1838 November: French forces occupy Veracruz, Mexico.

1845 March 1: U.S. Congress passes resolution to annex Texas to the United States. **December 2:** President James K. Polk issues his corollary to the Monroe Doctrine. Term "Manifest Destiny" appears in U.S. press.

1846 April 25: Clash between U.S. and Mexican forces marks beginning of the Mexican-American War. **December:** Bidlack Treaty signed between the United States and New Granada (Colombia).

1847 **September 14:** U.S. forces capture Mexico City. Caste War occurs in Yucatán.

1848 **February 2:** Treaty of Guadalupe Hidalgo ends the Mexican-American War.

1850 **April 19:** Clayton-Bulwer Treaty signed between the United States and Great Britain.

1853 **December 30:** Gadsden Purchase, in which Mexico sells additional territory to the United States.

1855 William Walker invades Nicaragua in filibustering expedition. Completion of construction of the U.S.-owned Panama Railroad across the Isthmus of Panama.

1860 **September 12:** Walker executed in Honduras.

1861 **April:** U.S. Civil War begins.

1862 French Intervention in Mexico begins.

1864 **April 10:** Archduke Maximilian of Austria crowned emperor of Mexico.

1865 **March 18:** Beginning of the War of the Triple Alliance between Argentina, Brazil, and Uruguay against Paraguay. **April:** U.S. Civil War ends. French troops begin withdrawal from Mexico.

1867 **June 19:** Execution of Archduke Maximilian in Mexico.

1868 Publication of legal studies by Carlos Calvo containing Calvo Doctrine.

1870 **March 1:** War of the Triple Alliance ends in defeat for Paraguay.

1877 **May 2:** Porfirio Diaz becomes president of Mexico.

1879 **April:** Beginning of the War of the Pacific between Bolivia and Peru against Chile. **May:** Paris International Congress approves Panama as best route for Central American canal. **August:** French Canal Company is organized with Ferdinand de Lesseps as its president.

1880 **March 8:** President Rutherford B. Hayes delivers Special Message to U.S. Congress on the Panama Canal. **December:** French Canal Company begins work on Panama Canal.

1883 **October 20:** Signing of the Treaty of Ancón ends fighting between Chile and Peru in the War of the Pacific.

1889 **October 2–April 19, 1890:** International American Conference (First Pan-American Conference) convenes in Washington. **November 15:** Military coup deposes Emperor Pedro II and establishes a republic in Brazil.

1890 **April 14:** International American Conference establishes Bureau of American Republics. 14 April designated as annual "Pan-American Day." **October 1:** McKinley Tariff becomes law and includes an amendment empowering the president to negotiate commercial reciprocity arrangements with foreign nations.

1891 **April 1:** Reciprocity arrangement between the United States and Brazil comes into effect. **October 16:** Attack on U.S. sailors from the USS *Baltimore* in Valparaíso, Chile.

1892 French Canal Company becomes bankrupt and ends construction work at Panama. **January 25:** President Benjamin Harrison demands official apology and financial compensation for injuries to U.S. sailors resulting from the "Baltimore Affair."

1893 **September:** Brazilian Naval Revolt begins.

1894 **March:** Brazilian Naval Revolt ends. **August:** Passage of the Wilson Tariff terminates reciprocity arrangements negotiated by the U.S. government under the McKinley Tariff.

1895 **July 20:** Secretary of State Richard Olney sends note to London concerning Venezuela Boundary Dispute. **December 17:** President Grover Cleveland sends Special Message to Congress insisting that Great Britain submit Venezuelan Boundary Dispute to arbitration; British government complies.

1898 **April–August:** Spanish-American War takes place between the United States and Spain.

1900 Publication of *Ariel* by José Enrique Rodó.

1901 **October 22–January 31, 1902:** Second Pan-American Conference meets in Mexico City. **November 18:** Hay-Pauncefote Treaty signed between the United States and Great Britain to replace 1850 Clayton-Bulwer Treaty.

1902 **December:** Venezuela Incident begins when Great Britain, Germany, and Italy send gunboats to blockade Venezuelan ports. **December 29:** Drago Doctrine communicated to U.S. State Department.

1903 **January 22:** Hay-Herrán Treaty signed between the United States and Colombia. **February:** Great Britain and Germany lift naval blockade of Venezuela. **August:** Colombian Senate refuses to ratify Hay-Herrán Treaty. **November 4:** Independence of Panama declared. **November 10:** United States recognizes independence of Panama. **November 19:** Hay-Bunau-Varilla Treaty signed between the United States and Panama.

1904 **February:** Panama adopts Constitution, which includes right of the United States to intervene to maintain political order. **December 6:** Roosevelt Corollary to the Monroe Doctrine announced in President Theodore Roosevelt's Annual Message to Congress.

1906 **July 23–August 27:** Third Pan-American Conference meets in Rio de Janeiro, Brazil.

1907 **November 14–December 20:** Central American Peace Conference meets in Washington.

1909 U.S. State Department creates a separate Division of Latin American Affairs.

1910 Insurgency against rule of President Porfirio Díaz marks beginning of the Mexican Revolution. **July 12–August 30:** Fourth Pan-American Conference meets in Buenos Aires, Argentina; Buenos Aires Conference approves reorganization of the Bureau of American Republics as the Pan-American Union.

1911 **May 25:** Overthrow of President Porfirio Díaz in Mexico. **November 6:** Francisco Madero elected president of Mexico.

1912 **August:** U.S. marines intervene in Nicaragua to maintain order.

1913 **February 18:** Madero is murdered during military coup in Mexico organized by General Victoriano Huerta. **October 27:** President Woodrow Wilson delivers Mobile Address.

1914 **April 21:** U.S. marines occupy Veracruz, Mexico. **May–June:** Conference at Niagara Falls, Canada, between United States and Mexico as a result of ABC diplomatic mediation. **August 15:** Panama Canal opens to international shipping. **September:** Boundary of U.S. Panama Canal Zone defined. **November 23:** U.S. troops evacuate Veracruz.

1916 **March 9:** Armed incursion by Francisco "Pancho" Villa into Columbus, New Mexico. **March–February 1917:** U.S. forces under General Pershing pursue Villa into northern Mexico.

1917 **January 31:** Mexican Constitution adopted. **March 1:** Publication of Zimmermann Telegram. **April 6:** United States declares war on Germany. **October 26:** Brazil declares war on Germany (the only South American country to do so).

1918 **November 11:** World War I hostilities cease.

1919 **January–June:** Paris Peace Conference. League of Nations established.

1920 **March 19:** U.S. Senate fails to ratify Treaty of Versailles.

1921 **April 20:** U.S. Senate ratifies treaty with Colombia providing compensation for loss of Panama.

1923 **March 25–May 3:** Fifth Pan-American Conference meets in Santiago de Chile.

1926 **May:** U.S. marines sent to Nicaragua to maintain order. **June 14:** Brazil withdraws from the League of Nations.

1927 Arrival of reinforcements of U.S. marines in Nicaragua sparks local guerrilla resistance led by Augusto Sandino.

1928 **January 16–February 20:** Sixth Pan-American Conference meets in Havana, Cuba. **November–December:** President-elect Herbert Hoover makes 10-week visit to Central and South America.

1929 **June 3:** Chile and Peru settle the Tacna-Arica Dispute.

1930 **March 31:** Publication of the Clark Memorandum on the Monroe Doctrine.

1932 Chaco War between Bolivia and Paraguay begins.

1933   **March 4:** In his Inaugural Address, President Franklin D. Roosevelt states that the United States will act as a "good neighbor" in its foreign policy. **December 3–26:** Seventh Pan-American Conference meets in Montevideo, Uruguay.

1934   **February 21:** Murder of Augusto Sandino in Nicaragua.

1935   **June 14:** Bolivia and Paraguay agree to a truce in the Chaco War.

1936   **December 1–23:** Inter-American Conference on the Maintenance of Peace meets in Buenos Aires, Argentina.

1938   **March 18:** Mexican government nationalizes the properties of U.S. oil companies. **December 9–27:** Eighth Pan-American Conference meets in Lima, Peru.

1939   **September 23–October 3:** Inter-American Conference of Foreign Ministers meets in Panama City: Declaration of Panama declares a safety zone around the Western Hemisphere.

1940   **July 21–30:** Inter-American Conference of Foreign Ministers meets in Havana, Cuba: Havana Conference approves No Transfer principle.

1941   **March 11:** U.S. Congress passes Lend-Lease Act. **September:** United States and Mexico agree to compromise over compensation for nationalization of U.S. oil companies. **December 7:** Japanese attack on Pearl Harbor brings United States into World War II.

1942   **January 15–28:** Inter-American Conference of Foreign Ministers meets in Rio de Janeiro, Brazil. **March:** Inter-American Defense Board established. **August 22:** Brazil joins World War II.

1943   **January 29:** President Franklin D. Roosevelt meets President Getúlio Vargas in Brazil. **June 5:** Military coup takes place in Argentina and results in a new government that includes Colonel Juan Perón.

1944   **October:** Guatemalan Revolution begins. **December:** Juan José Arévalo becomes president of Guatemala.

1945   **February 21–March 28:** Inter-American Conference on the Problems of War and Peace meets in Chapultepec Palace, Mexico City, and approves the Act of Chapultepec. **March 27:** Argentina declares war on Germany and Japan. **August 15:** World War II ends.

1946 **February 24:** Perón elected president of Argentina despite U.S. criticism that he had been a Nazi sympathizer during World War II.

1947 **August 15–September 2:** Inter-American Conference on the Preservation of Hemispheric Peace and Security meets in Rio de Janeiro, Brazil, and is attended by President Harry Truman; Rio Conference approves the Inter-American Treaty of Reciprocal Assistance or Rio Treaty.

1948 **March 30–May 2:** Ninth Pan-American Conference meets in Bogotá, Colombia; Bogotá Conference approves the Charter of the Organization of American States (OAS).

1950 **June 25:** Korean War begins. **November:** Jacobo Arbenz elected president of Guatemala.

1952 **April:** Bolivian Revolution begins. **June:** Guatemalan President Arbenz signs Agrarian Reform Bill.

1953 **July 27:** Korean War armistice announced.

1954 **March 1–28:** Tenth Pan-American Conference meets in Caracas, Venezuela. **June 18–27:** Overthrow of Guatemalan President Arbenz in Central Intelligence Agency (CIA)-backed Operation PBSUCCESS. Colonel Castillo Armas becomes president.

1957 **July 26:** Guatemalan President Castillo Armas is assassinated.

1958 **May:** Vice President Richard Nixon makes "goodwill visit" to Argentina, Peru, and Venezuela. Brazilian President Juscelino Kubitschek proposes economic program known as "Operation Pan-America."

1959 **January:** Fidel Castro takes power in Cuba.

1961 Formation of the Sandinista National Liberation Front (FSLN) in Nicaragua. **March 13:** President John F. Kennedy announces Alliance for Progress. **April 17–20:** CIA-backed Operation Zapata fails at Bay of Pigs, Cuba. **August 5–17:** Alliance for Progress Charter drawn up at Inter-American Conference held in Punta del Este, Uruguay. **August 25:** Jânio Quadros resigns as president of Brazil. **September 7:** Vice President João Goulart becomes president of Brazil.

1962 **January 23–31:** Organization of American States (OAS) foreign ministers meeting at San José, Costa Rica, confirm that Cuba has excluded itself from OAS activities. **October 15–28:** Cuban Missile Crisis occurs.

1963   November 22: President John F. Kennedy assassinated in Dallas, Texas.

1964   January: Anti-American riots in Panama. **March 31–April 2:** João Goulart overthrown in military coup in Brazil. **July 21–26:** Organization of American States (OAS) Conference approves economic embargo and the breaking of diplomatic relations with Cuba.

1965   April–May: U.S. military intervention in Dominican Republic.

1967   October 8: Death of Che Guevara in Bolivia.

1969   September 4: Guerrillas kidnap U.S. Ambassador C. Burke Elbrick in Brazil.

1970   September 4: Salvador Allende wins presidential election in Chile.

1973   September 11: Allende killed in military coup in Chile led by General Augusto Pinochet.

1975   November: Church Committee issues its Report on Governmental Operations with Respect to Intelligence Activities.

1976   March 1976–1979: "Dirty War" occurs in Argentina. **September 21:** Chilean political exile, Orlando Letelier, is killed by car bomb in Washington, D.C.

1977   January: President Jimmy Carter announces that observation of human rights will be a priority of his administration. **September 7:** Signing by President Jimmy Carter and General Omar Torrijos of the Panama Canal Treaties between the United States and Panama.

1978   March: President Carter visits Brazil. **April:** U.S. Senate ratifies Panama Canal Treaties.

1979   July 16: President Anastasio Somoza Debayle leaves Nicaragua to go into exile. **July 18:** Junta of National Reconstruction, including Sandinistas, assumes government in Nicaragua.

1980   Formation of the Farabundo Martí National Liberation Front (FMLN) in El Salvador.

1981   President Ronald Reagan orders massive increase in U.S. military aid to government of El Salvador and terminates U.S. financial aid to Sandinista government in Nicaragua. CIA organizes army of counterrevolutionaries known as the "Contras" to destabilize Sandinista government in Nicaragua.

1982   **April–June:** South Atlantic War between Argentina and Great Britain over possession of Falkland Islands. **August:** Mexico suspends servicing of foreign debt and initiates "Debt Crisis." **December:** U.S. Congress passes Boland Amendment.

1983   **January:** Foreign ministers of Mexico, Panama, Venezuela, and Colombia hold a meeting on Contadora Island to discuss means of ending the fighting in Central America.

1985   **October:** Baker Plan issued to relieve Debt Crisis.

1986   **November:** Iran-Contra affair revealed.

1987   **August 7:** Central American Presidents propose the Esquipulas II Accord or Arias Peace Plan to end fighting in Central America.

1988   Contras agree to cease-fire in Nicaragua.

1989   **March:** Brady Plan issued to relieve Debt Crisis. **December 20–January 4, 1990:** Operation Just Cause launched by United States to arrest Panamanian dictator Manuel Noriega.

1990   **February:** Violeta Barrios de Chamorro defeats Sandinista leader, Daniel Ortega, and wins presidential election in Nicaragua. **15 February:** President George H. W. Bush and presidents of Bolivia, Colombia, and Peru sign an agreement in Cartagena, Colombia, to cooperate in suppressing the trade in illegal narcotics. **June:** President Bush launches "Enterprise for the Americas Initiative" envisaging a free trade area covering the Western Hemisphere.

1991   **March 26:** Signing of free trade agreement to establish Mercosur (Mercosul) by Argentina, Brazil, Paraguay, and Uruguay.

1992   **January 16:** Government of El Salvador and Farabundo Martí National Liberation Front (FMLN) agree to end fighting. **June 3–14:** Meeting of the United Nations (UN) Conference on Environment and Development, also known as the Earth Summit, held in Rio de Janeiro,

Brazil. **December 17:** Mexico signs North American Free Trade Agreement (NAFTA).

1993   May 27: Canada formally approves North American Free Trade Agreement (NAFTA). **November:** U.S. Congress ratifies NAFTA.

1994   December 9–11: First Summit of the Americas meets in Miami, Florida. Attended by President Bill Clinton.

1997   October: President Clinton visits Venezuela, Brazil, and Argentina.

1998   April 18–19: Second Summit of the Americas meets in Santiago de Chile. Attended by President Clinton. **October 16:** Former Chilean dictator General Augusto Pinochet arrested and detained in Great Britain. **October 30:** Hurricane Mitch strikes Nicaragua and causes severe economic damage. **November:** International Environmental Conference held in Buenos Aires, Argentina. **December 6:** Hugo Chávez wins presidential election in Venezuela.

1999   January 15: President Chávez of Venezuela and President Andres Pastrana of Colombia visit Cuba to improve diplomatic relations. **December 31:** United States formally hands over control of the Panama Canal to Panama.

2000   January: Pinochet released from detention in Great Britain. **November:** George W. Bush is elected U.S. president.

2001   April 20–22: Third Summit of the Americas meets in Quebec City, Canada. Attended by President Bush.

2003   January: Lula Inacio da Silva is inaugurated as president of Brazil.

2004   November: George Bush is reelected as U.S. president.

2005   November 4–5: Fourth Summit of the Americas meets in Mar del Plata, Argentina. Attended by President Bush, who later visits Brazil and Panama.

Introduction

Since the achievement of their independence, the historical relationship between the United States and the nations of mainland Latin America has been one of unequals. In terms of political stability, economic achievement, and military power, the United States can be represented as the all-powerful "giant," while the several Latin American nations have been the lesser "pygmies." American military prowess has been convincingly demonstrated in victories in the Mexican-American War (1846–1848) and the Spanish-American War (1898). The huge American economy has made the United States the largest single commercial market and by far the biggest investor in Latin America. In addition, a vibrant society has led to the export of American culture and the phenomenon of "Americanization."

Relations have tended to be more rough than smooth. Notably, the exercise of American diplomacy has often been characterized as being unilateral and one in which prior consultation with Latin American governments about policy initiatives has been rare. From the assertion of the Monroe Doctrine in 1823 to the Reagan Doctrine of the 1980s, the United States has simply presumed a position of political leadership and preeminence in the Western Hemisphere. While American presidents have acknowledged that their country's policy has been motivated by national interest, they have contended that it has also been altruistic in seeking to protect the whole hemisphere from foreign invasion and to promote general economic growth and the advance of democratic government.

Latin American critics have argued that the policy of the United States has frequently been insensitive, aggressive, and imperialistic. They have been particularly incensed by armed interventions, both overt and covert, in their domestic affairs. Political leaders from Simón Bolívar to Hugo Chávez have proposed their own alternative ideal of

Spanish-American political unity that excludes the United States. Some nations such as Argentina have stressed the importance of maintaining close links with Europe and the wider world. Others have tried to form their own separate regional trading blocs. Resistance, however, has been constrained by recognition that the United States was also a world power whose guidance and protection was important during periods of international crisis, such as the two world wars and the Cold War. Moreover, the formation of a united front against the United States has proved impossible because individual Latin American governments have appreciated the value of American diplomatic support, especially in territorial disputes with neighboring states. In addition, there has been the general desire for more trade with the United States and gaining access to what has been the world's largest source of capital investment.

Emerging at the end of World War II with the status of the world's superpower, the United States developed a global foreign policy that included a new and active interest in the affairs of Europe, Southeast Asia, and the Middle East. While U.S. officials still directed close attention to the Middle America–Caribbean region because of its strategic importance, the rest of Latin America was relatively neglected and ignored. At times Latin Americans have complained about American indifference, but in some ways, and in a relationship of unequals, a "sleeping giant" can be preferable to one that is "wide awake."

THE DIPLOMATIC ENVIRONMENT

The mainland countries of the Western Hemisphere can be divided into three broad geographical sections. Starting at the top is North America, which contains Canada and the United States. Middle America ranges from Mexico in the north to Panama in the south and also includes the Central American countries of Guatemala, Honduras, El Salvador, Nicaragua, Belize, and Costa Rica. To the south of Panama is South America, whose northern region contains Colombia, Venezuela, Guyana, Suriname, and French Guiana. In the middle of South America are Bolivia and Paraguay. Brazil, Uruguay, and Argentina face the Atlantic Ocean, while Ecuador, Peru, and Chile look toward the Pacific Ocean.

Of these nations, the United States is the acknowledged "colossus" because of its vast territorial and natural resources, a stable political system, and a dynamic and prosperous economy. Drawing inspiration from the American Revolution, the United States has pursued an expansionist diplomacy that has led to frequent military intervention in the domestic affairs of neighboring states, especially those in Middle America and the Caribbean. By contrast, the countries of Latin America have lacked similar political stability and economic cohesion so that, in terms of relative power, they have been unable to prevent the rise of the United States to a position of political, economic, and military preeminence in the Western Hemisphere.

The northern neighbor of the United States, Canada, has historically been closely linked to Great Britain and the British Commonwealth and chose not to play an active role in inter-American diplomatic affairs until the 1980s. The southern neighbor of the United States, Mexico, is a large country that has been adversely affected by lengthy periods of political instability. Sharing a common border with the United States has meant that Mexico has experienced a close and often tense diplomatic relationship with its powerful neighbor. As a result of the Mexican-American War (1846–1848), Mexico lost half its national territory to the United States.

In terms of its considerable territorial size and resources, Mexico might have expected to be the dominant regional power in Middle America, but its political and military weakness encouraged the countries of Central America to break away and declare their independence. These nations initially found the idea of a common federation appealing. However, the federation collapsed in 1838 and resulted in the formation of the independent states of Guatemala, Honduras, Nicaragua, El Salvador, and Costa Rica. Panama declared its independence from Colombia in 1903. Belize, formerly a British colony, can also be considered as part of this region after achieving its full independence from Great Britain in 1981. Often afflicted by political disorder and economic crisis, the nations of Middle America have been vulnerable to frequent military intervention and financial supervision by the United States.

In South America, the most economically developed and militarily powerful nations are Brazil and Argentina. On account of its Portuguese background, Brazil has felt ethnically apart from the Spanish-American countries and has sought to compensate for this by seeking the diplomatic support of external powers, especially the United States. Argentina has experienced friction with Brazil over the control of the adjoining territory of Uruguay, but it has been Argentina's pretensions to regional leadership that have provoked diplomatic rivalry with Brazil and, at times, also with the United States. In the northern region, Colombia came into direct diplomatic contact with the United States over schemes for the construction of a canal at the Isthmus of Panama. This resulted, however, in the secession of Panama from the Colombian Union in 1903 and the building of the Panama Canal by the United States. Venezuela was involved in a boundary dispute with Great Britain that prompted the diplomatic intervention of the United States in 1895. In the middle of South America, the geographical remoteness of Bolivia and Paraguay has meant that their relations with the United States have been relatively insignificant. American interest in Ecuador has been similarly limited. Except for the War of the Pacific (1879–1884) and the subsequent Tacna-Arica Dispute, Peru and Chile have rarely attracted sustained diplomatic attention from the United States. A notable exception, however, was the presidency of Salvador Allende (1970–1973) when Chile was perceived by the U.S. government as a serious geopolitical threat to the security of the hemisphere.

FROM COLONIES TO INDEPENDENT NATIONS

During the late 18th century, the North American colonies successfully fought a war for their political independence from Great Britain. The result was the formation of the United States of America, a republic that came into existence in 1787 as the first independent state in the Western Hemisphere. Although the event would have enormous significance for the future diplomatic history of the region, its initial impact was negligible. Little affinity existed between the people of the United States and those of the Spanish and Portuguese colonies in the New World because they had been kept apart from each other for so long by geographical distance, different rulers, race, religion, and culture. Nevertheless, the winning of independence and the subsequent survival of the United States as a living example of republicanism and democratic government were tangible achievements that attracted notice and some admiration in a Western world characterized by belief in the superiority of the monarchical system of government.

The struggle for Latin American independence effectively began in 1808 when French Emperor Napoleon Bonaparte forced the abdication of the Spanish ruling family and declared his brother, Joseph, as the new king of Spain. Insurgency erupted in Spain and spread overseas to the Spanish-American empire, causing a crisis of authority that encouraged local movements first for economic and later for full political independence. By fighting to overthrow European monarchical tyranny, the Latin American insurgents were visibly following the example set earlier by the American colonists. The U.S. government was outwardly sympathetic but would not contribute any material military support. It maintained friendly relations with Spain and adopted a neutral attitude toward the Latin American wars for independence. The policy of neutrality was attractive because it served American national self-interest. Most of all, it facilitated the purchase from Spain of the coveted borderland territory of Spanish Florida. This was achieved in the Adams-Onís Treaty, which was concluded in 1819 but not formally ratified by the Spanish government until 1821. Only after ratification was definitely secured did the United States proceed to recognize the independence of the new states. The first official act took place in 1822 when President James Monroe received the chargé d'affaires representing the Republic of Colombia.

Despite waiting until after the ratification of the Adams-Onís Treaty, the United States was still the first outside power to accord official diplomatic recognition to the Latin American states. The timing of American action ahead of that by Great Britain represented not so much enthusiasm for the cause of Latin American independence than a calculation to gain political and especially commercial advantages in the new states. A similar motivation was evident in Monroe's decision to reject British Foreign Minister George Canning's proposal for a joint Anglo-American warning against rumored European military intervention to restore the authority of the Spanish king over his empire. Instead of diplomatic cooperation with Great Britain, Monroe decided on an independent course of action that he expressed in his Annual Message to Congress on December 2, 1823. Basing his argument on the idea that the New World had a political system separate from that of the Old World of Europe, the president warned against interference by the European powers. The message also asserted a superior leadership role for the United States. Even though there had been no prior consultation with Latin American governments, the new nations were simply declared to be under the protection of the United States.

In time, the message would develop into the "Monroe Doctrine." In 1823, however, Monroe's words represented only a presidential statement of policy that had no force in international law. The question was whether they would be challenged, but this did not materialize because Great Britain did not publicly oppose the statement. In fact, the president's words attracted little attention. Indeed, Latin Americans generally believed that Canning had done more than Monroe to help them both win and maintain their independence. The external power that they most admired was not the United States but Great Britain, the world's leading financial, commercial, and maritime nation. The distant and somewhat awkward diplomatic relationship between the United States and its southern neighbors was illustrated by the 1826 Panama Congress. At first, the United States was not included in the invitations sent by the "Liberator," Simón Bolívar, in 1824. The exclusion indicated the continuance of political and cultural division between the United States and the Spanish-American countries. When an invitation was eventually extended in 1825, the U.S. Congress debated for four months before deciding to appoint two delegates. The delay demonstrated that the people of the United States were clearly very ambivalent over participating in inter-American schemes even when advocated by such a prominent figure as Bolívar.

DIPLOMATIC DETACHMENT

Although Monroe's 1823 message proclaimed his country's intention to act as the protector of the Latin American nations, this did not result in active American involvement in hemispheric affairs. The detached diplomatic relationship that had existed during the colonial period persisted throughout most of the 19th century. Moreover, a stable balance of power existed in the Western Hemisphere where the fragmentation of the former Spanish-American empire into several separate states meant that there was no serious local military rival to threaten the United States. Indeed, instead of establishing viable democratic systems of government, most of the new republics provided examples of political instability. This outcome merely confirmed the pessimistic predictions of American political leaders such as Thomas Jefferson and John Quincy Adams that the people of Latin America would not be able to break free from their repressive and debilitating Spanish heritage. The frequent occurrence of violent coups and the rise to power of military rulers further reinforced this negative view.

In addition, the Latin American economy conspicuously failed to live up to its "el dorado" image. Like their European counterparts, American politicians and merchants had equated the achievement of Latin American independence with grand opportunities for profitable trade and investment. Apart from Mexico, Cuba, and Brazil, however, there was very little commercial contact between the United States and the new nations. The economic reality was that for much of the 19th century, the United States was similar to the countries of Latin America in being primarily an agrarian economy concentrating on the production of foodstuffs and raw materials. American merchants were particularly envious and critical of the powerful influence exercised by Great Britain in all aspects of commercial activity in Latin America. In the 19th century, however, they could do little to upset British economic preeminence.

During the 1830s and 1840s, the Texas question emerged as the most pressing diplomatic issue for the United States in its relations with Latin America. In 1836, American settlers in Texas successfully achieved secession from Mexico, declared a republic, and sought annexation to the United States. When annexation eventually took place in March 1845, protests from the Mexican government culminated in the outbreak of the Mexican-American War in May 1846. Mexico was defeated and ceded to the United States a vast portion of national territory extending from Texas to the Pacific coastline. The war was significant in demonstrating the military weakness of Mexico and its inability to prevent the emergence of the United States as the preeminent power in the Middle American–Caribbean region. It also served to strengthen the American belief in their military and cultural superiority over the people of Mexico and, by extension, over Latin Americans in general.

Acute alarm was aroused in Latin America by the scale of the American military victory and incorporation of huge amounts of Mexican territory. Similarly disturbing were the aggressive activities of American filibusters, such as those led by William Walker that sought land and treasure in Central America. Despite their notoriety, the actual examples of filibusters and their successful seizure of territory were limited in both duration and geographical location. They were confined to Mexico, Central America, and the Caribbean islands. By contrast, the South American countries that were more distant geographically from the United States were not directly affected by filibusters or American military action throughout most of the 19th century. In fact, the people of the United States felt no compelling desire to enter into close political cooperation with the countries and peoples beyond the Middle American–Caribbean region. For most of the 19th century, their energies were absorbed in westward territorial expansion, the sectional conflict leading to the Civil War, Reconstruction, and urban and industrial growth.

PAN-AMERICANISM

Americans began to show an unaccustomed attention to Latin American affairs during the last quarter of the 19th century. Prominent politicians such as the Republican presidential candidate James G. Blaine made "Pan-Americanism" a domestic political issue. He advocated that the United States must protect and lead its "sister" nations of the New World by establishing an informal political alliance and commercial union. The latter aspect was particularly well received in the United States because it provided a means of alleviating a current economic depression. Indeed, Latin America was now perceived as a natural market for American exports. In 1888, the U.S. Congress passed an act authorizing the president to invite Latin American governments to an International American Conference to be held in Washington. For a nation that had historically sought to avoid foreign entanglements and had been reluctant to attend the 1826 Panama Congress, the decision of the United States to call an inter-American conference was most unusual and an event of major diplomatic significance in the Western Hemisphere.

Delegates from the United States and the Latin American countries assembled in Washington in October 1889. Despite positive reports in the American press, the International American Conference was marked as much by divergence as by convergence. Argentina notably emerged as the focus of opposition to the United States and set the tone for a competitive if not adversarial relationship that would last well into the 20th century. The conference closed in April 1890 after being in session for more than six months. Its sole tangible achievement was the formation of a small commercial bureau located in Washington that would ultimately grow into the Pan-American Union. Nevertheless, the very fact that the conference had actually taken place was a significant demonstration of the prestige and powerful influence of the United States within the Western Hemisphere and provided a precedent for the holding of future inter-American meetings.

The importance of economic motivation in American policy was demonstrated by the reciprocity amendment to the 1890 McKinley tariff bill. President Benjamin Harrison and Secretary of State Blaine were especially keen to use the amendment to gain commercial advantages over European competitors and advance their plans for a hemispheric commercial union that would be ultimately dominated by the United States. The aim was far too ambitious to achieve. While treaties were concluded with the Central American and Caribbean countries whose trade was already mostly with the United States, no agreements were signed with Mexico or with any of the nations of South America, excluding Brazil. Moreover, the cavalier manner in which the treaties were abruptly terminated in 1894 not by diplomatic agreement but by the unilateral action of the U.S. Congress demonstrated that the policy of commercial reciprocity, both in formulation and in execution, had been dictated primarily by internal political pressures to expand American trade.

The 1890s also featured a growing disposition for the United States to intervene in Latin American domestic affairs. When American sailors were injured in the Baltimore Affair in Chile in 1891, President Benjamin Harrison responded by sending warships and demanding a humiliating apology from the Chilean government. Intervention in the Brazilian Naval Revolt of 1893–1894 gave a further demonstration of the growing naval power of the United States and how it could be projected, if required, to assert American rights in Latin America. In 1895, a diplomatic ultimatum from President Grover Cleveland persuaded Great Britain to arbitrate its long-standing boundary dispute with Venezuela and essentially recognize American political preeminence in the Western Hemisphere. While the Cleveland administration claimed to be unselfishly defending Venezuela against European imperialism, it also acted unilaterally and did not consult the Venezuelan government over its policy.

The new activism shown in American foreign policy caused dismay in Latin America. Those countries also had to take into account the impressive demonstration of military power by the United States in the Spanish-American War (1898). The unexpectedly swift military defeat of Spain, followed by the initial denial of home rule to Cuba and Puerto Rico and the establishment instead of American military governments in those islands, served to strengthen anti-American sentiment in Latin America. The Latin American predicament was eloquently expressed by the Uruguayan writer José Enrique Rodó, who likened the United States to Caliban, a monster that was respected for its great energy and strength but feared for its insensitivity and seemingly insatiable appetite for material expansion.

DOLLAR DIPLOMACY

Latin American nations were disturbed by the Venezuela Incident of 1902–1903, in which European powers resorted to gunboat diplomacy in an attempt to compel Venezuela to repay its foreign debt. While the U.S. government was critical of European military intervention, it would not rule out the legal right of foreign powers to use force to recover public debt in cases where arbitration was refused. The contingency, however, would not occur if the United States acted preemptively. In his Annual Message to Congress on December 6, 1904, President Theodore Roosevelt declared that United States had a duty to intervene in cases where Latin American governments committed what he described as "chronic wrongdoing." European nations readily appreciated the value of what became known as the "Roosevelt Corollary" to the Monroe Doctrine because it implied that the United States was prepared to act as a self-appointed policeman to ensure that Latin American governments behaved responsibly and, most important, met their financial obligations to foreign investors.

Theodore Roosevelt's forceful style was also evident in his action supporting the independence of Panama in 1903. In a later speech, he even boasted that he had "taken" the Canal Zone in 1903. While many Americans approved Roosevelt's actions, deep resentment against the

United States was stirred throughout Latin America at what was interpreted as his blatant aggression. Instead of Pan-Americanism, the United States was now associated with "dollar diplomacy," a policy characterized by the sending in of marines and financial supervisors. Dollar diplomacy reflected the expanding geopolitical power of the United States and conversely the relative weakness and vulnerability of the Latin American countries. It was also imperialistic in seeking to establish a framework of political order and stability specifically designed to promote the development of American trade and financial interests.

During the second decade of the 20th century, President Woodrow Wilson sought to repair the damage caused by dollar diplomacy. In his Mobile Address delivered on October 27, 1913, he spoke of his aim to cultivate a new relationship with the "sister republics" that was firmly based on reason and trust. Wilson discovered, however, that his good intentions were not so easy to put into practice. Moreover, idealistic rhetoric conflicted with more pragmatic considerations of national self-interest as exemplified by his decisions to intervene with armed force in Mexico and in the Middle American–Caribbean region.

When war broke out in Europe in 1914, Wilson declared that the United States would adopt a policy of strict neutrality. The Latin American governments looked to Wilson for leadership in the unfolding world crisis, but he appeared indifferent to Latin American opinion and left those nations to evolve their own separate policies of neutrality toward the war. The Wilson administration, however, showed a keen interest in promoting closer economic links with Latin America. Indeed, the serious economic dislocation caused by the world war provided a historic opportunity for the extension of American commercial influence throughout Latin America at the expense of its European competitors. Wartime conditions boosted American trade and investment, particularly with the countries of South America, where Europeans had traditionally been commercially well established and predominant.

On April 6, 1917, the U.S. Congress declared war on Germany. Although the decision to go to war had not involved prior consultation with the Latin American governments, Wilson hoped that they would join the war against Germany. But Wilson's idealistic justification for his country's entry into war evoked a disappointing response. Only eight nations formally entered the war, seven of which were Middle American–Caribbean states already strongly under American influence.

Mexico conspicuously chose to remain neutral. Brazil was the only South American country to declare war on Germany. Throughout the world, Wilson was popularly acclaimed a hero and a great statesman. But Latin American diplomatic opinion was more critical. Wilson's high moral principles and his image as a peacemaker sat awkwardly with his record of ordering so many military interventions.

During the 1920s, American foreign policy displayed an inward-looking mentality that was symbolized by the decision not to become a member of the League of Nations. The Latin American countries hoped that the League would offer a means of reducing American political and military interference in hemispheric affairs. But this was not realized because the United States did not join. Moreover, the geopolitical reality was that as a result of the world war, the United States had significantly increased its economic and political influence, especially in South America. The Republican presidential administrations of the 1920s, however, pursued a less military interventionist policy toward Latin America than their Democratic predecessors had done. The exception was in Nicaragua, where the dispatch of marines in 1926 provoked determined local guerrilla resistance led by Augusto Sandino. Latin American governments used the Pan-American conferences that were held at Santiago de Chile in 1923 and Havana in 1928 to voice their criticism of American diplomacy and especially of the practice of military intervention. By the close of the 1920s, U.S. diplomatic relations with Latin America appeared to have reached their nadir.

GOOD NEIGHBORS

Prior to assuming office, President-elect Herbert Hoover made a good-will tour of Latin America in December 1928. As president, Hoover genuinely wanted to improve diplomatic relations with Latin America, but his efforts were undermined by the impact of domestic events such as the Wall Street crash and the Great Depression. His successor, Franklin D. Roosevelt, attracted attention in his inaugural address in 1933 when he stated that his aim was to act as a "good neighbor" in foreign affairs. Consequently, it was Roosevelt and not Hoover who has been usually regarded as the originator of what became known as the Good Neighbor Policy. The concept was deliberately vague, but it was well received in Latin America because it implied equality and mutual respect among all nations. Roosevelt gave the idea tangible form in January 1934 by declaring his opposition to armed intervention. Behind his uplifting rhetoric, however, was a calculated strategy to expand hemispheric trade and help the American economy recover from the impact of the Great Depression. Particularly important was the passage in the U.S. Congress in June 1934 of the Reciprocal Trade Agreements Act. Beginning with Cuba in August 1934, the United States concluded bilateral reciprocity arrangements with 11 Latin American countries by 1939.

Although Great Britain remained the leading economic competitor of the United States in Latin America, the mid-1930s saw a rising challenge from other European countries, notably Nazi Germany. Furthermore, Germany was perceived as a growing strategic threat because of its fascist ideology and its attempts to strengthen political and cultural links with the large communities of immigrants of German extraction resident in parts of Central and South America. When war broke out in Europe in 1939, the United States and the Latin American nations responded with proclamations of neutrality. Roosevelt pursued a proactive policy that was much more sensitive to Latin America than Wilson had shown during World War I. A conference of foreign ministers at Panama adopted Roosevelt's suggestion of declaring a safety zone around the coastline of the Western Hemisphere. The inter-American cooperation that was evident at the conference was attributed to the success of the Good Neighbor Policy. When the United States formally entered the war in December 1941, it was joined shortly afterward by nine Central American and Caribbean countries. In contrast to their attitudes during World War I, the majority of South American nations also affirmed their solidarity with the United States by breaking off relations with the Axis powers and subsequently entering the war.

The Roosevelt administration valued Latin American diplomatic support in the fight against fascism. However, all military aspects involved in prosecuting the war effort were placed very firmly under American control. Just like World War I, little was required in the way of a Latin American contribution to actual military operations in World War II. Nevertheless, the wartime policy of close cooperation bordering on subordination to the United States contained distinct material benefits for many Latin American countries. This was particularly exemplified by

Brazil, which received the largest share of the Lend-Lease aid given by the United States to Latin America during the war. In a similar fashion to World War I, the Latin American countries were again highly appreciated as suppliers of strategic raw materials and minerals. The United States also compensated for the drastic decline of the region's prewar trade with Europe by purchasing large quantities of Latin American agricultural produce.

A feature of American policy that directly impinged on Latin America was the pursuit of economic warfare in the form of the Black List containing the names of suspected pro-Axis companies and individuals with whom American companies and individuals were instructed not to do business. Agents from the Federal Bureau of Investigation (FBI) were dispatched to Latin America to assist in identifying local Axis agents and sympathizers and restricting their activities. The Roosevelt administration also made a conscious effort to persuade Latin American governments to replace any existing military missions from the Axis powers with advisers from the United States. American military missions also developed programs to help modernize local military and police forces in terms of their training and equipment. Some Latin American governments, especially those headed by authoritarian leaders, saw such American aid as a valuable means of strengthening their own internal security forces. Another development was the closer professional and social association that was formed between Latin American military officers and their counterparts in the United States. A large number of Latin American junior officers received training at American military academies where they often acquired respect and admiration for the United States, especially its military and technological skills.

COLD WAR DIPLOMACY

World War II marked the transition of the United States from a nation historically on the margin of the international system centered on Europe to the new status of the world's superpower. As a result, the United States abandoned its isolationist tradition and accepted worldwide diplomatic and military commitments in Western Europe and the Far East. In terms of the Western Hemisphere, American preeminence was actually more secure than even before the war because of the dramatic economic and military decline of the great European powers, such as Great Britain, France, and Germany. In fact, Latin American governments confidently expected that the close wartime relationship with the United States would continue into the postwar period. Indeed, American financial assistance was considered as vital to prevent a recurrence of the economically depressed years of the 1930s. After 1945, however, American officials considered Western Europe the priority for economic reconstruction because it had suffered so much more extensive damage and destruction than Latin America during the war. They were much less sympathetic to Latin American pleas for assistance and characteristically believed that the economic difficulties of the region could be directly linked to local incompetence and inefficiency in political and economic management.

Following the articulation of the Truman Doctrine in 1947, the United States adopted the strategy of "containing" the perceived expansive tendencies of international communism. American officials assumed that the countries of Latin America would play a supportive role in the emerging Cold War between the United States and the Soviet Union. This was reflected in the creation of the Rio Pact and the Organization of American States (OAS), which became part of the evolving policy of the global containment of communism. In terms of an actual strategic threat to Latin America, what caused most concern to American officials was not the prospect of Soviet military aggression but rather political infiltration and subversion by local communists and their sympathizers. The first major clash was in Guatemala, where the Eisenhower administration feared that a communist beachhead was about to be established. The Central Intelligence Agency (CIA) organized Operation PBSUCCESS and overthrew the Guatemalan government in 1954. Latin American governments were dismayed by the use of armed force in the guise of a covert operation. In effect, Operation PBSUCCESS marked a reversion by the United States to the policy of unilateral armed interventionism and thereby the definitive end of the Good Neighbor Policy. What the coup and its aftermath also demonstrated was that, in its desire for political and economic stability and resistance to communism, the United States was prepared to destabilize elected governments and give material support to the reactionary dictators in Latin America, especially those military leaders who were not only pro-American but also strongly anticommunist.

Anti-American sentiment erupted at its most virulent during Vice President Richard Nixon's "goodwill tour" of Latin America in 1958. A shocked Eisenhower administration acknowledged the need to improve the American image in Latin America. Change became more urgent as a result of the rise to power in Cuba of Fidel Castro and the serious challenge that the Cuban Revolution presented to American democracy and the capitalist system. Eisenhower and his successor, John F. Kennedy, instructed the CIA to prepare for the overthrow of Castro. They also developed a policy of economic aid that Kennedy called the Alliance for Progress. Although the scheme was generous in representing a substantial financial commitment, it was proclaimed unilaterally, and its contents very much reflected traditional American values and sense of democratic mission.

During the Cold War, the United States increasingly stressed military aid as a means of containing the spread of communism in the hemisphere. The relationship that was established with the Brazilian military was so close that American complicity was suspected in the coup that overthrew President João Goulart in 1964. In the following year, President Lyndon Johnson intervened with massive military force in the Dominican Republic to defeat what he regarded as a communist conspiracy. Fearing the rise of anti-American sentiment and the spread of communism in Chile, President Richard Nixon determined to destabilize the government of Salvador Allende. The overthrow of Allende in a coup in 1973 caused political controversy in the United States. A congressional investigation carried out by the Church Committee in 1975 revealed that not only Nixon but also several of his predecessors had resorted to covert operations, including bribery and attempted assassinations, to achieve their foreign policy aims in Latin America. The Church Committee argued that, by acting in this way, presidents had betrayed their country's historic sense of moral purpose and idealism. As a result, the United States had thereby suffered a severe reduction in its prestige and influence in the Western Hemisphere.

TRANSITION TO A NEW CENTURY

The hearings of the Church Committee occurred at a time when the United States appeared to be losing its political and economic preeminence in the Western Hemisphere. This was visibly demonstrated by the successful survival of the Castro regime in Cuba and the desire of Latin American governments to develop closer diplomatic and economic relations with Western Europe and nations in the communist bloc and the Third World. Among the people of the United States, there was a sense of national malaise that was symbolized by the trauma of the Vietnam War. As a result, the United States became less assured and more conciliatory in its diplomacy toward Latin America. This was illustrated in the conclusion of new treaties concerning the future of the Panama Canal.

Implicit in the negotiations with Panama was the willingness of the United States to schedule a definite date for the ending of its control over the canal and also the confirmation of Panamanian sovereignty over the Canal Zone. But the prospect of giving up what was popularly perceived as "American territory" provoked a right-wing political backlash in the United States. President Jimmy Carter, however, employed his political skill and personal prestige to secure the ratification of the canal treaties by the U.S. Senate in 1978. Carter also insisted that nations respect human rights. The high political priority that he gave to this issue attracted a mixed response in Latin America because violations of human rights, including torture and disappearances, were a well-publicized occurrence in that region, especially during the 1970s. The right-wing governments of Argentina, Brazil, El Salvador, and Guatemala were so annoyed that they suspended their existing military assistance agreements with the United States.

Another salient example of the decline of American preeminence in the hemisphere was Carter's inability to prevent the Sandinista revolutionary movement from coming to power in Nicaragua in 1979. In the United States, the growing criticism of Carter's foreign policies contributed to the election of Ronald Reagan in 1980. Reagan was deeply distrustful of communism and determined to confront and defeat what he described as the "evil empire" of the Soviet Union. While relatively little attention was given to the countries of South America, the Reagan administration closely monitored events in Central America. In Nicaragua, Carter's conciliatory attitude toward the Sandinistas was changed to one of outright American hostility in which both overt and covert measures were employed to destabilize a regime that was viewed as an agent of Soviet expansion. The forceful policy, however, was constrained by the fact that the U.S. Congress and American public opinion were sharply divided over the issue. The dispatch of American combat troops was ruled out by the anxiety that Nicaragua might become another "Vietnam." This led the Reagan administration to organize a proxy army of Nicaraguan exiles known as the Contras.

Reagan called the Contras courageous "freedom fighters" who were engaged in a struggle to liberate their country from communist control. Some Latin American leaders, however, considered Reagan too confrontational. Forming the Contadora Group, they believed that the Central American crisis could never be resolved by military means alone and that a diplomatic approach was preferable. Reagan, however, was intent on pursuing a military solution. The exposure of illegal methods to fund the Contras, however, led in 1986 to the Iran-Contra affair, which raised the possibility of Reagan's resignation or even impeachment. The scandal also made it more difficult for him to reject the recommendations emerging from the peace process started by the Contadora Group and that had evolved into the Arias Peace Plan in 1987.

The East–West focus of the Reagan administration so evident in the Central American crisis was also demonstrated in its response to the South Atlantic War between Great Britain and Argentina in 1982. The war illustrated the predisposition of the United States during the Cold War to attach more importance to its European allies than its Latin American neighbors. The Reagan administration similarly neglected the growing problem of external debt that was adversely affecting most of Latin America and resulted in the debt crisis in August 1982. While emergency loans were made to Mexico, American officials were inclined to criticize the leaders of other Latin American countries for being reckless and profligate in their borrowing. As part of its strategy to isolate the Sandinistas in Nicaragua, the Reagan administration was prepared to offer preferential financial aid to the countries of Central America and the Caribbean in the form of the Caribbean Basin Initiative, but there was no sign of a similar aid program for the rest of Latin America.

After a period of relative decline during the 1970s, the prestige and power of the United States in the Western Hemisphere were visibly increased by events in Europe that brought a dramatic end to the Cold War and led to the disintegration of the Soviet Union in 1991. The end of East–West conflict meant that Central America notably lost its significance as a priority issue in American national security policy. During the

1990s, the focus of American diplomatic activity became firmly fixed on Europe, the Middle East, and Asia. Programs of economic and military aid for Latin America were correspondingly reduced or even terminated. New issues emerged, however, that pointed to the desirability of a closer and cooperative relationship between the United States and the countries of Latin America. For example, the development of a hemispheric free trade area was proposed in response to the emergence of powerful international trading blocs such as the European Union and concern over the ramifications of the increasing globalization of the world economy. Following on from the "Enterprise for the Americas Initiative" launched in 1990 by President George H. W. Bush, the United States, Canada, and Mexico negotiated the North American Free Trade Agreement (NAFTA) in 1992. NAFTA was generally regarded as the first step in a process toward the formation of the "Free Trade Area of the Americas."

The promotion of hemispheric trade was also valued as a means of persuading potential Latin American immigrants to the United States to stay in their home countries. The large numbers of illegal immigrants, especially from Mexico, continued to cause considerable political controversy in the United States. Decades of immigration and improvements in communications, however, had brought about major historical change. At the beginning of the 19th century, little affinity had existed between the people of the United States and those of the new Latin American nations. What was visibly different two centuries later was the rising number of Hispanics living in the United States, a historical development that meant that the barriers of distance and of racial and cultural difference would no longer be such a potent factor in the future diplomatic relationship between the United States and Latin America.

THE DICTIONARY

– A –

ABC. Acronym for **Argentina**, **Brazil**, and **Chile**. The ABC came into being as an active diplomatic entity in April 1914 as a result of the crisis caused by the military intervention of the United States in **Mexico**. As part of his strategy to compel General **Victoriano Huerta** to give up power in Mexico, President **Woodrow Wilson** had ordered U.S. marines to occupy the Mexican port of **Veracruz**. The potential escalation of the conflict into a full-scale war between Mexico and the United States became a distinct possibility and was avoided by the timely offer of diplomatic mediation from the three most powerful South American nations: Argentina, Brazil, and Chile (the ABC). The offer was speedily accepted by both Wilson and Huerta. It resulted in a cessation of hostilities in Mexico and a peace conference held at Niagara Falls, **Canada**, in May–June 1914.

Wilson, however, maintained the traditional American reluctance to endorse an inter-American resolution of a dispute in which the United States was an active participant. He also refused to consider an early withdrawal of his troops from Veracruz and continued to demand that Huerta be removed from office. Huerta later agreed to resign and leave Mexico in July 1914, after which American troops were withdrawn from Veracruz. The ABC had successfully achieved their immediate purpose of preventing a relatively small local conflict from escalating into a larger war, but their actual diplomatic influence on subsequent events was limited and temporary so long as the United States clearly preferred and was insistent on pursuing a unilateral policy in its relations with Mexico. A similar pattern of diplomatic events occurred during the 1980s when the **Contadora Group** of Latin American nations attempted to mediate the **Central**

American Crisis and received limited cooperation from President **Ronald Reagan**. *See also* MEXICAN REVOLUTION.

ACT OF CHAPULTEPEC (1945). An inter-American military agreement. At the Special Conference on the Problems of War and Peace held at the Chapultepec Palace in Mexico City in February–March 1945, the delegates discussed the issue of hemispheric defense. In the resulting Act of Chapultepec, they declared in favor of maintaining the existing policy of collective security for the duration of **World War II**. They also agreed that, shortly after the world war came to a formal end, a special inter-American meeting would be convened to discuss the establishment of a permanent treaty system of military alliance to provide for the future defense of the **Western Hemisphere**. This meeting was eventually held at Rio de Janeiro in 1947 and resulted in the formulation of the collective defensive arrangement known as the **Inter-American Treaty of Reciprocal Assistance** and also often referred to as the **Rio Treaty**. *See also* CHAPULTEPEC CONFERENCE (1945).

ADAMS, JOHN QUINCY (1767–1848). American political leader and president from 1825 to 1829. The eldest son of President John Adams, John Quincy Adams was born in Massachusetts and educated at Harvard University. A prominent member of the Federalist Party, he held several prestigious diplomatic appointments, including those of minister to Holland, Prussia, and **Great Britain**, before being appointed as secretary of state by President **James Monroe**. While serving as Monroe's secretary of state from 1817 to 1825, Adams successfully negotiated in 1819 the **Adams-Onís Treaty**, considerably expanding the territorial size of the United States. In 1823, he played a key role in the formulation of the policy that became known as the **Monroe Doctrine**. At the time, this represented the decision of the Monroe administration to reject British Foreign Minister **George Canning**'s proposal for a joint Anglo-American protest to prevent the prospective military intervention by **France** to reestablish Spanish monarchical rule over its former colonies in the New World. Adams was particularly influential in arguing that the United States should not be seen to be acting as a junior partner to Great Britain.

While mindful of Anglo-American political and commercial rivalry in the **Western Hemisphere**, Adams showed reluctance, however, to grant early diplomatic recognition to the new Latin American states. In this, he reflected traditional North American Anglo-Saxon attitudes that were influenced by the "**Black Legend**" that looked down on Latin Americans for their Spanish and Catholic background and regarded this as a major obstacle to their ever achieving a stable form of democratic government. As president from 1825 to 1829, however, Adams wished to improve diplomatic and commercial relations with the new Latin American nations and, despite opposition in the U.S. Congress, advocated the sending of U.S. delegates to the **Panama Congress** in 1826. *See also* WARS FOR LATIN AMERICAN INDEPENDENCE (1808–1826).

ADAMS-ONÍS TREATY (1819). A treaty between the United States and **Spain**. Involvement in the French revolutionary wars seriously depleted Spain's financial resources and persuaded the Spanish government to consider the sale of Spanish Florida to the United States. Negotiations started in 1817 between Secretary of State **John Quincy Adams** and the Spanish minister to the United States, Luis de Onís, and eventually resulted in the conclusion of the Adams-Onís Treaty, also known as the Transcontinental Treaty, on February 22, 1819. Formal ratification of the treaty by both governments took place on February 14, 1821. The treaty was regarded in the United States as a great personal success for Adams. Spain not only ceded Florida to the United States but also recognized the 42nd parallel (the border between Oregon and California) as dividing the two countries in the west. The drawing of the boundary on the Pacific coast was highly significant in indicating that the United States was for the first time officially recognized by foreign powers as a transcontinental nation rather than a country mainly based around the Atlantic seaboard. The territorial expansion of the United States raised some concern in Latin America, where it was also noted that the administration of President **James Monroe** was unwilling to recognize the achievement of Latin American independence until the treaty had been ratified by the Spanish government. *See also* WARS FOR LATIN AMERICAN INDEPENDENCE (1808–1826).

AGENCY FOR INTERNATIONAL DEVELOPMENT (AID). An agency of the U.S. government. AID was established in 1961 as one of several foreign policy initiatives launched by the administration of President **John F. Kennedy** to improve relations between the United States and the countries of the Third World. AID's designated function was to coordinate and monitor the overseas implementation of U.S. economic assistance programs. While AID provided money and technical assistance for social and economic needs such as education and health care, it also developed programs of promoting public safety that resulted in gathering political and military intelligence and in training internal security forces in counterinsurgency techniques. This meant that AID was often treated with suspicion in Latin America, where it was regarded not so much as the agency of economic assistance implied by its title but more an adjunct to the covert activities of the **Central Intelligence Agency** and an instrument of **Cold War** politics. *See also* ALLIANCE FOR PROGRESS; PEACE CORPS.

ALL-MEXICO MOVEMENT. A political movement seeking to acquire **Mexico** for the United States. During the 1830s and 1840s, American advocates of their country's territorial expansion were greatly encouraged by the question of the annexation of **Texas** to the United States and the resulting **Mexican-American War** (1846–1848). Prior to the end of the conflict with Mexico, an "all-Mexico" movement lobbied for total annexation of the whole of Mexico to the United States. One strong argument in favor was that Americans had a revolutionary duty to replace Spanish despotism with freedom just as they had overthrown British monarchical control in the **American Revolution** of the previous century. **Manifest Destiny** was also invoked because Mexico was regarded as part of the North American continent. But opponents likened the annexation of all Mexico to an unjustifiable and illegal act of conquest. They also pointed out that the incorporation of Mexico into the United States contained potentially heavy financial costs and raised the dangerous prospect of internal racial and religious conflict. As a result, annexation proved to be unacceptable to the U.S. Congress. *See also* FILIBUSTERS.

ALLENDE GOSSENS, SALVADOR (1908–1973). Chilean political leader and president from 1970 to 1973. A physician by training, Allende joined the Socialist Party and was an unsuccessful presidential candidate on three occasions before eventually winning a narrow victory in the 1970 presidential election in which he represented the left-wing coalition Alliance of Popular Unity. In office, Allende duly introduced radical and controversial measures designed to transform **Chile** into a socialist state. President **Richard Nixon** was alarmed by the election of a Marxist and the example of a communist government being legally established for the first time in a South American country. Particularly worrying for Washington also was the friendly relationship existing between Allende and **Cuba**'s **Fidel Castro**, who was invited to make a state visit to Chile in November 1971. Nixon implemented a policy of overt economic pressure to undermine Chile's economy combined with instructions to the **Central Intelligence Agency** to pursue covert political activities to destabilize Allende's government and remove him from office.

In September 1973, General **Augusto Pinochet** led a military coup during which Allende committed suicide. The new military government declared that decisive action had been necessary to save Chile from communism. While Allende's radical policies had undeniable popular support in Chile, especially among the workers, they also aroused considerable internal political controversy and opposition. The president's violent death, however, helped him acquire the image of a martyr among his supporters in Chile and to the wider world as a victim of American imperialism. *See also* CHURCH COMMITTEE; HELMS, RICHARD (1913–2002); KISSINGER, HENRY A. (1923–); VELASCO ALVARADO, JUAN (1910–1977).

ALLIANCE FOR PROGRESS. A major program of social reform and economic development largely funded by the United States and designed to counter the perceived threat of communist expansion in Latin America. The Alliance for Progress (La Alianza para el Progreso) was proposed by President **John F. Kennedy** in a speech at the White House on March 13, 1961. The idea resembled "**Operation Pan-America**," made in 1958 by Brazilian President **Juscelino Kubitschek**, which had been studiously ignored by the **Dwight Eisenhower** administration. In fact, the Latin American nations warmly welcomed an initiative coming from the new U.S. president and in August 1961 at a meeting in **Uruguay** signed the Charter of

Punta del Este, which formally established the alliance. The United States agreed to provide loans of $20 billion over a period of 10 years. The scheme essentially represented a belated **Marshall Plan** for Latin America and was similarly politically motivated in seeking to contain the advance of communism in what was regarded by U.S. officials as a strategically important region of the world that was visibly suffering from poverty and destitution. Moreover, by firmly linking the United States on the side of movements for democratic reform and social justice, the Kennedy administration was confident that it would successfully counter the challenge of the **Cuban Revolution** and prevent the occurrence of "another **Cuba**" in the hemisphere.

The degree of American support for the alliance was notably weakened by the assassination of Kennedy in 1963. In contrast to his predecessor, President **Lyndon Johnson** was not closely associated with the program, and he did not consider it a political priority of his administration. Johnson's growing preoccupation was with winning and also financing the Vietnam War. Moreover, the goals of social and economic advancement stated in the 1961 Charter proved much too ambitious to achieve, and in marked contrast to the success of the earlier Marshall Plan in Western Europe, the results of the alliance in its initial years were generally perceived as very disappointing. In addition, there was evidence of considerable internal resistance within Latin America from elite and conservative elements whose existing privileges were adversely affected by radical programs of land redistribution, the extension of democratic reforms, and the prospect of having to pay higher personal income taxes to fund large programs of social welfare. The economic statistics were invariably gloomy. During the decade of the 1960s, total unemployment in Latin America actually increased, while annual economic growth remained stuck at 1.5 percent and was outstripped by the population explosion. By the early 1970s, the program was widely considered as having failed, and it was quietly brought to an end. *See also* CHILE; GOODWIN, RICHARD (1931–); GORDON, LINCOLN (1913–).

AMERICAN REVOLUTION. A military conflict that occurred between 1774 and 1783 in which the North American colonies successfully won their independence from **Great Britain**. The result was the creation of the United States of America, which formally came into existence in 1787 as the first sovereign independent state in the **Western Hemisphere**. The rebellion was considered a "revolution" because it reflected radical ideas of republicanism and anticolonialism that were stated in the Declaration of Independence made in Philadelphia on July 4, 1776, and posed a challenge to the existing monarchical systems of Europe.

For Americans, it also came to express a sense of inherent American virtue and moral superiority, especially over what were perceived to be the reactionary political practices of the Old World of Europe.

The initial impact of the American Revolution on Latin America, however, was muted because popular awareness of the event was extremely limited. The educated creole elite knew little about the United States and attached more significance to political developments in Europe arising from the French Revolution in 1789. Nevertheless, the success of the North American colonists in winning independence—and especially the fact that the United States successfully remained in existence as a living example of freedom and republicanism—were recognized in Latin America as an impressive political achievement that deserved respect and could not be ignored. Moreover, the legacy of the American Revolution was evident in many presidential statements of U.S. policy toward Latin America ranging from **James Monroe**'s presidential message to the U.S. Congress in 1823 to the **Reagan Doctrine** of the 1990s. *See also* BOLÍVAR, SIMÓN (1783–1830).

ARANHA, OSVALDO (1894–1960). Brazilian political leader and diplomat. Born in Rio Grande do Sul, the same state as **Getúlio Vargas**, Aranha participated in the 1930 revolution that brought **Vargas** to power. After holding positions in the Vargas administration at the Ministry of Justice and the Treasury, he was appointed ambassador in Washington from 1933 to 1938 and minister of foreign affairs from 1938 to 1944. He followed the tradition of **Rio Branco** and **Joaquim Nabuco** in stressing that the priority of Brazilian foreign policy should be the pursuit of "alignment" with the United States. During the 1930s, Aranha sought to deflect criticism in the United States that **Brazil** was a fascist dictatorship. Later, as minister of foreign affairs, he was a key figure in bringing Brazil into **World War II** in 1942 on the side of the United States. The decision resulted in a massive increase in American economic and military assistance for Brazil.

Aranha hoped that the close wartime relationship with the United States would continue into peacetime. After 1945, however, Brazil was not so strategically important to the United States as it had been during the war. Consequently, Aranha was disappointed to find a lack of American diplomatic support for Brazil's request for a permanent seat on the Security Council of the newly formed **United Nations Organization**. He continued, however, to stress the importance of maintaining close relations with the United States and was able to express this in the economic policies that he pursued when he served as finance minister in the government of Getúlio Vargas from 1953 to 1954.

ARBENZ GUZMÁN, JACOBO (1913–1971). Guatemalan political leader and president from 1950 to 1954. A career army officer, Arbenz served as defense minister from 1945 to 1950 and was elected president in 1950. As president, he sought to continue and significantly expand the program of radical agrarian reform begun by the 1944 **Guatemalan Revolution**. However, his controversial expropriation of land owned by the Boston-based **United Fruit Company (UFCO)** and his personal association with Guatemalan communists provoked the hostility of officials in the administration of President **Dwight Eisenhower**. A covert operation, code-named **Operation PBSUCCESS**, was organized by the **Central Intelligence Agency (CIA)** and overthrew Arbenz in 1954. Shortly after the CIA-sponsored invasion began, Arbenz was informed by military colleagues that he did not have the support of the senior generals in the Guatemalan army. Consequently, he chose to resign the presidency and leave the country. He lived in exile until his death in 1971. Arbenz was an example of a left-wing Latin American leader whose ideas were considered too radical by the U.S. government. Fearful of the spread of international communism during the **Cold War**, American officials also considered Arbenz a procommunist. The decision was therefore made by the Eisenhower administration to destabilize his government and remove him from power. *See also* ARÉVALO BERMEJO, JUAN JOSÉ (1904–1990); ARMED INTERVENTIONS; COLD WAR.

ARÉVALO BERMEJO, JUAN JOSÉ (1904–1990). Guatemalan political leader and president from 1945 to 1951. A former teacher, Arévalo chose to live in exile in Argentina during the dictatorship of

Jorge Ubico. His political speeches and writings provided much of the inspiration for the period of radical economic and social reform beginning in 1944 and known as the **Guatemalan Revolution**. As president from 1945 to 1951, Arévalo introduced measures designed to promote greater political democracy but delayed the implementation of major land reform. He was, however, an outspoken and articulate critic of American interference in Latin American domestic affairs and blamed American imperialism for the region's political instability and economic backwardness. His view of the highly unequal and exploitative relationship between the United States and Latin America was well summed up in the title of his book *The Shark and the Sardines*, which was first published in Spanish in 1956 and then in English translation in 1961.

ARGENTINA. A country facing the Atlantic Ocean and along with **Chile** forms the southern cone of South America. On account of its relatively large territorial size, strategic location, and considerable economic achievement, Argentina has sought to pursue an active and at times assertive foreign policy commensurate with its claim to be the leading regional power in South America. It has also expected to play an important role in hemispheric affairs and in the wider world, an ambition frequently resulting in diplomatic tension and conflict not only with neighboring countries but also with the United States.

The first U.S. minister to serve in Argentina was Cesar A. Rodney, who presented his credentials to the Argentine government on December 23, 1823. For most of the 19th century, however, Argentina had little tangible contact with the United States. Both countries were separated by vast geographical distance and poor shipping communications. In addition, they shared few common diplomatic and commercial interests. By contrast, during the 19th century, Argentina developed a close and prosperous economic relationship with **Great Britain** based on the profitable export of meat and the import of British textiles, manufactured goods, and capital investment. Argentine confidence and sense of national achievement were evident at the 1889–1890 **International American Conference** held in Washington, where Argentina emerged as the focal point of Latin American opposition to the perceived attempts of the United States to control the proceedings. This provided a foretaste of the competitive and frequently adversarial relationship between Argentina and the United States that would emerge during the first half of the 20th century. By contrast, Argentina's great South American rival, **Brazil**, developed an alternative and calculated strategy of seeking close cooperation with the United States.

Argentine diplomatic divergence with the United States was clearly illustrated in attitudes toward the outbreak of war in Europe in 1914. Argentina initially followed the United States in adopting a policy of neutrality. When the United States entered the war against **Germany** in 1917, however, Argentina held firm to the policy of neutrality and insisted on continuing to observe normal diplomatic relations with all the nations at war. Moreover, in order to maintain hemispheric solidarity among the neutral nations, Argentine diplomats proposed the idea of hosting a Latin American peace conference from which belligerent powers such as the United States would be pointedly excluded. Brazil, however, effectively sabotaged the prospect of achieving united action by ending its neutrality and joining the war on the side of the United States.

As expressed in the **Calvo Doctrine** and the **Drago Doctrine**, both originating from the ideas of prominent Argentines, Argentina was prominent in arguing that foreign nations did not have automatic rights in international law to intervene forcibly in the domestic affairs of sovereign nations to recover public debt. This meant that Argentina, in marked contrast to Brazil, was frequently critical of the U.S. policy of **dollar diplomacy**, that resulted in the dispatch of U.S. marines to assume control over the government of countries in the Central American–Caribbean region. At the 1928 Havana Pan-American Conference, Argentine delegates were openly and bitterly critical of U.S. intervention in **Nicaragua**. The debate became so acrimonious that it was believed that the holding of future conferences would be so difficult that the **Pan-American Conference System** might well have come to an end.

A further period of serious diplomatic friction between Argentina and the United States ensued during **World War II**. Reminiscent of its actions in the previous world war, Argentina adopted an independent position at the Rio Conference of foreign ministers in 1942 and refused American requests to assent to a unanimous resolution mandating the immediate breaking of relations with the Axis powers.

While the action of the Argentine government characteristically reflected a proud desire not to be seen to be subservient to the United States, its attitude was also understandably influenced by profascist sympathies and a belief that Germany would win the war. Consequently, despite American political and economic pressure, Argentina insisted on its right to maintain diplomatic relations with the Axis powers. By contrast, Brazil was once again openly supportive of the United States and was rewarded with substantial **lend-lease** military assistance. Argentina was excluded from such aid. Only in March 1945, at a time when the Axis powers faced imminent military defeat, did Argentina finally declare war on Germany and Japan.

The legacy of the wartime ill feeling between Argentina and the United States persisted into peacetime when U.S. officials unsuccessfully sought to prevent the election of **Juan Perón** to the presidency in March 1946. Perón responded with anti-American rhetoric and during his presidency took a number of foreign policy initiatives that directly challenged the leadership role of the United States in the **Western Hemisphere**. Argentina's postwar financial prosperity, however, was brief and unsustainable so that Perón and his presidential successors not only abandoned ambitions of regional predominance but also often found themselves being compelled to seek financial aid from the United States.

There were few major issues affecting diplomatic relations between the two countries in the late 20th century with the exception in the 1970s of the controversy over the violation of human rights arising from the "**dirty war**" in Argentina, which led to protests from the Argentine military governments against the imposition of an arms embargo by the U.S. Congress. Another divisive issue arose later from the pro-British attitude adopted by the **Ronald Reagan** administration during the **South Atlantic War** (1982), in which Argentina resorted to aggressive military measures in a failed attempt to take possession of the **Falkland Islands** (**Islas Malvinas**) from Great Britain. *See also* HUMAN RIGHTS; RIVADAVIA, BERNARDINO (1780–1845); SÁENZ PEÑA, ROQUE (1851–1914); SARMIENTO, DOMINGO FAUSTINO (1811–1888).

ARIAS SÁNCHEZ, ÓSCAR (1940–). Costa Rican political leader and president from 1986 to 1990. Elected president in 1986, Arias sought to revive the stalled Latin American diplomatic efforts to resolve the **Central American Crisis**. He first presented his Peace Plan in May 1986 at a meeting of Central American presidents at Esquipulas in **Guatemala**. A further meeting was held in August 1987, resulting in the Esquipulas II Accord, or **Arias Peace Plan**. The accord called on governments in the region to negotiate directly with guerrilla movements to end all fighting. Similar proposals had been made by the **Contadora Group** but had invariably been sidelined by the **Ronald Reagan** administration. On this occasion, however, President Reagan reluctantly accepted the accord. Fighting came to an end throughout the region, and national elections were later held in **El Salvador**, Guatemala, and **Nicaragua**. In 1987, Arias achieved international distinction when he was awarded the Nobel Peace Prize in recognition of his personal contribution to bringing about the peace settlement.

ARIAS PEACE PLAN (1987). A diplomatic initiative to mediate the **Central American Crisis** also known as the Esquipulas II Accord. In May 1986, the presidents of the Central American countries met at Esquipulas in Guatemala to discuss ways of mediating the Central American crisis. The exposure of the **Iran-Contra affair** later in the year brought President **Ronald Reagan** and his Central American policy into serious disrepute and provided an opportunity for a renewal of Latin American diplomatic mediation to resolve the Central American crisis. A second meeting was held in August 1987, resulting in the Esquipulas II Accord, or Arias Peace Plan, named after **Óscar Arias**, the president of **Costa Rica**. The accord called on governments in the region to negotiate directly with guerrilla movements in order to bring an end to all fighting.

Beset by the domestic political controversy arising from the revelation of the Iran-Contra affair, the Reagan administration reluctantly accepted the recommendations made in the accord. As a result, armed hostilities were brought to an end throughout the region, and elections subsequently took place in **El Salvador**, **Guatemala**, and **Nicaragua**. In 1987, President Arias was awarded the Nobel Peace Prize for his personal contribution to the peace settlement. The Arias Peace Plan was a significant diplomatic event in the **Western Hemisphere** because it was the first major Latin American peace initiative to be accepted by the United States since the **ABC** mediation in President **Woodrow Wilson**'s dispute with **Mexico** in 1914.

ARMED INTERVENTIONS. Military interventions in Latin America by foreign powers. During 19th century, several Latin American countries experienced armed intervention by the great European powers and also by the United States. Only a few of the interventions, such as those launched by the British in the River Plate (1806–1807) and the French in **Mexico** (1862–1867), were military expeditions designed to occupy and control territory in Latin America. The large majority involved a show of limited naval force designed to protect the property and lives of endangered nationals during periods of serious local disorder. On occasion, intervention took the form of "gunboat diplomacy" in which warships were deliberately deployed to secure redress for perceived insults to national honor or grievances allegedly suffered by foreign nationals.

The United States was opposed to European military intervention that intended to acquire territory. This was made clear in President **James Monroe**'s message to the U.S. Congress in 1823 that became known as the **Monroe Doctrine**. Monroe's warning was not challenged because the military threat posed by the **Holy Alliance** did not materialize. In fact, with the exception of the **French Intervention** in Mexico (1862–1867), the European powers were reluctant to become involved in large-scale military actions in distant Latin America. Their interventions were confined to the brief use of naval force to secure specific objectives. Indeed, the United States carried out similar coercive naval measures where American interests were threatened. Citing Article 35 of the 1846 **Bidlack Treaty** with Colombia, the U.S. government sent military forces on 10 occasions to maintain order on the Isthmus of **Panama** during the second half of the 19th century. In 1903, U.S. warships aided the independence of Panama by preventing Colombian forces from suppressing the local rebellion.

Latin American governments regarded acts of foreign intervention as unjustifiable on the ground that they violated their sovereign rights as nation-states. When European powers resorted to gunboat diplomacy in the **Venezuela Incident** (1902–1903), Argentine Foreign Minister Luis María Drago argued that there was no automatic legal right to use military force to recover public debt. President **Theodore**

Roosevelt, however, would not endorse the **Drago Doctrine**. Instead, he declared that the United States had a duty to ensure order in the **Western Hemisphere** and that his government would act unilaterally if necessary to achieve this. The declaration, known as the **Roosevelt Corollary** to the Monroe Doctrine, was welcomed by the European powers because it meant that the United States would act as a self-appointed policeman to ensure that Latin American countries acted responsibly and, most important, continued to meet their financial obligations to foreign investors. The first implementation of this policy by Theodore Roosevelt was the sending of U.S. marines to restore order in the Dominican Republic in 1905. Most subsequent U.S. armed interventions involved countries in the Caribbean, but marines were sent to **Nicaragua** on the Central American mainland in 1912.

During the 1920s, there was growing criticism in Latin America over the U.S. policy of armed intervention. Particularly contentious was the deployment of U.S. marines in Nicaragua, an action that sparked off local guerrilla resistance led by **Augusto Sandino**. The issue of intervention aroused heated debate between the U.S. and Latin American delegates at the **Pan-American Conference** held at Havana in 1928. Inter-American relations were considerably improved, however, by President **Franklin D. Roosevelt**'s adoption of the **Good Neighbor Policy**. In January 1934, Roosevelt publicly declared that his government disavowed the policy of armed intervention in the affairs of sovereign states. He later announced the abrogation of the notorious **Platt Amendment** (1901), which had given the United States a constitutional right to intervene in **Cuba**.

Armed intervention by the United States in Latin America was revived during the **Cold War**, when it took the form mostly of covert military operations. Fearing that a communist beachhead was about to be established in **Guatemala**, the **Central Intelligence Agency (CIA)** organized **Operation PBSUCCESS** and overthrew Guatemalan President **Jacobo Arbenz** in 1954. A similar covert operation was prepared to overthrow **Fidel Castro** in **Cuba** but failed at the **Bay of Pigs** in April 1961. In the following year, President **Lyndon Johnson** resorted to overt armed intervention when he sent 20,000 U.S. troops to the Dominican Republic to defeat what he regarded as a communist conspiracy to seize the government. A similar action occurred almost two decades later in 1983 when **President Ronald Reagan** dispatched more than 7,000 troops to Grenada. Reagan also favored covert operations and was responsible for creating the army of political exiles known as the **Contras**, which sought to destabilize the **Sandinista** regime in Nicaragua.

The U.S. armed interventions that took place during the Cold War were intended to defeat the perceived threat of international communism. A different motive lay behind **Operation Just Cause**, which was approved by President **George H. W. Bush** in 1989. In this military action, more than 25,000 U.S. troops invaded **Panama** to arrest the Panamanian general **Manuel Noriega** and bring him to trial for narcotics trafficking. The fact that the operation aroused widespread criticism in Latin America, including condemnation by the **Organization of American States (OAS),** showed that armed intervention by the United States still remained a highly controversial and divisive issue in inter-American relations. This was demonstrated in 1982 by the attitudes toward the **South Atlantic War**; these attitudes were reminiscent of the different views held by Theodore Roosevelt and Luis María Drago regarding the right of foreign powers to resort to armed intervention at the beginning of the 20th century. While the United States condemned **Argentina**'s aggression and supported **Great Britain**'s decision to send a large military task force to regain the **Falkland Islands**, the Latin American governments were critical of European armed intervention in the **Western Hemisphere**. *See also* BIG STICK; CENTRAL AMERICAN CRISIS; DOMINICAN INTERVENTION (1965); DRAGO DOCTRINE; FRANCE; HUGHES, CHARLES EVANS (1863–1948); SOUTH ATLANTIC WAR (1982).

– B –

BAKER, JAMES A., III (1930–). American politician and secretary of state from 1989 to 1992. Born in Texas and trained as a lawyer at the University of Texas, Baker joined the Republican Party and was a senior adviser in **Ronald Reagan**'s successful campaign to win the presidency in 1980. During the Reagan administration, he served as White House chief of staff from 1981 to 1985 and secretary of the treasury from 1985 to 1988. In order to help alleviate the Latin American **debt**

crisis, Baker proposed what became known as the **Baker Plan** at a meeting of the **International Monetary Fund** in October 1985. Baker later served as secretary of state from 1989 to 1992 during the administration of President **George H. W. Bush**. *See also* GARCÍA PÉREZ, ALÁN (1949–).

BAKER PLAN (1985). A U.S. financial scheme to help resolve the Latin American **debt crisis**. The debt crisis began in 1982 and seriously affected the economies of many Latin American countries. In order to reschedule debt payments to their foreign creditors, these countries negotiated loans from the **International Monetary Fund (IMF)**. The total debt owed, however, continued to grow at the same time as economic growth sharply contracted for most countries. At the annual meeting of the IMF in South Korea in October 1985, the U.S. delegation unveiled the Baker Plan, named after Secretary of the Treasury **James Baker**. With the aim of stimulating international economic growth, the Baker Plan proposed that the **World Bank** make available $20 billion in new loans over a period of three years to the developing countries, most of which were located in Latin America. The debtor countries, however, were expected to adopt austerity economic policies in return. The financial arrangements of the Baker Plan helped alleviate the current shortage of foreign loans but were merely a short-term emergency solution. Another scheme known as the **Brady Plan** was adopted in 1990.

BALTIMORE AFFAIR (1891). Diplomatic crisis between the United States and **Chile**. In October 1891, a group of American sailors from the cruiser USS *Baltimore* on shore leave in Valparaíso, Chile, were involved in a fray with local Chileans in which one American sailor was killed and five were seriously wounded. The commander of the USS *Baltimore*, Captain Winfield F. Schley, reported to Washington that his men had been unarmed and had given no provocation for the attack. President **Benjamin Harrison** chose to react in an aggressive manner by sending warships to Chile and threatening to break off diplomatic relations. Since the **War of the Pacific** (1879–1884), diplomatic relations between Chile and the United States had been tense. Further conflict had arisen during the 1891 Chilean civil war. In the circumstances, the new Chilean government agreed to apologize to the United States for the incident and to pay financial compensation to the American sailors. While the American press applauded Harrison's firmness in defending national honor, it did not go unnoticed in Latin America that the president's resort to the threat of military force and his evident determination to humiliate Chile contradicted the Pan-American rhetoric and affirmations of goodwill that had marked the beginning of his presidential administration in 1889 and the **International American Conference** subsequently held in Washington.

BAY OF PIGS. A covert operation organized by the **Central Intelligence Agency (CIA)** to overthrow **Fidel Castro**. The covert military operation to remove Castro from political power in **Cuba** was based on **Operation PBSUCCESS**, which had overthrown President **Jacobo Arbenz** of **Guatemala** in 1954. The landing at the Bay of Pigs in Cuba took place on April 17, 1961. In marked contrast to the Guatemalan operation, however, the landing was a military failure. In fact, Castro's close colleague, **Ernesto "Che" Guevara**, had been present in Guatemala in 1954 and considered the example of Arbenz's abject surrender a grievous error. By contrast, Castro was determined to fight and personally directed the military operations that overwhelmed the invading force. In so doing, he greatly boosted his personal prestige throughout Latin America and the wider world. For the United States and President **John F. Kennedy**, the Bay of Pigs was an unmitigated disaster. Kennedy sought to counter Castro's success by launching a program of massive economic assistance for Latin America known as the **Alliance for Progress**. He also sought Latin American endorsement of plans to isolate Cuba both politically and economically. At the same time, a covert operation concentrating on internal sabotage in Cuba, known as "Operation Mongoose," was organized to destabilize Castro's regime. *See also* ARMED INTERVENTIONS.

BELAÚNDE TERRY, FERNANDO (1912–2002). Peruvian political leader and twice president from 1963 to 1968 and 1980 to 1985. Belaúnde studied architecture at the University of Texas and became a professor at the Catholic University of Lima. He was also active in politics and was the founder of the Popular Action Party (Acción

Popular) in 1956. He became president in 1963. His first administration sought to reduce poverty by promoting economic development, especially public works. The most controversial action, however, was Belaúnde's decision to reach a financial arrangement with the U.S.-owned International Petroleum Company. Nationalist opinion was inflamed by what was regarded as an act of surrender to the unpopular American company. The resulting political uproar resulted in a military coup that brought about Belaúnde's overthrow in 1968 and his replacement by General **Juan Velasco**.

After a period of political exile in the United States, Belaúnde returned to **Peru** and successfully won the 1980 presidential election. At a time of growing economic difficulty and insurgency made worse by the **debt crisis**, Belaúnde sought close diplomatic relations with the United States. He did, however, choose a divergent diplomatic course from Washington during the **South Atlantic War** in 1982. Initially, Belaúnde called for Latin American solidarity in support of **Argentina** against **Great Britain**. He offered Peruvian diplomatic mediation in order to prevent full-scale fighting breaking out between Argentina and Britain. The offer, however, was rejected by the British government, which proceeded to send a military task force and recapture the Falkland Islands. Belaúnde's pro-Argentine attitude contrasted markedly with the policy of the **Ronald Reagan** administration toward the conflict. *See also* OIL.

BELIZE. A country on the eastern coast of Central America bordered by **Mexico** to the north and **Guatemala** to the west and south. The possession of Belize by **Great Britain** dated from British settlements that were established in the 17th century. The United States showed minimal interest in the area until the 1840s and 1850s, when U.S. diplomats protested against Great Britain's attempt to extend its hold over Belize to include the Bay Islands and the port of Greytown. The conflict was motivated by Anglo-American commercial rivalry and American suspicion that Britain was seeking to possess territory that might be part of a future Central American canal. In 1859, Britain agreed that **Nicaragua** should control Greytown and that the Bay Islands would be returned to **Honduras**. A territorial dispute with **Guatemala**, however, was not resolved and has occasionally resulted in border incidents up to the present day. The territory of Belize was renamed British Honduras and became an official British colony in 1862. The country took the name of Belize in 1973 and achieved full independence in 1981.

BETANCOURT, RÓMULO (1908–1981). Venezuelan political leader and twice president. One of the founders and leaders of the radical political party known as Democratic Action (Acción Democrática), Betancourt served as president from 1945 to 1948 and from 1959 to 1964. A strong advocate of economic and social reform, Betancourt was openly admired by President **John F. Kennedy**. Moreover, the Venezuelan president was regarded as a key Latin American figure in helping to achieve the successful implementation of the **Alliance for Progress**. Betancourt was conscious that **Fidel Castro** viewed Venezuela as the leading target for the "export" of the **Cuban Revolution** to the mainland of Latin America. Consequently, he fully supported the United States in its controversial policy of seeking to isolate **Cuba** both politically and economically. *See also* INTERNATIONAL BANK FOR RECONSTRUCTION AND DEVELOPMENT (IBRD).

BIDLACK TREATY (1846). A canal treaty between the United States and **Colombia**. In 1846, the U.S. minister in Bogotá, Benjamin Bidlack, responded to the initiative of the Colombian foreign minister, Manuel Laria Mallarino, and negotiated a treaty with New Granada (renamed the United States of Colombia in 1863). The treaty was concerned mostly with commercial matters, but in Article 35 the United States agreed to guarantee Colombian sovereignty over the Isthmus of **Panama** and the protection of transit across the isthmus from either external or internal interference. It was expected that **Great Britain** and **France** would shortly conclude similar treaties with Colombia and thereby join in the guarantee of Colombian sovereignty. The failure of such treaties to materialize gave the United States by default a claim to a special position in isthmian affairs. This proved significant in 1880 when Article 35 was cited to justify the policy of President **Rutherford B. Hayes** to seek an "American" canal. It was also used by President **Theodore Roosevelt** to provide a legal basis for U.S. protective military intervention in the 1903 Panama revolt for the province's independence from Colombia.

BIG STICK. Policy associated with President **Theodore Roosevelt**. In his Annual Message to the U.S. Congress on December 6, 1904, Roosevelt stated that the United States had a duty to intervene in cases where Latin American governments committed "wrongdoing." Knowing that, in conversation, Roosevelt had used the maxim "Speak softly and carry a big stick," the American press described his new policy as one of wielding a "big stick" over Latin America. The policy was also referred to as the **Roosevelt Corollary** to the **Monroe Doctrine** and later as **dollar diplomacy** during the **William H. Taft** and **Woodrow Wilson** administrations. *See also* ARMED INTERVENTIONS.

BISSELL, RICHARD (1910–). Senior American official of the **Central Intelligence Agency (CIA)**. After working on the European Recovery Program (**Marshall Plan**) and for the Ford Foundation, in 1953 Bissell joined the CIA, where he soon established a reputation for outstanding technical expertise by organizing U-2 spy flights over the **Soviet Union**. In 1958, he became the head of the Directorate for Plans, which involved him in organizing and implementing covert operations. In an attempt to imitate the success of **Operation PBSUCCESS** in **Guatemala** in 1954, President **Dwight Eisenhower** instructed the preparation of a similar plan for the overthrow of **Fidel Castro** in **Cuba**. Bissell duly organized an operation code-named ZAPATA, which was approved by President **John F. Kennedy**, but in contrast to Operation PBSUCCESS, it ended in disaster at the **Bay of Pigs** in April 1961. Bissell left the CIA in February 1962 and later became a consultant for the Ford Foundation.

BLACK LEGEND. A historical belief held by many North Americans to explain and justify their assumed superiority over Spanish Americans. Also referred to as the "Spanish Fury," the "Black Legend" signified the deep religious differences and antagonism between Protestants and Catholics during the colonial period. It was particularly promoted in the North American colonies by the conviction that Spaniards had been responsible for the vicious persecution and deaths of thousands of Protestant civilians, including women and children, in the Netherlands in the 16th century. The idea of inherent Spanish depravity and religious extremism was later used by Americans to provide a simplistic explanation for the perceived backwardness of Latin American political and economic institutions when compared to those of the United States. *See also* ADAMS, JOHN QUINCY (1767–1848); JEFFERSON, THOMAS (1743–1826); KENNAN, GEORGE F. (1904–2005); WARS FOR LATIN AMERICAN INDEPENDENCE (1808–1826).

BLACK LIST. A U.S. wartime economic policy. During **World War II**, the United States followed the example of **Great Britain** and implemented policies of economic warfare against German and Italian business interests in Latin America. In July 1941, the **State Department** issued a "Proclaimed List of Certain Blocked Nationals," popularly known as the "Black List." The Black List contained the names of suspected pro-German and pro-Italian companies and individuals with whom American companies and citizens were instructed to boycott and to avoid having business relations with. Agents from the **Federal Bureau of Investigation (FBI)** were dispatched to Latin America to assist governments in identifying and restricting the activities of local German and Italian agents and their supporters.

The enforcement of the Black List, especially the handing over of hundreds of German nationals for wartime internment in the United States, provoked controversy in Latin America. The practice was criticized as unwarranted interference in domestic affairs and contrary to the policy of the **Good Neighbor** proclaimed by President **Franklin D. Roosevelt**. On the other hand, the restrictions placed on German and Italian activities were generally seen not only as sensible precautions but also as necessary for the successful prosecution of the war effort.

BLAINE, JAMES G. (1830–1893). American political leader and secretary of state in 1881 and also from 1889 to 1892. Born in Pennsylvania, Blaine moved to Maine, where he was active in the local Republican Party and secured election to the U.S. Congress first as a representative from 1863 to 1876 and then as a senator from 1876 to 1881. He was similar to **Henry Clay** in being unusual among American leading politicians of the 19th century in showing a special personal interest in Latin American affairs. Stressing the idea of the separation of the New World from the Old World of Europe, Blaine actively promoted the concept of **Pan-Americanism**. When he became secretary of state in 1881, he announced that the United States should protect and lead its "sister" nations of Latin America and that **Great Britain** posed the biggest threat to these aspirations. This was particularly evident in his attitude toward the **War of the Pacific** (1879–1884) and his determination that American diplomacy should become actively involved to bring about a peace settlement between **Chile** and **Peru**. Blaine, however, was known to be personally sympathetic toward Peru. A principal reason was his suspicion that British business interests were secretly supporting Chile to gain special favors.

Acting on his own personal initiative in early December 1881, Blaine proposed the assembly of a Pan-American peace conference in Washington to discuss and resolve the differences between Chile and Peru. A special diplomatic mission was dispatched to Santiago de Chile to secure Chile's agreement. But the initiative was badly timed. Blaine left the State Department on December 19, 1881, so that he was out of office when the mission reached South America in January 1882. The new secretary of state, Frederick Frelinghuysen, repudiated Blaine's policy and withdrew the invitations to the proposed conference. The outcome not only was personally humiliating for Blaine but also served to fuel the anti-American suspicions of Latin American political leaders. Although he was still generally regarded as an example of **Yankee** forcefulness and insensitivity, Blaine's image in Latin America was later improved by his leading role in organizing the **International American Conference** (1889–1890) and his advocacy of increased inter-American trade by the conclusion of bilateral **reciprocal trade agreements**.

BOLAND AMENDMENTS (1982–1984). Attempts by the U.S. Congress to restrict the power of the president in the conduct of foreign affairs. The revelation in the press in 1982 that officials in the administration of **Ronald Reagan** in Washington were conducting a "secret war" in **Nicaragua** prompted suspicion in the United States that the country was being stealthily dragged into "another Vietnam War." The House of Representatives responded in December 1982 with the passage of an amendment to a defense appropriations bill. Named after its sponsor, the Democratic Congressman from Massachusetts, Edward P. Boland, the Boland Amendment prohibited agencies of the federal government connected with intelligence activities from using congressional funds to attempt to overthrow the government of Nicaragua. The amendment expired after one year in December 1983.

A second Boland amendment was passed in October 1984 to prevent the federal government from supporting the paramilitary operations of the **Contras** in Nicaragua. The passage of a second amendment indicated the depth of congressional opposition toward President Ronald Reagan's policy in Nicaragua. The Reagan administration, however, was determined to continue providing aid for the Contras, and in order to circumvent the restrictions of the Boland Amendment, it resorted to covert and illegal methods to raise finances. This resulted in 1986 in the **Iran-Contra affair**, the public exposure of which threatened the president with the possibility of having to face impeachment. *See also* CASEY, WILLIAM J. (1913–1987); NORTH, OLIVER (1943–).

BOLÍVAR, SIMÓN (1783–1830). Revolutionary Latin American hero known as the "Liberator." From a wealthy and educated upper-class creole background, Bolívar was a charismatic figure who fought for the cause of Spanish-American independence from Spanish colonial rule. In his most successful military campaign, he commanded an army that started out from **Venezuela** in 1819, crossed the Andes, and eventually marched triumphantly into Lima, **Peru**, in 1823. After his outstanding military achievements, Bolívar was disillusioned by the frustrations of political life as he attempted to bring order and liberal reforms in the countries that he had liberated. Disillusioned and embittered, he decided to leave for Europe but died while still on Venezuelan soil in 1830.

Bolívar's fame as a military leader and political revolutionary spread far beyond his native Venezuela. In particular, his desire to retain the unity of the former Spanish-American colonial empire by creating a political federation of the new Latin American nations made him the celebrated champion and spokesperson of Spanish-American union. In 1820, he had united New Granada with Venezuela to form the new state of Gran Colombia, which was later joined by **Ecuador**. He attempted to implement his vision of an even larger union by convening the **Panama Congress** in 1826. The meeting was poorly attended and generally judged at the time as unsuccessful, but the Bolivarian ideal of hemispheric union remained an enduring influence on those political leaders who have sought to promote closer relations between the states in the **Western Hemisphere**.

The Bolivarian ideal has often been cited by Latin American politicians as a counter to the perceived hemispheric domination of the Anglo-Saxon United States. Indeed, Bolívar was typical of many Creoles of his era and afterward in displaying a curious attitude toward the United States. While he greatly admired the political achievements of the people of the northern republic in achieving and maintaining a republican system of government, he was severely critical of American indifference and diplomatic passivity during the Spanish-American struggle for independence. This ambivalence was reflected in the fact that he did not initially invite U.S. representation at the Panama Congress. *See also* CHÁVEZ, HUGO (1954–); INTERNATIONAL AMERICAN CONFERENCE (1889–1890); PAN-AMERICANISM; WARS FOR LATIN AMERICAN INDEPENDENCE (1808–1826); WESTERN HEMISPHERE.

BOLIVIA. A landlocked country located in the center of South America and named after **Simón Bolívar**. Official diplomatic relations between the United States and Bolivia were opened in 1849. However, contact between the two countries has been limited and largely commercial in nature. The principal issue has been over access to the country's natural resources. In general, the U.S. government has pursued a conciliatory policy toward Bolivia as exemplified by the acceptance during the 1930s of the nationalization of the U.S. oil company Standard Oil.

The administration of President **Dwight Eisenhower** was similarly accommodating toward the **National Revolutionary Movement** (Movimento Nacional Revolucionario [MNR]), which had risen to power in 1952. Although the MNR proclaimed its intention of implementing a "Bolivian Revolution" based on the example of the Mexican Revolution, the new government was willing to compensate the foreign-owned tin companies that suffered nationalization. In return, the Eisenhower administration continued programs of financial aid, including substantial purchases of Bolivian tin. The United States did not therefore encounter the same diplomatic difficulties in Bolivia that it had experienced earlier in **Mexico** over the control of natural resources.

Events in Bolivia also brought reassurance for U.S. diplomats in October 1967, when it was reported that the revolutionary **Ernesto "Che" Guevara** had been captured and killed in the interior of the country. Although Guevara would achieve international martyrdom status, his death was interpreted as a decisive setback for **Fidel Castro**'s policy of "exporting" the **Cuban Revolution** to the mainland of South America.

BRADEN, SPRUILLE (1894–1978). American diplomat. After serving in diplomatic posts in **Colombia** and **Cuba**, Braden was appointed ambassador to **Argentina** from May to September 1945. During this period, he developed a personal antipathy toward **Juan Perón**, who was then vice president. Recalled to Washington to serve as assistant secretary of state, Braden sought to prevent Perón's election to the Argentine presidency in March 1946. Two weeks before the election, he released for publication a **State Department** document titled *Consultation among the American Republics with Respect to the Argentine Situation* (more popularly known as the "Blue Book") detailing Perón's alleged wartime collusion with the Nazis. Perón responded by accusing the United States of blatant interference in Argentine domestic affairs and eagerly grasped the opportunity to state that the choice facing the Argentine people in the election was either "Perón or Braden." Perón duly won the election. Braden's ill-timed intervention not only damaged his own personal reputation within the State Department but also stimulated anti-American sentiment by portraying the United States as arrogant and interfering in its attitude toward the nations of Latin America.

BRADY PLAN (1990). A U.S. financial scheme to help resolve the **debt crisis**. The debt crisis, which began in 1982 and adversely affected the economies of the Latin American nations, had still not been resolved by the end of the decade. The election of **George H. W. Bush** in 1988 brought into office a new president who was prepared to endorse fresh initiatives designed to deal with the issues of hemispheric debt relief and trade. This was exemplified by the Brady Plan, named after Secretary of the Treasury Nicholas Brady, which was proposed in March 1989. In contrast to the earlier **Baker Plan** (1985), the new measure emphasized debt reduction by the elimination of arrears and, in effect, represented a tacit acknowledgment that the debt would never be repaid in full. The Brady Plan was more successful than the Baker Plan because it was implemented at a time when a strong revival in the world economy was already helping to promote economic recovery in Latin America and thereby diminish the severity of the debt crisis. *See also* INTERNATIONAL MONETARY FUND (IMF).

BRAZIL. The largest country in South America. As a former colony of Portugal, Brazil has historically believed itself to be different and apart from the Spanish countries of Latin America. In particular, it has felt strategically threatened by its powerful neighbor, **Argentina**, and to counter this anxiety has looked for external diplomatic and military support, especially from the United States. In 1824, when the administration of **James Monroe** established formal diplomatic relations with the newly independent Brazilian empire, the Brazilian minister in Washington suggested the conclusion of a military alliance between Brazil and the United States. The proposal was declined. For the next half century, contact between the two countries revolved mainly around trade and, in particular, the steady increase in sales of Brazilian coffee, for which the United States became the biggest single market. Political relations considerably improved during the period of **Pan-Americanism** at the end of the 19th century. The timing was propitious because the new Brazilian republic that came into being in 1889 desperately wanted diplomatic endorsement from the United States. Brazil therefore responded positively to proposals to negotiate a reciprocity treaty and in so doing greatly facilitated the implementation of the policy of commercial reciprocity pursued by the administration of **Benjamin Harrison**.

Brazil's friendly attitude toward the United States was further illustrated during the **Spanish-American War** (1898) when U.S. warships were allowed to take on fuel and to refit in Brazilian ports. The high point was the period of "approximation" at the beginning of the 20th century during which Brazilian Foreign Minister **Rio Branco** and the Brazilian ambassador in Washington, **Joaquim Nabuco**, developed a strategy that sought to align their country's foreign policy as closely as possible to that pursued by the United States. Diplomatic relations were upgraded to ambassadorial level and Secretary of State **Elihu Root** personally attended the Pan-American Conference held at Rio de Janeiro in 1906. Root even hinted at the possibility of an alliance between the two countries. The idea of a special relationship with the United States excited Brazilian diplomats, but their hopes of it materializing were soon disappointed. As in 1824, the United States traditionally sought to avoid diplomatic entanglements. Moreover, U.S. diplomats did not want to disturb Argentina by giving the impression that they were taking sides and favoring Brazil.

Brazil's economic and diplomatic importance to the United States increased during **World War I** when the country was valued as a supplier of vital raw materials for the war effort. American officials were also gratified by Brazil's decision to join the war in 1917 and hoped that the example would be followed by the other South American countries, especially Argentina. Indeed, Brazilian officials calculated that close wartime association with the United States would not only produce economic benefits but also enhance their country's diplomatic status in South America and in the wider world. Economic gains, however, proved to be temporary, and the rejection of the Versailles Treaty in the United States meant that Brazil was deprived of U.S. diplomatic backing in its bid to secure a permanent seat on the Council of the newly created **League of Nations**.

After a period of neglect, Washington's diplomatic interest in Brazil notably revived during the 1930s as apprehension arose over the perceived fascist sympathies of **Getúlio Vargas** and the marked increased in commercial relations between Brazil and Nazi **Germany**. Brazilian diplomacy, however, continued to stress through Ambassador **Osvaldo Aranha** its desire to maintain close and friendly relations with the United States. The relationship was boosted in 1939 by the outbreak of war in Europe, a development that greatly enhanced the strategic significance of Brazil's long coastline bordering the Atlantic Ocean. After the United States entered the war in 1941, the northeast of Brazil became a large U.S. military base and logistical bridge for the North African campaign. Massive quantities of **lend-lease** aid were received that contributed to Brazil surpassing Argentina as the leading military power in South America. But U.S.

preferential treatment for Brazil was withdrawn after 1945. Washington desired friendly relations but did not want Brazil to become too powerful and upset the existing balance of power in South America. Brazil's annoyance was exemplified in the refusal to send a token military expeditionary force to join U.S. forces in the **Korean War** (1950–1953).

During the 1950s, as part of the growing concern over the rise in the influence of international communism in the hemisphere, U.S. officials focused on the particular vulnerability of the poverty-stricken northeast of Brazil. Another cause for anxiety was the rise of the left-wing political leader **João Goulart** to the presidency in 1961. President **Lyndon Johnson** welcomed the fall of Goulart in 1964 and proceeded to endorse the new military government with diplomatic support and a substantial increase in financial aid and investment. The new military leadership regarded U.S. economic aid as vital for the development and modernization of the Brazilian economy. They also admired the political institutions of the United States and considered that country as the leader of the free world in the battle against international communism. The close relationship was demonstrated by Brazilian support for Johnson in his controversial military intervention in the Dominican Republic in 1965. But the convergence did not persist for very long. The geopolitical reality had not changed in that the United States was concerned more with **Cuba** and Central America than with a country that was considered too geographically distant and peripheral to U.S. national security.

Brazil's response to U.S. indifference followed the pattern of the past. While Brazilian governments acknowledged the preeminent influence of the United States in hemispheric affairs, they stressed their determination to pursue independent policies where necessary to promote not only Brazil's hemispheric but also its own global interests. Consequently, in 1991 Brazil joined with Argentina, **Paraguay**, and **Uruguay** in forming a customs union known as **Mercosul**. Brazil also looked outward for alternative trading markets and sources of capital in Western Europe, Japan, and the Third World. Where diplomatic friction arose with the United States over controversial issues such as **human rights**, the debt question, and the environment, Brazil was not averse to criticizing U.S. policy. *See also* BRAZILIAN NAVAL REVOLT (1893–1894); DOMINICAN INTERVENTION

(1965); LULA DA SILVA, LUIZ INÁCIO (1945–); RECIPROCAL TRADE AGREEMENTS.

BRAZILIAN COUP (1964). Change of government by military coup in **Brazil**. On April 2, 1964, senior Brazilian army officers staged a coup that overthrew the government of President **João Goulart**. Local U.S. officials, including Ambassador **Lincoln Gordon** and the defense attaché, **Vernon Walters**, had been given prior information of the coup. Indeed, Walters was known to be on very friendly terms with a number of Brazilian generals. Consequently, American complicity in the coup was strongly suspected, although this was publicly and firmly denied by the U.S. ambassador. Although it was not public knowledge at the time, officials in the **Lyndon Johnson** administration had secretly prepared a contingency plan code-named "Operation Brother Sam" that involved mobilizing a U.S. naval task force offshore with instructions to intervene in Brazil to protect American citizens should the military coup fail and serious violence ensue.

In fact, in 1964, President Johnson was delighted to learn of Goulart's fall from power. Even though Goulart was known to be still in Brazil, Johnson quickly telegraphed his good wishes to the new interim Brazilian president. No objection was made by American officials as the strongly anticommunist Brazilian military installed themselves in government and proceeded ruthlessly to suppress any signs of political opposition.

BRAZILIAN NAVAL REVOLT (1893–1894). Revolt in **Brazil** involving U.S. naval intervention. In 1889, the Brazilian empire came to an end, and the country became a republic. The event was especially welcomed in the United States because it signified the collapse of the last remaining monarchical system of government in Latin America. But political instability followed. The threat by the Brazilian navy to bombard Rio de Janeiro in November 1891 brought about the resignation of the first president of the republic, Deodoro da Fonseca. In September 1893, the Brazilian navy mutinied again and mounted a naval blockade of the harbor of Rio de Janeiro. The government of Floriano Peixoto, however, refused to resign and alleged that the revolt represented a secret European plot to restore the monarchy. Peixoto hoped that his allegation would gain not only

American sympathy but also material support. Although Secretary of State Walter Q. Gresham doubted the idea of a European conspiracy, he increased the U.S. naval presence in Rio de Janeiro to five warships. The small American squadron commanded by Admiral Andrew Benham was given the task of protecting American merchant shipping from interference by the naval insurgents. When he subsequently fired on the insurgents and thereby prevented them from stopping and searching American merchant ships in January 1894, Benham effectively broke the attempted blockade and rendered the position of the insurgent fleet in the harbor basically untenable.

The Naval Revolt finally collapsed in March 1894 when the rebels admitted defeat and withdrew from the harbor. Floriano Peixoto was so grateful to the United States that he made July 4, 1894, a national holiday. Gresham, however, was careful to stress that the aim of the American naval action undertaken by Benham had not been to take sides in an internal political dispute but to uphold the right of American merchants to carry out commercial operations in the harbor without interference. Whatever Gresham's exact motive, the naval action in Brazil was similar to the **Baltimore Affair** in 1891 in demonstrating the growing military power of the United States and how it could be projected, if required, to assert American rights throughout Latin America. *See also* PEDRO II, EMPEROR OF BRAZIL (1825–1891).

BRYAN, WILLIAM JENNINGS (1860–1925). American political leader, celebrated public speaker, and secretary of state from 1913 to 1915. Born in Illinois, Bryan moved to Nebraska, where he worked as a lawyer and journalist. A charismatic political figure and famous public speaker, he was defeated as Democratic presidential candidate on three occasions in 1896, 1900, and 1908. In 1912, he accepted the invitation of President-elect **Woodrow Wilson** to become secretary of state in his administration. The choice reflected Wilson's aim of pursuing a new and idealistic foreign policy.

As secretary of state, Bryan promoted the cause of international peace by emphasizing the conclusion of arbitration agreements to settle disputes between nations quickly and amicably. The scheme was intended to be worldwide, but it also complemented Wilson's broad vision of a peaceful and prosperous **Western Hemisphere** outlined in his **Mobile Address**. While most Latin American states joined the United States in signing what were popularly called "cooling off" arrangements, only 10 countries formally ratified the treaties. Furthermore, Bryan's diplomatic efforts to promote hemispheric peace and cooperation were seriously undermined by the outbreak of **World War I**. He disagreed with Wilson over policy on the German submarine question and resigned from the cabinet on June 9, 1915.

BUNAU-VARILLA, PHILIPPE (1859–1940). French engineer and Panama canal lobbyist. During the 1880s, Bunau-Varilla worked as an engineer on the French canal scheme in Panama and acquired large financial interests in the **Panama Canal Company** after it emerged from bankruptcy and was reorganized in 1894. On learning that the U.S. government intended to construct a canal through Central America, he came to the United States to lobby American politicians to decide in favor of the route through **Panama**. Particularly persuasive was his information that the existing canal concessions possessed by the Panama Canal Company could be purchased at very reasonable financial terms. This considerably aided the choice of Panama rather than Nicaragua as the preferred route.

When Colombia chose not to ratify the **Hay-Herrán Treaty**, Bunau-Varilla supported moves for the independence of Panama. As the representative of the new republic in Washington, he speedily negotiated a convention with Secretary of State **John Hay** in November 1903 that was ratified as the **Hay-Bunau-Varilla Treaty** in November 1903. This agreement achieved Bunau-Varilla's purpose of ensuring that the canal was constructed at Panama. On the other hand, he had accepted financial terms and rights to control territory that were regarded as very favorable to the United States and would later be contested by Panamanian political leaders. *See also* ROOSEVELT, THEODORE (1858–1919).

BUNKER, ELLSWORTH (1894–1984). American diplomat. A career diplomat, Bunker's first ambassadorial appointment was to **Argentina** from 1951 to 1952. He later held several important posts, including service in India and South Vietnam. While generally regarded as an expert on Asian affairs, Bunker maintained an active involvement in U.S. policy toward Latin America. From 1964 to

1966, he served as ambassador to the **Organization of American States**. During the **Richard Nixon** administration, he was put in charge of conducting discussions with **Panama** over the renegotiation of the 1903 Canal Treaty. In 1977, Bunker's specialist knowledge of the canal issue and his diplomatic skills resulted in his appointment by President **Jimmy Carter** to join with Ambassador **Sol Linowitz** and negotiate new canal treaties with the Panamanian government. The talks were complex but resulted in the **Panama Canal Treaties**, which were signed by Carter and the Panamanian leader, **Omar Torrijos**, in September 1977 and eventually ratified by the U.S. Senate in 1978.

BUREAU OF THE AMERICAN REPUBLICS. *See* PAN-AMERICAN UNION (PAU).

BURNHAM, FORBES (1923–1985). Guyanese political leader and prime minister from 1964 to 1980 and president from 1980 to 1985. Of African ethnic background, Burnham was educated at the University of London and became a lawyer. When he returned to **Guyana**, he joined with **Cheddi Jagan** to form the left-wing People's Progressive Party in 1950. When Jagan was elected prime minister in 1953, Burnham became a member of the executive government. Forced out of office by the reimposition of British colonial rule in October 1953, Burnham subsequently became a political rival of Jagan.

In 1958, Burnham formed the People's National Congress. His party received the support of U.S. officials who believed that Jagan intended to turn Guyana into a communist state. The covert activities of agents of the **Central Intelligence Agency (CIA)** helped bring about electoral defeat for Jagan in 1964 and his replacement by Burnham. In return for economic aid from the **Lyndon Johnson** administration, Burnham adopted pro-American policies, including the placing of an embargo on trade with **Cuba**. During the 1970s, however, Burnham changed political course and began to cultivate friendly relations with Cuba and the **Soviet Union**. The **Richard Nixon** administration retaliated by cutting off economic aid in 1971. Burnham, however, retained his political ascendancy in Guyana, increased his presidential powers, and ruled as a virtual dictator until his death in 1985.

BUSH, GEORGE H. W. (1924–). American political leader and president from 1989 to 1993. Born in Massachusetts but raised in Connecticut, Bush moved to Texas, where he became active in the oil industry and in politics as a member of the Republican Party. After being successfully elected as the Republican candidate for vice president in 1980 and again in 1984, Bush won the presidential election in 1988. Taking office at a time when the **Cold War** was coming to an end, Bush was less concerned about the threat of international communism and was more receptive than his predecessor, **Ronald Reagan**, to proposals for taking initiatives in hemispheric issues, especially those relating to trade and investment.

In June 1990, he announced the "Enterprise for the Americas Initiative" (EAI), which envisaged the creation of a free trade area covering all of the **Western Hemisphere**. As a first step, Bush welcomed the proposal of Mexican President **Carlos Salinas** to begin negotiations leading to the **North American Free Trade Agreement (NAFTA)** consisting of the United States, Mexico, and Canada. The Bush administration also produced the **Brady Plan** to help resolve the Latin American **debt crisis**. However, in a manner much more reminiscent of old-fashioned **dollar diplomacy**, Bush approved **Operation Just Cause** in 1989, a military and unilateral intervention that involved more than 25,000 U.S. troops invading **Panama** to arrest the Panamanian general **Manuel Noriega**. *See also* ARMED INTERVENTIONS; NARCOTICS TRAFFICKING.

BUSH, GEORGE W. (1946–). American political leader and president since 2001. The son of President **George H. W. Bush**, George W. Bush was born in New Haven, Connecticut, and educated at Yale and Harvard. He served as Republican governor of **Texas** before securing election as president in 2000 and reelection in 2004. In foreign affairs, the Bush administration has been preoccupied mainly with fighting international terrorism in the aftermath of the attacks of September 11, 2001, on the United States. In this respect, the war in Iraq and postwar events in that country have been a dominant issue. While Bush's Texan background has made him more conscious of the issue of managing the problem of increasing numbers of illegal immigrants from Mexico, his administration has shown relatively little sustained interest in other Latin American affairs. A notable exception, however, has been Washington's attempts to secure regular supplies of **oil** from **Venezuela** while also seeking to counter the anti-American propaganda of Venezuelan President **Hugo Chávez**.

– C –

CALLES, PLUTARCO ELÍAS (1877–1945). Mexican political leader and president from 1924 to 1928. A supporter of **Francisco Madero**, Calles was one of the prominent political leaders of the **Mexican Revolution**. As president from 1924 to 1928, he experienced difficult relations with the United States because of his attempt to implement Article 27 of the 1917 Mexican Constitution, which declared that rights to property acquired by foreigners prior to 1917 were to be limited to a time period of 50 years, after which ownership would revert to the state. The measure directly affected U.S. **oil** companies that complained that the proposed action was unfair because it was retrospective. Diplomatic relations became strained as the **Calvin Coolidge** administration sought to protect U.S. interests until a compromise agreement was reached in December 1927. After leaving the presidency in 1928, Calles continued to be a force in Mexican politics and is regarded as the founder in 1929 of the National Revolutionary Party (Partido Nacional Revolucionario), which later was renamed the PRI and has long been the dominant political party in the country.

CALVO DOCTRINE. Statement concerning the right of intervention by foreign powers. During the 19th century, the newly independent nations of Latin America felt vulnerable to external interference by foreign powers in their domestic affairs. A particular concern was "gunboat diplomacy" in the form of military intervention by the warships of the leading European powers to protect the rights of their foreign nationals and recover public debt. In 1868, the Argentine international lawyer Carlos Calvo argued that a nation's sovereignty was inviolable and that foreign governments did not have an automatic legal right to intervene to protect their nationals because this gave foreigners a privileged status over local citizens. The resulting Calvo Doctrine provided the basis for the later **Drago Doctrine** (1902) and became a feature of Latin American claims to secure international recognition of and respect for the sovereign rights of all nations. The United States declined to recognize both doctrines and preferred to reserve the right to take armed intervention where circumstances warranted. *See also* ARGENTINA; ARMED INTERVENTIONS; ROOSEVELT COROLLARY; ROOSEVELT, THEODORE (1858–1919); VENEZUELA INCIDENT (1902–1903).

CANADA. A country in North America bordered by the United States to the south. A former colony of **Great Britain**, Canada was given dominion self-governing status in 1867. Regarding itself as part of the British Commonwealth, Canada pursued a foreign policy that was aligned to that of Great Britain and traditionally took more interest in British and Commonwealth than in hemispheric affairs. For example, Canada joined both world wars at their commencement as an ally of Great Britain and became a founding member of the North Atlantic Treaty Organization (NATO) in 1948. The close identification with Great Britain meant that Canada was not invited to attend the **International American Conference** in 1889 and did not become a member of either the **Pan-American Conference System** or later of the **Organization of American States (OAS)** when it was created in 1948.

During the late 20th century, Canada modified its diplomatic strategy and chose to develop closer political and economic relations with the nations of the **Western Hemisphere**. In 1989, Canada became a full member of the OAS. In the same year, Canada signed a free trade agreement with the United States that, with the addition of **Mexico** in 1992, became the **North American Free Trade Agreement (NAFTA).**

CANNING, GEORGE (1770–1827). British political leader and supporter of Latin American independence. In 1823, British Foreign Minister George Canning proposed a joint Anglo-American protest to forestall the threat of military intervention in Latin America by the European powers known as the **Holy Alliance**. The suggestion was considered but rejected by the **James Monroe** administration. Canning, however, sought to advance his country's political and commercial interests over those of the United States by claiming that

Great Britain wished to be the foremost friend, protector, and example for the newly independent Latin American nations. In fact, he effectively marginalized the public relations impact of the **Monroe Doctrine** by stating that it was the deterrent of the British navy, the world's most powerful naval force, and his own diplomatic skill in securing a private understanding with the French foreign minister in October 1823 that had prevented the Holy Alliance from undertaking military intervention to restore Spanish rule in the New World. Canning was successful in that Latin Americans generally believed that he had actually done much more than Monroe to help them in both winning and maintaining independence from Europe. *See also* ADAMS, JOHN QUINCY (1767–1848); WARS FOR LATIN AMERICAN INDEPENDENCE (1808–1826).

CÁRDENAS, LÁZARO (1895–1970). Mexican political leader and president from 1934 to 1940. A former army officer, Cárdenas became active in politics and was elected president in 1934. His presidency was notable for its determined efforts to accelerate the implementation of the **Mexican Revolution**, especially land reform. In 1938, he provoked diplomatic controversy with the United States by unilaterally announcing the nationalization of the foreign-owned **oil** companies in **Mexico**. This resulted in a serious clash with the **Franklin D. Roosevelt** administration over the exact amount of compensation to be paid to the U.S. oil companies. Relations became extremely tense as Cárdenas resisted President Roosevelt's threat of economic sanctions and insisted on carrying out his program of nationalization. Roosevelt eventually accepted the recommendation of the U.S. ambassador in Mexico, **Josephus Daniels**, that a policy of conciliation be adopted. In September 1941, after Cárdenas had left the presidency, a satisfactory agreement was finally reached between the two governments on the amount of compensation to be paid to the oil companies.

CARNEGIE, ANDREW (1835–1919). American businessman and philanthropist. Born in Dunfermline, Scotland, Carnegie immigrated as a child to the United States and in a true story of "rags to riches" went on to acquire a vast fortune as an iron and steel industrialist. A member of the Republican Party, he was a supporter of **James G.**

Blaine and the policy of **Pan-Americanism** that was adopted by the **Benjamin Harrison** administration (1889–1893). Carnegie advocated the development of closer relations with Latin America and was a member of the U.S. delegation at the **International American Conference** (1889–1890). As a celebrated philanthropist, Carnegie took a close personal interest in international affairs and especially in supporting the promotion of world peace that was exemplified by the establishment of the Carnegie Endowment for International Peace. Nevertheless, he also retained a desire to assist the cultivation of improved relations between the United States and Latin America. This was demonstrated in 1910 by his generous donation of almost $1 million toward the cost of constructing a new building in Washington that became the permanent home of the **Pan-American Union (PAU)**.

CARRANZA, VENUSTIANO (1859–1920). Mexican political leader and president from 1915 to 1920. A landowner and politician, Carranza joined the insurgency led by **Francisco Madero** to challenge the oppressive rule of President **Porfirio Díaz** in 1910. After Madero's death in 1913, Carranza was one of the principal leaders of the revolutionary movement to overthrow **Victoriano Huerta** and restore constitutional government. In 1915, Carranza was recognized as president and held this office until his murder in 1920.

Carranza exemplified the anti-Americanism that was such a visible feature of the **Mexican Revolution**. He was strongly nationalist and was severely critical of President **Woodrow Wilson**'s decision to send U.S. troops to occupy **Veracruz** in April 1914 and later to order the armed pursuit of **Pancho Villa** into Mexican territory in 1916. A clash between Mexican and U.S. troops in June 1916 briefly raised the possibility of war between **Mexico** and the United States. Moreover, as demonstrated by the **Zimmermann Telegram** (1917), the German government sought to exploit Carranza's well-known anti-American attitude by seeking to persuade Mexico to join **World War I** on the side of **Germany**. The Mexican government, however, preferred to maintain its policy of neutrality. In 1920, Carranza was overthrown in a military coup and killed.

CARTER, JIMMY (1924–). American political leader and president from 1977 to 1981. Born in Plains, Georgia, "Jimmy" Carter was a successful local businessman who served as Democratic governor of Georgia from 1970 to 1974. His election to the presidency in 1976 as a political outsider raised the prospect of radical changes occurring in both the domestic and the foreign policy of the United States. In diplomacy, this included a new emphasis on closer relations with Latin America, a region that Carter and his wife Rosalyn had visited several times and had long had a personal interest in. Moreover, Carter included an overtly Christian ethos in his early foreign policy speeches and stated that his administration would place considerable importance on the international observation of **human rights**. This aim was likely, however, to cause conflict with those Latin American governments that were dominated by the military and pursued repressive authoritarian policies.

In his policy toward the Latin American nations, Carter saw **Panama** as a test case of his intention to improve the image of the United States. Influenced by the **Linowitz Report**, he particularly wanted to expedite discussions with that country and finally resolve the long-standing controversy over the ownership of the canal and the exact status of the **Canal Zone**. This was achieved by his active involvement in the process of negotiation and ratification of the **Panama Canal Treaties** in 1977–1978. The canal issue, however, was very controversial in the United States, and Carter secured the ratification of the treaties only at considerable political cost.

Carter's insistence on respect for human rights also proved highly contentious and was often likened by his critics to the preaching of his Democratic predecessor, President **Woodrow Wilson**. It particularly irritated military governments in Latin America who complained that Carter was deliberately adopting double standards by placing punitive sanctions on them but neglecting to put the same pressure on communist countries. A similar argument was made by political conservatives in the United States who were especially critical of what they described as Carter's naive and mistaken policy of alienating friendly authoritarian governments while accommodating anti-American left-wing regimes such as the **Sandinistas** in **Nicaragua**. The "loss of Nicaragua" was added to the list of alleged foreign policy disasters, including the Iranian embassy hostage crisis and the Soviet invasion of Afghanistan, all of which contributed to Carter's defeat by **Ronald Reagan** in the 1980 presidential election.

After leaving the presidency, Carter maintained an interest in foreign affairs and acted as a roving international ambassador. He was appointed on a number of occasions to act as an observer in the monitoring of elections held in Latin America. *See also* DIRTY WAR; KIRKPATRICK, JEANE (1926–); PANAMA CANAL; SANTA FE REPORT (1980); SOMOZA DEBAYLE, ANASTASIO (1925–1980); TORRIJOS HERRERRA, OMAR (1929–1981).

CASEY, WILLIAM J. (1913–1987). American diplomat and director of the **Central Intelligence Agency (CIA)** from 1981 to 1987. During **World War II**, Casey served in the Office of Strategic Services. In 1980, he managed the successful presidential campaign of the Republican candidate, **Ronald Reagan**, and was rewarded in 1981 with appointment as director of the CIA. As director, he enthusiastically sought to implement the **Reagan Doctrine**. In Latin America, this resulted in the secret recruitment and training of the **Contras** as an army to destabilize the **Sandinistas** in **Nicaragua**. Casey's attempts to circumvent congressional restrictions on funding the Contras became public knowledge when the **Iran-Contra affair** was revealed in 1986. However, Casey's exact role in the scandal could not be fully investigated by the U.S. Congress because he suffered a terminal illness in May 1987 and was not able to testify in congressional hearings. *See also* BOLAND AMENDMENTS (1982–1984); CENTRAL AMERICAN CRISIS; NORTH, OLIVER (1943–).

CASTILLO ARMAS, CARLOS (1914–1957). Guatemalan army officer and president from 1954 to 1957. A staunch anticommunist and critic of radical agrarian reform, Colonel Castillo Armas was opposed to the policies of the government of President **Jacobo Arbenz**. He was chosen by the **Central Intelligence Agency (CIA)** to head the army of Guatemalan exiles recruited and trained by the CIA in **Honduras** as part of **Operation PBSUCCESS**. Castillo Armas commanded the exile army that invaded **Guatemala** in June 1954 and was instrumental in forcing Arbenz to resign the presidency.

With the backing of the United States, Castillo Armas became the new president. His government was strongly pro-American and anticommunist and essentially brought an end to the **Guatemalan Revolution** by reversing the policies of agrarian reform, arresting alleged communists, and restricting the activities of labor unions. Castillo Armas, however, was soon overthrown by assassination in July 1957. He provided an example of the Latin American authoritarian figure usually originating from a military background whose anticommunist attitude gained the political endorsement and material support of the United States during the **Cold War**. *See also* DULLES, JOHN FOSTER (1889–1959).

CASTRO, CIPRIANO (1858–1924). Venezuelan general and president from 1899 to 1911. After staging a military coup in 1899, Castro ruled as a virtual dictator until 1911. His cavalier attitude toward payment of the country's foreign debt and insistence that the Venezuelan courts should decide cases where foreigners claimed for losses incurred as a result of civil disorder provoked the **Venezuelan Incident** (1902–1903). **Great Britain**, **Germany**, and Italy sent a squadron of gunboats to impose a punitive naval blockade of the main Venezuelan ports. In the face of Castro's indifference, the European powers ended the blockade and agreed to seek arbitration at The Hague Court of Permanent Arbitration. The resort to arbitration pleased President **Theodore Roosevelt**, but he also found Castro extremely difficult to deal with over the matter of claims made by American citizens against Venezuela. American officials were relieved when Castro left the presidency in 1911. *See also* DRAGO DOCTRINE; VENEZUELA.

CASTRO RUZ, FIDEL (1927–). Cuban communist political leader and president since 1959. Fidel Castro's rise to power in **Cuba** in 1959 marked a significant step in the development of the **Cold War** in the **Western Hemisphere** because he was determined to implement the **Cuban Revolution** and transform Cuba rapidly into a socialist society. At the same time, he wanted to export the social revolution to the mainland of Latin America and advocated armed struggle to achieve this. Castro was also severely critical of the United States and, in the tradition of **José Martí**, blamed American imperialism for inflicting economic backwardness not only on Cuba but also on the whole of Latin America. President **John F. Kennedy** responded by denouncing the violent extremism of the Cuban Revolution and advocated the **Alliance for Progress** as the best way for Latin America to achieve peaceful economic development, democratic government, and social reform. At the same time, the United States attempted to destabilize the Castro regime by conducting covert operations involving acts of sabotage and a military invasion at the **Bay of Pigs**. A number of assassination attempts against Castro were also organized by the **Central Intelligence Agency (CIA)**.

Fidel Castro reacted to American hostility by openly describing himself as a Marxist-Leninist. He also entered into close political and economic ties with the **Soviet Union**. At times, it seemed that Fidel Castro had become a puppet of the Soviet Union, but his skill in successfully maintaining Cuba's independence of the United States earned him admiration in Latin America and throughout the Third World. With his beard and cigar and dressed in army fatigues, he successfully cultivated the image of the revolutionary hero and guerrilla fighter.

Although the Soviet Union never entered into a formal military alliance with Castro, his support was very useful in serving as a means of challenging American preeminence in Latin America. In this sense, the continued existence of Castro's Cuba was a persistent irritation to the Americans just as the Western presence in West Berlin annoyed the Soviets. Moreover, Castro regularly appeared at international meetings where he berated American imperialism and offered aid and encouragement to national liberation movements in Latin America, especially in Central America and the Caribbean. *See also* CHURCH COMMITTEE; CUBAN MISSILE CRISIS (1962); GUEVARA, ERNESTO "CHE" (1928–1967).

CENTRAL AMERICAN COURT OF JUSTICE. A conference to promote peace in Central America. After successfully mediating a conflict between **El Salvador**, **Guatemala**, and **Honduras** in 1906, President **Theodore Roosevelt** and Mexican President **Porfirio Díaz** invited the governments of **Costa Rica**, El Salvador, Guatemala, Honduras, and **Nicaragua** to send delegates to a Central American Peace Conference. The conference took place in Washington from November 14 to December 20, 1907. A General Treaty of Peace and Amity was concluded, providing for the compulsory settlement of disputes between the Central American countries. The delegates also agreed to establish a Central American Court of Justice, which remained in existence until 1918.

CENTRAL AMERICAN CRISIS. A period of political instability in Central America. During the 1970s and 1980s, political discontent in Central America was reflected in the emergence of "national liberation fronts" based on guerrilla movements exemplified by the **Farabundo Martí National Liberation Front** (Frente Farabundo Martí para la Liberación Nacional [FMLN]) in **El Salvador** and the **Sandinista National Liberation Front** (Frente Sandinista de Liberación Nacional [FSLN], or "Sandinistas") in **Nicaragua**. Officials in the **Jimmy Carter** and especially the **Ronald Reagan** administrations observed events in Central America primarily in terms of **Cold War** politics and saw both the FMLN and FSLN not as internal movements seeking political reform but as agents of international communism.

Consequently, the Carter administration pursued an ambivalent policy toward the repressive rule of **Anastasio Somoza Debayle** in Nicaragua because it did not want to see him replaced by the pro-Marxist Sandinistas. After Somoza resigned in 1979, Carter's apparent tolerance of the Sandinista government in Nicaragua was one of the controversial foreign policy issues that contributed to his defeat in the presidential election of 1980. On assuming the presidency in 1981, Ronald Reagan referred to Central America as America's "backyard" and interpreted the struggle taking place there as an East–West confrontation whose outcome would play a significant part in the global crusade to defeat the "evil empire" of the **Soviet Union**.

Although disturbances occurred throughout the whole of Central America, Reagan's biggest concerns were El Salvador and Nicaragua. In El Salvador, the danger of "another Cuba" was the main worry. The conflict in that country was attributed not to internal factors but to deliberate communist interference. The priority of American policy was the total military destruction of the FMLN. While the FMLN was never actually militarily defeated and continued to survive as a credible fighting force in the countryside, Reagan's policy was successful to the extent that it prevented the guerrillas from achieving the same degree of military and especially political success as the Sandinistas in Nicaragua. Nevertheless, criticism of his strategy was provoked not only in the United States but also in Latin America and Western Europe as civil unrest and violence in El Salvador continued unabated throughout the 1980s, resulting in extensive economic destruction, violations of human rights, and massive civilian casualties, including an estimated 1 million people forced to become refugees. A large number moved north and eventually migrated to Mexico and the United States.

In Nicaragua, Carter's policy of seeking political accommodation with the Sandinistas was changed by Reagan to one of outright hostility in which both overt and covert measures, notably the organization of a private army known as the "Contras," were employed to overthrow a regime whose leader, **Daniel Ortega**, was regarded a younger version of **Fidel Castro**. The confrontational approach, however, was constrained by the fact that the U.S. Congress, American public opinion, and even senior members of the Reagan administration and the armed services were sharply divided over the issue of Nicaragua. In particular, anxiety over the nightmare scenario of being sucked into "another Vietnam [War]" effectively ruled out the deployment of American combat troops in Central America.

Latin American leaders, notably the **Contadora Group**, engaged in diplomatic efforts to end the fighting. In 1987, the presidents of the Central American nations signed the Esquipulas II Accord, or **Arias Peace Plan**. The accord called on governments in the region to negotiate directly with guerrilla movements to end all fighting. The Reagan administration reluctantly accepted the accord. Elections subsequently took place in Nicaragua in 1990 and unexpectedly resulted in victory for an anti-Sandinista coalition. A negotiated ending of the war in El Salvador was also achieved in January 1992. These events brought a close to the Central American crisis but did not attract very much public notice in the United States, where the sudden end of the Cold War with the Soviet Union meant that the region lost the geopolitical significance that it had been given by American officials during the 1980s. *See also* BOLAND AMENDMENTS (1982–1984); CASEY, WILLIAM J. (1913–1987); CHAMORRO, VIOLETA BARRIOS DE (1929–); DUARTE, JOSÉ NAPOLEÓN (1925–1990); IRAN-CONTRA AFFAIR; NORTH, OLIVER (1943–).

CENTRAL INTELLIGENCE AGENCY (CIA). Agency of the U.S. government responsible for the collection and analysis of secret intelligence. The 1947 National Security Act created the CIA and gave it the primary function of gathering and analyzing secret intelligence that would be used by the president in the formulation and execution of foreign policy. A second function was the conduct of covert overseas operations involving espionage and counterintelligence. This latter activity proved politically controversial because it resulted in covert actions designed to influence the domestic political affairs of foreign countries. This activity ranged from financing anticommunist propaganda and lobbying activities to the recruitment, training, and financing of paramilitary mercenaries to overthrow governments. At the height of **Cold War** tension in the early 1950s, the CIA was regarded in the United States as an important and necessary instrument of American foreign policy. Moreover, there was general admiration for its success in overthrowing suspected procommunist governments, such as in **Guatemala** in 1954.

The professional reputation of the CIA was seriously damaged, however, by the failure at the **Bay of Pigs** in 1961 and by revelations during the 1970s that it had been involved in several attempts to assassinate foreign leaders, most notably **Fidel Castro**. During the 1980s under President **Ronald Reagan**, the CIA became more active in a manner reminiscent of the 1950s, but controversy and scandal revived over the secret financing in violation of federal law of the **Contra** rebels in **Nicaragua**. Congress attempted to increase its oversight of the CIA and its activities by passing the **Boland Amendments**. *See also* BISSELL, RICHARD (1910–1994); CASEY, WILLIAM J. (1913–1987); CHURCH COMMITTEE; DULLES, ALLEN (1893–1969); FREI MONTALVA, EDUARDO (1911–1982).

CHACO WAR (1932–1935). War between **Bolivia** and **Paraguay**. The long-standing territorial dispute between Bolivia and Paraguay for possession of the Chaco Boreal region erupted into armed hostilities in 1932. The United States had no major strategic or economic interest in the remote region but joined with other Latin American nations in seeking to bring an end to the fighting by offering their diplomatic good offices. After these efforts failed, the United States reluctantly accepted the involvement of the **League of Nations** in mediating the conflict. A cease-fire was accepted in 1935, and the subsequent peace negotiations eventually resulted in a treaty in 1938 that awarded most of the disputed territory to Paraguay.

CHAMORRO, VIOLETA BARRIOS DE (1929–). Nicaraguan political leader and president from 1990 to 1997. The widow of the newspaper editor Pedro Joaquín Chamorro, who had been assassinated in 1978, Violeta Chamorro used the family newspaper, *La Prensa*, to present liberal political views often conflicting with the policies of the government in power. She briefly served as a member of the Junta for National Reconstruction in 1979 but disagreed with the policies of the **Sandinistas**. In 1990, she accepted the presidential nomination of the newly formed anti-Sandinista political coalition known as the National Opposition Union. In the election, Chamorro won 54.7 percent of the popular vote to **Daniel Ortega**'s 40.8 percent. Her presidency continued until 1997 and was marked by an end of the "**Contra** War," the disbandment of the Contras, and the reestablishment of friendly relations with the United States. *See also* CENTRAL AMERICAN CRISIS.

CHAPULTEPEC CONFERENCE (1945). An inter-American conference of foreign ministers. A Special Pan-American Conference on the Problems of War and Peace was held at the Chapultepec Palace in Mexico City from February 21 to March 8, 1945. Conscious of the imminent end of **World War II**, the foreign ministers regarded the meeting as providing an important opportunity for the discussion of postwar matters. Particular significance was attached to the proposals for a new world organization unveiled the previous year at a conference in Dumbarton Oaks in Washington and how this would affect the future working of regional associations such as the existing **Pan-American Conference System**. While the delegates reaffirmed their support for regional associations, they endorsed the principle of establishing a new world organization known as the **United Nations (UN)**. They also discussed the issue of future hemispheric defense, and in the **Act of Chapultepec**, it was agreed that, when the world war came to a formal end, an inter-American meeting would be convened to discuss the establishment of a permanent treaty system of military alliance based on the principle of collective security. This meeting duly took place at Rio de Janeiro in 1947 and resulted in the conclusion of the **Rio Treaty**.

CHÁVEZ, HUGO (1954–). Venezuelan political leader and president since 1998. Founder in 1994 of the Movement for the Fifth Republic, Chávez was elected president in 1998 and reelected in 2002. An open admirer of **Fidel Castro** and the **Cuban Revolution**, Chávez has sought to bring about a socialist revolution in **Venezuela**. In foreign affairs, he has claimed to be following the ideas of the Venezuelan hero, **Simón Bolívar**, in urging Latin American countries to unite against the capitalist system of the United States, which he argues has inflicted a state of "neocolonialism" on Latin America. Chávez, therefore, has opposed proposals for a "Free Trade Area of the Americas" on the ground that it will lead only to a strengthening of U.S. imperialism. *See also* TRADE.

CHILE. A country facing the Pacific Ocean and with **Argentina** forms the southern cone of South America. Diplomatic relations between the United States and Chile were officially opened when the U.S. minister, Heman Allen, presented his credentials to the Chilean government in April 1824. It was not until the **War of the Pacific** (1879–1884), however, that a period of unfriendly diplomatic relations began. The United States had no direct national interest in the conflict between Chile, **Peru**, and **Bolivia** but became diplomatically involved because Secretary of State **James G. Blaine** was convinced that **Great Britain** was secretly supporting Chile in order to gain special privileges for local British business interests. Consequently, Blaine sided with Peru and in partisan fashion sought to put diplomatic pressure on Chile to end the war. Chile resisted and eventually concluded a peace settlement with Peru in 1883 without the participation of the United States. Chilean troops were withdrawn from Peru, but in return Peru ceded the southern provinces of **Tacna** and **Arica** to Chile. The outcome illustrated the independence of action that Chile had enjoyed and maintained ever since the beginning of the war. By contrast, Blaine's diplomatic meddling appeared reckless and proved embarrassing for U.S. diplomacy.

Chile's irritation at U.S. interference during the War of the Pacific was increased in 1891 by the **Baltimore Affair**. The crisis arose when a group of American sailors from the cruiser USS *Baltimore* on shore leave in Valparaíso were involved in a fray with a Chilean mob in which one American sailor was killed and five were seriously wounded. President **Benjamin Harrison** chose to respond in an aggressive manner by sending warships to Chile and threatening to break off diplomatic relations. Recovering from a recent and destructive civil war, the new Chilean government agreed to apologize for the incident and to pay financial compensation to the American sailors. The legacy of humiliation felt by Chile over the Baltimore Affair contributed to that country's unwillingness to join the United States in **World War I**.

During the 1920s the United States adopted an evenhanded approach when it attempted to break the diplomatic impasse between Chile and Peru over their respective claims to possess Tacna and Arica. In 1922, both countries accepted President **Warren Harding**'s offer of good offices and agreed to attend a conference in Washington where it was decided that the question should be settled by holding a plebiscite in the disputed territories. The plebiscite would be organized and held under U.S. supervision. A succession of American officials, including General **John J. Pershing**, attempted to organize a plebiscite but were frustrated by Chilean and Peruvian objections. Finally, in April 1929, a satisfactory settlement was reached after direct negotiations between the Chilean and Peruvian governments in which Chile retained Arica but returned Tacna to Peru.

In the 1950s, there was an upsurge in nationalist sentiment in Chile against the large profits made by the foreign owners of the copper industry and the belief that only a small share of this money was reinvested in local economic activity. Particular targets of criticism were the huge U.S.-owned companies, Anaconda and Kennecott. The question of nationalization of these companies became an issue in the 1964 presidential election, which was fought between the Christian Democratic leader **Eduardo Frei** and the pro-Marxist **Salvador Allende**. American officials closely monitored an election that was seen as part of the **Cold War** and in which the **Central Intelligence Agency (CIA)** secretly contributed more than $3 million to Frei's successful campaign. In office, Frei proclaimed himself a nationalist and declared that his aim was the "Chileanization" of the copper industry. Instead of full nationalization of foreign companies, however, he entered into negotiations that resulted in the Chilean government purchasing a majority share of 51 percent while the companies continued to extract and sell copper on the world market. Frei's moderation was well received in Washington and was rewarded with an increase in U.S. financial assistance under the **Alliance for Progress**. According to the Chilean Constitution, presidents could only serve for one term. Frei was not, therefore, a candidate in the 1970 election.

Diplomatic relations between the United States and Chile once again became particularly tense after Salvador Allende narrowly won the presidency in 1970. As president, Allende introduced radical and controversial measures designed to transform Chile into a socialist state. In Washington, Allende's Chile was viewed as posing a geopolitical threat to the security of South America. President **Richard Nixon** responded by implementing a policy of overt economic pressure on Chile combined with instructions to the CIA to pursue covert political activities to destabilize Allende's government and remove him from office. In September 1973, amid growing political and economic discontent, General **Augusto Pinochet** seized power in a military coup during which Allende committed suicide. The new military government declared that Chile had been saved from communism. Diplomatic recognition was quickly forthcoming from a delighted Nixon administration, but the personal reputations of U.S. officials, particularly Secretary of State **Henry Kissinger**, were damaged by their unwillingness to voice any public criticism of the brutal and repressive policies subsequently pursued in Chile by Pinochet's government. *See also* HELMS, RICHARD (1913–2002); TACNA-ARICA DISPUTE.

CHURCH COMMITTEE. A U.S. congressional investigating committee. The exact role of the **Richard Nixon** administration in the overthrow of Chilean President **Salvador Allende** in 1973 became a matter of investigation in the U.S. Congress in 1975. Hearings were held in the Senate by the Select Committee to Study Governmental Operations with Respect to Intelligence Activities, chaired by Senator Frank Church of Idaho and popularly known as the "Church Committee." While the Church Committee eventually reported that there was no hard evidence of direct American participation in the 1973

Chilean coup, it was highly critical of the Nixon administration's use of covert methods to destabilize the Allende government.

The investigation also covered the activities of previous presidential administrations and disclosed that the **Central Intelligence Agency (CIA)** had organized at least eight assassination attempts against **Fidel Castro** during the period from 1960 to 1965. By the resort to covert methods extending even to attempts at the violent removal of heads of state, the Church Committee argued that U.S. governments, headed by both Democratic and Republican presidents, had brought American prestige and influence in the **Western Hemisphere** to their lowest point for some decades. *See also* ARMED INTERVENTIONS.

CLARK, J. REUBEN (1871–1961). American lawyer and under secretary of state from 1928 to 1929. Clark was a lawyer who served as solicitor in the **State Department** during **World War I**. As under secretary of state in the **Calvin Coolidge** administration, he was responsible for the preparation of a historical study of U.S. policy toward Latin America. Known as the "**Clark Memorandum**," the study was critical of the past policy of military interventionism. In 1930, Clark was appointed U.S. ambassador to **Mexico**, a position he held until February 1933. *See also* GOOD NEIGHBOR POLICY; MONROE DOCTRINE.

CLARK MEMORANDUM (1930). A statement of foreign policy prepared by the U.S. **State Department**. As part of the reappraisal of its policy toward Latin America, the **Calvin Coolidge** administration instructed Undersecretary of State **J. Reuben Clark** to prepare a study of the history of the **Monroe Doctrine**. The resulting **Clark Memorandum**, which was published in 1930, considered that the recent policy of military intervention in Latin America had actually been counterproductive to U.S. national interests and had seriously damaged the international image of the United States. In effect, the memorandum represented an official repudiation of the **Roosevelt Corollary** to the Monroe Doctrine and the policy of **dollar diplomacy**. President **Herbert Hoover** approved the memorandum and sought to implement some of its ideas by announcing the phased withdrawal of all American marines who were currently stationed in Nicaragua and

Haiti. In effect, this marked the beginning of what would become known as the **"Good Neighbor Policy."** *See also* ARMED INTERVENTIONS.

CLAY, HENRY (1777–1852). American political leader and advocate of hemispheric unity. A congressman from Kentucky, Clay became Speaker of the U.S. House of Representatives and was twice an unsuccessful presidential candidate in 1824 and 1832. He was unusual among American politicians of his time in showing a personal interest in Latin American affairs and in advocating early diplomatic recognition of the Latin American states in their fight for independence from Spain. He regarded U.S. recognition as a means of confirming the existence of an "American system" based on republicanism and clearly separate both politically and geographically from that of Europe. Clay, however, showed little active interest in implementing his "Pan-American" views when he served as U.S. secretary of state from 1825 to 1829 in the **John Quincy Adams** administration. *See also* BLAINE, JAMES G. (1830–1893); WESTERN HEMISPHERE.

CLAYTON, JOHN M. (1796–1856). American diplomat and secretary of state from 1849 to 1850. Born in Delaware, Clayton was a lawyer who served as U.S. senator for Delaware from 1829 to 1836 and 1845 to 1849. A Quaker, he objected to the annexation of **Texas** to the United States and was initially a critic of the **Mexican-American War** (1846–1848). In March 1849, he was appointed secretary of state by President **Zachary Taylor**. Clayton's tenure of office was brief, but it was important in the history of U.S. relations with Latin America because it included the conclusion of a canal treaty with **Great Britain**. This treaty became known as the **Clayton-Bulwer Treaty** because it was negotiated by Clayton and the British minister in Washington, Sir Henry Lytton Bulwer. *See also* PANAMA CANAL.

CLAYTON-BULWER TREATY (1850). A canal treaty between the United States and **Great Britain**. The discovery of gold in California in 1848 and the ensuing gold rush in 1849 resulted in a greatly increased use of the Isthmus of **Panama** as the shortest and quickest means of traveling to and from the east and west coasts of the United States. Numerous schemes were announced by private companies and entrepreneurs to construct a sea-level canal across the isthmus. Conscious of close British diplomatic interest in the question and the fact that the involvement of British financiers was essential to ensure the successful construction of any canal, the United States sought the diplomatic cooperation of the British government. A treaty was negotiated with Great Britain in April 1850. Known as the Clayton-Bulwer Treaty after the principal negotiators, Secretary of State **John M. Clayton** and the British minister to the United States, Henry Lytton Bulwer, it included terms that amounted to an Anglo-American undertaking to guarantee the neutrality of the projected isthmian canal with a joint disclaimer that neither power would ever erect fortifications or seek to acquire exclusive privilege or control of the waterway. Despite the treaty providing what amounted to an unprecedented Anglo-American political undertaking to cooperate in canal construction, major engineering difficulties and lack of finance still proved to be insuperable barriers to prevent any serious canal work from being undertaken. Instead, a railroad was constructed. Interest in the Clayton-Bulwer Treaty, however, revived, and it became a contentious diplomatic issue between the two governments when the United States sought to pursue a policy of securing an exclusive "American" canal at the end of the 19th century. In 1881, the claim made by Secretary of State **James G. Blaine** that the United States possessed special canal rights provoked a rejoinder from the British government pointing out that this was contrary to the provisions of the 1850 treaty.

After the **Spanish-American War** in 1898, the **William McKinley** administration formally proposed a revision of the treaty in order to secure a canal to be constructed and controlled exclusively by the United States. Not wishing to obstruct the building of the canal and impressed by the display of American military power against Spain in 1898, the British government approved the negotiation of a new treaty in 1901. Known as the **Hay-Pauncefote Treaty**, the arrangement abrogated the 1850 treaty and meant that the United States could now build, fortify, and exercise exclusive control over the projected canal. The **Panama Canal** was completed and opened to international shipping in 1914.

CLEVELAND, GROVER (1837–1908). American political leader and president from 1885 to 1889 and 1893 to 1897. Born in New Jersey but raised in upstate New York, Cleveland was a lawyer who was elected Democratic governor of New York in 1882. He won the presidential election in 1884 but failed to secure reelection in 1888. He was, however, successful in winning the 1892 election. During his second presidential administration from 1893 to 1897, Cleveland was conscious of public criticism that his foreign policy was perceived as weak. As a result, his administration showed determination to protect American shipping from interference during the **Brazilian Naval Revolt** of 1893–1894. He also notably intervened in the boundary dispute between **Great Britain** and **Venezuela** in 1895 by demanding that the dispute between the two countries go to arbitration. A minor Latin American issue was thereby transformed into an international crisis that even posed, if only briefly, the possibility of war between the United States and Britain. While invoking the **Monroe Doctrine** and ostensibly claiming to represent the interests of Latin America against European imperialism, Cleveland did not consult with the Venezuelan government and was in reality—like President **James Monroe** in 1823—unilaterally enforcing the political preeminence of the United States in the **Western Hemisphere**. *See also* OLNEY, RICHARD (1835–1917); OLNEY MEMORANDUM (1895); SCRUGGS, WILLIAM L. (1836–1912); VENEZUELA BOUNDARY DISPUTE (1895).

CLINTON, WILLIAM J. (1946–). American political leader and president from 1993 to 2001. Born in Arkansas, "Bill" Clinton joined the Democratic Party and served as governor of Arkansas from 1979 to 1980 and 1983 to 1992. On assuming the presidency in 1993, Clinton stressed that one of his major foreign policy objectives would be the development of closer commercial relations with Latin America. He was a strong supporter of the **North American Free Trade Agreement (NAFTA)** and saw its ratification by the U.S. Congress in November 1993 as a major achievement for his administration. Conscious of the bitter political controversy generated by NAFTA, he refrained from publicly endorsing proposals to promote further hemispheric economic integration.

COLBY, BAINBRIDGE (1869–1950). American politician and secretary of state from 1920 to 1921. Born in St. Louis, Missouri, and educated at Columbia University, Colby practiced law in New York and joined the Republican Party. A strong supporter of **Theodore Roosevelt**, he left the Republicans in 1912 for the Progressive Party after Roosevelt failed to secure the Republican presidential nomination. During **World War I**, Colby served in the **Woodrow Wilson** administration in the U.S. Shipping Board and was appointed secretary of state in March 1920. In an attempt to improve the image of the United States in the hemisphere, he undertook a goodwill mission by visiting **Brazil**, **Uruguay**, and **Argentina** in December 1920. Although Colby received a friendly reception, the political impact of his visit was considerably diminished by the fact that Woodrow Wilson's presidential term of office was shortly about to end. Nevertheless, Colby's trip can be viewed as part of the sequence of diplomatic events leading to the adoption by the United States of the **Good Neighbor Policy** during the 1930s.

COLD WAR. A period of international conflict between the United States and the **Soviet Union**. Emerging at the end of World War II with the new status of the world's superpower, the United States extended the protection offered by the **Monroe Doctrine** in the **Western Hemisphere** to include new worldwide diplomatic and military commitments in Western Europe and the Far East. This resulted in a state of conflict with the Soviet Union that became known as the "Cold War." American officials confidently anticipated support from the countries of Latin America. This was reflected in the creation of inter-American institutions such as the **Rio Pact** and the **Organization of American States (OAS)**, which became part of the evolving policy of the global containment of international communism.

In terms of an actual strategic threat to Latin America, U.S. officials were concerned not so much with the prospect of direct Soviet military aggression as with political infiltration and subversion by local communists and their sympathizers. The first major test was during the early 1950s in **Guatemala**, where President **Dwight Eisenhower** feared that a communist beachhead was about to be established. The **Central Intelligence Agency (CIA)** organized

Operation PBSUCCESS and overthrew President **Jacobo Arbenz** in 1954. A similar covert operation was attempted against **Fidel Castro** in **Cuba** but failed at the **Bay of Pigs** in April 1961. In 1965, however, President **Lyndon Johnson** decided on overt intervention by U.S. forces to defeat what he regarded as a communist conspiracy to seize political control in the Dominican Republic.

The United States used its substantial economic wealth in its battle with the Soviet Union during the Cold War. In Latin America, this was exemplified in the **Alliance for Progress**. Another notable feature of U.S. policy was the stress on developing close and cooperative links with the Latin American military. The relationship appeared so friendly that U.S. complicity was suspected in the military coups that overthrew Brazilian President **João Goulart** in 1964 and Chilean President **Salvador Allende** in 1973. The overthrow of Allende stimulated considerable anti-Americanism in Latin America and occurred at a time when the United States appeared to be losing its traditional political and economic preeminence in the Western Hemisphere. This was visibly demonstrated by the successful survival of the Castro regime in Cuba in spite of American hostility and the desire of Latin American governments to develop closer diplomatic and economic relations with Western Europe and nations in the communist bloc and the Third World.

During the 1970s, a mood of national malaise was evident among the people of the United States that was symbolized by the trauma of the Vietnam War. As a result, U.S. diplomacy became less confident and more conciliatory in its dealings with Latin America. This was illustrated in President **Jimmy Carter**'s acquiescence of the rise to power in **Nicaragua** of the **Sandinista** revolutionary movement in 1979. In the United States, the growing perception of Carter's foreign policies as weak contributed to the election of **Ronald Reagan** in 1980. Cold War tensions were markedly increased as Reagan announced his determination to confront and defeat what he described as the "evil empire" of the Soviet Union. In Nicaragua, Carter's conciliatory attitude toward the Sandinistas was changed to one of outright American hostility in which both overt and covert measures were employed to destabilize a regime that was viewed as an agent of the Soviet Union seeking to spread international communism throughout Central America.

Reagan's policies, especially toward Nicaragua, were condemned by his critics in both the United States and Latin America as too aggressive and confrontational. The exposure of illegal methods to fund the CIA-backed **Contras** led in 1986 to the **Iran-Contra affair**, which raised the possibility of Reagan's resignation or even impeachment. The president's difficulties in resolving the **Central American crisis**, however, were overshadowed by unexpected events occurring not in Latin America but in Europe. In fact, the prestige and power of the United States in the Western Hemisphere were visibly increased by the dramatic collapse of communist regimes in Eastern Europe and eventually the political disintegration of the Soviet Union in 1991. The end of the Cold War meant that Central America was no longer viewed in East–West terms and consequently lost its significance in American national security policy. During the 1990s, the focus of American diplomatic activity became firmly fixed on Europe, the Middle East, and Asia. Programs of economic and military aid for Latin America were correspondingly reduced or even terminated. *See also* ARMED INTERVENTIONS; CUBAN MISSILE CRISIS (1962); DOMINICAN INTERVENTION (1965); MILITARY ASSISTANCE; UNITED NATIONS ORGANIZATION (UN).

COLOMBIA. A country in northern South America bordered by **Panama** to the north, **Venezuela** to the northeast, Brazil to the southeast, and **Ecuador** and **Peru** to the south. Colombia was the first Latin American nation on which the United States conferred diplomatic recognition on June 19, 1822. During the 19th century, diplomatic relations between the United States and Colombia revolved mainly around the question of the location and construction of an isthmian canal in the northern province of Panama. In Article 35 of the **Bidlack Treaty** (1846), the United States agreed to guarantee both Colombian sovereignty over the Isthmus of Panama and the protection of transit across the isthmus from either external or internal interference. The stipulation gave the United States a claim to possess a special protective role in isthmian affairs. This proved significant in 1880 when Article 35 was cited to endorse the policy of President **Rutherford B. Hayes** in seeking an "American" canal.

After the U.S. Congress chose Panama over **Nicaragua** as the best route for a canal linking the Atlantic and Pacific oceans, the

Hay-Herrán Treaty was negotiated with Colombia in 1903 to transfer the existing canal concessions held by the French **Panama Canal Company**. The treaty secured ratification by the U.S. Senate in March 1903 but was later defeated in the Colombian Senate. An angry President **Theodore Roosevelt** let it be known that he would not be averse to Panama breaking away from Colombia. Indeed, the collapse of the treaty had grave implications for the future economic prosperity of the isthmian region and provoked political demonstrations in Panama that resulted in the independence of the province in November 1903. The new republic of Panama quickly concluded a canal treaty that granted the United States the canal rights that it had failed to secure from the Colombian government. The canal was successfully completed and opened to the world on August 15, 1914. While Theodore Roosevelt proudly boasted that he had "taken" the canal, a feeling persisted among U.S. diplomats that Colombia had been unfairly treated. In 1921, the U.S. Senate approved a treaty giving compensation of $25 million to Colombia for the loss of income arising from the secession of Panama.

It was not until the late 20th century that Colombia once more became a significant issue in U.S. Latin American policy. This reflected the determination of the United States to prevent the trafficking in illegal narcotics. Colombia was known to be a major transshipment point for cocaine originating from **Bolivia** and **Peru** and destined for the United States. Indeed, massive financial profits led to the emergence of large organized drug cartels in Colombia, the most notorious of which were located in the cities of Cali and Medellín. The United States negotiated agreements with the Colombian government in which agents of the U.S. Drug Enforcement Administration (DEA) provided training and equipment for Colombian police and paramilitary forces to locate and destroy illegal narcotics at the source of production and shipment. Success proved elusive because the drug cartels possessed considerable local political influence extending even to the highest officials in the Colombian government. In fact, the trade continued to flourish so long as the demand for illegal narcotics in the United States constantly remained high and offered opportunities to make lucrative financial profits. Moreover, the United States was accused of arrogantly and insensitively interfering in Colombian domestic affairs. Critics in the United States even drew parallels with

Nicaragua in the 1980s and argued that the increasing activities of DEA agents meant that the United States was becoming involved in a "secret war" in Colombia. *See also* HAY-BUNAU-VARILLA TREATY (1903); NARCOTICS TRAFFICKING.

CONTADORA GROUP. A Latin American diplomatic initiative to mediate the **Central American crisis** during the 1980s. A number of Latin American leaders regarded President **Ronald Reagan** as too ideological and too confrontational in his approach to the Central American crisis. They believed that civil unrest in the region would never be resolved by military means alone and that a peaceful diplomatic approach was preferable. In January 1983, the foreign ministers of **Mexico**, **Panama**, **Venezuela**, and **Colombia** held a meeting on Contadora Island, off the coast of Panama, to discuss means of assisting a negotiated peace settlement. For public relations reasons, Reagan appeared to welcome the subsequent formation of the "Contadora Group," but he frustrated and effectively negated their diplomatic efforts by refusing to enter into substantive negotiations with the **Sandinista** government in **Nicaragua**. Many of the proposals of the Contadora Group were later successfully incorporated into the **Arias Peace Plan** (1987). *See also* ARIAS SÁNCHEZ, ÓSCAR (1940–); EL SALVADOR.

CONTRAS. A secret army funded by the U.S. government. As part of the policy of the **Ronald Reagan** administration to destabilize the **Sandinista** government in **Nicaragua**, the **Central Intelligence Agency (CIA)** secretly organized and financed an army of Nicaraguan exiles. This force, numbering initially around 500 and rising at one point to 15,000, called itself the "Nicaraguan Democratic Force" but became more popularly known as the "counterrevolutionaries," or "Contras." From their bases in **Honduras** and **Costa Rica**, the Contras launched low-intensity military operations inside Nicaragua aimed at blowing up bridges, mining harbors, carrying out industrial sabotage, and destroying agricultural crops. The Contras, however, remained dependent on continuing American financial backing. Heavily outnumbered by the Sandinista army, they avoided battles and never acquired or held any actual territory in Nicaragua. Furthermore, because of their previous association with the hated

Somoza regime and their links with the CIA, they attracted insignificant popular support in the countryside. While they gained little tangible military success, the Contras did damage the Nicaraguan economy and compelled the Sandinistas to maintain large military forces and divert scarce resources to fighting the "Contra War."

President Ronald Reagan admiringly complimented the Contras as courageous "freedom fighters" who were engaged in the patriotic struggle to liberate their country from communist control. However, the revelation in the press in 1982 that the Reagan administration was conducting a "secret war" in Nicaragua prompted suspicion and concern in the United States that the country was being dragged into "another Vietnam War." In 1982, the U.S. Congress passed the **Boland Amendment** to limit funds going to the Contras. In order to circumvent the restrictions of the amendment, the Reagan administration resorted to covert methods leading to revelation of the **Iran-Contra affair** in 1986. Congress eventually agreed to allow funding for the Contras but only in limited amounts and specifically allocated for humanitarian purposes, such as the provision of food and medical supplies. Deprived of significant American material support, the Contras were compelled to agree to a cease-fire in 1988. In return, the Sandinista government offered a general amnesty. After the holding of national elections in 1990, arrangements were made for the demobilization, under the supervision of the **United Nations (UN)**, of the remaining Contra forces. *See also* CASEY, WILLIAM J. (1913–1987); NORTH, OLIVER (1943–).

COOLIDGE, CALVIN (1872–1933). American political leader and president from 1923 to 1929. Born in Vermont, Coolidge was a lawyer who joined the Republican Party and became governor of Massachusetts in 1991. In 1920, he was elected vice president and succeeded to the presidency on the death of **Warren G. Harding** in 1921. As the head of an administration dedicated to the expansion of American business, Coolidge sought to promote and protect the interests of U.S. trade and investment in Latin America. It was the decision of the Coolidge administration in 1927 to send additional U.S. marines to **Nicaragua** that sparked off local guerrilla resistance led by **Augusto Sandino**. Coolidge was also determined to support the interests of American oil companies in Mexico.

Nevertheless, Coolidge was aware of the damage being caused to the image of the United States in Latin America and adopted a more conciliatory policy in the final years of his presidency. For example, he ruled out proposals for U.S. military intervention in Mexico and secured a diplomatic resolution to the dispute between the oil companies and the Mexican government in December 1927. Undersecretary of State **J. Reuben Clark** was also instructed to prepare a historical study of the **Monroe Doctrine** to aid in a reappraisal of policy toward Latin America. As a gesture of friendly feeling and conciliation, Coolidge personally attended the opening ceremonies of the Pan-American Conference at Havana in 1928. The gesture, however, was spoiled by the fact that the president arrived in a large battleship. Moreover, so long as U.S. marines sought to hunt down and capture Sandino in Nicaragua, the Coolidge administration could do little to stem the rise of anti-American sentiment in Latin America. Coolidge's term of office ended in 1929, and he retired from politics. *See also* CALLES, PLUTARCO ELÍAS (1877–1945); PAN-AMERICAN CONFERENCE SYSTEM.

COSTA RICA. A country in Central America bordered by **Nicaragua** to the north and **Panama** to the south. Formerly part of the United Provinces of Central America, Costa Rica became independent after the collapse of the federation in 1838. Official diplomatic relations were established between the United States and Costa Rica in 1853. In marked contrast to its neighbors in Central America, Costa Rica has experienced impressive political and financial stability so that relations with the United States have remained friendly and have not been disturbed by American military intervention.

During the late 1940s and early 1950s, U.S. officials were concerned by civil unrest in the country and attributed this to the rise of communist influence, especially in the Costa Rican labor unions. Unlike President **Jacobo Arbenz** in **Guatemala**, however, Costa Rican President **José Figueres** pleased Washington by acting vigorously to restrict local communist activities. During the 1980s, a diplomatic divergence with the United States emerged when the Costa Rican government criticized President **Ronald Reagan**'s emphasis on pursuing a military solution to end the fighting in **El Salvador** and Nicaragua. President **Óscar Arias** used his diplomatic skill and his country's prestige to secure acceptance of the **Arias Peace Plan** and thereby bring a peaceful end to the warfare in the region. For his work in aiding the peace process, the Costa Rican president was awarded the Nobel Peace Prize in 1987. *See also* CENTRAL AMERICAN CRISIS; CONTADORA GROUP; KEITH, MINOR C. (1848–1929).

CUBA. The largest island in the Caribbean Sea. For Latin Americans, Cuba has often been cited as the foremost example of the employment of forceful American diplomacy. The victory over Spain in the **Spanish-American War** (1898) and the subsequent military occupation and administration of Cuba until 1902 demonstrated the political and military preeminence of the United States in the **Western Hemisphere**. Although Latin American governments had adopted policies of neutrality during the 1898 war, there was a general distrust of the idealistic motives proclaimed by President **William McKinley** to justify U.S. intervention. There was also a suspicion that the "**Yankees**" were characteristically intent on seizing territory and humiliating the Spanish race. These ideas were expressed in the influential writings of **José Martí** and **José Enrique Rodó**. While the United States soon withdrew its military forces from Cuba, it retained the right of intervention under the **Platt Amendment** until 1934. Cuba, therefore, provided an example to the rest of Latin America of **dollar diplomacy**, a policy by which the United States sought to dominate the Central American–Caribbean region politically, militarily, and economically.

A serious challenge to U.S. preeminence occurred in 1959 with the rise of **Fidel Castro** to power. Castro proceeded rapidly to transform Cuba from a capitalist to a socialist society. Moreover, he directly provoked the United States by stating that he would "export" the **Cuban Revolution** to the mainland of Latin America. The United States responded with a variety of policies ranging from overthrowing Castro by covert operations, securing hemispheric agreement to isolate Cuba politically and economically, and launching a massive aid program known as the **Alliance for Progress** to demonstrate the superior benefits of capitalism over socialism.

Fidel Castro's defiance of the United States attracted considerable admiration in Latin America, especially among left-wing groups, some of whom followed his example of forming national liberation movements in the countryside and pursuing the strategy of armed struggle. This only alarmed the conservative ruling elites of Latin America who were traditionally hostile to communism and fearful of guerrilla movements. Preferring to maintain friendly relations with the United States, they cooperated in the policy of isolating Cuba. A very different approach was evident in **Chile** under President **Salvador Allende** and in **Nicaragua** and **El Salvador**, where local national liberation movements acknowledged the importance of maintaining their links with Cuba. The disintegration of the **Soviet Union** and the end of the Cold War delivered, however, a devastating blow to the welfare of the Cuban economy and to the claims of Fidel Castro that the Cuban Revolution was more successful than American capitalism. *See also* GUEVARA, ERNESTO "CHE" (1928–1967); PERU; VELASCO ALVARADO, JUAN (1910–1977).

CUBAN MISSILE CRISIS (1962). A crisis between the superpowers in October 1962 that directly affected Latin America. As part of the **Cold War** struggle, in 1962 the Soviet leader, Nikita Khrushchev, secretly attempted to gain a strategic advantage over the United States by placing nuclear missiles in Cuba. On learning that missile sites were under construction in Cuba, President **John F. Kennedy** established an American naval blockade around the island. The action was typical of American policy in that it was taken unilaterally and without consultation with Latin American governments. Kennedy, however, subsequently invoked the 1947 **Rio Treaty** and sought the endorsement of the **Organization of American States (OAS)** to approve the use of armed force should it be necessary. An affirmative vote was forthcoming from the Latin American countries who were shocked at the prospect of Soviet nuclear missiles being placed in Cuba and the threat that this posed to the security of the whole **Western Hemisphere**. There was, however, some criticism of what was regarded as Kennedy's technically illegal action in mounting a naval blockade. **Bolivia**, **Brazil**, and **Mexico** abstained in one of the votes at the OAS in order to express their opposition. On the other hand, the peaceful resolution of the crisis was attributed to Kennedy's diplomatic skill and contributed to enhancing the president's prestige after the earlier disaster at the **Bay of Pigs**. By contrast, **Fidel Castro** exercised little influence on events and appeared as a puppet of the Soviet Union.

CUBAN REVOLUTION. A revolutionary movement in **Cuba**. The revolutionary policy of transforming Cuba from a capitalist to a socialist society was begun by Fidel **Castro** in 1959 and made Cuba a focal point of the **Cold War**. The resulting restriction of political rights in Cuba and especially the nationalization of foreign-owned companies provoked the hostility of the U.S. government. In an attempt to destroy the Cuban Revolution, President **John F. Kennedy** imposed an economic embargo, secured Cuba's expulsion from the **Organization of American States (OAS)**, and engaged in a policy of covert operations to undermine the Castro regime from within Cuba.

Castro defiantly talked of "exporting" the revolution to the mainland of Latin America. Some of the policies of the Cuban Revolution were adopted in neighboring Caribbean islands, such as Jamaica and Grenada, but they exerted little political impact on the rest of Latin America, whose ruling elites were traditionally suspicious of communism and wanted friendly relations with the United States. The notable exceptions were in **Chile** under President **Salvador Allende** and in Central America, where guerrilla movements in **Nicaragua** and **El Salvador** acknowledged the material support and ideological encouragement that they had received from Cuba. The national liberation movements in Central America, however, emphasized independence of action and claimed that their greatest inspiration originated from their own national heroes, such as **Augusto Sandino** and **Augustín Farabundo Martí**.

The sudden withdrawal of Soviet financial subsidies at the end of the Cold War dealt a devastating blow to the Cuban economy and to the claims of Fidel Castro that the Cuban Revolution was more successful than capitalism. Instead of a model for future economic and social development, the Cuban Revolution appeared inefficient and anachronistic. *See also* GUEVARA, ERNESTO "CHE" (1928–1967); SOVIET UNION.

CURTIS, WILLIAM E. (1850–1911). American journalist and author. Curtis was the Washington correspondent of the *Chicago Inter-Ocean* and served as the secretary to the U.S. Latin American Trade Commission that visited Latin America in 1884–1885. From his travel experiences, Curtis published *The Capitals of Spanish America* in 1888 and gained the reputation in the United States of an expert on Latin American affairs. The book, however, was not so well received in Latin America, where critics judged it superficial and ill informed. They also derisively noted his inability to speak the Spanish language. Nevertheless, President **Benjamin Harrison** put Curtis in charge of the administrative preparations for the 1889–1890 **International American Conference**. Curtis later served as the first director of the Commercial **Bureau of the American Republics** from 1890 to 1893.

– D –

DANIELS, JOSEPHUS (1862–1948). American editor and diplomat. Daniels served as secretary of war during the **Woodrow Wilson** administration from 1913 to 1921 and was involved in implementing U.S. naval interventions in **Mexico** and the Central American–Caribbean region. On the return of the Democrats to political power in 1933, he was appointed ambassador to Mexico, an office that he held until 1941. As ambassador, Daniels sought to promote the **Good Neighbor Policy**. When the Mexican government announced its intention of nationalizing U.S.-owned **oil** companies operating in Mexico, he was influential in persuading President **Franklin D. Roosevelt** to resist pressure to retaliate with forceful economic sanctions and to adopt a conciliatory policy instead. A compromise was eventually reached between the two governments in 1941. A further demonstration of the personal success of Daniels in improving diplomatic relations was the cooperative attitude adopted by the Mexican government in support of Roosevelt's policy to counter the spread of fascism in the **Western Hemisphere** and, after he had left Mexico, the decision in 1942 to join **World War II** as an ally of the United States.

DARÍO, RUBÉN (1867–1916). Nicaraguan poet. Darío was the founder of the influential literary movement known as "modernism" (modernismo). Writing during the same period as **José Enrique Rodó**, his views were similar in identifying the Anglo-Saxon United States as an aggressive and arrogant power. Many of Darío's ideas were formed by his observations on the triumphalist attitude and insensitive policy that the United States showed toward **Cuba** and its Spanish culture after the end of the **Spanish-American War** (1898). *See also* MARTÍ, JOSÉ (1853–1895).

DEBT CRISIS. A period of serious economic difficulty during the 1980s. An abundance of international liquidity during the 1970s meant that many Latin American countries were able to contract large external loans at relatively low interest rates from private commercial banks in North American and Europe. The result was a substantial increase in the total external foreign debt of Latin America from $27 billion in 1970 to $370 billion in 1984. The annual servicing of the debt became extremely difficult at the beginning of the 1980s as a result of a sudden world economic recession that brought a big rise in international interest rates combined with a sharp fall in the income earned from traditional exports, especially commodities and agricultural products. In 1984, the cost for Latin America of servicing the external debt was estimated to be nearly 50 percent of the annual income derived from exports.

The debt crisis came suddenly to the world's attention in August 1982 when **Mexico** defaulted on repayments of the annual interest on its external debt. **Brazil** followed Mexico's example three months later. The debt problem was not just confined to Mexico and Brazil and extended beyond Latin America to most of the countries in the Third World. Nevertheless, so much publicity was given to the particular Mexican and Brazilian defaults and so great was the total amount of debt owed by Latin American countries that the crisis was often misleadingly referred to as the "Latin American debt crisis."

Concerned over the stability of the American banking system and that potential civil disorder might spread from Mexico to the U.S.–Mexican border, the **Ronald Reagan** administration reacted quickly to Mexico's default and made available emergency loans so that Mexico could reschedule its debt repayments. As part of its strategy to isolate the **Sandinistas** in **Nicaragua**, the Reagan administration was prepared to extend similar financial aid and preferential commercial terms to the countries of Central America and the Caribbean in the form of the Caribbean Basin Initiative (1982). There was, however, no sign of a similar major aid program for the rest of

Latin America. In fact, American officials generally considered that the leaders of the Latin American governments had been characteristically reckless and profligate in their borrowing and that they must face up to the consequences. In effect, this meant that those governments would have to request aid directly from the **International Monetary Fund (IMF)** and accept the financial conditions that were required by that institution.

In the absence of U.S. support, several Latin American governments felt compelled to resort to regional cooperation and, prompted by **Fidel Castro**, even threatened to cancel all debt payments. The possibility of collective action by the debtor nations to repudiate their debts posed a challenge to the stability of the world banking system and persuaded the Reagan administration to propose the **Baker Plan** in October 1985. This was followed in 1990 by the **Brady Plan**, which represented a tacit acknowledgment that the debt would never be repaid in full. As international trade and investment recovered during the second half of the 1980s, the export earnings of the Latin American countries steadily increased. At the same time, interest rates fell, and more private capital gradually became available for loans so that the debt crisis essentially came to an end. Looking back, however, the Latin American economies had suffered what was called the "lost decade" of the 1980s. *See also* GARCÍA PÉREZ, ALÁN (1949–).

DECLARATION OF HAVANA (1940). Statement of inter-American policy also known as the "Act of Havana concerning the Provisional Administration of European Colonies and Possessions in the Americas." In the spring of 1940, stunning German military victories in Western Europe dramatically posed the prospect of **Germany** assuming future control of the existing French and Dutch colonies in the Caribbean. A Pan-American meeting of foreign ministers was held at Havana on July 21–30 to discuss this issue. Aware that the U.S. Congress had already passed a joint resolution on June 17–18 affirming the **No-Transfer Resolution** (1811), the foreign ministers endorsed the policy of the United States by similarly resolving not to recognize the transfer of any European colony in the Caribbean to Germany.

At the same time, the conference adopted the principle of collective security and agreed that any attack by an external power on an

American state should be regarded as an act of aggression against all the American countries. But no specific military commitment was proposed. In the event of an external attack, foreign ministers would meet to consult on possible courses of action just as they had done in convening the Havana conference. When Japan attacked the U.S. Pacific Fleet at Pearl Harbor in December 1941, the United States put this procedure into effect and called for a meeting of foreign ministers that was subsequently held at Rio de Janeiro in January 1942.

DECLARATION OF PANAMA (1939). Statement of inter-American policy toward the war in Europe. When war broke out in Europe in September 1939, the governments of the United States and the Latin American nations responded with declarations of neutrality. A meeting of foreign ministers was convened at Panama City from September 23 to October 3 to discuss measures of hemispheric self-defense. The foreign ministers agreed to the "Declaration of Panama" proclaiming the establishment of a neutrality or "safety" zone averaging 300 miles in width around the coastline of the **Western Hemisphere** (excluding **Canada** and European colonies in the Caribbean) into which the warships of the belligerents should not enter.

President **Franklin D. Roosevelt** was very much in favor of the idea of hemispheric isolationism, which he hoped would protect and insulate the United States and the Latin American nations from the war in Europe. Some observers predicted, however, that the sheer size of the zone made the declaration practically unenforceable and that it would not be recognized by the nations at war. This proved correct in December 1939 when the German battleship *Graf Spee* was engaged in a battle with British cruisers 200 miles off the coast of Uruguay and therefore clearly within the proclaimed safety zone. A Pan-American note of protest was delivered to the belligerents but was rejected by both the British and the German government. During 1940, the diplomatic controversy subsided, however, as growing sympathy in the United States for the plight of **Great Britain** and especially Roosevelt's desire to help that country against **Germany**, with all material means short of actually going to war, meant that the concept of the neutrality zone effectively became redundant.

DÍAZ, PORFIRIO (1830–1915). Mexican political leader and seven times president. Porfirio Díaz was reelected president seven times from 1876 to 1910 and dominated the period of Mexican history known as "the Pofiriato." In seeking to promote a strong national government and a prosperous "modern" economy, Díaz particularly welcomed foreign investment and participation in the development of the country's natural resources and transportation infrastructure. American entrepreneurs and companies were especially prominent in placing large investments in Mexican railroads, mining, and the search for **oil**. Despite some successful industrial growth, the large majority of the local population remained dependent on agriculture and lived at a subsistence level. Growing popular discontent and armed uprising resulted in the overthrow of Díaz in May 1911. The policy of cultivating the inflow of foreign capital had stimulated anti-Americanism and also a more general xenophobia that was illustrated in the **Mexican Revolution** and especially in Article 27 of the Mexican Constitution (1917), which asserted Mexican sovereign rights over its own natural resources. *See also* MADERO, FRANCISCO (1873–1913); MEXICO; ROMERO, MATÍAS (1837–1898).

DIRTY WAR. A period of political oppression by the state occurring in **Argentina** from 1976 to 1983. On seizing political power in Argentina in 1976, the new military government proclaimed a state of "ideological war" to bring an end to the increasing urban violence and terrorist activities associated with left-wing guerrilla movements. The army and police subsequently pursued a policy of systematic and brutal repression that affected not only known guerrillas but also political critics and opponents of the military government. In the process, a "dirty war" occurred in which thousands were arrested, with many suffering torture and summary execution in the form of their "disappearance."

The reports of repression in Argentina attracted growing criticism in the United States where President **Jimmy Carter** had made the issue of observing **human rights** a priority of his administration. In 1977, the U.S. Congress voted to reduce American military aid to Argentina as a punitive measure. Like their military counterparts in **Brazil** and **Chile**, the military governments in Argentina expressed irritation at what they regarded as unwarranted American interference in their internal political affairs. They refused to be deflected from their "war" on terrorism, which came to an end only after the senior military leaders suffered humiliation in the **South Atlantic War** (1982) and elections were held in 1983 to restore civilian government.

DOLLAR DIPLOMACY. Descriptive term for U.S. foreign policy during the early 20th century. The term "dollar diplomacy" derived from a speech in 1911 by Assistant Secretary of State Francis Huntington Wilson, who remarked that "the substitution of dollars for bullets" was an aim of American foreign policy. The promotion and protection of overseas trade and investment became regarded as one of the main functions of the **State Department** and coincided with a period at the beginning of the 20th century in which the American economy was eager to take advantage of the growing commercial opportunities in Latin America and especially in the Caribbean–Central American region. In the process, dollar diplomacy assisted the development of the Caribbean–Central American region into an "American lake," an exclusive sphere of influence that the United States sought to dominate politically, militarily, and economically.

The pursuit of dollar diplomacy directly followed on from the **Roosevelt Corollary** to the **Monroe Doctrine** and the policy of the **Big Stick**. It reflected the expanding geopolitical power of the United States exemplified in the **Spanish-American War** (1898) and conversely the relative weakness and vulnerability of the Latin American countries. The policy was often implemented in a forceful and insensitive manner through the sending in of U.S. marines and financial supervisors. Latin American critics condemned dollar diplomacy as imperialistic and argued that it showed how the lofty ideals of **Pan-Americanism** had evolved into the reality of "the American peril." *See also* ARMED INTERVENTIONS; DARÍO, RUBÉN (1867–1916); RODÓ, JOSÉ ENRIQUE (1871–1917); ROOSEVELT, THEODORE (1858–1919).

DOMINICAN INTERVENTION (1965). Example of unilateral U.S. military intervention. In April 1965, when political chaos escalated into violence in Santo Domingo, the capital of the Dominican Republic, President **Lyndon Johnson** was informed that a communist conspiracy was responsible. More than 20,000 American troops were dispatched to restore order, the first overt military intervention by the United States in Latin America since **Nicaragua** in the late 1920s. The intervention provoked controversy both in the United States and throughout Latin America. Critics pointed out that Johnson had not consulted the **Organization of American States (OAS)** prior to his decision to send in troops and that his unilateral intervention signified the return of the **Roosevelt Corollary**, which was now scathingly referred to as the "Johnson Doctrine."

Johnson, however, stated that he had no intention of establishing an American protectorate in the **dollar diplomacy** style of previous presidents. Although somewhat belatedly, he brought the issue to the OAS and, despite considerable misgivings being expressed from some members of the council, secured agreement for the dispatch of an OAS military presence in the form of token contingents of troops from six Latin American nations under the command of Brazilian General Hugo Panasco Allvim to supervise peacekeeping arrangements. The arrangement effectively signified retrospective OAS endorsement of Johnson's armed intervention. In return, American troops were withdrawn from the Dominican Republic within six months. *See also* ARMED INTERVENTIONS.

DRAGO DOCTRINE. Latin American statement concerning the right of intervention. Alarmed by the resort of European powers to gunboat diplomacy in the **Venezuela Incident** (1902–1903), Argentine Foreign Minister Luis María Drago wrote a diplomatic note to the **State Department** dated December 29, 1902, that argued that foreign nations did not automatically possess the legal right to use military force to recover public debt. Following the ideas expressed in 1868 by the Argentine international lawyer Carlos Calvo, Drago stated that the use of force directly challenged the principle of respect for the sovereignty and independence of nations. Latin American nations sought collective hemispheric recognition of the Drago Doctrine. President **Theodore Roosevelt**, however, announced his preference to act unilaterally in the form of the **Roosevelt Corollary** to the **Monroe Doctrine**. Latin American support for the Drago Doctrine was also undermined by acknowledgment that the use of force by external powers had legal justification as a final resort in cases where arbitration was refused. *See also* CALVO DOCTRINE.

DUARTE, JOSÉ NAPOLEÓN (1925–1990). Salvadoran political leader and president from 1984 to 1989. A graduate of the University of Notre Dame and founder of the Christian Democratic Party, Duarte served as mayor of San Salvador from 1964 to 1970. After a period of political exile, he returned to **El Salvador** in 1980 to join the Revolutionary Government Junta that had taken power in a coup during the previous year. In 1984, he was elected president and held this office until 1989. A supporter of political reform and land redistribution, Duarte presented a pro-American and liberal image that made him popular in the United States. However, his political influence in his own country was challenged by the pro-Marxist **Farabundo Martí Liberation Front** (Frente Farabundo Marí para la Liberación Nacional [FMLN]), which was determined to overthrow his government by armed struggle. In addition, Duarte's condemnation of human rights violations by the Salvadoran military provoked the bitter enmity of right-wing political groups. While publicly endorsing Duarte's rule, officials in the **Ronald Reagan** administration were frustrated by his political weakness and preferred to work directly with senior Salvadoran military figures in implementing their military strategy to defeat the FMLN. *See also* CENTRAL AMERICAN CRISIS.

DULLES, ALLEN (1893–1969). American spymaster and director of the **Central Intelligence Agency (CIA)** from 1953 to 1963. The younger brother of the diplomat **John Foster Dulles**, Allen Dulles was an expert on intelligence activities and espionage who contributed to the founding of the CIA in 1947 and eventually became director in 1953. During his tenure as director, the CIA greatly expanded its size and international activities and was involved in a series of covert operations, including **Operation PBSUCCESS**, the successful overthrow of the government of President **Jacobo Arbenz** in **Guatemala** in 1954. But a similar attempt to overthrow **Fidel Castro** in Operation ZAPATA culminated in disaster at the **Bay of Pigs** in 1961. Although President **John F. Kennedy** had personally approved the operation, the setback was initially attributed to the internal failings of the CIA and seriously damaged the professional reputation and prestige of both Dulles and the agency. Dulles subsequently resigned as director of the CIA in 1963. *See also* BISSELL, RICHARD (1910–).

DULLES, JOHN FOSTER (1889–1959). American diplomat and secretary of state from 1953 to 1959. The grandson of Secretary of State **John W. Foster**, Dulles was a successful international lawyer and prominent member of the "Eastern Establishment" who frequently served in government and undertook special missions on behalf of several presidential administrations. As secretary of state in the **Dwight Eisenhower** administration from 1953 to 1959, Dulles acted as the archetypal "cold warrior" who condemned international communism as evil and intent on world conquest. Dulles, therefore, readily subscribed to the belief that communists were seeking to control Guatemalan President **Jacobo Arbenz** in order to establish a Soviet satellite state in Central America.

In March 1954, Dulles attended the Tenth Inter-American Conference at Caracas but was unsuccessful in gaining unanimous Latin American support for a resolution condemning foreign intervention in the form of international communism. Latin American diplomats recognized that he was seeking their backing for action against the Guatemalan government. Moreover, they were generally uncomfortable with his strident anticommunism and confrontational style. In addition, there was suspicion that the policy of the Eisenhower administration toward **Guatemala** was motivated by selfish economic considerations, such as support for the **United Fruit Company (UFCO)** in its dispute with the Guatemalan government. Dulles was reported to have once done legal work for UFCO when he had been an international lawyer, a charge that critics used to query his denial of American complicity in the coup that overthrew Arbenz in 1954. Dulles characteristically claimed that the new Guatemalan government represented an important victory for democracy in the struggle against the evil influence of international communism. *See also* CASTILLO ARMAS, CARLOS (1914–1957); COLD WAR.

– E –

ECUADOR. A country on the west coast of South America bordered by **Colombia** to the north and **Peru** to the south. Diplomatic relations between the United States and Ecuador have been uneventful because of the country's relative lack of political, commercial, and military significance. During **World War II**, Ecuador acquired strategic importance because of its proximity to the Panama Canal. As a result, the United States was temporarily given rights to convert the Galapagos Islands into a military base. Military cooperation between the two countries continued after the war and was exemplified in 1951 by Ecuador signing the first defense agreement with the United States under the 1951 **Mutual Security Act**.

EISENHOWER, DWIGHT (1890–1969). American general, political leader, and president from 1953 to 1961. Born in Abilene, Kansas, Eisenhower was a career army officer who rose to become Supreme Allied Commander in Europe during **World War II**. In 1952, he won the Republican presidential nomination and was elected president in a landslide victory. He was similarly reelected for a second term in 1956. As president, Eisenhower's foreign policy concentrated primarily on dealing with Cold War tensions in Europe, the Middle East, and Asia. By contrast, Latin American affairs were accorded relatively little importance. The main exception was **Guatemala**, where American officials feared the expansion of communist influence. As a result, Eisenhower instructed the **Central Intelligence Agency (CIA)** to mount a covert operation known as **Operation PBSUCCESS**, which overthrew the Guatemalan government in June 1954.

Eisenhower's general attitude of indifference toward Latin American affairs was shaken in May 1958 by the outbreak of violent anti-American demonstrations during Vice President **Richard Nixon**'s visit to **Venezuela**. A reassessment of U.S. Latin American policy subsequently occurred, during which Eisenhower sent his brother, Dr. **Milton Eisenhower**, on a fact-finding tour. He also sought to improve the image of the United States by making a personal visit to several Latin American countries in February–March 1960. At the same time, the provision of U.S. financial aid allocated to the region was considerably increased. But the fight against international communism still remained a priority. Before he left presidential office in January 1961, Eisenhower had observed with dismay the spread of communist influence in **Cuba**. He broke off diplomatic relations with the Cuban government in January 1961 and approved the preparation by the CIA of a covert operation similar to Operation PBSUCCESS to remove **Fidel Castro** from power. The operation took place under

Eisenhower's successor, **John F. Kennedy**, and ended in failure at the **Bay of Pigs** in April 1961. *See also* DULLES, JOHN FOSTER (1889–1959); NIXON VISIT TO LATIN AMERICA (1958).

EISENHOWER, MILTON S. (1899–1985). American educator and diplomat. The younger brother of President **Dwight Eisenhower**, Milton Eisenhower was born in Abilene, Kansas, and became a distinguished educator who served at various times as president of Kansas State University, Pennsylvania State University, and Johns Hopkins University. He also had experience of working in the **State Department** during **World War II** and served as an adviser to his brother on foreign affairs, especially relating to Latin America. Dr. Eisenhower made two fact-finding missions to Latin America, the first in 1953 to Central America and the second in 1958 to South America to assess the implications for U.S. policy of Vice President **Richard Nixon**'s recent visit that had provoked strong anti-American protests. To prevent the advance of international communism, Dr. Eisenhower believed that the United States should considerably increase its financial assistance to the region to raise living standards and promote sustainable economic development. His influence was evident in the program of economic aid devised by President Eisenhower and later in **John F. Kennedy**'s **Alliance for Progress**. In 1963, Dr. Eisenhower published *The Wine Is Bitter*, which recounted the views expressed in his report of his visit to Latin America in 1958. *See also* NIXON VISIT TO LATIN AMERICA (1958).

ELBRICK, C. BURKE (1908–1983). American diplomat. Born in Kentucky, Elbrick was a career diplomat who became ambassador to Portugal from 1958 to 1963 and Yugoslavia from 1964 to 1969. In 1969, he was appointed ambassador to **Brazil**. Only a short time after his arrival in Brazil, Elbrick was kidnapped by a group of revolutionary guerrillas. Elbrick was released unharmed after four days of captivity in return for the agreement of the Brazilian government to release 15 political prisoners and fly them to Mexico. The action against Elbrick reflected left-wing bitterness in Brazil against the United States over its support for the military government. It also illustrated the personal danger often faced by U.S. diplomats arising from the outbreak of urban terrorism that was often a feature of parts of South America during the late 1960s and early 1970s. The story of the kidnapping was later made into a movie titled *Four Days in September* and released in 1997.

EL SALVADOR. The smallest country in Central America bordered by **Guatemala** and **Honduras**. Formerly part of the United Provinces of Central America, El Salvador became an independent republic in 1842. Because of the country's geographical remoteness and relatively small size, diplomatic relations between the United States and El Salvador were conducted via the U.S. legation in Guatemala City until 1853. In fact, El Salvador did not attract much diplomatic significance for the United States until the 1970s and 1980s when it temporarily became a focal point of the **Cold War**. Officials in the **Ronald Reagan** administration were alarmed by the guerrilla activities of the **Farabundo Martí Liberation Front** (Frente Farabundo Martí para la Liberación Nacional [FMLN]) in El Salvador and regarded the movement as an insurgency masterminded by the **Soviet Union** and indirectly aided by procommunist **Cuba** and **Nicaragua**. The result was massive American financial and especially military assistance for the democratic government of El Salvador to suppress and destroy the FMLN. The stress on purely seeking a military solution was only partly successful. While the guerrillas failed to emulate the military success of the **Sandinistas** in Nicaragua, they remained in existence as a credible fighting force in the countryside. The fierce fighting, however, meant that violence became virtually endemic in El Salvador with more than 75,000 Salvadoran civilians estimated to have been killed during the 1980s. The U.S. government eventually accepted the Esquipulas II Accord, also known as the **Arias Peace Plan**, which resulted in a cease-fire and the holding of national elections in 1992. By this time, however, the Cold War had ended, and El Salvador was no longer perceived as a significant issue in U.S. politics or Latin American policy. *See also* CENTRAL AMERICAN CRISIS; DUARTE, JOSÉ NAPOLEON (1925–1990).

EXPORT-IMPORT BANK (EXIM). A U.S. government agency providing export credits. As part of the administration's New Deal measures designed to promote economic recovery from the **Great Depression**, an executive order issued by President **Franklin D.**

Roosevelt in February 1934 created EXIM to provide foreign countries with long-term dollar credits for the purchase of imports from
the United States. In addition to its primary purpose of expanding
trade, the bank gave loans for industrial development and thereby
served as a useful tool of American diplomacy. Although initially designed to finance trade with the **Soviet Union**, EXIM's activities
proved highly successful during the late 1930s in promoting U.S.
trade with Latin America and in countering the attempts of **Germany**
and Japan to take control of these markets. Latin America was also an
important aspect of EXIM's activities during **World War II** when it
provided essential credits for the purchase of U.S. capital goods.

– F –

FALKLAND ISLANDS. A group of islands also known as the **Islas
Malvinas** located in the South Atlantic Ocean off the southern tip of
South America. The islands were geographically remote and lacking
in known natural resources, but control over them was historically
contested between **Great Britain** and **Spain**, whose territorial claim
was later assumed by **Argentina**. Despite **President James Monroe**'s 1823 message warning against future European colonization in
Latin American political affairs, a new European colony was formally established in the **Western Hemisphere** when Great Britain
declared its sovereign control over the Falkland Islands in 1833. The
U.S. government made no objection to Britain's action.

British control over the Falklands, however, was vigorously disputed by Argentina from 1833 on but not subject to an overt military
challenge until April 1982 when Argentine troops invaded and took
possession of the islands without giving any prior warning. A British
military task force was sent to recapture the islands. In the mean-
time, the **Ronald Reagan** administration attempted to mediate the
conflict. While Latin American governments were critical of Argentina's deliberate act of aggression and military conquest, they
were alarmed by the arrival of the large British task force in the
South Atlantic. There was also disappointment with the United
States for allowing this development to occur and a belief that the
Reagan administration was too sympathetic to its European ally. The

issue, however, was effectively decided by Britain's overwhelming military victory over the Argentine forces. Consequently, British control over the Falklands was fully restored in June 1982. *See also* HAIG, ALEXANDER M., JR. (1924–).

FARABUNDO MARTÍ, AUGUSTÍN (1893–1932). Salvadoran revolutionary leader. A political exile in **Guatemala**, Farabundo Martí helped to found the Central American Communist Party in 1925. After traveling to Nicaragua, where he joined **Augustín Sandino** in his struggle against the U.S. occupying forces, Farabundo Martí returned in 1930 to **El Salvador**. In 1932, he led an unsuccessful guerrilla revolt after which he was captured and executed. His reputation and legacy as a revolutionary hero of the Salvadoran people were demonstrated in 1980 when his name was used as the title of the **Farabundo Martí Liberation Front** (Frente Farabundo Martí para la Liberación Nacional). *See also* CENTRAL AMERICAN CRISIS.

FARABUNDO MARTÍ NATIONAL LIBERATION FRONT (FMLN). A guerrilla movement operating in **El Salvador**. In 1980, the various Marxist guerrilla groups in El Salvador came together to form the Farabundo Martí National Liberation Front (Frente Farabundo Martí para la Liberación Nacional [FMLN]), named in honor of the celebrated revolutionary leader **Augustín Farabundo Martí**. The **Ronald Reagan** administration regarded the FMLN as an agent of international communism and sought its complete destruction through a program of massive military aid to the democratic government of El Salvador. Although the FMLN was never actually militarily defeated and continued to operate as a credible fighting force in rural areas, Reagan's strategy was successful in that it prevented the guerrillas from achieving the same military and political success as the **Sandinistas** in **Nicaragua**. The military impasse was eventually broken in 1992 when the FMLN accepted the Esquipulas II Accord, abandoned the armed struggle, and agreed to take the form of a political party and participate in the country's political system. *See also* CENTRAL AMERICAN CRISIS.

FAREWELL ADDRESS (1796). Influential presidential statement on U.S. foreign policy. The Farewell Address was a statement made by

President George Washington that was published in September 1796 shortly before he gave up his presidential office. It advised that the future foreign policy of the United States should always seek to preserve independence of diplomatic action and to avoid entering into damaging entanglements with the powers of the Old World of Europe. Washington, however, did not advocate complete isolation in foreign affairs because he expected the new American republic to expand its overseas trade with European nations and to pursue territorial expansion within the North American continent. The statement also had application to future relations with the countries of Latin America because it signified ideas of U.S. exceptionalism and determination to pursue a unilateral attitude in diplomatic affairs. *See also* AMERICAN REVOLUTION; FRANCE.

FEDERAL BUREAU OF INVESTIGATION (FBI). An agency of the U.S. government. The FBI was responsible primarily for law enforcement within the United States. During **World War II**, however, FBI agents were dispatched to Latin America to assist governments in identifying local Nazi activists and sympathizers and to cooperate in efforts to restrict Nazi activities. By the end of World War II, more than 300 FBI agents were stationed in Latin America. Acting as a precursor of the **Central Intelligence Agency (CIA)** and providing a foretaste of future U.S. clandestine operations during the Cold War, they often gathered intelligence and conducted their own independent investigations rather than collaborating with local government officials.

FIGUERES FERRER, JOSÉ (1906–1990). Costa Rican political leader and three-time president from 1948 to 1974. A successful coffee planter, Figueres became a political exile in 1942 but returned to **Costa Rica** and seized political power in the 1948 civil war. After resigning the presidency in 1949, he formed the Partido de Liberación Nacional (National Liberation Party) and won the presidential election in 1953. American officials were concerned by civil unrest in the country and attributed this to the rise of communist influence, especially in the Costa Rican labor unions. Figueres was critical of the excessive profits made by foreign corporations and threatened to nationalize the Boston-based **United Fruit Company (UFCO)**. Unlike

President **Jacobo Arbenz** in **Guatemala**, however, he was staunchly anticommunist and acted vigorously to restrict local communist activities. Consequently, the **Dwight Eisenhower** administration supported Figueres when his quarrel with Nicaraguan President **Anastasio Somoza García** erupted into a military invasion of Costa Rica by Nicaraguan forces in 1955. With the approval of Washington, the **Organization of American States** intervened to bring about a cease-fire and settlement of the dispute. Although his term as president ended in 1958, Figueres continued to be active in politics and served another presidential term from 1970 to 1974.

FILIBUSTERS. Expeditions organized by American adventurers to seize land and precious metals in Latin America. Originating from the Dutch word for "free booter," filibusters were composed of groups of mostly American adventurers and soldiers of fortune who used force in attempts to seize land in **Mexico**, Central America, and **Cuba**. Aims were varied and ranged from a nationalistic desire to fulfill America's **Manifest Destiny** to assist the spread of democracy, establish colonies of settlers (sometimes as a means of perpetuating the institution of slavery), or the purely mercenary motive of taking possession of any easily available precious metal, such as gold or silver. Filibusters attracted most support in the southern states of the United States because of geographical proximity to Central America and the Caribbean and because they were viewed as a means of bringing new slave states into the Union and thereby strengthening the controversial institution of slavery. Prominent leaders were the Venezuelan-born Cuban patriot Narciso López, who launched a succession of unsuccessful military expeditions to **Cuba** starting out from New Orleans in 1848 and 1851. During the 1850s, **William Walker** organized an invasion of **Nicaragua**, where he briefly established a government in which he ruled as dictator.

The activities of the filibusters were sometimes portrayed by the press in the United States as in keeping with America's traditional sense of democratic mission. But the U.S. federal government did not wish to be seen to be endorsing forceful seizure of overseas territory because such action would almost certainly provoke diplomatic difficulties. Moreover, under existing American neutrality legislation, it was illegal to organize military expeditions to invade countries with which the United States was not at war. The federal authorities, however, did not always vigorously enforce the law, a practice that understandably raised suspicions in Latin America of American hypocrisy and ulterior motive. Already alarmed by the conquest and incorporation of huge amounts of Mexican territory resulting from the **Mexican-American War** (1846–1848), Latin Americans regarded the filibusters as little more than pirates in the tradition of Francis Drake and Henry Morgan. Instead of promoting democracy, they were viewed as examples of calculated American aggression and desire for territorial expansion. *See also* AMERICAN REVOLUTION.

FISH, HAMILTON (1808–1893). American diplomat and secretary of state from 1869 to 1877. Born in New York City, Fish was active in New York politics first as a Whig and later as a member of the Republican Party. While senator for New York from 1851 to 1857, he gained experience of foreign affairs by serving on the Senate Foreign Relations Committee. In 1869, Fish was appointed secretary of state, a position that he held for the duration of the **Ulysses S. Grant** administration from 1869 to 1877. While Fish carefully monitored events in **Cuba**, where rebels sought independence from **Spain** in what was known as the Ten Years' War (1868–1878), he had little active involvement in the diplomatic affairs of Central and South America. The principal exception was over proposals for schemes to construct a Central American Canal. In response to pressure from American politicians and business interests, Fish duly entered into diplomatic negotiations separately with the governments of **Colombia**, **Nicaragua**, and **Costa Rica** to aid the building of a canal. Fish, however, showed little personal enthusiasm for discussions that not only proved complex and time-consuming but also unsuccessful. *See also* PANAMA CANAL.

FLETCHER, HENRY P. (1873–1959). American diplomat. Born in Pennsylvania, Fletcher became a lawyer and fought as a volunteer in the **Spanish-American War** (1898). He joined the **State Department** in 1902 and acquired the reputation of an expert on Latin American affairs after serving first as minister and then ambassador to Chile from 1910 to 1916 and ambassador to Mexico from 1917 to 1919. In 1921, Fletcher was appointed undersecretary of state in the

Warren Harding administration. In 1923, when Secretary of State **Charles Evans Hughes** declined to attend the Pan-American Conference at Santiago de Chile, Fletcher was appointed to head the U.S. delegation in his place. From 1924 to 1929, Fletcher served as ambassador to Italy. His expertise on Latin American affairs continued to be highly valued in Washington, and he was seconded to the U.S. delegation that attended the Pan-American Conference held at Havana, **Cuba**, in 1928. After leaving the State Department in 1929, Fletcher remained a consultant on foreign policy matters. He notably traveled with President-elect **Herbert Hoover** on the latter's goodwill visit to Latin America during the interregnum prior to his assuming presidential office in 1929.

FORD, GERALD R. (1913–). American political leader and president from 1974 to 1977. A Republican congressman representing Michigan since 1948, Ford rose to be House Minority Leader in 1965 and was appointed vice president by President **Richard Nixon** in 1973. When Nixon resigned in August 1974, he became president. In foreign affairs, Ford concentrated mainly on dealing with **Cold War** issues, such as continuing the policy of détente with the **Soviet Union** and the negotiation of a new arms limitation treaty known as SALT II. The Ford administration publicly stated its intention of improving diplomatic and commercial relations with Latin America but found itself on the defensive as a result of the congressional hearings opened by the **Church Committee** to investigate the policies of previous presidential administrations and, in particular, alleged links with the Chilean coup that overthrew President **Salvador Allende** in 1973. In seeking his party's renomination as presidential candidate in 1976, Ford also faced considerable criticism from right-wing critics, notably former governor of California **Ronald Reagan**, who charged that the administration was involved in negotiations with **Panama** that would result in the humiliating surrender of U.S. control over the **Panama Canal Zone**. Despite successfully winning the Republican nomination, Ford lost the 1976 presidential election to the Democratic candidate, **Jimmy Carter**.

FORD MOTOR COMPANY. A prominent U.S. corporation. During the 1920s, the United States replaced **Great Britain** as the leading foreign investor in Latin America. A particular feature of American economic influence was the giant corporation such as Ford Motor Company, which brought not only investment for new factories and jobs but at the same time also spread American business skills and cultural values. In 1919 at its main factory in São Paulo, **Brazil**, the company assembled just over 2,000 automobiles. In 1925, production had increased to the same figure per month. By 1928, the company had authorized 700 agencies and more than 2,000 garages all over Brazil to market, distribute, and repair its products. The owner of the company, Henry Ford, had ambitions on the massive scale that was typically associated with the celebrated American entrepreneurs. Acquiring a concession of Brazilian territory almost the size of the state of Connecticut, he ordered work to commence in 1928 on his ultimately ill-fated scheme to create a prosperous rubber plantation in the new planned city of "Fordlandia" located in the remote Amazon jungle. A similar Amazonian scheme was attempted during the 1960s by the American shipping millionaire Daniel Ludwig.

FOSTER, JOHN W. (1836–1917). American diplomat and secretary of state from 1892 to 1893. Born in Indiana, Foster was a lawyer and journalist who was rewarded for his political services on behalf of the Republican Party in the 1872 elections with appointment as minister to **Mexico**. He went on to have a distinguished diplomatic career serving in Mexico from 1873 to 1880, **Russia** from 1880 to 1881, and **Spain** from 1883 to 1885. Foster's personal experience of Mexico and Spain gave him a knowledge of the Spanish language and expertise in Latin American affairs that were used during the **Benjamin Harrison** administration (1889–1893), when he was prominent in promoting the policy of commercial reciprocity and was placed in charge of negotiating the **reciprocal trade agreements** with **Brazil** and with **Spain** (for trade with Cuba). He was appointed secretary of state from 1892 to 1893. Foster's active involvement in U.S. diplomacy established a tradition in his family that was followed most notably by his grandson **John Foster Dulles**, who served as secretary of state under President **Dwight Eisenhower**.

FRANCE. A European great power. The significant involvement of France in diplomatic relations between the United States and Latin

America was confined to the 19th century. While retaining a close interest in its colonies in the Caribbean, especially Haiti, France had little direct contact with the Spanish-American colonial empire and the ensuing **wars for Latin American independence**. French detachment from affairs in the New World was demonstrated by Emperor **Napoleon Bonaparte**'s decision in 1803 to sell the vast **Louisiana** territory to the United States. In so doing, he greatly assisted the territorial expansion and ambitions of the new American republic to become a nation of continental extent. France was also instrumental in prompting American presidents to make public statements outlining their country's determination to take an independent line in foreign policy based on the separation of the New World from the Old World of Europe. This was exemplified in President George Washington's **Farewell Address** in 1796 warning his successors not to enter into diplomatic entanglements with European nations. Moreover, it was the rumored prospect of French troops being sent to the New World on behalf of the **Holy Alliance** to restore the monarchical rule of King Ferdinand VII of Spain that led to **President James Monroe**'s message to Congress in 1823 outlining what would become the **Monroe Doctrine**.

When French Emperor Napoleon III dispatched troops to **Mexico** in 1862, the U.S. government was preoccupied with fighting the American Civil War and did not issue any immediate protest. In fact, emboldened by his initial success, Napoleon III developed a scheme in which he sought to control Mexico by making an Austrian archduke emperor of the country. By 1865, however, when the American Civil War ended, Napoleon III had already decided to abandon his ambitious plans. Diplomatic pressure from Secretary of State **William H. Seward** merely expedited the emperor's decision that had already been taken to withdraw all French troops from Mexico.

American concerns that France still possessed designs on acquiring territory in the New World were revived in 1879 when the French **Panama Canal Company**, with the celebrated entrepreneur **Ferdinand de Lesseps** as its president, secured a concession from Colombia and started building a sea-level canal at the Isthmus of **Panama**. Several resolutions were passed in the U.S. Congress stating that France was violating the Monroe Doctrine. In March 1880, President **Rutherford B. Hayes** was prompted into sending a Special Message to the U.S. Congress affirming that the United States would seek to take control of any completed canal. De Lesseps argued correctly, however, that the canal company was a private and not a government venture. Although the French company proceeded with construction work at Panama, this was soon abandoned not because of American diplomatic pressure but because of major engineering difficulties and financial scandal. The company transferred its concessions and sold its assets to the U.S. government in 1904. Like the issue of the Holy Alliance in 1823 and the **French Intervention** in Mexico during the 1860s, U.S.–French rivalry over the **Panama Canal** was a relatively brief matter and one that was resolved peacefully. *See also* FRENCH INTERVENTION (1862–1867); VERACRUZ.

FREE TRADE AREA OF THE AMERICAS (FTAA). Proposed free trade covering the **Western Hemisphere**. Since the American Civil War (1861–1865), the United States has favored a protectionist economic policy exemplified by the maintenance of a high tariff on foreign imports. Although a hemispheric commercial union was proposed by the U.S. delegation at the **International American Conference** (1889–1890), the United States has preferred to make limited tariff changes either in bilateral **reciprocal trade agreements** or at a broader international level as part of the General Agreement on Tariffs and Trade (GATT). While Latin American nations have also pursued protectionist policies, they have generally been more receptive to joining free trade agreements. This has been illustrated in the creation of the Central American Common Market in 1960, the Latin American Free Trade Association (or Asociación Latinoamericana de Libre Comercio) in 1970, and **Mercosur** in 1991.

During the late 20th century, the emergence of powerful international trading blocs such as the European Union and concern over the ramifications of the increasing globalization of the world economy resulted in a series of meetings under GATT that were aimed at the liberalization of world trade. At the same time, the U.S. government also considered means of promoting hemispheric integration. In June 1990, President **George H. W. Bush** announced the "Enterprise for the Americas Initiative" (EAI), which envisaged the creation of a free trade area covering all of the Western Hemisphere. The EAI produced a positive response from Mexican President **Carlos Salinas** that led to the negotiation in 1992 of the **North American Free Trade Agreement (NAFTA)** comprising the United States, **Canada**, and **Mexico**. NAFTA was generally regarded as the first step in a process toward the formation of the "Free Trade Area of the Americas" (Área de Libre Comercio de las Américas). Discussions subsequently took place at the series of summit meetings of heads of state in Miami (1994), Santiago de Chile (1998), Quebec City (2001), and Mar del Plata (2005). While the concept of the Free Trade Area of the Americas has attracted general support, there has been general concern, especially among Latin American governments, that it will lead to increased economic influence for the United States. *See also* SUMMITS OF THE AMERICAS; UNITED NATIONS ECONOMIC COMMISSION FOR LATIN AMERICA (UNECLA or ECLA).

FREI MONTALVA, EDUARDO (1911–1982). Chilean political leader and president from 1964 to 1970. Frei was a lawyer who became the leader of the newly formed Christian Democratic Party in 1957. Defeated for the presidency in 1958 by Jorge Alessandri, he won election in 1964 against the socialist candidate, **Salvador Allende**. The 1964 election was closely monitored by U.S. officials because Allende was a Marxist and his campaign was highly critical of the economic influence possessed by the U.S.-owned copper companies, notably Anaconda and Kennecott. It was estimated that the Central Intelligence Agency secretly contributed in excess of $3 million to help fund Frei's successful campaign that won the election with more than 50 percent of the popular vote.

As president, Frei responded to nationalist sentiment by declaring that his aim was the "Chileanization" of the copper industry. Instead of announcing the full nationalization of foreign companies, however, he entered into negotiations that resulted in the Chilean government securing 51 percent ownership while the companies continued to extract and sell copper on the world market. Frei's moderation was well received in Washington and was rewarded with an increase in U.S. financial assistance under the **Alliance for Progress**. According to the Chilean Constitution, presidents could serve only one full term of office. Frei was not, therefore, a candidate in the 1970 election won by Salvador Allende. *See also* CHILE.

FRELINGHUYSEN, FREDERICK T. (1817–1885). American diplomat and secretary of state from 1881 to 1885. Born in New Jersey, Frelinghusyen pursued a legal career and then became active in politics. Representing the Republican Party, he won election to the U.S. Senate in 1866 and 1870. Frelinghuysen's involvement in foreign affairs occurred as the result of the resignation of **James G. Blaine** in December 1881 when he was appointed secretary of state by President Chester A. Arthur. A longtime political opponent of Blaine, Frelinghuysen sought to discredit the former secretary of state by publishing much of his controversial diplomatic correspondence with **Chile** and **Peru** concerning the role of the United States in the **War of the Pacific**.

While he adopted a more conciliatory role in the conflict between Chile and Peru, Frelinghuysen was similar to Blaine in personally favoring an active U.S. policy toward Latin America. He was a strong supporter of increased trade with the region and negotiated commercial reciprocity treaties with Mexico and Spain (for trade with Cuba). He was also an advocate of the building of a Central American Canal and secured a treaty with **Nicaragua** in 1884 that gave the United States special canal rights in violation of the terms of the **Clayton-Bulwer Treaty** (1850). The treaties, however, were politically controversial and were brought before the U.S. Senate for ratification just as the Arthur administration was coming to an end of its term of office. The treaties failed to secure congressional support and were withdrawn by the new Democratic President **Grover Cleveland**. *See also* PANAMA CANAL.

FRENCH GUIANA. A French colony in South America bordered by Suriname to the west and Brazil to the south and east. French Guiana has been a colony of France since the 17th century and became an overseas department in 1946.

FRENCH INTERVENTION (1862–1867). French attempt to establish a monarchy in **Mexico**. At a time when the United States was preoccupied with the American Civil War (1861–1865), French Emperor Louis Napoleon III implemented an ambitious scheme to place Mexico under French influence and guidance. Starting in 1862 initially as a display of gunboat diplomacy to secure the payment of financial debts to European bondholders, the French Intervention developed in 1864 into a major military operation to occupy **Mexico** and install an Austrian prince, Archduke Maximilian of Habsburg, as emperor of the country. The U.S. government adopted a neutral policy and did not wish to antagonize France. Unable to defeat the Mexican resistance forces led by **Benito Juárez** and concerned at the military implications of the end of the American Civil War in 1865 and also Prussia's victory over Austria in the Austro-Prussian War of 1866, Napoleon admitted military defeat and ordered the phased withdrawal of French troops from Mexico in 1866. Maximilian rejected advice to abdicate and leave Mexico. The final humiliation for Napoleon personally and for French prestige more generally occurred when Maximilian was captured and executed by a firing squad on June 19, 1867. *See also* FRANCE; SEWARD, WILLIAM H. (1801–1872).

– G –

GADSDEN, JAMES (1788–1858). American businessman and diplomat. A railroad entrepreneur from South Carolina, Gadsden was appointed as minister to **Mexico** from 1853 to 1856. He was instrumental in negotiating the **Gadsden Purchase**, a treaty with Mexico in which the United States purchased a considerable amount of Mexican territory. *See also* TREATY OF GUADALUPE HIDALGO (1848).

GADSDEN PURCHASE (1853). An arrangement in which the United States purchased territory from **Mexico**. In the **Treaty of Guadalupe Hidalgo**, which ended the **Mexican-American War** in 1848, Mexico accepted the Rio Grande River as its border with Texas and also ceded to the United States a vast portion of territory extending from the modern state of New Mexico to California. Additional land was gained later for the United States by the Gadsden Purchase in 1853 in which the American minister to Mexico, James Gadsden, negotiated a treaty with the Mexican government for the purchase of the Gila River valley in Arizona and New Mexico at the price of $10 million. The treaty was formally ratified by the U.S. Senate in April 1854.

GARCÍA PÉREZ, ALÁN (1949–). Peruvian political leader and president from 1985 to 1990. A member of the radical Popular Revolutionary Alliance Party (Alianza Popular Revolucionaria Americana), García was elected president of **Peru** in 1985. At the age of 36, his relative youth drew comparisons with **John F. Kennedy** and his U.S. presidential victory in 1960. At his presidential inauguration, he denounced the **International Monetary Fund (IMF)** for imposing excessive and damaging economic restrictions on Peru and declared that his country's repayments would be strictly limited to no more than 10 percent of the country's annual income that was earned from exports.

American officials in the **Ronald Reagan** administration were concerned by García's unilateral decision to reduce debt repayments. They were further alarmed by the prospect of the new Peruvian president joining forces with other Latin American leaders, including perhaps even **Fidel Castro**, to develop their own independent policy to deal with the **debt crisis**. In response, the Reagan administration prepared the **Baker Plan** to help alleviate financial difficulties.

García also adopted an independent approach in his diplomatic relations with the United States. He was severely critical of Washington's aggressive policy toward **Nicaragua** and professed sympathy for the **Sandinistas**. García's policies, however, were also controversial in Peru. Rapid inflation, increasing unemployment, and a marked upsurge in terrorism resulting from the activities of the guerrilla movement known as the "Shining Path" (Sendero Luminoso) led to the end of his presidency in 1990.

GERMANY. A European great power. During the 19th century, German interest in Latin America was limited mainly to modest amounts of trade and immigration. At the start of the 20th century, however, Germany and its head of state, Kaiser William II, gained a reputation for aggressive gunboat diplomacy and for harboring secret designs to acquire territory in Central America and the Caribbean. American officials suspected German ulterior motives in the **Venezuela Incident** (1902–1903), when Germany cooperated with **Great Britain** and Italy in sending a small squadron of gunboats to Venezuela to impose a punitive naval blockade for that country's refusal to service its foreign debt. After some initial hesitation, Germany agreed to go to arbitration to settle the dispute. President **Theodore Roosevelt** later claimed that his threat of American naval intervention had been responsible for Germany's change of policy. The Venezuela Incident was significant because, in order to prevent a repetition of similar acts of European gunboat diplomacy, Roosevelt declared that the United States would intervene militarily in cases where Latin American governments refused to meet their financial obligations to overseas creditors. This policy became known as the **Roosevelt Corollary** to the **Monroe Doctrine**.

Diplomatic relations between the United States and Germany were complicated by the outbreak of **World War I** in August 1914. While the United States proclaimed a policy of neutrality toward all the belligerent powers, it soon became evident that officials in the **Woodrow Wilson** administration and American public opinion were generally sympathetic to Great Britain and **France** and regarded Germany as the aggressor in the war. This view was reinforced in 1917 by the **Zimmermann Telegram**, which revealed that German diplomats had secretly promised the Mexican government the restitution of territory lost as a result of the **Mexican-American War** (1846–1848) should Mexico join Germany in a war against the United States. The revelation of German intrigues in Latin America was shocking and contributed to the decision of the U.S. Congress to vote to go to war against Germany in April 1917.

After its defeat in World War I, Germany was not regarded as a real threat either to hemispheric security or to U.S. interests in Latin America until the 1930s. During that decade, the **Franklin D. Roosevelt** administration sought to expand American trade in the region and regarded Germany as a major economic competitor. Indeed, German businessmen were very successful in making inroads into South American markets, especially **Brazil**. American officials were also concerned by the spread of Nazi influence and its effect on the large local communities of German extraction resident in parts of Central and South America. Fears of a potential German "fifth column" were particularly worrying. The task of countering Nazi propaganda in Latin America was allocated to the Office of Inter-American Affairs that was created in August 1940 and renamed in July 1941 the **Office of the Coordinator of Inter-American Affairs (OCIAA)**. While OCIAA pursued a strategy of psychological warfare, the **State Department** issued a **Black List** containing the names of suspected pro-German companies and individuals whom American companies and citizens were instructed to boycott and to avoid having business relations with. In addition, agents from the **Federal Bureau of Investigation (FBI)** were dispatched to Latin America to assist governments in identifying and restricting the activities of local German agents and their associates.

World War II greatly enhanced the position of the United States as the preeminent political, economic, and military power in the **Western Hemisphere**. The German political challenge, which had appeared so serious during the 1930s, was diminished and effectively destroyed. Not only was Nazism discredited as a political system and ideology, but Germany also lost the economic markets that it had gained during the previous decade. It was not until the 1970s that "Germany," in the form of West Germany, would again become one of the world's leading economic powers and a major competitor of the United States in Latin American markets.

GOOD NEIGHBOR POLICY. A term used to describe U.S. policy toward Latin America from 1933 to 1945. In foreign affairs, President **Franklin D. Roosevelt** advocated an active internationalist role for the United States. In terms of his policy toward Latin America, he basically continued the conciliatory approach of his Republican predecessor, **Herbert Hoover**, as part of the strategy designed to rebut the view that the United States was an aggressive and overbearing power. The policy, however, acquired a new name as a result of a section taken from Roosevelt's inaugural address as president on March 4, 1933, in which he referred to "the policy of the good neighbor." Consequently, it was Roosevelt and not Hoover who has been regarded as the originator of the Good Neighbor Policy.

Prominent examples of good neighborliness were Roosevelt's speech in January 1934 publicly declaring that his government disavowed the policy of armed intervention in the affairs of sovereign states; the abrogation in 1934 of the notorious **Platt Amendment** (1901), which had given the United States a constitutional right to intervene in **Cuba**; and the president's personal attendance at the Special Pan-American Conference for the Maintenance of Peace held in Buenos Aires in December 1936.

The marked improvement in inter-American relations brought about by the Good Neighbor Policy resulted in the conclusion of several **reciprocal trade agreements** that brought direct benefits for the United States in terms of increased trade and economic recovery from the **Great Depression**. In addition, American officials were most gratified by the willingness of the Latin American governments to offer military cooperation. For example, most countries agreed to join the United States in organizing resistance against the fascist threat posed by **Germany** and Italy both before and during **World War II**. Moreover, in marked contrast to their attitudes during **World War I**, all the South American nations, with the exception of **Argentina** and **Chile**, readily affirmed their support for the United States by either joining the war against or breaking off relations with the Axis powers by the end of 1942. After the close of World War II in 1945, however, the Good Neighbor Policy was quietly sidelined as the United States paid much more attention to political and economic developments occurring in Europe rather than in Latin America. A complacent attitude was adopted toward the Latin American nations whose support for the United States in the emerging **Cold War** was taken for granted. *See also* ACT OF CHAPULTEPEC (1945); CHAPULTEPEC CONFERENCE (1945); CLARK MEMORANDUM (1930); COLD WAR; HULL, CORDELL (1871–1955).

GOODWIN, RICHARD (1931–). American diplomat. Born in Boston, Massachusetts, Goodwin was a lawyer who worked as a speechwriter in **John F. Kennedy**'s successful campaign for the presidency in 1960. He was subsequently appointed a member of Kennedy's task force to recommend options on Latin American policy. In the Kennedy administration, Goodwin advised the president on Latin American affairs and served as deputy assistant secretary of state for inter-American affairs from 1961 to 1963. He was an enthusiastic advocate of developing a major program of U.S. economic aid for Latin America and was credited with first suggesting the title "**Alliance for Progress**."

GORDON, LINCOLN (1913–). American economist and diplomat. Born in Massachusetts, Gordon was a professor of economics at Harvard University who gave advice to the **John F. Kennedy** administration on the formulation and implementation of the **Alliance for Progress**. Appointed ambassador to **Brazil** in 1961, he was present when President **João Goulart** was deposed in a military coup in 1964. Although he was known to have been in close contact with senior Brazilian military officers, Gordon vigorously denied charges of U.S. complicity in the coup. In 1966, he returned to Washington to take up the post of assistant secretary for inter-American affairs. After leaving the **State Department**, he served as a consultant on international affairs and was president of Johns Hopkins University. *See also* WALTERS, VERNON (1917–2002).

GOULART, JOÃO (1918–1976). Brazilian political leader and president from 1961 to 1964. A political protégé of **Getúlio Vargas**, Goulart succeeded to the presidency on the surprise resignation of **Jânio Quadros** in August 1961. Known for his left-wing ideas and close associations with left-wing labor unions, Goulart had long aroused the suspicion of American officials that he was a procommunist. They were also disturbed by his decision to continue the independent approach to foreign policy that had been initiated by Quadros. As president, Goulart formally renewed Brazil's diplomatic relations with the **Soviet Union** and was critical of American efforts to expel Cuba from the **Organization of American States (OAS)**. Fearing that Goulart was deliberately creating an internal political and economic crisis that would stimulate the rise of communist influence in Brazil, the **Lyndon Johnson** administration was openly critical of his policies and welcomed his fall from power by a military coup in April 1964. Goulart left Brazil and lived in exile in Uruguay.

GRANT, ULYSSES S. (1822–1885). American general and president from 1869 to 1877. A career army officer, Grant rose to command the Union army during the American Civil War (1861–1865) and became a popular military hero. Representing the Republican Party, he was elected president in 1868 and reelected in 1872. In U.S. policy toward Latin America, the Grant administration was significant in attaching the "No-Transfer" stipulation to the **Monroe Doctrine**. This occurred when Grant, responding to rumors that European powers were interested in annexing the Dominican Republic, sent a Special

Message to the U.S. Senate on May 31, 1870, declaring that no territory in the **Western Hemisphere** should be transferred to a European nation.

Grant was also personally interested in the question of a Central American Canal. He had crossed the isthmus as a young army officer in 1852 and was receptive to the lobbying of American politicians and business interests to involve the U.S. government in the building of a canal. This resulted in diplomatic negotiations with the governments of **Colombia**, **Nicaragua**, and **Costa Rica** to acquire canal rights. Secretary of State **Hamilton Fish**, however, showed little enthusiasm for discussions that not only proved complex and time-consuming but also were ultimately unsuccessful. *See also* PANAMA CANAL.

GREAT BRITAIN. A European great power. Anglo-American rivalry was a salient feature of the diplomatic history of the **Western Hemisphere** during the 19th century. In fact, the fulfillment of U.S. claims to a preeminent political position required the displacement of European powers, especially Great Britain, which was also a well-established "American" power because of its colonial possessions in **Canada**, in the Caribbean, and on the mainland of Central and South America. Moreover, Britain was the "workshop of the world," and British merchants and investors were eager to seize what were perceived to be major economic opportunities presented in Latin America by the collapse of the protectionist-minded Spanish and Portuguese empires.

Anglo-American political rivalry was evident in the decision of President **James Monroe** in 1822 to grant diplomatic recognition to the new Latin American states ahead of Britain. In 1823, the Monroe administration rejected British Foreign Minister **George Canning**'s proposal to issue a joint Anglo-American protest against the rumored intervention of the **Holy Alliance**. Canning argued, however, that his own diplomatic skill in securing a prior understanding with the French government, combined with the threat to use British naval power, had been the decisive factors in defeating the threat of European military intervention. He claimed that Britain wished to be the foremost friend, protector, and example for the new Latin American states. In fact, the latter appreciated the importance of possessing military power and judged Britain to be much stronger in this particular respect than the United States. Accordingly, Canning's statements were given more credence than those of Monroe, especially in Latin America, where the British were generally regarded as the real friends of Latin American independence, while the Americans were considered as diplomatically self-serving.

Furthermore, Latin American countries, especially **Brazil**, were willing to conclude preferential commercial treaties with Great Britain, the world's leading industrial and commercial nation and one that had more to offer than the United States. For much of the 19th century, American merchants provided weak competition to their British rivals because they lacked similar knowledge of local markets, manufacturing capacity, shipping lines, and credit facilities.

The United States, however, steadily gained in hemispheric political influence. This reflected mainly the fact that British diplomats were preoccupied with European and their own imperial issues in Africa, India, and Asia and did not regard Latin America as a region of correspondingly important national interest. Consequently, Britain sought cooperation rather than conflict with the United States in political affairs involving the Western Hemisphere. For example, the British government agreed to the **Clayton-Bulwer Treaty** in 1850 as a means of aiding the proposed construction of a Central American Canal. In 1859, diplomatic tension between the two countries over Central American affairs was alleviated when Britain agreed that **Nicaragua** should control the port of Greytown and that the Bay Islands should be returned to **Honduras**.

The most serious Anglo-American crisis occurred over the **Venezuela Boundary Dispute** in 1895. Believing that Britain was violating the Monroe Doctrine by secretly seeking to acquire territory at Venezuela's expense, the **Grover Cleveland** administration demanded that Britain agree to submit the dispute to binding arbitration. When Britain refused, war suddenly became a possibility. The war scare, however, was short lived. The British government agreed to arbitration and thereby acknowledged the right of the United States to intervene in the boundary dispute. In the process, not only was Cleveland's assertion of the **Monroe Doctrine** vindicated, but American political preeminence in the **Western Hemisphere** was also finally recognized by Britain.

In fact, Britain and other European nations were economic benefici-
aries of the assertive policy adopted by the United States after the
Spanish-American War (1898). By agreeing to the **Hay-Pauncefote
Treaty** (1901) and thereby abrogating the Clayton-Bulwer Treaty,
Britain allowed the United States to build and exercise exclusive control over the projected **Panama Canal**. The result was the construction
of a major canal that greatly boosted international trade. Similarly, the
exercise of **dollar diplomacy** promoted political order and stability in
the often turbulent Central American–Caribbean region and, consequently, both protected and assisted British trade and investment. The
rise of U.S. political preeminence, however, was also accompanied by
the advance of American business and investment as the United States
displaced Britain as the leading economic power in the hemisphere. For
a time, the British maintained their well-established leading economic
position in South America, especially **Argentina**, but this was considerably weakened by the liquidation of many British investments because of two costly world wars during the first half of the 20th century.

While a British diplomatic representative had attended the **Panama
Congress** (1826), Britain was not invited to the **International American Conference** (1889–1890). During the 20th century, Britain had little direct impact on the political affairs of Latin America and was not
a member of the **Pan-American Conference System** or the inter-
American movement. While no longer a political rival in Latin American affairs, Britain was the principal ally of the United States in the
wider world. In fact, Britain was often more favored than Latin America. For example, substantial **lend-lease** aid was given by the United
States to Latin America during **World War II**, but it was only a small
fraction of the huge amount that Britain received. The importance attached by American diplomacy to the "special relationship" with
Britain had visible repercussions in Latin America in 1982 when the
Ronald Reagan administration provided diplomatic and material sup-
port to Britain in the prosecution of its **South Atlantic War** against
Argentina. *See also* BLAINE, JAMES G. (1830–1893); CANADA;
FALKLAND ISLANDS; ROOSEVELT COROLLARY; SCRUGGS,
WILLIAM L. (1836–1912).

GREAT DEPRESSION. An economic depression occurring during
the 1930s. The worst international economic crisis of the 20th cen-

tury began with the stock market crash on Wall Street in October 1929 and subsequently developed into the Great Depression, which lasted throughout the 1930s and was extremely damaging to the economies of the United States and all the Latin American countries. Governments throughout Latin America sought to combat the economic crisis by stimulating exports. This policy was regarded not only as the best means of generating increased earnings of foreign currency but also as essential to save particular export sectors from complete economic collapse.

Initially, the United States appeared unsympathetic to the economic plight of Latin American exporters because it maintained a strongly protectionist attitude that was symbolized by the passage of the Smoot-Hawley Tariff in 1930. However, President **Franklin D. Roosevelt**, who came to office in 1933, launched the **Good Neighbor Policy** in an attempt to improve hemispheric relations. A feature of the policy was closer economic contact to promote trade and help the American economy recover from the Great Depression. Starting with **Cuba** in 1934, the Roosevelt administration concluded a series of bilateral trade treaties with several Latin American countries. Although its share of the Latin American export trade actually declined slightly during the 1930s, the United States remained the largest single market for Latin American goods. The economic boom that occurred as a result of **World War II** not only effectively ended the Great Depression but also reinforced the leading economic role of the United States in the **Western Hemisphere**. *See also* EXPORT-IMPORT BANK (EXIM); HULL, CORDELL (1871–1955).

GRESHAM, WALTER Q. (1832–1895). American lawyer, politician, and secretary of state from 1893 to 1895. Born in Illinois, Gresham was a lawyer who joined the Republican Party. In 1883, he was appointed postmaster general by President Chester A. Arthur and later served as secretary of the treasury. Gresham disagreed with Republican policies on the protective tariff in 1892 and accepted appointment as secretary of state in the Democratic administration of President **Grover Cleveland**. Gresham adopted a highly principled approach to foreign policy issues as he showed in his condemnation of the proposal to annex the Hawaiian Islands as morally wrong. He demonstrated a similar attitude toward the **Brazilian Naval Revolt** (1893–1894). While the Brazilian government of Marshal Floriano Peixoto was grateful for U.S. naval intervention in the dispute and made July 4, 1894, a national holiday in Brazil, Gresham was careful to stress that the aim of the American action had been not to take sides in an internal political dispute but to uphold the legal right of American merchants to carry out their commercial operations at Rio de Janeiro without interference. *See also* ARMED INTERVENTIONS.

GUATEMALA. A country in Central America bordered by **Mexico** to the north and **Honduras** and **El Salvador** to the south. The regional importance of Guatemala was reflected in that fact that it provided the capital city of the United Provinces of Central America, which was created in 1821. Official diplomatic relations were established with the United States in 1824. Guatemala became an independent republic after the collapse of the federation in 1838. In the 19th century, however, Guatemala lacked strategic importance for the United States. It was geographically remote and offered very few commercial attractions for American merchants and investors. In fact, for most of the 1830s and 1840s, no U.S. minister actually took up official residence in Guatemala City.

At the beginning of the 20th century, the **United Fruit Company (UFCO)** of Boston acquired large plantations in Guatemala and began a flourishing business in the cultivation and export of bananas. However, it was only during the late 1930s, at a time of growing alarm over the rise of the fascist threat to the **Western Hemisphere**, that U.S. diplomatic officials began to show a particular interest in Guatemalan political affairs. This reflected their concern that German business interests dominated the local coffee industry and that this might influence the Guatemalan government to adopt a pro-Nazi foreign policy. The apprehension was unnecessary because President Jorge Ubico banned the Nazi Party and cooperated closely with the United States to the extent of joining the war against **Germany** in January 1942. In return, Guatemala received U.S. financial assistance in the form of **lend-lease** aid.

Ubico's overthrow in 1944 began the period of radical economic and social reform known as the **Guatemalan Revolution**. In foreign affairs, the new president, **Juan José Arévalo**, frequently adopted an anti-American approach and castigated American imperialism for his country's economic backwardness. American officials, however, were more disturbed by the election of **Jacobo Arbenz** as president in 1950 and his evident determination to implement a program of major land redistribution. Faced with the expropriation of considerable amounts of its land without the provision of adequate financial compensation, the United Fruit Company vigorously protested and appealed to the **State Department** for diplomatic assistance. In fact, Guatemala became a focal point of the **Cold War** as the **Dwight Eisenhower** administration became alarmed by reports that the policy of agrarian reform was the work of local communists who had infiltrated into influential positions in Arbenz's government. Fearing that a Soviet satellite state would soon be created in Guatemala, President Eisenhower instructed the **Central Intelligence Agency (CIA)** to prepare a covert military operation to remove Arbenz from power. A small army of Guatemalan political exiles was subsequently recruited, equipped, and trained in neighboring Honduras.

In June 1954, a force numbering just over 200 under the command of Colonel **Castillo Armas** entered Guatemala, and though no significant fighting took place, President Arbenz was persuaded to resign and leave the country. The pro-American Castillo Armas became president and proceeded to arrest alleged communists and reverse the policy of agrarian reform. Castillo Armas, however, was soon overthrown by assassination in 1957. Guatemala subsequently experienced long periods of internal disorder and a series of repressive military governments. With the exception of the period of **Jimmy Carter**'s presidency (1977–1981), American presidents generally saw the high incidence of political violence in Guatemala simply as a reflection of the Cold War and an unfortunate aspect of the struggle to defeat international communism. Critics countered with the argument that the CIA-backed 1954 coup had arrested Guatemala's peaceful political development and that, by supporting a series of brutal military dictators, U.S. policy had actually promoted further political unrest and economic destruction in the country. *See also* ARMED INTERVENTIONS; BELIZE; RÍOS MONTT, JOSÉ EFRAÍN (1926–).

GUATEMALAN REVOLUTION. A revolutionary political movement occurring in **Guatemala**. In 1944, a left-wing political coalition overthrew the dictatorship of Jorge Ubico and, under the leadership of President **Juan José Arévalo**, inaugurated a period of radical economic and social reform known as the Guatemalan Revolution. After winning the presidential election in 1950, **Jacobo Arbenz** proceeded to go much further than his predecessor in implementing schemes of major agrarian reform. A particularly controversial measure was the expropriation of uncultivated land owned by the Boston-based **United Fruit Company (UFCO)**, the major exporter of bananas. The dispute had ramifications beyond Guatemala because American officials regarded the agrarian reform measure as having been deliberately instigated by local communists who were alleged to have infiltrated into influential positions in the government. A growing anxiety emerged in Washington over the prospect that a Soviet satellite state was about to be established in Central America.

The **Dwight Eisenhower** administration responded by organizing a covert military operation, code-named **Operation PBSUCCESS**, that brought down the government of President Arbenz in June 1954. Arbenz was replaced by Colonel **Castillo Armas**, who was strongly anticommunist and the choice of the United States. The new government of Castillo Armas essentially brought an end to the 1944 Guatemalan Revolution by carrying out the policies that the Eisenhower administration had wanted Arbenz to follow. It arrested suspected communists, renegotiated UFCO's financial contracts, reversed the policies of agrarian reform, and severely restricted the activities of labor unions. Despite the optimistic prediction of Secretary of State **John Foster Dulles**, the rule of Castillo Armas did not bring political stability for Guatemala. The assassination of the Guatemalan president in 1957 only led to further unrest and a series of military governments. Critics of U.S. diplomacy argued that, by bringing an end to the Guatemalan Revolution, the 1954 coup had significantly contributed to the creation and perpetuation of a culture of political violence in the country. *See also* ARMED INTERVENTIONS.

GUEVARA, ERNESTO "CHE" (1928–1967). Marxist revolutionary hero and guerrilla fighter. Despite his close identification with **Cuba** and the **Cuban Revolution**, Guevara was not of Cuban nationality but born in Rosario, Argentina. After completing a medical degree at the University of Buenos Aires, he traveled to Guatemala in 1954 and was present during the **Central Intelligence Agency**'s **(CIA)** operation that overthrew President **Jacobo Arbenz**. Guevara met **Fidel Castro** in Mexico in 1955 and became one of Castro's closest aides. His Cuban colleagues called him the nickname of "Che," an Argentine term for "buddy."

When Fidel Castro came to power in Cuba in 1959, he appointed Guevara as minister of industry. Ill suited to administration and determined to promote the armed struggle overseas, Guevara soon gave up governmental office. After spending a short period training guerrilla forces in the Congo in 1965, he returned to South America in 1966 and attempted to organize a guerrilla movement in the countryside in Bolivia. In October 1967, he was captured by Bolivian troops and executed. Guevara's grave was later discovered in 1997, and his remains were brought back to be enshrined in Cuba. Despite his conspicuous failure to arouse local support for the national liberation movement in Bolivia, "Che" Guevara acquired legendary status and an international reputation for personal heroism and great skill in conducting and achieving success in guerrilla warfare.

GUYANA. A country in northeastern South America. As a colony of **Great Britain**, British Guiana was part of the **Venezuela Boundary Dispute** (1895), which involved the diplomatic intervention of the United States. The colony remained under British rule until it achieved full independence as Guyana in 1966. Prior to independence, local self-government was established in which the left-wing political leader, **Cheddi Jagan**, won election as prime minister in 1953. Pressure from the British government brought about Jagan's resignation in October 1953 and the reimposition of British colonial rule. The restoration of elections in 1957 resulted in victory for Jagan. An uneasy relationship existed with the United States. American mining companies such as Kennecott and Reynolds warned that Jagan was planning nationalization of their assets. Moreover, the **John F. Kennedy** administration was suspicious of Jagan because he had visited **Cuba** and was known to be an admirer of **Fidel Castro** and the **Cuban Revolution**. Fearing the expansion of communism to the mainland of South America, American officials sought to destabilize Jagan's government by covert action in which agents of the **Central**

Intelligence Agency (CIA) encouraged major strikes and political demonstrations. In 1964, Jagan was defeated in national elections. The **Lyndon Johnson** administration welcomed the election of the new prime minister, **Forbes Burnham**, and greatly increased U.S. economic aid to the country. Burnham responded by affirming his support for the U.S. policy of placing an embargo on trade with Cuba.

During the 1970s, however, Burnham changed political course and began to cultivate friendly relations with Cuba and the **Soviet Union**. The **Richard Nixon** administration retaliated by cutting off economic aid. In the process, Guyana became one of the poorest countries in the **Western Hemisphere**. After the end of the **Cold War**, elections took place in 1992 that resulted in Jagan's return to power. In contrast to his earlier policies, Jagan sought to cooperate with the U.S. government in order to assist the development of the Guyanese economy.

– H –

HAIG, ALEXANDER M., JR. (1924–). American general and secretary of state from 1981 to 1982. After military service in Vietnam, General Haig became a staff member of the National Security Council and for a period from 1973 to 1974 served as President **Richard Nixon**'s chief of staff in the White House. In 1981, he was appointed secretary of state in the **Ronald Reagan** administration. As secretary of state, he showed particular concern at the perceived expansion of communist influence in Central America and advocated a policy of substantially increasing military aid to the democratic government of **El Salvador** in order to defeat the guerrilla movement in that country. Haig also took on a high-profile and active diplomatic role in trying to mediate the conflict between **Great Britain** and **Argentina** over the **Falkland Islands** in 1982. Personal differences with some of Reagan's key aides resulted in Haig's resignation as secretary of state in June 1982. *See also* SOUTH ATLANTIC WAR (1982).

HARDING, WARREN G. (1865–1923). American political leader and president from 1921 to 1923. Born in Ohio, Harding was a newspaper publisher who joined the Republican Party and was elected to the

U.S. Senate in 1914. In his successful campaign for the presidency in 1920, he promised the American people a return to "normalcy." In foreign policy, this meant an inward-looking mentality that was symbolized by the decision not to become a member of the **League of Nations**. While his administration gave relatively little attention to Latin American affairs, Harding adopted a conciliatory and much less moralistic attitude toward the region than had been shown by his Democratic predecessor, **Woodrow Wilson**. In 1921, Harding approved the passage by the U.S. Senate of a treaty that paid compensation of $25 million to **Colombia** toward the financial loss arising from the independence of **Panama** in 1903. Just before Harding's death in 1923, public announcements were made of plans to withdraw the garrisons of U.S. marines serving in **Nicaragua** and the Caribbean republics.

HARRISON, BENJAMIN (1833–1901). American political leader and president from 1889 to 1893. The grandson of President William Henry Harrison, Benjamin Harrison joined the Republican Party in Indiana and won election to the U.S. Senate in 1880. In 1888, he defeated his Democratic opponent, **Grover Cleveland**, in the presidential election. As president from 1889 to 1893, Harrison sought closer political and commercial relations with Latin America. This was exemplified by the importance that he attached to the success of the **International American Conference** (1889–1890) and his subsequent conclusion of reciprocal trade agreements with several Latin American nations. His image as a friend of Latin America, however, was seriously impaired by the **Baltimore Affair** (1891). Harrison reacted to reports that American sailors had suffered an unprovoked assault in **Chile** by sending warships and threatening to break off diplomatic relations. Harrison secured Chile's full apology for the attack on the sailors, but his insensitive and forceful attitude contradicted the Pan-American rhetoric that had been such a feature at the beginning of his presidential administration. *See also* BLAINE, JAMES G. (1830–1893); PAN-AMERICANISM.

HAY, JOHN (1838–1905). American diplomat and secretary of state from 1898 to 1905. In U.S. diplomatic history, Hay is best known for his description in July 1898 of the **Spanish-American War** as "a splendid little war" for the United States. As secretary of state, he was also well known for promoting the policy of the "open door" in China. While Hay showed relatively less concern for Latin American affairs, he was successful in advancing the policy of securing an isthmian canal built and controlled by the United States. In 1901, he negotiated the **Hay-Pauncefote Treaty**, which abrogated the 1850 **Clayton-Bulwer Treaty** with **Great Britain**. He followed this in 1903 with the **Hay-Herrán Treaty**, in which **Colombia** agreed to transfer existing French canal concessions to the United States. The treaty, however, was not ratified by the Colombian Senate. When **Panama** declared its independence from Colombia in November 1903, Hay entered into negotiations with the new republic's representative in the United States, **Philippe Bunau-Varilla**, and quickly concluded a new and highly satisfactory canal arrangement. The **Hay-Bunau-Varilla Treaty** was ratified by the United States and Panama in November of 1903. The United States was therefore able to proceed with the construction of the **Panama Canal**.

HAYA DE LA TORRE, VÍCTOR RAÚL (1895–1979). Peruvian political leader. As a political exile in **Mexico** in 1924, Haya de la Torre founded the American Popular Revolutionary Alliance Party (Alianza Popular Revolucionaria Americana [APRA]) in 1924. The political movement that became known as Aprismo advocated major agrarian reform and especially respect for the indigenous people not just in Peru but for the whole of Latin America. It was also severely critical of American interventionist policies, particularly in **Nicaragua**, and called on Latin Americans to unite in opposition to U.S. imperialism. Haya de la Torre, however, was strongly opposed to communism. His belief that he could win political power by democratic election proved mistaken. In Peru, he experienced arrest, curtailment of political rights, and periods of exile, while APRA was frequently declared an illegal organization. Although never allowed to exercise political power in Peru, Haya de la Torre was an influential figure whose speeches and writings significantly contributed to the growth of anti-American sentiment in Latin America during the 1920s and 1930s.

HAY-BUNAU-VARILLA TREATY (1903). A canal treaty between the United States and **Panama**. The failure of the Colombian Senate to ratify the **Hay-Herrán Treaty** in 1903 was a major influence in stimulating demands in Panama for its independence from **Colombia**. Without the canal, Panama would have a bleak economic future. Violence erupted on November 3, 1903, and a new republic of Panama was established. A canal treaty was quickly concluded between Secretary of State **John Hay** and **Philippe Bunau-Varilla**, who represented the new republic of Panama in the United States. The treaty was ratified by both governments in February 1904. The treaty granted the United States rights to administer an area of land across the isthmus that would become known as the **Panama Canal Zone**. Panamanians welcomed their independence from Colombia and recognized the financial benefits brought by the canal after its opening in 1914. Nevertheless, there was also concern that the Hay-Bunau-Varilla Treaty infringed their country's sovereign rights and had turned it into an American protectorate. A long struggle ensued to persuade the U.S. government to revise the treaty. This was eventually achieved by the negotiation and ratification of the **Panama Canal Treaties** in 1977–1978.

HAY-HERRÁN TREATY (1903). An incomplete canal treaty between the United States and **Colombia**. After deciding on **Panama** as the best location for the projected Central American canal, the United States sought to conclude a treaty with Colombia that would transfer the existing French canal rights to the United States. Negotiations between Secretary of State **John Hay** and the Colombian minister in Washington, Tomás Herrán, resulted in the Hay-Herrán Treaty in January 1903. The treaty was ratified by the U.S. Senate in March but defeated by the Colombia Senate. The collapse of the Hay-Herrán Treaty contributed to the growing demand in Panama for independence from Colombia. When the new republic of Panama was formed in November 1903, the United States was able to conclude the **Hay-Bunau-Varilla Treaty** (1903), which allowed the building of an isthmian canal under American ownership and control. *See also* PANAMA CANAL.

HAY-PAUNCEFOTE TREATY (1901). A canal treaty between the United States and **Great Britain**. In 1898, the **William McKinley** administration decided that the successful completion of an isthmian canal required the direct involvement of the U.S. government. It was necessary, however, to remove the constraint of the 1850 **Clayton-Bulwer Treaty** in order to allow the canal to be constructed, fortified, and controlled exclusively by the United States. Negotiations were begun in Washington between Secretary of State **John Hay** and the British ambassador, Julian Pauncefote. Not wishing to provide an obstacle to the building of a canal and impressed by the display of American military power in the recent **Spanish-American War** (1898), the British government consented to a new treaty in 1901. Known as the Hay-Pauncefote Treaty, the arrangement abrogated the 1850 treaty and enabled the United States to construct and fortify a canal and also exercise exclusive control so long as full provision was made for international shipping to use the completed waterway. *See also* PANAMA; PANAMA CANAL.

HAYES, RUTHERFORD B. (1822–1893). American political leader and president from 1877 to 1881. Born in Ohio, Hayes trained as a lawyer and was elected Republican governor of Ohio from 1868 to 1872 and from 1875 to 1876. As president from 1877 to 1881, he was preoccupied mainly with domestic affairs and gave little consideration to Latin America. However, responding to public alarm over the emergence of a French scheme to construct a canal across the Isthmus of **Panama**, Hayes sent a Special Message to the U.S. Congress on March 8, 1880, declaring that he regarded the proposed canal to be virtually part of the coastline of the United States and that the policy of his government would be to secure control of this canal when it was completed. In justification, Hayes cited not the **Monroe Doctrine** but Article 35 of the 1846 **Bidlack Treaty** with New Grenada.

In practice, the impact of the message was limited because it was a presidential statement that did not specifically call for any immediate action or response from the U.S. Congress or even from foreign governments. The message, however, underscored the unilateral nature of U.S. policy toward Latin America. It also affirmed the abandonment of the policy of seeking an international canal that was implicit in the **Clayton-Bulwer Treaty** (1850) with **Great Britain** and its replacement by the idea of an "American canal" in which the waterway would be owned and controlled by the United States. *See also* LESSEPS, FERDINAND DE (1802–1894); PANAMA CANAL COMPANY.

HELMS, RICHARD (1913–2002). American intelligence officer and director of the **Central Intelligence Agency (CIA)** from 1966 to 1973. Helms pursued a career in secret intelligence and in 1962 was appointed to replace **Richard Bissell** as head of the directorate for plans. He became director of the CIA in 1966 and held this post until 1973. His period as director coincided with growing public criticism of the CIA that resulted in a series of congressional investigations, notably exemplified by the **Church Committee**, which were both seriously embarrassing and damaging to the agency. In Latin American affairs, Helms became known to the public for his attempts to carry out President **Richard Nixon**'s private instructions to destabilize the government of President **Salvador Allende** in **Chile**. Helms was convicted in 1977 of lying to the U.S. Senate four years earlier in an investigation on American policy toward Allende.

HOLY ALLIANCE. An informal alliance of European monarchies. By 1823, just as Spanish control over its American empire appeared to be on the brink of collapse, the prospect of military assistance suddenly appeared in the form of the Holy Alliance of **Russia**, **France**, Austria, and Prussia, an organization of European rulers that had been established at the Congress of Vienna in 1815 and whose proclaimed aim was to restore legitimate monarchs to their rightful positions of authority. French troops had already achieved this in Spain for King Ferdinand VII in 1822–1823 and were judged capable of performing a similar task in Latin America for the same monarch. However, the Holy Alliance faced the opposition of **Great Britain**, whose foreign minister, **George Canning**, proposed a joint Anglo-American protest to prevent military intervention by France.

Instead of diplomatic cooperation with Great Britain, President **James Monroe** preferred to adopt an independent course of action that he expressed in his annual presidential message to Congress on December 2, 1823. The French military expedition to the New World never actually materialized. In effect, it was arguably the deterrent of the British navy, the world's most powerful naval force, and Canning's diplomatic skill in securing a private diplomatic understanding with the French government in October 1823 that persuaded the Holy Alliance to abandon the idea of military intervention in Latin America. *See also* ADAMS, JOHN QUINCY (1767–1848); MONROE DOCTRINE.

HONDURAS. A country in Central America bordered by Guatemala to the northwest and **El Salvador** and **Nicaragua** to the south. Formerly part of the United Provinces of Central America, Honduras became an independent republic after the collapse of the federation in 1838. While diplomatic relations were officially established between the United States and Honduras in 1853, there was subsequently little actual political or commercial contact between the two countries. This changed at the beginning of the 20th century when U.S. companies, including the **United Fruit Company (UFCO)** established sizable plantations to cultivate and export tropical fruit. Moreover, the prospect of Honduras defaulting on its foreign debt and thereby provoking European military intervention led the **William H. Taft** administration to implement the policy of **dollar diplomacy**. A treaty was concluded with Honduras in 1911 by which the country's finances were placed under U.S. supervision, an arrangement that lasted until the 1920s. The dependent relationship continued throughout the 20th century and was reflected in Honduran foreign policy, which generally sought close alignment with that of the United States. For example, Honduras joined the United States in **World War II** and adopted a cooperative attitude during the **Cold War** to the extent of allowing the **Central Intelligence Agency (CIA)** to establish secret bases on Honduran territory for the preparation of **Operation PBSUCCESS** in 1954 and later to organize and equip the Nicaraguan **Contras** in the 1980s.

HOOVER, HERBERT (1874–1964). American political leader and president from 1929 to 1933. Born in West Branch, Iowa, Hoover moved to California and was educated at Stanford University. He became an engineer and millionaire before the age of 40. As secretary of commerce from 1921 to 1928, he personally symbolized the dynamism and ruthlessness of American capitalism in his urging of American business to seek commercial opportunities all over the world. Particular stress was placed on Latin America, which was regarded as a valuable source of raw materials and a receptive market for American investment capital. Consequently, Hoover's election as president in 1928 aroused some apprehension in Latin America. Hoover, however, sincerely wished to cultivate friendly relations with the region and demonstrated this by using the interregnum period before he became president to make a goodwill tour to Latin America lasting 10 weeks and visiting 10 countries.

As president, Hoover showed a genuine desire to counter anti-American feeling by implementing a conciliatory policy. The long-standing controversy over the legality of armed intervention was eased by the publication in 1930 of the **Clark Memorandum**. Hoover also publicly announced a schedule for the phased withdrawal of all U.S. marines to be completed in **Nicaragua** by January 1933 and in Haiti by December 1934. The president's interest in hemispheric relations waned, however, as he became increasingly preoccupied with dealing with domestic events arising from the 1929 Wall Street Crash and the ensuing **Great Depression**, an event that seriously damaged Hoover's reputation as a "wonder-worker" and resulted in his heavy defeat in the 1932 presidential election.

Despite Hoover's best intentions, his administration was unable to bring about a marked improvement in inter-American relations or understanding. A similar conciliatory approach was continued by Hoover's presidential successor, **Franklin D. Roosevelt**, that acquired the name of "the policy of the good neighbor." While it could be argued that Hoover had actually started the process of improving relations between the United States and Latin America, it was Roosevelt and not Hoover who became popularly regarded as the president who was the architect and instigator of the **Good Neighbor Policy**. *See also* ARMED INTERVENTIONS.

HOUSTON, SAM (1793–1863). American political leader and president of Texas. Born in Virginia but raised in Tennessee, Houston served in the U.S. Congress from 1823 to 1827, when he was elected governor of Tennessee. In 1832, he moved to **Texas** and became one of the leaders in the movement for independence from **Mexico**. In 1836, Houston took command of the Texas forces and defeated the Mexican army of General **Antonio López de Santa Anna** at the Battle of San Jacinto on April 21, 1836. Houston's victory secured revenge for the earlier defeat suffered by the Texans at the Alamo. Texas also gained its independence, and Houston was rewarded with election as the first president of the "lone star republic."

HUERTA, VICTORIANO (1854–1916). Mexican general and president from 1913 to 1914. In February 1913, General Huerta staged a military coup that resulted in the murder of **Francisco Madero**, who had been elected president in 1911. President **Woodrow Wilson** condemned the assassination as a barbaric act and refused to recognize the new military government. Unable to persuade Huerta to resign voluntarily, Wilson exploited an incident involving the arrest of American sailors at Tampico to send a naval squadron to occupy the port of **Veracruz** in April 1914. The intervention met resistance and resulted in the death of 19 Americans and more than 200 Mexicans. It also greatly stimulated anti-Americanism in Mexico and transformed Huerta temporarily into a national hero. To prevent hostilities from escalating further, Wilson accepted the offer of mediation made by the governments of **Argentina**, **Brazil**, and **Chile** (the **ABC**). The diplomatic intervention produced a settlement leading to Huerta's resignation and departure from **Mexico** for exile in Europe in July 1914. *See also* MEXICAN REVOLUTION.

HUGHES, CHARLES EVANS (1863–1948). American diplomat and secretary of state from 1921 to 1925. A distinguished lawyer and governor of New York from 1906 to 1910, Hughes was the Republican presidential candidate in 1916 and narrowly lost the election to **Woodrow Wilson**. As secretary of state, he adopted a legalistic approach to the conduct of foreign policy. He had little personal interest in Latin American affairs, and after attending **Brazil**'s centennial celebrations in 1922, he bluntly informed President **Warren G. Harding** that he did not wish to make another trip to Latin America to attend the forthcoming Pan-American Conference at Santiago de Chile. His negative response considerably diminished the prestige of the conference and was interpreted in Latin America as an indication of the lack of importance that the United States attached to meetings with its southern neighbors. Hughes relented in 1928 and agreed to head the American delegation to the Pan-American Conference at Havana, **Cuba**. Responding to criticism from Latin American delegates in a debate over the right of external powers to intervene in domestic affairs, Hughes robustly asserted the traditional U.S. opinion that intervention was justified by international law in cases where order had broken down and the normal processes of government had collapsed. In 1930, Hughes was appointed chief justice of the U.S. Supreme Court, a position he held until his retirement in 1941. *See also* ARMED INTERVENTIONS; DRAGO DOCTRINE; PAN-AMERICAN CONFERENCE SYSTEM.

HULL, CORDELL (1871–1955). American diplomat and secretary of state from 1933 to 1944. Born in Tennessee, Hull was a lawyer and politician who served as a volunteer in the **Spanish-American War** (1898). From 1907 on, he was a congressman and senator representing Tennessee until his appointment as secretary of state in 1933. As secretary of state, Hull was active in implementing the **Good Neighbor Policy** of President **Franklin D. Roosevelt**. Hull personally headed the U.S. delegation at the Pan-American Conference held at Montevideo in December 1933 in order to indicate the importance attached to the meeting by the Roosevelt administration. Hull was also a strong advocate of expanding trade with Latin America and supported the passage of the **Reciprocal Trade Agreements** Act by the U.S. Congress in June 1934. By 1939, he had negotiated reciprocal trade treaties with 11 Latin American countries. In 1944, he resigned his office as secretary of state for health reasons.

HUMAN RIGHTS. A U.S. foreign policy objective closely associated with President **Jimmy Carter**. The promotion of political rights for individual citizens has long been a feature of American foreign policy, ranging from the 1776 Declaration of Independence during the **American Revolution** to U.S. leadership of the "free world" in the **Cold War**. What was different and highly controversial about Jimmy Carter's foreign policy during the late 1970s was his insistence on the moral obligation of all nations to respect human rights. Unlike many American political leaders during the Cold War, he refused to condone violations of human rights on the ground that they were a regrettable but necessary evil in the war against communism. The public priority that he gave to the issue, however, raised high expectations and also bitter controversy in Latin America where torture, summary executions, disappearances, and the violent activities of military and police forces referred to as "death squads" were frequent and well-publicized occurrences, especially during the 1970s.

In the aftermath of the Vietnam War, the Watergate scandal, and the damning report of the **Church Committee**, the U.S. Congress was favorably disposed to participate in the making of a more ethically based foreign policy. In a manner reminiscent of President **Woodrow Wilson**, Carter and Congress believed that Latin America was particularly amenable to pressure from the United States and would therefore agree to change its policies more readily than other regions of the world. Consequently, Congress voted to reduce American military aid to repressive governments that were judged to have violated human rights, starting with **Argentina** in 1977. In fact, the decrease of military aid was counterproductive in the short term because it exerted little visible impact on the domestic policies of authoritarian regimes that simply turned to other available sources for their supplies of weapons. Indeed, the military governments of Argentina, **Brazil**, and **Chile** condemned what they regarded as unwarranted American interference in their internal political affairs. They also complained that Carter unfairly adopted double standards by not putting the same pressure on communist countries where the violation of human rights was known to be a deliberate state policy. *See also* DIRTY WAR; MILITARY ASSISTANCE.

– I –

IMMIGRATION. Historic movement of people to the United States. During the colonial period, immigrants to the American colonies came mainly from Europe. The migration of Latin Americans to the United States, largely in search of economic opportunity, began in the 19th century. It consisted mostly of Mexicans moving back and forward across the U.S.–Mexican border in response to the rise and fall of the American business cycle. For example, immigration was sharply reduced during the **Great Depression** of the 1930s but rose rapidly when the American economy recovered at the beginning of **World War II**. The policy of the federal government sought to manage this movement of people by encouraging the recruitment of temporary contract labor in the 1942 Bracero Accord. After 1964, the Bracero Accord was replaced by a policy of granting visas to legal immigrants who either were blood relatives of U.S. citizens or had secured employment or sponsorship prior to entering the country. At the same time, the U.S. Congress passed a series of legislative measures to prohibit the local employment of undocumented immigrants and to restrict entry to the United States by guarding and policing the American side of the border.

During the 1970s, the pattern of immigration changed in that the largest source of both legal and illegal immigration from Latin America was no longer from Mexico but from the countries of Central America and the Caribbean islands. By the end of the 20th century, not only did the flow of immigration increase in absolute numbers, but a growing proportion of immigrants began to arrive from South America. Migration was still motivated mainly by economic factors, but the impact of political repression and violence associated with the **Central American crisis** during the 1980s was also influential. At times and especially during periods of economic recession in the United States when unemployment was increasing, the number of illegal immigrants entering the country from Latin America was perceived by the public as overwhelming. This resulted in demands for restrictions on immigration. American politicians at both state and federal levels, however, have not been able to offer a solution to the problem. In fact, the steady growth of the "Latino" population within the United States and its concentration in particular states such as Florida, Texas, and California have made the issue politically divisive. Moreover, the border with Mexico is so extensive that it can never be effectively policed or fortified with fences and barriers. Programs of economic assistance, such as the **North American Free Trade Agreement (NAFTA)**, have been implemented in order to promote economic growth so that Mexicans would have less reason to emigrate. However, the migration of Latin Americans to the United States, both legal and illegal, has continued to flourish so long as the American economy requires workers, and even for unskilled jobs, it offers the prospects of a much higher standard of living than in the home country. In 2005, it was estimated that half a million undocumented Mexicans entered the United States during the year. Estimates of the number of illegal Latin Americans in the United States ranged up to 20 million.

INTER-AMERICAN DEFENSE BOARD (IADB). An inter-American agency. The United States took the lead in organizing the practical measures for hemispheric defense during **World War II**. At the Pan-American meeting of foreign ministers held at Rio de Janeiro in January 1942, a resolution was approved to establish an Inter-American Defense Board (IADB) in Washington to direct military preparations and strategy for the defense of the **Western Hemisphere**. Latin American military attachés served on the IADB. Although limited to a mainly advisory function, the IADB provided a public symbol of inter-American unity and military cooperation. In fact, all military aspects involved in prosecuting the war effort were placed very firmly under American control. Just like **World War I**, little was required in the way of a Latin American contribution to actual military operations in World War II. The IADB continued to function after the end of World War II and was incorporated within the structure of the **Organization of American States** in 1948. Individual governments, including the United States, were unwilling to transfer substantial military resources to the IADB so that it remained largely a technical and advisory agency.

INTER-AMERICAN TREATY OF RECIPROCAL ASSISTANCE. *See* RIO TREATY (1947).

INTERNATIONAL AMERICAN CONFERENCE (1889–1890). The first meeting of the **Pan-American Conference System**. The idea that the United States should host a meeting to include all the Latin American nations of the **Western Hemisphere** attracted increasing bipartisan support among American political leaders during the 1880s. In 1888, the U.S. Congress passed an act providing appropriations for an "International American Conference" to be held in Washington in 1889. While much of the agenda for the conference revolved around specific commercial matters, the inclusion of proposals to form an inter-American customs union and to establish arbitration machinery to resolve disputes between nations signified the ambition of the United States to lead a movement to exclude European political and economic influence from the Western Hemisphere.

Given its well-known reluctance to attend the 1826 **Panama Congress**, the decision of the United States to convene an inter-American conference was regarded as most unusual and an event of major diplomatic significance in the Western Hemisphere. With the sole exception of the Dominican Republic, all the Latin American countries accepted the invitations. The conference opened in Washington in October 1889 and continued until April 1890. In the United States, the meeting was adjudged to have been so successful in promoting Pan-American fellowship that in reporting the event, the U.S. press preferred to adopt the popular term "Pan-American Conference" instead of the official title of "International American Conference." The meeting, however, produced few results. The concept of a hemispheric customs union and an agreement to accept compulsory arbitration proved much too ambitious and had not been adequately prepared to allow for substantive discussion. Several of the Latin American delegates, particularly those representing **Argentina**, were highly critical of the United States for what they claimed was inadequate management of the conference. Their speeches and actions indicated the existence of a significant divergence of national interests between Latin America and the United States.

In fact, the sole tangible achievement of the conference was agreement to fund the establishment of a small commercial information bureau to be located in Washington and that ultimately became the **Pan-American Union (PAU)**. Nevertheless, the very fact that the conference had actually taken place successfully provided a precedent for future inter-American meetings. Most of all, it had proved to be a significant demonstration of the growing prestige and leading influence of the United States within the Western Hemisphere. *See also* BLAINE, JAMES G. (1830–1893); CARNEGIE, ANDREW (1835–1919); CURTIS, WILLIAM E. (1850–1911); RECIPROCAL TRADE AGREEMENTS; SÁENZ PEÑA, ROQUE (1851–1914).

INTERNATIONAL BANK FOR RECONSTRUCTION AND DEVELOPMENT (IBRD). An international economic organization also known as the World Bank. As part of postwar economic planning, the World Bank was conceived at a conference held at Bretton Woods, New Hampshire, in July 1944. The bank came into existence in 1945 with the initial purpose of providing finance for the reconstruction of war-damaged Europe. From the 1950s on, its activities spread beyond Europe and became targeted at providing loans and grants for large-scale enterprises intended to promote the economies of developing nations, including those in Latin America.

The World Bank was very much an American initiative and originated from a conference held in the United States. Much of its funding also came from U.S. sources. Moreover, its headquarters were located in Washington, and many of senior staff members were U.S. citizens. Consequently, the bank has often been regarded in Latin America and the wider world as an instrument of U.S. foreign policy. Latin American governments favored by the United States, such as **Venezuela** under President **Rómulo Betancourt** (1959–1964) or the military government that seized power in **Brazil** in 1964, have received large loans and generous treatment. By contrast, the government of President Salvador **Allende** in **Chile** found that its request for loans were denied by the bank. *See also* INTERNATIONAL MONETARY FUND (IMF); NIXON, RICHARD (1913–1994).

INTERNATIONAL MONETARY FUND (IMF). A major financial organization to promote international monetary cooperation. The IMF originated at a conference held in Bretton Woods, New Hampshire, in July 1944. It came into being in December 1945 with the stated aim of promoting international trade and cooperation in monetary affairs. The IMF soon acquired importance as the major international financial institution able to assist countries that were experiencing serious economic difficulties, usually arising from problems with balance of payments or repayments of foreign debt. Loans were provided to member nations on condition that they accepted Structural Adjustment Programs (SAPs) and allowed IMF officers to examine their financial accounts. SAPs usually entailed the adoption of policies of fiscal austerity, such as financial restraint, leading to a balanced budget.

The IMF acquired a negative image in Latin America. For example, Brazilian President **Juscelino Kubitschek** sought an IMF loan during the late 1950s and broke off negotiations, complaining that the proposed conditions were too exploitative and restrictive. During the **debt crisis** of the 1980s, several Latin American governments were compelled to negotiate agreements with the IMF. The terms were often so unpopular that they provoked popular demonstrations and riots. In Peru, President **Alán García** declared that the level of repayment was extortionate.

Although the IMF was a truly international organization whose membership extended to almost every nation in the world, it was often suspected of being too much under the influence of the U.S. government. This reflected the fact that it had been very much an American initiative and had originated from a conference held in the United States. Not only were its headquarters located in Washington, but much of its funding was derived from U.S. sources. Consequently, the United States was often linked with the IMF in Latin American criticism that the conditions imposed by the institution made economic conditions worse rather than better. *See also* INTERNATIONAL BANK FOR RECONSTRUCTION AND DEVELOPMENT (IBRD).

INVESTMENT. Export of capital by the United States to Latin America. The achievement of independence at the beginning of the 19th century marked the end of Spanish mercantilist restrictions and opened the former colonies in Latin America to contact with the world economy. Stimulated by the prospect of rapid economic development, a boom in foreign capital investment occurred. **Great Britain** was the leading investor because of its economic strength and the importance of the London capital market. However, Latin America experienced only a short economic boom, one that soon turned to bust, so that all loans were in default by 1827. The bursting of the economic "bubble" was a warning to investors and set a pattern for the future.

Great Britain remained the major source of capital for Latin American investment throughout the 19th century and into the 20th. For much of this period, the United States was itself a borrower of foreign capital, and it was only toward the end of the 19th century that surplus capital was generated for overseas investment. Initially, this was mostly directed to **Mexico** and **Cuba**. American investment, however, greatly expanded during **World War I** (1914–1918), when many British investments in Latin America were liquidated to pay the costs of fighting the war.

In fact, the world war witnessed the emergence of New York as the world's leading capital market. During the 1920s, American investments flooded the world, and substantial sums were directed toward Latin America, where the total amount of U.S. investment more than tripled. Indeed, U.S. investment in the region grew at a faster rate than that of Great Britain so that by the end of the decade the United States finally replaced Britain as the nation with the largest total investment in Latin America. A significant aspect of this development was its geographical spread, which now included South America instead of concentrating, as before, mainly on the Central American–Caribbean region.

The financial preeminence of the United States was further strengthened by **World War II** (1939–1945), which further weakened the financial investments of Britain and the other European powers by compelling them to sell many of their assets. Moreover, after the war the U.S. government exercised considerable influence over decisions on loans made by new international institutions such as the **International Monetary Fund (IMF)** and the **International Bank for Reconstruction and Development (IBRD)**. Substantial amounts of money for economic development were also forthcoming from such U.S. initiatives as the **Alliance for Progress**. For a while during the 1960s and 1970s, some Latin American governments turned to rising economic powers, such as Germany and Japan, for loans, but overall the United States still remained the main source of capital. In 1990, the total of U.S. investments in Latin America was estimated to be in excess of $70 billion.

IRAN-CONTRA AFFAIR. A political scandal during the **Ronald Reagan** administration. Beginning in 1984, Lieutenant Colonel **Oliver North**, a staff member of the National Security Council, secretly arranged the sale of American military equipment to Iran. The proceeds were used to purchase military equipment for use by the **Contras** in **Nicaragua**. This action, however, violated the 1982 **Boland Amendment** and was revealed to the public in 1986 first by press reports and then by an investigation by the Department of Justice. The resulting "Iran-Contra affair" greatly embarrassed the Reagan administration and compelled President Reagan to be more accommodating in his attitude toward the **Arias Peace Plan**. In fact, the scandal resulted in a number of criminal prosecutions and convictions, including North, and while Reagan ultimately served out his full term of office, for a time the Iran-Contra affair raised the possibility of either his resignation or impeachment. *See also* CASEY, WILLIAM J. (1913–1987); CENTRAL AMERICAN CRISIS.

ISLAS MALVINAS. *See* FALKLAND ISLANDS.

– J –

JAGAN, CHEDDI (1918–1997). Guyanese political leader and prime minister in 1953 and from 1957 to 1963 and president from 1992 to 1997. Of ethnic Indian background, Jagan was a left-wing political radical who joined with **Forbes Burnham** to found the People's Progressive Party in 1950. In 1953, Jagan won election as prime minister. Pressure from the British government brought about his resignation in October 1953 and the reimposition of British rule. The restoration of elections in 1957 resulted in victory for Jagan. He faced hostility from Washington because of his public support for **Fidel Castro** and the **Cuban Revolution**. American officials responded by seeking to destabilize Jagan's government by covert action in which agents of the **Central Intelligence Agency (CIA)** encouraged major strikes and political demonstrations. In 1964, Jagan was defeated in national elections and replaced by Forbes Burnham. After a long period in political opposition, Jagan was elected president in 1992. Although still a strong supporter of labor unions and workers' rights, Jagan recognized that the **Cold War** had ended and that friendly relations with the United States were necessary to assist the development of the Guyanese economy. Jagan died in 1997 while in presidential office.

JEFFERSON, THOMAS (1743–1826). American revolutionary leader and president from 1801 to 1809. Born in Virginia, Jefferson was responsible for the drafting of the Declaration of Independence in 1776 and was one of the most important of American revolutionary leaders. He served as president for two terms from 1801 to 1809. His period in office coincided with the beginning of the **wars for Latin American independence**. In principle, Jefferson welcomed the emergence of political revolt in Spanish America, which he saw as a stimulus to promoting the worldwide advance of liberty and republican government already exemplified by the United States. On the other hand, he shared the traditional North American attitude dating from the colonial period of looking down on Latin Americans because of their Spanish and Catholic background.

    As president, Jefferson agreed to receive the Venezuelan revolutionary leader **Francisco de Miranda** in Washington but refused to give him any prospect of official assistance from the U.S. government. Jefferson insisted on pursuing a policy of neutrality and maintaining friendly relations with **Spain**. The policy of acting correctly allowed Jefferson to take advantage of **France**'s need for money and conclude the **Louisiana Purchase** in 1803. The acquisition of this large territory promoted his vision of a United States that would in the future expand to become a nation of continental extent. *See also* FRANCE; NAPOLEON BONAPARTE (1769–1821).

JOHNSON, LYNDON (1908–1973). American political leader and president from 1963 to 1969. A New Deal Democrat and senator from Texas, Johnson rose to become Senate majority leader in 1955. He accepted the invitation to become **John F. Kennedy**'s running mate and was elected vice president in 1960. Johnson succeeded to the presidency on November 22, 1963, on the assassination of Kennedy in Dallas. Johnson was staunchly anticommunist and notably escalated American military participation in the Vietnam War. In the **Western Hemisphere**, he particularly detested Cuban leader **Fidel Castro** and was determined to resist the expansion of communism. When confronted by anti-American demonstrations in **Panama** in January 1964, Johnson suspected Castro's involvement and refused to make any concessions to the Panamanian government. Another concern was the spread of communist influence in **Brazil**. Johnson considered Brazilian President **João Goulart** a procommunist and welcomed the military coup that overthrew Goulart from power in 1964. While he denied any direct involvement in assisting the coup, Johnson had instructed a U.S. naval task force to be prepared to intervene in Brazil should serious civil disorder occur.

In the case of internal political crisis in the Dominican Republic in 1965, Johnson intervened directly by sending in more than 20,000 U.S. troops to bring an end to the fighting and prevent what he feared would be a communist takeover of the government. Latin American critics condemned the decision to intervene and scathingly referred to it as an example of the "Johnson Doctrine." Controversy in the United States over the Vietnam War persuaded Johnson not to run for presidential office in 1968. He retired from politics in 1969. *See also* DOMINICAN INTERVENTION (1965); MANN DOCTRINE; PANAMA CANAL; PANAMA CANAL ZONE.

JUÁREZ, BENITO (1806–1872). A political leader, national hero, and president of **Mexico** from 1861 to 1872. A pure Zapotec Indian, Juárez became a lawyer and a prominent leader of the movement for liberal reform, serving as governor of the state of Oaxaca from 1847 to 1852 and president of Mexico from 1861 to 1872. Juárez was a strong nationalist and fought against the attempt of the French emperor Napoleon III to impose an Austrian archduke as emperor of Mexico in 1864. Juárez was sympathetic to the cause of the Union during the American Civil War (1861–1865) and welcomed the end of slavery in the United States. He hoped for material aid from the United States in his fight against the French and was disappointed when this was not forthcoming. Juárez attributed this lack of support to the overriding and selfish concern of President Abraham Lincoln to avoid disturbing his country's diplomatic relations with **France** during the period of the American Civil War.

– K –

KEITH, MINOR C. (1848–1929). American entrepreneur. During the 1870s, Keith became involved in building railroads in **Costa Rica**. At the same time, he purchased local plantations, mainly for the cultivation and export of bananas. In 1899, he merged his companies with the Boston Fruit Company to form the **United Fruit Company (UFCO)**. The new company soon became the world's largest producer of bananas and dominated the export trade in this product. Keith was a prominent example of the American entrepreneur whose initiative and energy contributed to the economic development of the Central American–Caribbean region and also made it a profitable market for U.S. trade and investment during the early 20th century. *See also* DOLLAR DIPLOMACY.

KELLOGG, FRANK B. (1856–1937). American diplomat and secretary of state from 1925 to 1929. Born in New York, Kellogg was raised in Minnesota and became a lawyer. Joining the Republican Party, he represented Minnesota in the U.S. Senate from 1917 to 1923. Kellogg was a member of the U.S. delegation to the Pan-American Conference held at Santiago de Chile in 1923 and served as ambassador to **Great**

Britain from 1923 to 1925. As secretary of state in the **Calvin Coolidge** administration, Kellogg was prominent in working for world peace and, with the French diplomat Aristide Briand, was the coauthor of the Kellogg-Briand Peace Pact. In Latin American affairs, Kellogg was well known for expressing his suspicions of the growth of Bolshevist influence in the region. This concern led him to advocate a firm policy against Mexican attempts to expropriate the property of U.S. **oil** companies and also to support U.S. military intervention to maintain political order in **Nicaragua**. *See also* MEXICAN REVOLUTION.

KENNAN, GEORGE F. (1904–2005). American diplomat and academic writer. Born in Wisconsin and educated at Princeton University, Kennan was a career diplomat who specialized in U.S. relations with the **Soviet Union**. From 1947 to 1949, he headed the Policy Planning Staff in the **State Department**. On his retirement from the State Department in 1950, he visited Latin America for the first and only time. Unimpressed by his experiences there, he compiled a negative report for the secretary of state that simplistically attributed the political, economic, and cultural backwardness of the region and its people to the "**Black Legend**." Kennan's condescension and ingrained pessimism about the political future of Latin America echoed the views similarly expressed by **Thomas Jefferson** and **John Quincy Adams** more than a century earlier and indicated that there had been little substantive change in the attitudes of U.S. officials toward their southern neighbors.

When Kennan later returned to the foreign service, it was as an expert on relations with the Soviet Union and Eastern Europe. During the **John F. Kennedy** administration, he served as ambassador to Yugoslavia from 1961 to 1963. Kennedy spent most of his later years in Princeton and was a celebrated author of works on American foreign policy. *See also* COLD WAR; DEBT CRISIS.

KENNEDY, JOHN F. (1917–1963). American political leader and president from 1961 to 1963. Born in Massachusetts, Kennedy joined the Democratic Party and was elected to the U.S. House of Representatives in 1946 and the Senate in 1952. In 1960, Kennedy won the Democratic presidential nomination and defeated the Republican candidate, **Richard Nixon**, in the presidential election. As president,

Kennedy carried out his campaign promise to provide vigorous leadership in foreign affairs to contain and reverse the expansion of international communism. Kennedy talked of "winning the minds" of the people of the Third World in what he claimed was a battle between the "free world" led by the United States against the forces of international communism led by the **Soviet Union**. He was particularly concerned about the extent of economic backwardness in Latin America and how this made the region vulnerable to communist infiltration. While Kennedy basically continued President **Dwight Eisenhower**'s policy of financial aid to the region, he greatly expanded the amount of funds to be allocated and also sought to make this appear as his own personal initiative in what he called the **Alliance for Progress**. Programs designed to achieve this were the Alliance for Progress, the work of the **Agency for International Development (AID)**, and the **Peace Corps**.

Just as he did in Southeast Asia, Kennedy was attracted to the use of military means to counter the perceived threat of communist expansion in Latin America. The most serious challenge that he identified was the rise of communist influence in **Cuba**. In April 1961, a covert operation organized by the **Central Intelligence Agency (CIA)** to overthrow **Fidel Castro** ended in failure at the **Bay of Pigs** in Cuba. The setback was damaging for Kennedy's personal prestige in the **Western Hemisphere**, but his reputation was restored a year later by the firmness and diplomatic skill that he showed during the peaceful resolution of the **Cuban Missile Crisis** in 1962. Kennedy was assassinated in Dallas on November 22, 1963. *See also* CUBAN REVOLUTION; GOODWIN, RICHARD (1931–); PEACE CORPS; RUSK, DEAN (1909–1994).

KIRKPATRICK, JEANE J. (1926–). American political scientist and diplomat. A professor of political science at Georgetown University, Kirkpatrick was an active member of the Democratic Party who became disillusioned with the foreign policy of President **Jimmy Carter**. She believed that the United States should be prepared as a matter of policy to maintain friendly right-wing "authoritarian" governments in power and oppose left-wing "totalitarian" regimes. In her opinion, Carter had failed to make this distinction in his Latin American policy with the result that he had allowed the overthrow of a pro-Western government in **Nicaragua**, only for it to be replaced by an anti-American left-wing regime. Kirkpatrick's views attracted the attention of the Republican presidential candidate **Ronald Reagan**, who invited her to become one of his leading foreign policy advisers during the 1980 presidential election. In 1981, Reagan appointed Kirkpatrick as American ambassador to the **United Nations (UN)**, a post she held until 1985. During the 1980s, Kirkpatrick's strident anticommunism and combative personal style were influential in both shaping and exemplifying the forceful U.S. foreign policy that became known as the **Reagan Doctrine** and was notably employed in attempting to resolve the **Central American crisis**. *See also* SANTA FE REPORT (1980).

KISSINGER, HENRY A. (1923–). American diplomat and secretary of state from 1973 to 1977. Born in Germany, Kissinger came to the United States in 1938. A professor of government at Harvard University and an eminent expert on nuclear weapons and foreign policy, he acted as a consultant for the **State Department** and was appointed national security adviser by President **Richard Nixon** in 1969. Kissinger worked with Nixon to launch important initiatives in foreign policy, most notably the pursuit of détente with the **Soviet Union** and the renewal of diplomatic relations with Communist China.

Kissinger showed little sustained interest in Latin American affairs with the exception of developments in **Cuba** and in **Chile** that directly affected **Cold War** politics. He was particularly concerned by the election to the Chilean presidency in 1970 of the Marxist political leader **Salvador Allende** and regarded this development as posing a geopolitical threat to the security of the whole hemisphere. While Kissinger was not responsible for the instructions given to the Central Intelligence Agency, he had administrative oversight of the Nixon administration's secret efforts to destabilize Allende's government. Kissinger was delighted with the overthrow of Allende in 1973, but his own personal reputation was damaged by his unwillingness to express any public criticism of the brutal and repressive policies subsequently pursued by the military government headed by **Augusto Pinochet** in Chile.

Kissinger left government office in 1977 but continued to act as an influential consultant, writer, and lecturer on foreign policy. He was appointed by President **Ronald Reagan** in 1983 to chair the National Bipartisan Commission on Central America to study the **Central American crisis** and make recommendations for U.S. policy. The report of what became known as the "Kissinger Commission" was published in January 1984. *See also* KISSINGER REPORT (1984); LETELIER, ORLANDO (1932–1976).

KISSINGER REPORT (1984). A U.S. report on policy toward Latin America, also known as the Kissinger Commission or the Bipartisan Commission on Central America. Chaired by former Secretary of State **Henry Kissinger**, the bipartisan commission was appointed by President **Ronald Reagan** in July 1983 to study and propose recommendations for ways of resolving the **Central American crisis**. The report was published in January 1984. While the report mentioned the importance of promoting political reform and social and economic change, it was well received by Reagan because it confirmed the seriousness of the communist threat to the region and advocated a massive increase in U.S. economic aid and military aid.

KNOX, PHILANDER C. (1853–1921). American diplomat and secretary of state from 1909 to 1913. Born in Pennsylvania, Knox was a corporate lawyer and Republican politician who served as attorney general in the **William McKinley** and **Theodore Roosevelt** administrations. He was typical of many American leaders of his time in having a negative opinion of Latin Americans, especially for what he regarded as their lack of administrative and business skills. As secretary of state in the **William H. Taft** administration, Knox readily implemented the policy of **dollar diplomacy** by dispatching U.S. marines and financial supervisors to **Nicaragua**, **Honduras**, **Guatemala**, **Cuba**, Haiti, and the Dominican Republic. During Knox's period of office, the **State Department** was reorganized into divisions based on geographical regions. This resulted in the creation of a new and separate Division of Latin America Affairs. After leaving office in 1913, Knox represented Pennsylvania in the U.S. Senate from 1917 until his death in 1921. *See also* ARMED INTERVENTIONS.

KOREAN WAR (1950–1953). A major international war taking place in the Korean peninsula. The war began on June 25, 1950, when

North Korean forces launched a surprise invasion of South Korea. The United States secured the passage of resolutions at the **United Nations (UN)**, calling on North Korea to withdraw its forces from South Korea and asking UN members to supply troops to drive back the invaders. On June 27, 1950, President **Harry Truman** announced that the United States would deploy its military forces on behalf of the United Nations. The Korean War exposed, however, a divergence of inter-American opinion over how to respond to the external communist threat. While most Latin American nations initially joined the United States in approving the condemnation of North Korea's aggression both by affirmative votes in the United Nations and the **Organization of American States (OAS)**, attitudes became much more ambivalent when the war was widened after the military intervention of the People's Republic of China in November 1950. Like **World War II**, the Truman administration suggested a modest Latin American military contribution to demonstrate the region's symbolic support for the war and for U.S. policy. However, with the exception of a small token force consisting of an infantry battalion from **Colombia**, Latin American governments were unwilling to participate directly in the Korean War. In part, this reflected the current annoyance of some governments that, in terms of dispensing military and economic aid, the United States was showing much more favor to the countries of Western Europe than to those of Latin America. More significant, however, was the geopolitical reality that, in marked contrast to the United States, the fight against the expansion of international communism in Europe or the Far East was not a pressing strategic concern of Latin American governments. *See also* COLD WAR.

KUBITSCHEK, JUSCELINO (1902–1976). Brazilian political leader and president from 1955 to 1961. A former mayor of Belo Horizonte and governor of Minas Gerais, Kubitschek served as president from 1955 to 1961. His administration emphasized massive economic development, including most famously the construction of a new capital city called Brasília. In May 1958, Kubitschek attracted diplomatic attention beyond Brazil when he proposed that economic growth should be pursued at the hemispheric level and that the United States should lead a major economic recovery program. The idea, which was reminiscent of the **Marshall Plan**, would be known as **Operation Pan-America** because it would seek to aid all the economies of Latin America. The proposal was politely welcomed but studiously ignored by officials in the **Dwight Eisenhower** administration who preferred to devise their own solutions to hemispheric problems. An alternative U.S. scheme eventually emerged in 1961 at the beginning of the **John F. Kennedy** administration and was titled the **Alliance for Progress**. After leaving the presidency in 1961, Kubitschek served as a state senator, but his political activities were curtailed after the military coup in 1964 when the new government withdrew his political rights for a period of 10 years.

– L –

LAW OF THE SEA. Rights over adjacent seas and seabeds. Nations with seas adjacent to their coastline have historically recognized that their national sovereignty extends to a limit of three miles. In 1947, this limit was contested by the governments of **Chile** and **Peru**, which claimed that their sovereign control extended to a distance of 200 miles. **Ecuador** took a similar position in 1952. In order to test this claim, some American fishing vessels entering the 200-mile zone during the 1950s were seized for illegal fishing and became the subject of diplomatic protest and lengthy correspondence.

The issue, however, was not solely between the United States and individual South American governments. In fact, it acquired wider global ramifications as several nations in other parts of the world became concerned about the exploitation of their adjacent seas for fishing and their seabeds for mineral resources. Under the auspices of the **United Nations (UN)**, a number of Conferences on the Law of the Sea were held to resolve the issue. After two decades of complex discussions, the UN Convention on the Law of the Sea was agreed in 1982, stating that coastal nations possessed sovereign rights up to a 12-mile limit in their adjacent seas and a 200-mile zone for their exclusive economic use.

LEAGUE OF NATIONS. An international organization. The Latin American nations approved the proposal made at the 1919 Versailles

Peace Conference to create a new world organization to be known as the League of Nations with its headquarters located in Geneva, Switzerland. In contrast to the United States, they all duly became members of the Assembly of the League. **Brazil**, as the largest Latin American nation and a cobelligerent in **World War I**, was honored with a temporary seat on the Council of the League. The Latin American nations welcomed the establishment of the League because membership conferred international recognition and prestige. In addition, the League appeared as a means of reducing the political and military preeminence of the United States in the **Western Hemisphere**. This belief, however, was not realized because the United States did not join the League and was not therefore bound by either the rules or the resolutions passed in Geneva. Indeed, it soon became evident that the great European powers, which dominated the Council, had no desire to discuss any controversial Latin American questions that might cause possible diplomatic conflict with the United States. Consequently, Latin American countries quickly became disillusioned with the League and questioned its relevance to their affairs. In 1921, **Peru** and **Bolivia** withdrew their membership over the refusal of the League to debate their boundary dispute with **Chile**. In 1926, Brazil left the League as a result of its failure to secure permanent membership of the Council. The League of Nations and its functions were replaced by the establishment of the **United Nations Organization (UN)** in 1946. *See also* TACNA-ARICA DISPUTE.

LEND-LEASE. American military assistance program to Latin America during **World War II**. On March 11, 1941, the U.S. Congress passed the Lend-Lease Act authorizing President **Franklin D. Roosevelt** to lend or lease armaments and military materials to countries whose defense was deemed vital to the national security of the United States. The intention of the policy was primarily to aid **Great Britain** in its fight for survival against Nazi **Germany**, but lend-lease agreements were eventually signed with 18 Latin American governments. Countries such as **Brazil** that fully cooperated with the United States during **World War II** received preferential treatment in the distribution of lend-lease aid. After Brazil's formal declaration of war against Germany in 1942, American assistance was increased to such an extent that Brazil received more than $350 million or 70 percent of the total lend-lease aid given by the United States to the whole of Latin America during World War II. Under lend-lease, Latin American countries received a total of more than $450 million in military assistance. The sum was substantial, but it represented only 1 percent of total U.S. lend-lease aid that amounted to more than $40 billion. This comparative neglect by the United States of Latin America in favor of its European allies was continued into the postwar period and was notably exemplified by the European Recovery Program, also known as the **Marshall Plan.**

LESSEPS, FERDINAND DE (1805–1894). French diplomat and canal entrepreneur. De Lesseps became famous as a result of his success in supervising the construction of the Suez Canal, which opened to world shipping in 1869. In 1879, he was appointed president of the French **Panama Canal Company**, whose stated aim was to construct "a second Suez" across the Isthmus of Panama. Despite his advanced age, De Lesseps traveled to **Panama** and made a tour of the United States in 1880 designed to persuade American investors to support the canal scheme. There was considerable admiration for De Lesseps in the United States, but Americans were generally critical of the scheme and suspected that **France** was secretly seeking to establish a protectorate over the isthmus. President **Rutherford B. Hayes** sent a Special Message to the U.S. Congress in March 1880 declaring that the United States would seek to control the canal when it was completed.

Although the amount of financial subscriptions raised in the United States proved relatively meager, the fact that De Lesseps was seen to be in personal charge of the project meant that sufficient capital was forthcoming from French investors. Consequently, actual construction work was begun by the end of 1881. By 1892, however, work had ceased, and the canal company had gone into bankruptcy. Subsequent revelations of serious mismanagement and financial corruption created a major scandal in France. De Lesseps was indicted for misappropriation of funds and convicted in 1893. The sentence of five years' imprisonment was not imposed because of the advanced age and frailty of De Lesseps. *See also* PANAMA CANAL.

LETELIER, ORLANDO (1932–1976). Chilean diplomat. A member of the left-wing Popular Unity Party and supporter of Chilean President

Salvador Allende, Letelier was appointed ambassador to the United States in 1971. He returned to **Chile** in 1973 to serve in Allende's government, first as foreign minister and then as defense minister. As a result of the 1973 military coup that overthrew Allende, Letelier was arrested and imprisoned. He was released in 1974 and chose to go into political exile in the United States. On September 21, 1976, he was killed by a car bomb explosion in Washington. Although it was strongly suspected that the explosion had been organized by Chilean secret service agents operating in the United States, the **Gerald Ford** administration did not issue a formal protest to the Chilean government. This reflected the fact that U.S. officials had welcomed the overthrow of Allende and his replacement by the anticommunist General **Augusto Pinochet**. After the departure of Pinochet from the presidency in 1990, it became possible to undertake legal investigations in Chile that resulted in the indictment and conviction of a number of Chileans for the murder of Letelier. *See also* KISSINGER, HENRY A. (1923–).

LINOWITZ REPORT (1976). A U.S. report on the **Panama Canal** question. Prepared by the bipartisan Commission on U.S.–Latin American Relations and named after the commission's chairman, **Sol Linowitz**, the Linowitz Report was published in 1976. It identified the current difficulties between the United States and **Panama** over canal rights as the most pressing issue in current U.S.–Latin American relations. The publication of the report coincided with the election to the presidency of **Jimmy Carter**. Carter praised the report and accepted its recommendation that speedy diplomatic action be taken by the U.S. government to resolve the controversy with Panama over the operation of the Panama Canal and the status of the **Panama Canal Zone**. The result was the negotiation of the Panama Canal Treaties in 1977. *See also* BUNKER, ELLSWORTH (1894–1984); TORRIJOS HERRER, OMAR (1929–1981).

LINOWITZ, SOL (1913–2005). American lawyer and diplomat. A lawyer and businessman, Linowitz served as ambassador to the **Organization of American States** from 1966 to 1969. In 1976, he chaired the privately funded Commission on U.S.–Latin American Relations, which prepared a study of U.S. policy toward Latin America. Known as the **Linowitz Report**, the study recommended that urgent diplomatic action be taken by the U.S. government to resolve the controversy with **Panama** over the operation of the **Panama Canal** and the status of the **Panama Canal Zone**. After examining the report, President-elect **Jimmy Carter** said that the canal question would be given high priority in his forthcoming administration. Linowitz was appointed by Carter along with Ambassador **Ellsworth Bunker** as one of the principal U.S. negotiators and assisted in the discussions that resulted in the successful conclusion of the Panama Canal Treaties in 1977.

LOUISIANA PURCHASE (1803). Act of territorial purchase by the United States. The large territory of 827,000 square miles to the west of the Mississippi River and stretching from and including the port of New Orleans to the northern border with **Canada** was sold by **France** to the United States in 1803 for $15 million during the **Thomas Jefferson** administration. The purchase more than doubled the existing size of the United States and indicated the desire of its political leaders to expand their republic so that it became a nation of continental extent. The fact that Louisiana bordered Spanish Florida also resulted in diplomatic pressure on **Spain** to conclude a similar arrangement and sell that territory to the United States. *See also* ADAMS-ONÍS TREATY (1819); NAPOLEON BONAPARTE (1769–1821); WARS FOR LATIN AMERICAN INDEPENDENCE (1808–1826).

LULA DA SILVA, LUIZ INÁCIO (1945–). Brazilian political leader and president since 2003. From a poor background, Luiz Inácio or "Lula" da Silva became a factory worker and a leading trade unionist representing the automotive workers in São Paulo. In 1980, he helped found the left-wing Workers' Party (Partido do Trabalhadores [PT]). Lula was the unsuccessful presidential candidate for his party on three occasions (in 1989, 1994, and 1998) but finally won the presidential election in 2002. Lula's left-wing background and proclaimed determination to pursue a program of radical economic and social reform aroused apprehension in U.S. political and business circles. A particular worry was that Brazil would default on payments to service its foreign debt and thereby precipitate a global economic crisis. As president, however, Lula has maintained existing financial arrangements and has aimed to achieve a budgetary surplus. On the other hand, he has been active in criticizing Western nations, including the United States, for their protectionist attitudes and unwillingness to lower tariff barriers to help less developing nations such as Brazil.

– M –

MADERO, FRANCISCO (1873–1913). Mexican revolutionary leader and president from 1911 to 1913. A wealthy landowner, Madero was a prominent liberal reformer who protested against the oppressive rule of President **Porfirio Díaz**. In November 1910, Madero sought political refuge in **Texas** but soon returned to Mexico to lead an armed revolt that forced Díaz to resign. Madero became president but was murdered on February 22, 1913, during a military coup organized by General **Victoriano Huerta**. The murder was condemned in the United States, particularly by **Woodrow Wilson**, who made Huerta's removal from office one of the priorities of his first presidential administration. *See also* MEXICAN REVOLUTION.

MANIFEST DESTINY. A popular idea justifying U.S. territorial expansion in the mid-19th century. During the 1840s, the issue of annexing **Texas** to the United States became fused with the powerful movement of people westward across the North American continent that was popularly known as Manifest Destiny. Westward expansion pre-dated the 1840s, but the public imagination was captured, if only briefly, by the new term, which was coined in July 1845 by the magazine editor John Louis O'Sullivan. He wrote that America's territorial expansion and transformation into a transcontinental nation was divinely ordained because it was "our manifest destiny." *See also* ALL-MEXICO MOVEMENT; FILIBUSTERS.

MANN DOCTRINE. Statement of U.S. Latin American policy. Named after **Thomas Mann**, who served in the **Lyndon Johnson** administration as assistant secretary of state for inter-American affairs from 1964 to 1965, the "Mann Doctrine" declared that U.S. Latin American policy would first and foremost stress an anticommunist approach. This meant that it intended to be pragmatic in its dealings with governments in the region and would no longer follow the policy of the previous **John F. Kennedy** administration (which also had been a feature of the **Alliance for Progress**) of putting pressure on authoritarian regimes to implement political reforms. In effect, the Mann Doctrine was acknowledging that during the **Cold War** the United States found it easier to work with right-wing authoritarian governments often headed by military figures who could be depended on to adopt anticommunist policies. A very similar view was later presented by **Jeane Kirkpatrick** and adopted during the 1980s by the **Ronald Reagan** administration. *See also* MILITARY ASSISTANCE.

MANN, THOMAS C. (1912–1999). American diplomat. Born in Texas, Mann trained as a lawyer and joined the **State Department** during **World War II**. Because of his fluent knowledge of Spanish, he was appointed to Latin American posts, including ambassador to **El Salvador**, during the **Dwight Eisenhower** administration and ambassador to Mexico during the **John F. Kennedy** administration. In January 1964, he became assistant secretary of state for inter-American affairs, a position he held until March 1965. In an attempt to clarify the Latin American policy of the new **Lyndon Johnson** administration, Mann stated that it would be guided by political realism and refrain from putting pressure on right-wing governments to enact democratic reforms. Called the "**Mann Doctrine**," the statement implied that President Lyndon Johnson intended to pursue a different policy toward Latin America from that of his predecessor, John F. Kennedy. Mann retired from the State Department in 1966.

MARSHALL PLAN. American aid program for the economic recovery of Western Europe, also known as the European Recovery Program. Named after Secretary of State George C. Marshall and first proposed in 1947, the Marshall Plan was the means by which the United States provided massive financial assistance for the postwar economic recovery of Western Europe. Latin American governments, however, frequently complained that there was no counterpart of the Marshall Plan for their region and that, despite their cooperation with the United States during **World War II**, they had been subsequently allocated an inferior status to the countries of Western Europe. The attitude of indifference shown by American officials toward Latin

America markedly began to change during the late 1950s as communism gained ground in **Cuba**. In effect, the **Alliance for Progress**, proposed by the **John F. Kennedy** administration in 1961, represented a belated Marshall Plan for the region and was similarly politically motivated in seeking to contain and defeat the spread of international communism.

MARTÍ, JOSÉ (1853–1895). Cuban national hero and poet. Born in **Cuba**, Martí was committed to the cause of securing Cuban independence from **Spain**. As a political exile after 1871, he lived for long periods in the United States, where he became a journalist and writer in New York. Martí was typical of many Latin Americans going back to **Simón Bolívar** in respecting the achievements of the United States, but he was also repelled by what he regarded as the destructive impact of economic materialism on American politics and culture. He described the United States as "the monster" and warned that it would seek political, economic, and cultural domination over the nations and people of Latin America. Martí's ideas exercised considerable influence on the growing literature of anti-Americanism expressed in the works of Latin American writers such as **Rubén Darío** and **José Enrique Rodó**. Martí returned to Cuba in 1895 and was killed in the fight for Cuban independence from Spain. *See also* CASTRO RUZ, FIDEL (1927–); CUBAN REVOLUTION.

MCKINLEY, WILLIAM (1843–1901). American political leader and president from 1897 to 1901. From 1877 to 1891, McKinley served as a Republican representative from Ohio in the U.S. Congress. As chairman of the House Ways and Means Committee, he drafted the highly protectionist measure that resulted in the 1890 Tariff Act, also known as the McKinley Tariff. In response to requests from President **Benjamin Harrison** and Secretary of State **James G. Blaine** to help stimulate American exports to Latin America, the act contained an amendment enabling the president to conclude **reciprocal trade agreements** that reduced tariff duties on staple products. Several agreements were subsequently signed with Latin American nations by the Harrison administration.

McKinley was elected president in 1896 and took the United States to war against **Spain** in 1898. As president, he also supported the expansion of trade with Latin America and sought to revive the policy of concluding reciprocity treaties. McKinley was assassinated in September 1901 while attending the Pan-American Exposition held at Buffalo, New York. *See also* INTERNATIONAL AMERICAN CONFERENCE (1889–1890); PAN-AMERICANISM; SPANISH-AMERICAN WAR (1898).

MERCOSUL. *See* MERCOSUR.

MERCOSUR. South American free trade agreement also known in Portuguese as **Mercosul**. After the signing of the **North American Free Trade Agreement (NAFTA)** in 1992, the United States showed little sustained interest in promoting further hemispheric economic integration. By default, Latin American governments attempted to protect themselves from the increasing globalization of the world economy by negotiating their own subregional agreements. The most successful example in South America was the Southern Cone Common Market (Mercado Común del Sur), known as Mercosur (Mercosul in Portuguese), the customs union formed earlier in 1991 and consisting of **Brazil**, **Argentina**, **Paraguay**, and **Uruguay**. *See also* FREE TRADE AREA OF THE AMERICAS (FTAA).

MEXICAN-AMERICAN WAR (1846–1848). Military conflict between Mexico and the United States, also known as the Mexican War. When **Texas** was eventually incorporated into the United States by a joint resolution passed by the U.S. Congress in March 1845, the Mexican government protested and refused to recognize the Rio Grande River as marking the border with the United States. Continued friction between Mexico and the United States eventually resulted in the Mexican-American War, which broke out between the two countries in May 1846.

While most of the initial fighting took place in northern Mexico, where General **Zachary Taylor** won victories at Palo Alto and Buena Vista, a separate American army under General **Winfield Scott** landed at and captured the port of **Veracruz** in March 1847. After a slow inland advance to Mexico City, the capital was successfully stormed and occupied in September. An American army of around 10,000 troops defeated a Mexican force of 30,000 soldiers defending the city. The fall of the capital to the U.S. forces was a decisive event. It resulted in the resignation of President **Santa Anna** and his replacement by a Mexican government that accepted the reality of military defeat and decided to seek peace terms. The war formally ended in February 1848 with the signing of the **Treaty of Guadalupe Hidalgo**. *See also* ALL-MEXICO MOVEMENT; POLK, JAMES K. (1795–1849).

MEXICAN REVOLUTION. A revolutionary movement occurring in **Mexico**. The challenge to the dictatorial rule of Mexican President **Porfirio Díaz** that began in 1910 unleashed a decade of political turmoil and violence that is referred to as the beginning of the "Mexican Revolution." For the United States, a pressing concern was the potential for instability to spread in its border region with Mexico. In 1916, a violent incursion into New Mexico by the Mexican general **Pancho Villa** prompted President **Woodrow Wilson** to retaliate by ordering American troops under the command of General **John J. Pershing** to pursue and apprehend Villa. In 1920, the period of excessive violence ended in Mexico when **Álvaro Obregón** became president.

Wilson's interference in Mexican internal politics stimulated anti-American sentiment in Mexico. In fact, antiforeign feeling was a visible feature of the Mexican Revolution and reflected the popular view among Mexicans that foreigners, especially Americans, had ruthlessly plundered Mexico's economic resources during the period of the Porfiriato (1876–1911). Consequently, the 1917 Mexican Constitution, in particular Article 27, vested ownership of the country's natural resources in the Mexican nation and imposed restrictions on foreign investment and property rights. Furthermore, the 1917 Constitution affirmed the aim of the Mexican Revolution to exercise control over the country's natural resources and implement radical policies of economic development. A clash with the United States emerged because American citizens and companies, notably landowners and those involved in the flourishing **oil** industry, feared that the enforcement of the Constitution would result in the expropriation of their property and investments. Moreover, the issue had international diplomatic and legal implications because Mexico appeared to be embracing the ideas of the Bolshevist Revolution by promoting an economic ideology that directly challenged the free-enterprise capitalist system favored and promoted by the United States.

The conflict that ensued between the American and Mexican governments centered on the extent of national control of the oil industry. Although Mexico claimed ownership of the subsoil oil, it was initially unable to operate the oil fields or to export and market the oil at a profit without the cooperation of the major international oil companies. Consequently, a series of compromises were negotiated in which the oil companies retained their property rights until the Mexican state declared its intention to nationalize the industry in 1938. At first, President **Franklin D. Roosevelt** opposed nationalization but eventually accepted Mexico's terms for compensation in 1941. By this time, the Mexican Revolution was no longer such a divisive issue in relations between the two countries. In fact, Roosevelt's desire to conciliate Mexico reflected his view that European fascism currently posed a greater danger to U.S. security and national interests than the Mexican Revolution. Moreover, the United States and Mexico soon joined together in a common struggle to defend democracy against Nazi **Germany** during **World War II**. *See also* DANIELS, JOSEPHUS (1862–1948); MADERO, FRANCISCO (1873–1913).

MEXICO. A country bordered by the United States to the north and **Guatemala** to the south. Sharing a common border with the United States has meant that Mexico has always experienced a close and often tense diplomatic relationship with its powerful neighbor. During the late 18th and early 19th centuries, the exact location of the boundary between the expansionist-minded United States and the declining Spanish empire was a matter of regular dispute and diplomatic negotiation. For independent Mexico, the first major clash with the United States was over the **Texas** question. Texas was a frontier province of Mexico and attracted groups of American settlers organized by Stephen Austin during the 1820s. In 1836, the Americans rose in rebellion, proclaimed the independent republic of Texas, and defeated a large Mexican army at San Jacinto. The new nation was officially recognized by the United States in March 1837 but not by Mexico. Insecure and fearful of Mexican military retaliation, the Texans desired annexation to the United States.

When Texas was eventually incorporated into the United States in 1845, Mexican protests resulted in the outbreak of the **Mexican-American War** in May 1846. The war ended in military victory for the United States and a peace settlement in 1848 in which a humiliated Mexico ceded a vast portion of territory equivalent in size to half the territory of the Mexican nation in 1848. The Mexican-American War demonstrated the relative weakness of Mexico in comparison to the United States and its inability to prevent the emergence of its powerful neighbor as the preeminent power in the Central American–Caribbean region.

During the rest of the 19th century, however, the United States showed little active diplomatic interest in Mexican affairs. For most of the period of the **French Intervention** in Mexico (1862–1867), the U.S. government was preoccupied with fighting the American Civil War and wished to avoid disturbing its friendly diplomatic relationship with **France**. Much more interest was shown later by American entrepreneurs and investors in responding to Mexican President **Porfirio Díaz**'s welcome to foreigners to develop his country's economic resources. American capitalists were especially prominent in placing substantial investments in Mexican railroads, mining enterprises, and the emerging **oil** industry.

The overthrow of Díaz in 1911 unleashed the **Mexican Revolution**, starting with a decade of political instability and major violence. For the United States, a major concern was the outbreak of civil disorder occurring in the border region. In 1914, President **Woodrow Wilson** sought to interfere directly in Mexican politics by ordering U.S. marines to occupy the port of **Veracruz**. In 1916, after a violent incursion into New Mexico by the Mexican general **Pancho Villa**, Wilson dispatched 6,000 American troops under the command of General **John J. Pershing** to invade northern Mexico and embark on what turned out to be a controversial and ultimately futile mission to apprehend Villa.

Wilson's interference in Mexican politics was counterproductive and merely provoked the antiforeign feeling that was a visible feature of the Mexican Revolution and reflected the widely held suspicion that foreigners, especially Americans, had systematically exploited the wealth of the country during the rule of Porfirio Díaz. As a result, the 1917 Mexican Constitution, in particular Article 27, declared that the ownership of the country's natural resources resided in the Mexican nation. Restrictions were also imposed on foreign investment and property rights. American citizens and companies, especially those involved in the new oil industry, feared that enforcement of Article 27 would lead to the seizure of their existing assets. Moreover, the issue had international diplomatic and legal implications because Mexico appeared to be endorsing the ideas of the Russian Revolution by promoting a particular economic ideology that challenged the right to own private property, an integral feature of the free-enterprise capitalist system favored by the United States. The awkward state of relations between the United States and Mexico was exemplified by the publication of the **Zimmermann Telegram** in 1917. The secret telegram revealed that the German minister had promised the Mexican government the restitution of territory lost as a result of the Mexican-American War (1846–1848) should Mexico join **Germany** in a war against the United States.

During the 1920s and 1930s, the state of diplomatic relations between the United States and Mexico was complicated by the oil question. Although Mexico claimed ownership of its oil, it was initially unable either to produce or to sell the oil at a profit without the active cooperation of the major international oil companies. Consequently, the Mexican government felt the need to agree to a series of compromises in which the American oil companies retained their property rights. In 1938, however, the Mexican government announced its intention to nationalize the industry. President **Franklin D. Roosevelt** initially opposed nationalization on the ground that the financial amounts offered were inadequate, but eventually, in 1941, he accepted Mexico's terms for compensating the U.S. oil companies. Roosevelt's decision reflected not so much financial considerations as his political concerns over the growing international conflict and his view that European fascism posed a greater threat to U.S. security than the ideology of the Mexican Revolution. The conciliatory policy was highly successful because Mexico proved to be a cooperative ally of the United States during **World War II**. In fact, a Mexican air force squadron served in the Philippines, and Mexico was one of only two Latin American countries to send combat troops overseas. Moreover, Mexicans made up the highest proportion of the several thousand Latin Americans who joined the U.S. armed forces as volunteers.

The economic boom in the United States arising from World War II stimulated a large increase in Mexican migration to the United States. The U.S. government sought to regulate this movement by permitting the legal recruitment of temporary contract labor in the 1942 Bracero Accord. After 1964, the Bracero Accord was replaced by the policy of granting visas to legal immigrants. At the same time, the U.S. Congress passed legislative measures designed to prohibit the employment of undocumented immigrants and to restrict their entry to the United States by guarding and policing the American side of the border. The policy worked satisfactorily during periods of economic prosperity when the American economy needed additional workers mostly for unskilled and semiskilled occupations. At times of economic recession, however, the number of illegal immigrants entering the country from Mexico and other areas of Latin America was perceived by American public opinion as overwhelming. Immigrants were perceived as taking away jobs from Americans and exploiting the federal and state provision of welfare for the unemployed and needy. This resulted in demands for the imposition of restrictions on immigration and deportation of illegal aliens.

During the last quarter of the 20th century, there was a notable convergence in economic relations between the United States and Mexico. The importance attached by the U.S. government to the maintenance of economic stability in Mexico was demonstrated in 1982 when the Mexican government defaulted on repayments of the annual interest on its external debt. In doing so, Mexico initiated what became known throughout the world as the **debt crisis**. Concerned over the stability of the American commercial banking system and the danger that potential civil disorder might spread from Mexico to the U.S.–Mexican border region, the **Ronald Reagan** administration reacted quickly to Mexico's default and made available emergency loans so that Mexico could reschedule its debt repayments.

The emerging special economic relationship with Mexico was reaffirmed in 1990 when President **George H. W. Bush** welcomed the proposal of Mexican President **Carlos Salinas** to enter into discussions to negotiate a free trade agreement similar to the treaty that had been signed by the United States and **Canada** in 1989. The scheme became known as the **North American Free Trade Agreement (NAFTA)** and provoked political controversy within the United States. Supporters of NAFTA stressed the value of promoting economic stability and development in Mexico, a nation of vital strategic importance to the United States. Opponents argued that free trade agreements would inevitably result in the relocation of many American jobs and factories to Mexico, where the cost of labor was known to be much lower than in the United States. The NAFTA treaty was signed in October 1992 and, after contentious political debate, was eventually ratified by the U.S. Congress in November 1993. *See also* IMMIGRATION; MADERO, FRANCISCO (1873–1913); OBREGÓN, ÁLVARO (1880–1928).

MILITARY ASSISTANCE. American policy of assisting the Latin American military. During the 19th century **France**, **Germany**, and **Great Britain** were the principal suppliers of armaments and professional instruction, in the form of military missions, to the Latin American military. Army officers traditionally looked to France, while naval personnel admired the British navy. The United States lacked large standing military forces and began a policy of giving military assistance to Latin American nations only during **World War I**. Most U.S. aid was directed to improving wartime naval operations and included the provision of equipment and training. In the case of **Brazil** and **Peru**, this led to the appointment of U.S. naval missions during the 1920s. However, the adoption of a systematic strategy of cultivating close and cooperative relations with the Latin American military dated from the administration of **Franklin D. Roosevelt** (1933–1945) and initially reflected its attempts to reduce the political influence of the fascist powers, Germany and Italy. In 1938, U.S. military missions were assigned to only five Latin American countries. By contrast, in December 1941, American advisers were officially attached to the military of every Latin American country. During **World War II**, the United States was allowed to establish large air and naval bases, especially in **Brazil**, **Mexico**, and **Ecuador**, for use in the contingency of an invasion by the Axis powers. In return, the Latin American governments received substantial economic benefits under the **lend-lease** program, amounting to more that $450 million.

Similar policies of military assistance were pursued by the United States amounting to around $5 billion for the period of the **Cold War** (1945–1991). American military missions no longer had to contend with European rivals in Central and South America. Their objective was not to duplicate U.S. national security policy and develop large conventional military forces capable of resisting external attack by the Soviet Union. They concentrated instead on developing programs to help modernize local military and police forces in terms of their training, their equipment, and especially their skill in developing counterinsurgency techniques to combat internal guerrilla activities. Latin America governments, especially those headed by authoritarian leaders in Central America, saw such American aid as a valuable means of strengthening not only their own internal security forces but also their personal positions of power. Another visible result was the closer association and identification between Latin American military officers and their counterparts in the United States. A large number of Latin American junior officers received training at U.S. military academies, such as the **School of the Americas** in **Panama**, where they often acquired considerable respect and admiration for the United States, especially its military and technological skills. This was particularly evident among officers in the Brazilian military who had served under U.S. command in Italy during World War II and resulted in the establishment in 1949 of the National War College (Escola Superior de Guerra [ESG]). Based on U.S. models of military education, this institution sought to promote instruction not only in military doctrine but also in national economic and social development.

Supporters of U.S. military assistance programs claimed that they enhanced hemispheric security and that the training and professionalization of the Latin American military contributed to the maintenance of political stability and the advance of democratic government. Critics argued, however, that these policies actually undermined democracy in Latin America because they encouraged, if not actively assisted, the rise to political power of authoritarian military regimes. This view attracted political support in the U.S. Congress during the **Jimmy Carter** presidency (1977–1981), when restrictions on the provision of U.S. military assistance were imposed on the governments of **Argentina**, Brazil, and **Chile** to change their policies regarding the observance of **human rights** and the holding of elections. *See also* MUTUAL SECURITY ACT (1951).

MIRANDA, FRANCISCO DE (1750–1816). Venezuelan revolutionary leader known as the "precursor" of Spanish-American independence. A former officer in the Spanish royal army, Miranda believed that the colonies of Spanish America should imitate the example of the North American colonists and seek independence from European monarchical rule. He was unusual among Latin Americans of his era in actually having visited the United States. In 1783–1784, Miranda traveled extensively from Boston to Charleston and met with several prominent American political leaders, including George Washington and Alexander Hamilton. But his stay was only temporary because he was en route to Europe, where he made his home in London for several years.

Miranda briefly came back to the United States in 1805 and sought support for a military expedition to liberate **Venezuela**. President **Thomas Jefferson** agreed to receive Miranda in Washington but declined to give him any official assistance. Miranda proceeded to launch an unsuccessful expedition to liberate Venezuela from Spanish rule in 1806. He returned to Venezuela in 1810 to take command of the revolutionary forces with **Simón Bolívar** as one of his leading subordinates. Miranda was captured in 1812 and eventually taken to **Spain**, where he died in prison in 1816. *See also* WARS FOR LATIN AMERICAN INDEPENDENCE (1808–1826).

MOBILE ADDRESS (1913). Celebrated speech by President **Woodrow Wilson** on U.S. relations with Latin America. On becoming president in 1913, Woodrow Wilson publicly declared his intention of reversing the aggressive foreign policy of **dollar diplomacy** associated with his Republican presidential predecessors. Singling out the nations of Latin America, Wilson declared that he would seek an improved relationship that was firmly based on the dictates of reason and trust. This view was expressed in Wilson's celebrated speech delivered to the meeting of the Southern Commercial Congress at Mobile, Alabama, on October 27, 1913. Wilson saw the occasion as an opportunity to reassure the people of Latin America that the United States would treat them on terms of equality and would not seek territory by conquest. Latin Americans, however, noted the moralistic and strident tone of the speech. Its uplifting ideas were later directly contradicted by Wilson's overt meddling in Mexican political affairs and his forceful interventionist policies that resulted in the sending of U.S. marines to take over the governments of several countries in the Central

American–Caribbean region. In fact, Wilson ordered more military interventions in Latin America than either of his Republican predecessors, **William H. Taft** or **Theodore Roosevelt**. *See also* CARTER, JIMMY (1924–); MEXICAN REVOLUTION; VERACRUZ.

MONROE, JAMES (1758–1831). American revolutionary leader and president from 1817 to 1825. Born in Virginia, Monroe was a member of the Continental Congress and served as minister to France from 1794 to 1796 and minister to **Great Britain** from 1803 to 1807. As secretary of state from 1811 to 1817, he conducted foreign relations during the **wars for Latin American independence** and was an advocate of the **No-Transfer Resolution** (1811). During his presidential administration from 1817 to 1825, Monroe recognized the independence of several of the new Latin American nations and also sent a presidential message to Congress in December 1823 that later became famous as the **Monroe Doctrine**. The message was historically significant in affirming the idea of the separation of the New World of the Americas from the Old World of Europe but also in stressing that the United States preferred to adopt an independent course of action in foreign affairs. *See also* FAREWELL ADDRESS (1796).

MONROE DOCTRINE. Historic statement on U.S. policy toward Latin America. The prospect of imminent European military interference to restore Spanish rule in the New World led President **James Monroe** to warn against such action in his annual presidential message delivered to the U.S. Congress on December 2, 1823. Although the message was directed at the European heads of state in the **Holy Alliance**, it also had specific relevance to the countries of Latin America. In fact, it presumed a leadership role for the United States even though there was no prior consultation about this with Latin American leaders or governments. The new countries were simply regarded as being under the protection of the United States, a presumption that implied American superiority in a relationship of unequals. In addition, the idea proclaimed by Monroe of a separate and distinctive Western Hemispheric political system in which the United States assumed a preeminent role reflected the rhetoric of the **American Revolution** and developed into a national symbol around which Americans could readily identify. Indeed, Monroe's statement eventually acquired the status of a "doctrine" and in the process became a venerated American political tradition.

Monroe's message initially appeared to have little significance because it never became a matter of public diplomatic correspondence between the United States and other governments. Moreover, its broader implications warning against European interference in Latin American political affairs were simply ignored by European powers. A new European colony was formally established in the **Western Hemisphere** when **Great Britain** assumed sovereign control over the **Falkland Islands** (**Islas Malvinas**) in 1833. Nevertheless, President **James K. Polk** drew attention to the message in 1845 when he asserted that the United States would not permit the establishment of a European colony in "the North American continent." Moreover, the acquisition of large amounts of Mexican territory as a result of the **Mexican-American War** (1846–1848) was a demonstration that American political leaders did not regard the proscriptions contained in Monroe's 1823 statement as applying to their country. The United States was evidently free to acquire territory in the New World by either military conquest or purchase.

The range of the Monroe Doctrine was steadily extended by the addition of "corollaries." The debate over the proposed annexation to the United States of the Dominican Republic prompted President Ulysses S. Grant to send a Special Message to the U.S. Senate on May 31, 1870, in which he added the "no-transfer" corollary to Monroe's 1823 message. Alarmed by the example of gunboat diplomacy employed by the European powers in the **Venezuela Incident** (1902–1903), President Theodore **Roosevelt** declared on December 6, 1904, that the United States had a duty to ensure order in the **Western Hemisphere** and that his government would act unilaterally if necessary to achieve this. This became known as the **Roosevelt Corollary** to the Monroe Doctrine, or the policy of the **Big Stick**, because it meant that the United States would act as a self-appointed policeman to ensure that Latin American governments acted responsibly and, most important, maintained their finances in order so as to meet their financial obligations to foreign investors.

The policy of sending American marines and financial supervisors to restore political and financial stability frequently aroused anger and resentment in Latin America and was condemned as "Monroeism." As part of the reappraisal of its policy toward Latin America, the **Calvin Coolidge** administration instructed Undersecretary of State **J. Reuben Clark** to prepare a study of the history of the Monroe Doctrine. The resulting **Clark Memorandum**, which was published in 1930, considered that the policy of military intervention in Latin America had been damaging and counterproductive to U.S. national interests. In effect, the memorandum represented an official repudiation of the Roosevelt Corollary. Starting with **Herbert Hoover**, subsequent U.S. presidents avoided making direct reference to the Monroe Doctrine and preferred to talk in terms of collective or multilateral action to combat external threats to the security of the Western Hemisphere. This was formalized by the 1947 **Rio Treaty**, which established a regional system of collective security. In cases of external threat, such as the **Cuban Missile Crisis** in 1962, the United States invoked the Rio Treaty rather than the Monroe Doctrine. A direct link with Monroe's 1823 message, however, was evident in the fact that the United States never abandoned its unilateral and preemptive approach. This was demonstrated by the decision not to consult Latin American governments and to resort instead to unilateral military intervention in the Dominican Republic in 1965 and Grenada in 1983. *See also* CANNING, GEORGE (1770–1827); DOMINICAN INTERVENTION (1965).

MORGAN, EDWIN (1865–1934). American diplomat. In 1900, Morgan joined the **State Department** and held various junior diplomatic posts until his appointment as minister to **Cuba** in 1905. He became minister to **Uruguay** in 1909 and was transferred to Portugal in 1911. In 1912, he was promoted to the post of ambassador to **Brazil** and held this appointment continuously for 21 years until his resignation in 1933. No American diplomat has served longer at a single ambassadorial post. Morgan was notably different from the majority of American diplomats of his time, especially those in Latin American posts, in displaying a genuine sensitivity to the opinion and customs of the people of the nation in which he served. Moreover, he used his considerable personal wealth and cultured background to cultivate close personal relations with members of the Brazilian elite. After his death in April 1934, he was buried in Petrópolis with a ceremony in which the Brazilian government accorded him full honors. As a further mark of tribute to his memory, a street in one of the most affluent residential sections of Rio de Janeiro was given the name "Rua Embaixador Morgan." During an era in which anti-American feeling was very pronounced in Latin America, it was remarkable for an American diplomat to be shown so much personal respect and affection.

MORGAN, JOHN TYLER (1824–1907). American politician. Born in Tennessee and raised in Alabama, Morgan was a lawyer and Confederate general during the American Civil War (1861–1865) before securing election as Democratic senator for Alabama from 1876 to 1907. As a member and later chairman of the Senate Foreign Relations Committee, he took a close interest in Latin American affairs. Morgan was a prominent example of the bipartisan political support that was evident in the U.S. Congress during the 1880s and that resulted in the passage of the appropriation to hold the **International American Conference** (1889–1890). He also believed that U.S. trade with Latin America would be greatly boosted by the construction of an isthmian canal and was an enthusiastic supporter of the Nicaraguan route. Despite Morgan's persistent lobbying over more than two decades for **Nicaragua**, the **Panama** route was eventually chosen. *See also* PANAMA CANAL; PAN-AMERICANISM.

MUTUAL SECURITY ACT (1951). U.S. congressional act authorizing military assistance agreements. The act was passed by the U.S. Congress in 1951 and was designed to promote the common defense of the hemisphere during the Cold War. In effect, the act supplemented the activities of the **Inter-American Defense Board** by authorizing the U.S. president to conclude military assistance agreements with individual Latin American countries. Beginning with **Ecuador** in January 1952, 12 Latin American governments subsequently signed treaties with the United States for the provision of military equipment and training. In the period from 1953 to 1961, the U.S. Congress voted appropriations of more than $500 million to fund the act. *See also* MILITARY ASSISTANCE.

– N –

NABUCO, JOAQUIM (1849–1910). Brazilian political leader and diplomat. A celebrated writer, orator, and leader of **Brazil**'s antislavery movement, Joaquim Nabuco was Brazil's first ambassador to the United States. From his arrival in Washington in 1905, he worked assiduously to cultivate friendly relations with American officials and notably established a cordial relationship with Secretary of State **Elihu Root**. Nabuco was particularly gratified at the choice of Rio de Janeiro ahead of Buenos Aires as the venue for the Third Pan-American Conference in 1906. The decision conferred considerable prestige on Brazil and reflected Nabuco's success in working with Brazilian Foreign Minister **Rio Branco** in promoting the policy of approximating their country's diplomacy to that of the United States. When Nabuco died in Washington in January 1910, President **William H. Taft** paid the signal tribute of providing an American warship to take the ambassador's body back home for burial in Brazil. *See also* PAN-AMERICAN CONFERENCE SYSTEM.

NAPOLEON BONAPARTE (1769–1821). Emperor of **France** from 1804 to 1814. Napoleon greatly assisted U.S. territorial expansion in the North American continent by agreeing in 1803 to the **Louisiana Purchase**, in which the United States bought 827,000 square miles of Louisiana for $15 million. Moreover, it was Napoleon's action in 1808 to force the abdication of the Spanish ruling family, and make his brother, Joseph, king of **Spain**, that provoked widespread protest and rebellion resulting in the movements for economic and political independence in Latin America. *See also* WARS FOR LATIN AMERICAN INDEPENDENCE (1808–1826).

NARCOTICS TRAFFICKING. The illegal trafficking of narcotics. During the second half of the 20th century, the United States was the world's biggest consumer of narcotics, such as cocaine, marijuana, and heroin, which were imported illegally. In response, the U.S. government developed a policy of narcotics control that sought to prevent narcotics from reaching the country by interdiction in transit, especially along the Mexican border with the United States, and also by destroying and eradicating the sources of supply in the producing countries. The main suppliers were located in Turkey and Southeast Asia, but Latin America was also implicated because the coca leaf had long been a traditional cash crop in **Bolivia** and **Peru**, while countries such as **Mexico** and **Colombia** provided staging posts for the reexport of coca leaves in the form of cocaine to the United States. A notable development in Colombia was the rise of organized drug cartels, the most notorious of which were located in the cities of Cali and Medellín.

In the U.S. government, the task of interdicting and destroying the supply of illegal narcotics lay primarily with the Drug Enforcement Administration (DEA), which had been established within the Department of Justice in 1973. The DEA worked with local Latin American governments and provided training and equipment for police and paramilitary forces. In addition, DEA agents were sent to Latin America to act as advisers and to offer tactical support. Financial aid programs were also established to educate and provide incentives for local farmers and peasants to switch production of narcotics to foodstuffs and staple goods. During the 1980 and 1990s, the **Ronald Reagan**, **George H. W. Bush**, and **Bill Clinton** administrations continued and expanded these policies but found that success was elusive so long as the demand for illegal narcotics in the United States constantly remained high and offered opportunities for Latin American drug cartels to make lucrative financial profits.

The policies of narcotics control also underscored many of the historical problems of inter-American relations, especially the preference of the United States for unilateral rather than multilateral action. Agents of the DEA were frequently regarded as foreigners whose forceful and often insensitive behavior did much to upset rather than cultivate a cooperative working relationship with local officials and people. Latin American governments were also irritated by American insistence on the extradition to the United States of Latin American nationals for alleged criminal activities. In the case of the Panamanian general **Manuel Noriega**, alleged involvement in illegal narcotics trafficking provided a justification for massive U.S. military intervention in **Panama** in 1989. Critics complained that the action was excessively violent and unjustified. *See also* PAZ ESTENSSORO, VÍCTOR (1907–2001).

NATIONAL REVOLUTIONARY MOVEMENT (MOVIMENTO NACIONAL REVOLUCIONIONARIO) (MNR). A revolutionary political movement occurring in **Bolivia**. The MNR was founded in 1941 and seized political power in a violent uprising in 1952. In office, however, the MNR showed caution in the implementation of its proclaimed radical policies of major land reform and economic nationalism, including the expropriation of the foreign-owned tin companies. Consequently, the "Bolivian Revolution" did not cause the same difficulties with the United States as the earlier **Mexican Revolution**. Moreover, not only was the MNR opposed to communism, but it also agreed to compensate the foreign-owned tin companies that suffered nationalization. In return, the United States consented to continue programs of financial aid and to maintain substantial purchases of Bolivian tin to the extent of having to stockpile large quantities. The MNR was overthrown by a military coup in 1964 but continued to play an active and prominent role in Bolivian politics. *See also* PAZ ESTENSSORO, VÍCTOR (1907–2001).

NICARAGUA. The largest country in Central America bordered by **Honduras** to the north and **Costa Rica** to the south. Formerly part of the United Provinces of Central America, Nicaragua became an independent republic after the dissolution of the federation in 1838. The first U.S. minister officially presented his credentials to the Nicaraguan government in 1852 at a time when American **filibusters** were showing an interest in the country. The most famous and notorious was **William Walker**, who arrived in 1855 with just over 50 men, took possession of the government, and called himself dictator of the whole country. However, Walker's political authority did not extend very far beyond his actual headquarters. Walker was forced to flee from Nicaragua in 1857 and return to the United States. He resumed his filibustering activities until they came to an end in 1860 when he was captured and executed by a firing squad in Honduras.

The U.S. government was embarrassed by the filibustering activities of Walker. While disavowing any intention of seizing territory, it showed a definite interest in Nicaragua as the potential site of a route for a canal linking the Atlantic and Pacific oceans. Although the Isthmus of Panama offered the shortest route, the inland river system in Nicaragua made a waterway easier to construct in that country and therefore less expensive. American business interests strongly favored Nicaragua and formed the Maritime Canal Company to lobby for that country. However, an international congress held at Paris in 1879 chose **Panama**. Construction work was started in 1881 and continued until the French **Panama Canal Company** became bankrupt in 1892. When interest in canal projects subsequently revived after the **Spanish-American War** (1898), the U.S. Congress debated the respective merits of Panama and Nicaragua and eventually chose the former. The possibility of building a canal in Nicaragua, however, was never entirely ruled out and was expressed in the conclusion of the Bryan-Chamorro Treaty (1916), which gave canal rights in the country to the United States.

In the early 20th century, continued political instability in Nicaragua and the resulting inability to service the country's foreign debt led to the exercise of **dollar diplomacy**. In 1912, U.S. marines landed in the country to support the pro-American government of President Adolfo Díaz. Military occupation and financial supervision continued until 1924 and made Nicaragua a virtual protectorate of the United States. The American military withdrawal in 1924 proved to be temporary. The return of U.S. marines in 1926 to quell local disturbances and the acceptance by the **Calvin Coolidge** administration of the military requirement to reinforce those forces in 1927 provoked an outbreak of local guerrilla resistance that was organized by the Nicaraguan political leader **Augusto Sandino**. While American officials denounced him as a bandit and a communist, Sandino acquired the image of a national hero in Nicaragua and soon became a symbolic figure throughout Latin America for those critical of the U.S. policy of military intervention.

The policy of training local Nicaraguan police forces to form a National Guard and assume the responsibility for maintaining civil order allowed the withdrawal of U.S. marines from Nicaragua in 1932. The commander of the National Guard, **Anastasio Somoza García**, particularly enjoyed American support and favor. In 1936, Somoza seized political power in a military coup and later became president in 1937, a position he held continuously until his assassination in 1956. Although Somoza imposed what amounted to a brutal dictatorship in Nicaragua, he gave the country the appearance of being politically stable and was, therefore, able to enjoy friendly relations with the United States. Moreover, in return for American financial and military aid, Somoza proved a most cooperative ally in assisting the United States during **World War II** and later in supporting policies of anticommunism during the **Cold War**, notably providing military bases for the **Central Intelligence Agency (CIA)** to organize covert operations against Guatemalan President **Jacobo Arbenz** in 1954.

Although notorious for their repressive rule, Somoza and his sons, who succeeded to the Nicaraguan presidency after their father's death in 1956, were helped with favorable publicity from the well-funded "Nicaragua lobby" in Washington, which pointed out that the family were staunch anticommunists and long-standing friends of the United States. It was not until **Jimmy Carter** assumed the presidency in 1977 that U.S. policymakers openly withdrew their political support of the Somoza family. A combination of American diplomatic pressure and a series of military defeats inflicted by the **Sandinista National Liberation Front (Sandinistas)** persuaded **Anastasio Somoza Debayle** to resign the presidency and leave Nicaragua in July 1979.

The change of political regime posed a dilemma to the United States because the Sandinistas took their name from Augusto Sandino, the national hero who had led anti-American resistance in the 1920s. Moreover, the Sandinistas were openly procommunist and admired the **Cuban Revolution**. They did not wish, however, to break off diplomatic relations with the United States or enter into a formal alliance with the **Soviet Union**. Nevertheless, the administration of President **Ronald Reagan** was implacably hostile and sought to destabilize the Sandinistas by applying a combination of external economic pressure and internal sabotage. The CIA organized and financed an army of exiles known as the **Contras** who operated from bases in neighboring Honduras and Costa Rica. The Contras gained little actual military success and remained heavily dependent upon the continuation of American financial assistance.

During the 1980s American political opinion was deeply divided over the issue of Nicaragua. The fear of being sucked into "another Vietnam [War]" not only ruled out the use of American combat troops in Central America but also seriously restricted the amount of financial support that Congress would vote to assist the military operations of the Contras. This prompted the Reagan administration to resort to covert methods of funding the Contras and led to the revelation of the **Iran-Contra affair** in 1986. The scandal was a serious political embarrassment to President Reagan and resulted in a softening of his opposition to the diplomatic peace process undertaken by Central American leaders, notably President **Óscar Arias** of Costa Rica. A peace settlement was concluded in which the Contras agreed to a cease-fire in 1988, and national elections were held in Nicaragua in 1990. The elections unexpectedly resulted in victory for an anti-Sandinista coalition headed by **Violeta Barrios de Chamorro**. The new government immediately reestablished friendly relations with the United States. The electoral outcome was very pleasing to U.S. officials. The apparent defeat of communism in Nicaragua, however, was overshadowed in news value by its coinciding with the collapse of the Soviet Union and the dramatic end of the Cold War. By comparison, events in Nicaragua were accorded much less significance as the country suddenly lost the geopolitical significance that it had possessed during the 1980s and, consequently, became a much less important issue in U.S. Latin American policy. *See also* CENTRAL AMERICAN CRISIS; GRANT, ULYSSES S. (1822–1885); MORGAN, JOHN TYLER (1824–1907); NORTH, OLIVER (1943–); PANAMA CANAL.

NIXON, RICHARD M. (1913–1994). American political leader and president from 1969 to 1975. Born in California, Nixon was a lawyer who joined the Republican Party and won election to the U.S. House of Representatives in 1946 and to the Senate in 1950. In 1952, he was chosen as **Dwight Eisenhower**'s vice-presidential candidate in the 1952 presidential election. Electoral victory in 1952 was repeated in 1956. As vice president from 1953 to 1961, Nixon was known for his attitude of staunch anticommunism. In 1958, he made a goodwill tour of Latin America that made front-page news in the United States because it aroused violent anti-American demonstrations, especially in Caracas, **Venezuela**. The event shocked officials in the Eisenhower administration and resulted in a reassessment of U.S. Latin American policy that led to the increased provision of economic aid to the region.

Nixon lost the presidential election to **John F. Kennedy** in 1960 but won against Hubert Humphrey in 1968. On becoming president in 1969, it was clear that his priority in foreign policy was to extricate the United States from the war in Vietnam through the diplomatic strategy of pursuing détente with the **Soviet Union**. Affairs in the rest of the world, including Latin America, attracted close American interest only when they directly interacted with **Cold War** politics. A notable example was in **Chile**, where Nixon and his national security adviser, **Henry Kissinger**, were taken aback by the victory of the Marxist politician **Salvador Allende** in the 1970 presidential election. Nixon instructed the **Central Intelligence Agency (CIA)** to implement a policy of economic pressure and covert political activity to destabilize Allende's government and remove him from office. In September 1973, General **Augusto Pinochet** seized power in a military coup during which Allende committed suicide. American complicity in the coup was widely suspected but has never been definitively proved. In fact, the controversy over Nixon's policy toward Chile was overshadowed in the United States by the unfolding Watergate scandal, which culminated in Nixon's unprecedented decision to resign the presidency in August 1974. *See also* EISENHOWER, MILTON S. (1899–1985); HELMS, RICHARD (1913–2002); NIXON VISIT TO LATIN AMERICA (1958).

NIXON VISIT TO LATIN AMERICA (1958). Example of a significant event that stimulated anti-American feeling in Latin America. Anti-American sentiment emerged at its most virulent during Vice President **Richard Nixon**'s goodwill tour of Latin America in May 1958. Nixon's itinerary included stops in **Argentina**, **Uruguay**, **Paraguay**, **Peru**, and **Venezuela**. The visit started peacefully in Buenos Aires, where Nixon attended the inauguration of President Arturo Frondizi. In Lima, however, Nixon was confronted by student riots. In Caracas, the protests were on a larger scale, and his life was endangered when a howling mob attacked his motorcade. Despite the attribution that the actions against Nixon were the work of a communist minority, the **Dwight Eisenhower** administration was startled by the depth of anti-American hostility that had been so openly displayed. A reassessment of Latin American policy took place in which Eisenhower decided to try to remedy the previous attitude of complacency by making a personal visit to several countries in February–March 1960. At the same time, the provision of financial aid allocated to the region was considerably increased. Eisenhower's successor, **John F. Kennedy**, continued this policy in the form of the **Alliance for Progress**. In his memoir, *Six Crises*, published in 1962, Nixon described his confrontation with the mob in Caracas as one of the major formative influences on his political career. *See also* EISENHOWER, MILTON S. (1899–1985).

NO-TRANSFER RESOLUTION (1811). Statement of U.S. policy toward Latin America. Fearing that **Great Britain** might exploit **Spain**'s weakness during the **wars for Latin American independence** and opportunistically gain possess of Spanish Florida, Secretary of State **James Monroe** requested the U.S. Congress to pass a joint resolution in January 1811 affirming that the United States would oppose the transfer of Florida to a foreign power. The No-Transfer Resolution clearly indicated American ambitions to expand territorially. Furthermore, by indicating the close interest of the United States in what should happen to the Spanish colonies the resolution also served as a precursor to the **Monroe Doctrine**.

The range of the No-Transfer Resolution was extended in 1870 when President **Ulysses S. Grant** sent a Special Message to the U.S. Senate declaring that no territory in the **Western Hemisphere** should be transferred to a European nation. Grant responded to what turned out to be unfounded rumors that European powers were interested in annexing the Dominican Republic. A similar external threat emerged in 1940 following the rapid German military victories in Western Europe that dramatically posed the prospect of **Germany** assuming future control of the existing French and Dutch colonies in the Caribbean and using these islands as bases for offensive military operations in the Western Hemisphere. To prevent this outcome, the U.S. Congress passed a joint resolution on June 17–18 reaffirming the No-Transfer Resolution. A pan-American meeting of foreign ministers was held at Havana on July 21–30 that endorsed the action of the U.S. Congress by similarly resolving not to recognize the transfer of any European colony in the Caribbean to Germany. *See also* DECLARATION OF HAVANA (1940); WORLD WAR II (1939–1945).

NORIEGA, MANUEL (1938–). Panamanian general and dictator. In 1983, Noriega took command of the Panamanian National Guard, which he renamed the Panamanian Defense Force, and from this position of military power ruled as a virtual dictator. Noriega aided the

Ronald Reagan administration in its covert operations against the **Sandinistas** in **Nicaragua**, but at the same time he allowed **Panama** to become a leading transshipment point for illegal narcotics destined for the United States and also a center for money laundering of the vast profits made from the trade in illegal narcotics. The brutality of Noriega's rule, his flagrant abuse of human rights, and his refusal to cooperate in interdicting the trade in narcotics made him an increasingly notorious figure in the United States. In 1988, the U.S. Department of Justice publicly named Noriega in an indictment for illegal **narcotics trafficking**. A U.S. military mission code-named **Operation Just Cause** was implemented in 1989 to arrest Noriega. It involved more than 25,000 U.S. troops who entered Panama to apprehend the general and secure his extradition to the United States. In 1992, Noriega was put on trial, convicted, and sentenced to 40 years in prison. *See also* BUSH, GEORGE H. W. (1924–).

NORTH, OLIVER (1943–). American military officer. Born in Texas, North joined the U.S. Marines and attained the rank of lieutenant colonel. In 1981, he became a staff member of the National Security Council (NSC). Acting as a liaison with the **Contras** in **Nicaragua**, he secretly arranged the sale of American military equipment to Iran and directed the financial proceeds to purchase military equipment for the Contras. North's actions were carried out without informing the U.S. Congress and were in violation of federal law prohibiting such funding of the Contras. Known as the **Iran-Contra affair**, the activities were publicly exposed in November 1986 and immediately became a major political scandal that greatly embarrassed the **Ronald Reagan** administration. Identified as a principal figure in the scandal, North was dismissed from the NSC and later convicted on criminal charges. The conviction was overturned on appeal. For a short time, North was a media celebrity and unsuccessfully attempted to win election to the U.S. Senate in 1994. *See also* CASEY, WILLIAM J. (1913–1987).

NORTH AMERICAN FREE TRADE AGREEMENT (NAFTA). Commercial agreement between the United States, **Mexico**, and **Canada**. In 1989, the United States signed a free trade agreement with Canada. During the following year, Mexican President **Carlos Salinas** announced his aim of negotiating a similar arrangement with the United States. President **George H. W. Bush** welcomed the proposal as fitting in with his own stated aim to bring about a free trade area covering all of the **Western Hemisphere**. The idea of hemispheric commercial union, however, traditionally provoked contentious political debate within the United States. In this case, the debate focused on the proposed extension of the existing free trade agreement with Canada to include Mexico in what would become the North American Free Trade Agreement (NAFTA). Supporters emphasized the importance of reducing tariffs as a means of promoting economic stability and development in Mexico, a nation of vital strategic importance to the United States. Opponents, especially the U.S. labor unions, argued that free trade agreements would inevitably result in the relocation of many current American jobs and factories to Mexico, where the cost of labor was considerably lower than in the United States. Both the Bush and **Clinton** administrations declared that the American economy would benefit greatly from NAFTA and strongly supported the measure.

The NAFTA treaty was signed by the leaders of the three governments in October 1992 and, after considerable political debate, was eventually ratified by the U.S. Congress in November 1993. NAFTA was generally regarded as the first step in a process toward what would become a hemispheric free trade area to be known as the Free Trade Area of the Americas (FTAA). Rapid progress in this direction was effectively ruled out, however, by the perceived constraints on U.S. presidential action arising from the bitter political controversy generated over NAFTA in the U.S. Congress. There was also criticism that the reductions in tariffs were too limited and selective and tended to favor the already well-established and big U.S. business interests. At the beginning of the 21st century, discussions to establish the FTAA were still taking place but had become further complicated by wider concerns over the economic effects of globalization. *See also* SUMMITS OF THE AMERICAS.

– O –

OBREGÓN, ÁLVARO (1880–1928). Mexican general and president from 1920 to 1924. A supporter of **Francisco Madero**, Obregón was one of the revolutionary leaders who sought to avenge Madero's death in 1913 and overthrow the military government of General **Victoriano Huerta**. Obregón's military skills, especially his victories over **Francisco "Pancho" Villa**, were important in allowing **Venustiano Carranza** to rise to political power and to bring an end to the violent period of the **Mexican Revolution**. In 1920, however, Obregón overthrew Carranza and became president. In office, he stressed the value of seeking friendly and cooperative relations with the United States. *See also* MEXICO.

OFFICE OF THE COORDINATOR OF INTER-AMERICAN AFFAIRS (OCIAA). A wartime agency of the U.S. government. Prior to **World War II**, the administration of President **Franklin D. Roosevelt** sought to combat the growing influence of Nazi propaganda in Latin America. The task was assigned to the Office of Inter-American Affairs, which was created in August 1940 and renamed in July 1941 the Office of Coordinator of Inter-American Affairs (OCIAA). The Republican political leader, **Nelson Rockefeller**, who held the office of coordinator from 1941 until December 1944, formulated a successful strategy of waging psychological warfare against the Nazis by extolling the virtues of democracy and the American way of life through radio broadcasting and the distribution of press releases, motion pictures, books, and newspapers. Care was taken, however, to stress a sense of mutual inter-American interest and common endeavor in keeping with the concept of the **Good Neighbor Policy**. Programs were also set up to promote and reinforce hemispheric unity by sponsoring art exhibitions, concerts, and educational and cultural exchanges.

In addition, OCIAA brought tangible economic and social benefits to Latin America during World War II. Funds were allocated for specific public health projects that led to marked improvements in sanitation, water supply, and health care facilities. Rockefeller's achievement as both an administrator and a fund-raiser for his agency was impressive. Starting in 1941 with an annual budget of $3.5 million, by 1945 OCIAA had a staff of more than 1,000 in Washington, and its activities were costing $45 million. The agency, however, had always been regarded as a temporary wartime emergency measure. At the end of World War II in 1945, most of OCIAA's responsibilities were transferred to the **State Department**. The agency was formally abolished in April 1946.

OIL. A controversial issue in U.S. diplomatic relations with Latin America. The production of raw materials and commodities in Latin America has frequently led to diplomatic controversy with the United States. A foremost example has been Mexican oil. At the beginning of the 20th century, U.S. oil companies operating in **Mexico** were alarmed by the implications of the 1917 Mexican Constitution, especially Article 27, which placed the ownership of all the country's natural resources including oil in the Mexican nation. The companies feared that enforcement of the constitutional provision would lead to nationalization of their existing assets without adequate financial compensation. Although Mexico claimed possession of the oil, the provisions of Article 27 were not immediately enforced because the continuance of government oil revenues depended on cooperation with the oil companies to extract the oil and sell it to foreign markets. The Mexican government was also mindful of international competition and that alternative supplies of oil for the American market were becoming available from countries such as **Venezuela**.

In 1925, Mexican President **Plutarco Elías Calles** declared that, under Article 27, rights to property acquired by foreigners prior to 1917 were to be limited to a time period of 50 years, after which ownership would revert to the state. American companies complained that the proposed action was unfair because it was retrospective. Diplomatic relations became strained as the **Calvin Coolidge** administration sought to protect the interests of the oil companies. An agreement was reached with the Mexican government in December 1927 stating that foreign interests that had already begun work on their subsoil properties should retain their existing property rights. Another major diplomatic crisis, however, arose in 1938 when Mexican President **Lázaro Cárdenas** unilaterally announced the nationalization of the foreign-owned oil companies. The companies did not contest Mexico's sovereign right to expropriate, but they rejected the amount of compensation offered as insufficient. At first, President **Franklin D. Roosevelt** backed the protests of the American oil companies. The fear was that if the Mexicans were successful, this would not only threaten the confiscation of all American property and investments in

Mexico but would also encourage other Latin American nations to take similar action and thereby restrict the access of American companies to oil and other raw materials. A particular concern was the effect of the dispute on Venezuela and **Bolivia**, whose governments were currently involved in negotiations with American companies over concessions to drill for oil.

Mindful of Latin American sensitivity over the issue of American interference in their internal affairs, Roosevelt ruled out the use of military force. He was also influenced by a desire to retain Latin American goodwill and to avoid damage to his country's image as a good neighbor. Moreover, the value of having friendly relations with Mexico was enhanced by the sense of international crisis arising from the outbreak of **World War II** in Europe in 1939. A compromise was eventually reached in September 1941 in which Roosevelt essentially accepted the act of expropriation on Mexico's terms. The oil companies received $24 million instead of the $600 million that they had previously insisted on. The long-running diplomatic controversy with Mexico provided a foretaste of similar awkward disputes that the United States would experience with other Latin American countries, such as **Peru** and Venezuela over oil and **Chile** over copper. *See also* FREI MONTALVA, EDUARDO (1911–1982); GOOD NEIGHBOR POLICY; DANIELS, JOSEPHUS (1862–1948); MEXICAN REVOLUTION; VELASCO ALVARADO, JUAN (1910–1977).

OLNEY MEMORANDUM (1895). A statement, also known as the Olney Doctrine, asserting the hemispheric power of the United States. On July 20, 1895, Secretary of State **Richard Olney** dispatched a diplomatic note to the British Foreign Office calling on **Great Britain** to submit its boundary dispute with **Venezuela** to binding arbitration. The note, also known as the Olney Memorandum or Olney Doctrine, justified American intervention in the dispute as based on the **Monroe Doctrine** and the claim that the United States was the preeminent power in the **Western Hemisphere**. At first, the British government rejected the note but later agreed to arbitrate the dispute. The Olney Memorandum was therefore instrumental in securing British recognition of the Monroe Doctrine and in affirming the predominant political position of the United States in the Western Hemisphere. The same idea was expressed in 1904 in the **Roosevelt**

Corollary to the Monroe Doctrine. *See also* VENEZUELA BOUNDARY DISPUTE (1895).

OLNEY, RICHARD (1835–1917). American lawyer and secretary of state from 1895 to 1897. Born in Massachusetts, Olney was a lawyer who served as attorney general in the **Grover Cleveland** administration from 1893 to 1895. His most celebrated action as secretary of state was to involve the U.S. government directly in the long-standing boundary dispute between **Great Britain** and **Venezuela**. In July 1895, Olney sent a diplomatic note, also known as the **Olney Memorandum**, to the British Foreign Office stating that the dispute should be submitted to binding arbitration. Olney declared that the United States was the leading power in the **Western Hemisphere** and that its intervention was justified because Britain was suspected of violating the **Monroe Doctrine**. *See also* SCRUGGS, WILLIAM L. (1836–1912); VENEZUELA BOUNDARY DISPUTE (1895).

OPERATION JUST CAUSE (1989–1990). A U.S. military operation in **Panama**. In 1988, the U.S. Department of Justice named the Panamanian general and dictator **Manuel Noriega** in an indictment for illegal narcotics trafficking. After the murder of an American officer by Noriega's police forces in Panama, President **George H. W. Bush** approved the implementation of Operation Just Cause for military intervention in Panama to apprehend Noriega and bring him before an American court. The mission commenced on December 20, 1989. It involved over 25,000 troops and 300 aircraft and was the largest deployment of American troops in combat action since the Vietnam War. Noriega sought political asylum but eventually surrendered on January 3, 1990. He was arrested, extradited to Miami, and put on trial in the United States and convicted in 1992.

The U.S. decision to intervene with massive military force in Panama aroused widespread criticism in Latin America. A resolution was passed in the **Organization of American States** condemning it as an act of aggression. To register the extent of its disapproval, the Peruvian government broke off diplomatic relations with the United States. Resolutions were also passed in the **United Nations (UN)** Security Council and the General Assembly describing the action as a violation of international law. In its defense, the Bush administration maintained that Noriega had to be brought to trial to face criminal charges that he was personally involved in illegal **narcotics trafficking**. In addition, Bush argued that Noriega's rule was known to be brutal and oppressive and that his forced removal was necessary to enable a democratically elected civilian president to take office in Panama. Critics noted, however, that American criticism of Noriega's dictatorial rule had remained curiously muted in the past when the **Ronald Reagan** administration had considered him a valued ally in the struggle to defeat the **Sandinistas** in **Nicaragua**.

OPERATION PAN-AMERICA. A Latin American proposal to fund major economic development. During the 1950s, Latin American governments sought external funding for large schemes of national economic development. In May 1958, Brazilian President **Juscelino Kubitschek** proposed that a large and systematic program for hemispheric economic growth should be adopted in which the United States would take the leading role. The concept was based on the postwar **Marshall Plan** for Europe and was called "Operation Pan-America" because it would seek to aid all the economies of Latin America. The idea received a negative response from officials in the **Dwight Eisenhower** administration who were suspicious of Latin American initiatives and preferred to devise their own solutions to hemispheric problems. A separate U.S. scheme eventually emerged in 1961 at the beginning of the **John F. Kennedy** administration and was known as the **Alliance for Progress**.

OPERATION PBSUCCESS (1954). A U.S. covert operation to overthrow the Guatemalan government in 1954. Fearing that **Guatemala** was falling under communist influence and was in danger of becoming a Soviet satellite state, President **Dwight Eisenhower** instructed the **Central Intelligence Agency (CIA)** to prepare a covert military operation, code-named "Operation PBSUCCESS," with the aim of overthrowing the government of Guatemalan President **Jacobo Arbenz**. A number of Guatemalan political exiles were duly recruited, equipped, and organized in the neighboring states of **Honduras** and **Nicaragua**. In June 1954, the CIA directed this force consisting of around 150 Guatemalans commanded by Colonel **Carlos Castillo**

Armas to invade Guatemala from Honduras. While the rebels were given air support by bombers supplied by the CIA and flown by privately contracted American pilots, no American troops were to be involved in combat operations on the ground. CIA agents, however, were active in taking over control of Guatemalan radio communications in order to broadcast anti-Arbenz propaganda. The broadcasts were also effective in persuading the Guatemala people that the tiny advancing rebel army was a large invasion force. Without any major battle being actually fought, Arbenz decided to resign and was replaced by Castillo Armas.

The significant role of the CIA in the coup was widely suspected but was not publicly revealed at the time. Instead, Secretary of State **John Foster Dulles** publicly denied American involvement and declared that the coup was internally motivated. Latin American governments, however, were generally dismayed by the employment of armed force in the guise of a covert operation to overthrow a legally elected government and suppress radical reforms. In effect, the Guatemalan episode marked a reversion of the United States to the policy of unilateral interventionism and thereby the definitive end of the **Good Neighbor Policy**. In Washington, however, the prestige of the CIA was greatly enhanced as a result of the perceived success of Operation PBSUCCESS. Consequently, the agency was given a similar task in 1959 to organize the removal of **Fidel Castro** from power in Cuba. This operation, however, ended in failure at the **Bay of Pigs** in April 1961 and considerably damaged the reputation of the CIA. *See also* ARMED INTERVENTIONS; PEURIFOY, JOHN E. (1907–1955).

ORGANIZATION OF AMERICAN STATES (OAS). A regional organization of all the nations of the **Western Hemisphere**. The Ninth Pan-American Conference held at Bogotá in 1948 replaced the longstanding but informal **Pan-American Conference System** and **Pan-American Union (PAU)** with a new political institution still located in the same headquarters in Washington but now consisting of a permanent headquarters and staff. This was to be known as the OAS and was created in accordance with Articles 52 to 54 of the **United Nations (UN)** Charter, allowing member states to enter into separate regional organizations to deal with their local security problems.

The Charter of the OAS affirmed the equality of its member nations. It also included a guarantee of the principle of nonintervention in the internal affairs of those members. The OAS was important in giving the Latin American governments what they had long desired in the form of a permanent forum and machinery to debate and directly influence issues affecting the Western Hemisphere. But the United States also stood to gain from the new institution. In fact, the OAS proved valuable for American diplomacy because it provided a convenient tool that could be used in the policy of containing international communism during the Cold War. On several occasions during the Cold War, such as the intervention in **Guatemala** in 1954 and the imposition of economic sanctions on **Cuba** in 1962, the United States used the OAS as an instrument to endorse and ratify its Latin American policies. On the other hand, the impotence of the OAS was visibly demonstrated in the crises in the Dominican Republic in 1965 and Grenada in 1983 when American military intervention took place unilaterally and without prior consultation with the governments of Latin America. *See also* DOMINICAN INTERVENTION (1965); FIGUERES FERRER, JOSÉ (1906–1990); JOHNSON, LYNDON (1908–1973); OPERATION JUST CAUSE (1989–1990); PANAMA; UNITED NATIONS ECONOMIC COMMISSION FOR LATIN AMERICA (UNECLA or ECLA).

ORTEGA SAAVEDRA, DANIEL (1945–). Nicaraguan political leader and president from 1984 to 1990. A prominent leader of the **Sandinista National Liberation Front (FSLN)**, Ortega was a political prisoner from 1967 to 1974. In 1979, he joined the Junta of National Reconstruction, which formed the new government that replaced the regime of **Anastasio Somoza**. In 1984, national elections were held in which Ortega was elected president. As president, he sought to implement the revolutionary ideals of the FSLN. The **Ronald Reagan** administration, however, was unrelentingly hostile. It regarded Ortega as identical to **Fidel Castro** and sought to destabilize his government. When elections were held in **Nicaragua** in 1990, Ortega unexpectedly lost the presidency to the candidate of the National Opposition Union, **Violeta Barrios de Chamorro**. Ortega continued to be active in Nicaraguan politics and ran for presidential election again in 1996 and 2001 but was defeated on both occasions. *See also* CENTRAL AMERICAN CRISIS.

– P –

PANAMA. A country in Central America bordered by **Costa Rica** to the northwest and **Colombia** to the southeast. Panama broke away from Spanish colonial rule in 1821 and became the most northerly province of New Grenada (renamed the United States of Colombia in 1863). Panama's importance to other countries lay in its geographical position straddling the Isthmus of Panama, the narrow strip of land that provided the shortest overland journey between the Atlantic and Pacific oceans. After the discovery of gold in California in 1848, there was a great increase in transit by Americans across the Isthmus because it provided the fastest route for those traveling between the east and west coasts of the continental United States. Consequently, American economic and political interest in Panama greatly increased. American capitalists funded the construction of a railroad across the isthmus, which opened in 1855. Moreover, citing Article 35 of the 1846 **Bidlack Treaty** with Colombia, the U.S. government claimed the right to intervene with military force in order to maintain the security of transit across the isthmus. Ten U.S. military interventions took place during the second half of the 19th century.

The Panama Railroad only partly satisfied the growing demand for travel between the oceans. The preferred solution was to build a sea-level canal, a daunting project in terms of finding sufficient finance and overcoming engineering obstacles but one that appeared much more feasible after the successful construction and opening of the Suez Canal in 1869. The vexing question, however, was to find the best location. While the Isthmus of Panama offered the shortest route, the inland river system in **Nicaragua** made a waterway much more straightforward to construct in that country and therefore less expensive and time-consuming. An international congress held at Paris in 1879 chose in favor of Panama. President **Rutherford B. Hayes** made it known that a French-owned canal was not acceptable. Without consulting any foreign government, he sent a Special Message to the U.S. Congress in March 1880 asserting that the United States would take control of any completed canal. Although construction work was started in 1881 by the French **Panama Canal Company**, it came to a halt in 1892 when the company fell into bankruptcy. American interest in canal projects notably revived during the **Spanish-American**

War (1898), especially among U.S. naval officers who argued the need for a canal in order to implement a two-ocean naval strategy.

Instead of looking to private enterprise as in the past, the U.S. government determined to become directly involved in the construction work. Diplomatic negotiations with **Great Britain** were necessary to conclude the **Hay-Pauncefote Treaty** (1901) to abrogate the **Clayton-Bulwer Treaty** (1850) and allow the United States to have exclusive rights over the projected waterway. After choosing Panama over Nicaragua, the **Theodore Roosevelt** administration negotiated a treaty with Colombia to transfer the existing French canal concessions to the United States. The treaty was ratified by the U.S. Senate in March 1903 but defeated by the Colombian Senate. This resulted in riots in Panama in November 1903. American warships prevented Colombian troops from suppressing the demonstrations so that Panama was able to declare its independence from Colombia. The new republic quickly concluded a treaty that granted the United States rights of virtual sovereignty to govern, fortify, and defend an area of land across the isthmus that would be known as the **Panama Canal Zone**. The task of constructing the waterway was assigned to the U.S. Corps of Engineers, under whose direction the canal was successfully completed and opened to the world on August 15, 1914.

Because of the canal, Panama possessed vital strategic, military, and commercial importance for the United States. In terms of diplomatic relations with Panama, however, much of the 20th century was concerned with revising the 1903 Treaty. The general sentiment in Panama was that the original financial terms were inadequate. There was also criticism that the United States governed the Canal Zone as if it was sovereign U.S. territory. As part of the **Good Neighbor Policy**, a new treaty was signed with Panama in 1936 that increased annual payments to that country arising from the operation of the canal. This arrangement, however, did not disturb American control over the Canal Zone. Consequently, Panamanian resentment lingered and erupted in anti-American riots in 1959 and 1964. Conscious of the fact that the canal had entered a period of relative economic decline because it was too small to accommodate the new generation of super oil tankers, the **Lyndon Johnson** administration was willing to enter into discussions to revise the existing treaty arrangements. Substantive negotiations, however, did not occur until the presidency of

Jimmy Carter. Two canal treaties were formally signed in September 1977 and after controversial debate were formally ratified by the U.S. Senate in March–April 1978. The treaties stated that the United States and Panama would manage the canal in joint partnership until it was handed over to Panama on December 31, 1999.

During the late 20th century, Panama was also an important issue in American diplomacy because of its notoriety as a prime location for the transshipment of illegal narcotics and a center for criminal money laundering. In 1988, the U.S. Department of Justice named the Panamanian general and dictator **Manuel Noriega** in an indictment for illegal **narcotics trafficking**. On December 20, 1989, **Operation Just Cause** was put into effect. More than 25,000 U.S. troops invaded Panama to apprehend Noriega and bring him to the United States to stand trial. Noriega surrendered on January 3, 1990. He was arrested, extradited to Miami and put on trial in the United States, and convicted in 1992.

The decision by President **George H. W. Bush** to intervene with overwhelming military force in Panama was characteristic of U.S. diplomacy in being unilateral and involving no prior consultation with neighboring governments. The response in Latin America was also typically one of outrage. A resolution was passed in the **Organization of American States (OAS)** condemning the intervention as an act of aggression. Just as ex-President Theodore Roosevelt had boasted in 1911 that he had "taken" the canal, President George H. W. Bush was similarly forthright when he declared that his decision to intervene militarily in Panama in 1989 was justified by the need to protect U.S. national interests. *See also* HAY-BUNAU-VARILLA TREATY (1903); LESSEPS, FERDINAND DE (1805–1894); TORRIJOS HERRERA, OMAR (1929–1981).

PANAMA CANAL. A waterway constructed across the Isthmus of Panama. Throughout the whole of the 19th century, plans for the construction of a canal linking the Atlantic and Pacific oceans were complicated by disagreement over the best route. While the Isthmus of Panama offered the shortest route, the river system in **Nicaragua** made a waterway easier to construct in that country and therefore less expensive. However, an international congress held at Paris in 1879 chose in favor of **Panama**, and construction work was started in 1881 by the French **Panama Canal Company**. By 1892, the company was bankrupt, and work on the canal was halted. American interest in canal projects notably revived during the **Spanish-American War** (1898), especially among U.S. naval officers who advocated the building of a canal in order to allow the adoption of a two-ocean naval strategy.

Instead of relying on private enterprise as in the past, the U.S. government decided to fund, manage, and execute the project itself. After choosing Panama over Nicaragua, a treaty was negotiated with Colombia to transfer the existing French canal concessions to the United States. The resulting **Hay-Herrán Treaty** was ratified by the U.S. Senate in March 1903 but was rejected by the Colombian Senate. The failure of the treaty contributed to demonstrations in Panama for the independence of the province from Colombia in November 1903. The new republic of Panama quickly concluded the **Hay-Bunau-Varilla Treaty**, which granted the United States rights of virtual sovereignty to administer, fortify, and defend an area of land across the isthmus that would be known as the **Panama Canal Zone**. The task of construction was assigned to the U.S. Corps of Engineers, under whose direction the canal was successfully completed and opened to the world on August 15, 1914. In 1921, the U.S. Senate approved a treaty giving compensation of $25 million to Colombia for the financial loss incurred by the independence of Panama.

A sense of grievance also existed among Panamanians that the terms of the Hay-Bunau-Varilla Treaty had been too favorable to the United States. A new treaty was signed with Panama in 1936 that abrogated the existing American legal right of intervention and increased annual payments to that country arising from the operation of the canal. This arrangement, however, did not affect American control over the Canal Zone. Panamanian resentment was rekindled during the 1950s and expressed itself in anti-American riots in 1959 and 1964. At the same time, the canal began a period of relative economic decline, as it proved too small to accommodate the new super oil tankers and also faced increasing competition for business from the system of federal highways that was being constructed in the United States. The **Lyndon Johnson** administration entered into discussions to revise the existing treaty arrangements, but substantive negotiations did not take place until the presidency of **Jimmy Carter**. The governments of the United States and Panama formally signed two canal treaties in September 1977 that were formally ratified by the U.S. Senate in March–April 1978 after contentious debate. According to the treaties, the United States and Panama would manage the canal in joint partnership until it was transferred to Panama on December 31, 1999. *See also* HAYES, RUTHERFORD B. (1822–1893); LESSEPS, FERDINAND DE (1805–1894); LINOWITZ REPORT (1976); MORGAN, JOHN TYLER (1824–1907); TORRIJOS HERRERA, OMAR (1929–1981).

PANAMA CANAL COMPANY. A French canal company. European interest in canal schemes was stimulated by the successful construction and opening of the Suez Canal in 1869. An international congress was held at Paris in May 1879 and recommended the construction of a sea-level canal across the Isthmus of Panama. The **Panama Canal Company**, whose official title was La Compagnie Universelle du Canal Interocéanique de Panamá (Universal Interoceanic Panama Canal Company), was quickly established, and the celebrated French entrepreneur and builder of the Suez Canal, **Ferdinand de Lesseps**, was appointed as its president. The company secured finance from public subscriptions, mostly from French investors, on the basis that the canal would be completed in 1889 in time to commemorate the centenary of the French Revolution. The company began construction work on schedule at the end of 1881, but progress was slow because of major engineering and climatic difficulties. In 1892, work halted, and the company declared itself bankrupt. The company was reformed in 1894 as the New Panama Canal Company. Construction work on the canal, however, was not resumed. In fact, the activities of the company were concerned mostly with attempts to sell its existing assets and concessions for building the canal. These were eventually purchased by the United States government in 1904. *See also* BUNAU-VARILLA, PHILIPPE (1859–1940); HAYES, RUTHERFORD B. (1822–1893).

PANAMA CANAL TREATIES (1977). Treaties establishing Panamanian sovereign rights over the **Panama Canal**. Shortly after winning the presidential election in 1976, **Jimmy Carter** announced that one of the foreign policy priorities of his forthcoming administration would be a resolution of the long-standing controversy between the United States and **Panama** over the operation of the canal and the status of the **Panama Canal Zone**. The diplomatic negotiations were complex but resulted in two canal treaties that were formally signed by **Carter** and the Panamanian leader **Omar Torrijos** in Washington in September 1977. The first treaty outlined the arrangements by which the United States and Panama would manage the canal in joint partnership until it was handed over to Panama on December 31, 1999. The second treaty stipulated the terms for the operation and defense of the canal after that date. While the treaties were speedily ratified in Panama, the same process was not so straightforward in the United States, where critics argued that the canal was not only "American" territory but also a vital strategic asset. To sway the vote in favor of ratifying the treaties, Carter found that he had to make significant concessions to his political opponents. The treaties were eventually ratified by the U.S. Senate in March–April 1978 though only narrowly, by 68 to 32 votes, just one vote more than the two-thirds necessary for ratification. *See also* LINOWITZ REPORT (1976).

PANAMA CANAL ZONE. An area of land in **Panama** under the control of the United States. In the **Hay-Bunau-Varilla Treaty** (1903), Panama granted the United States virtual sovereign rights to govern, fortify, and defend an area of land 10 miles wide across the isthmus that would become known as the Panama Canal Zone. While the United States paid Panama for canal rights, it did not purchase actual territory as had been done in respect of acquiring Louisiana in 1803 and Alaska in 1867. In fact, the question of defining sovereign rights proved to be a very contentious issue between the United States and Panama throughout the 20th century. Nevertheless, at its inception in 1904, the Canal Zone was administered essentially as a "colony" of the United States in which American authority was strictly imposed on the inhabitants. Construction of the canal involved massive improvements to the region in terms of the provision of housing, social and welfare facilities, and public health, especially sanitation and the successful treatment of tropical diseases. The canal was eventually opened on August 15, 1914.

While Panamanians welcomed their separation from **Colombia** and the construction of the canal with all its financial benefits, there was also concern that the 1904 Treaty infringed their country's sovereign rights and had turned Panama into an American protectorate. A new treaty was signed with Panama in 1936 that increased annual payments to that country arising from the operation of the canal from

$250,000 to $430,000 but did not affect American control over the Canal Zone. On occasions, criticism of the United States resulted in violent anti-American demonstrations, notably in 1959 and 1964. Substantive discussions to end American control, however, did not take place until the 1970s. The issue was complicated by the emergence of a right-wing backlash in the United States in which prominent political figures, such as the former governor of California, **Ronald Reagan**, insisted that the Canal Zone was the national territory of the United States and should never be given away.

During the **Jimmy Carter** administration and after much political controversy and debate, two new canal treaties were signed in 1977. They were narrowly ratified by the U.S. Senate in 1978. The treaties started a process in which Panama gradually assumed sole control of the operation of the canal and the administration of the Canal Zone. The final transfer was completed according to schedule on December 31, 1999. *See also* BUNKER, ELLSWORTH (1894–1984); JOHNSON, LYNDON (1908–1973); LINOWITZ REPORT (1976); TORRIJOS HERRERA, OMAR (1929–1981).

PANAMA CONGRESS (1826). The first official meeting of Latin American countries. The congress was the idea of **Simón Bolívar** and was intended to encourage arrangements to provide for the common defense of the former Spanish-American colonies. Bolívar's ultimate aim was the formation of a federation of Latin American states to replace and maintain the unity of the former Spanish-American empire. The congress met in **Panama** from June 22 to July 15, 1826, and was attended by delegates from only four Latin American states. The congress later reconvened in 1827 at Tacubaya, **Mexico**. The delegates discussed a range of issues, including the establishment of arbitration procedures to resolve disputes, the abolition of the slave trade, and even the formation of a multinational army and navy to deter the Holy Alliance. With the exception of Gran **Colombia**, however, no state ever ratified any of the agreements concluded at the meetings in Panama and later at Tacubaya. The United States played a minor role in the proceedings. At first, Bolívar did not envisage American participation. When an invitation was received, the U.S. Congress hesitated to send delegates because it feared that acceptance would lead to undesirable and restrictive diplomatic entanglements. Eventually, two delegates were appointed. One died en route to Panama. The other attended the reconvened meeting in Mexico.

The fact that the Panama Congress had actually taken place would have considerable symbolic value in the future for advocates of hemispheric unity. Nevertheless, in 1826, the evident disunion among the new Latin American states was a blow to Bolívar's dream of forming a federation based on a common language, religion, and historical traditions. In addition, the Panama Congress also demonstrated the awkward relationship that existed between the United States and the countries of Latin America. *See also* ADAMS, JOHN QUINCY (1767–1848); FAREWELL ADDRESS (1796); WESTERN HEMISPHERE.

PAN-AMERICAN CONFERENCE SYSTEM. The holding of conferences at regular intervals to promote inter-American cooperation and mutual interests. During the 1880s, a growing awareness of Latin American affairs in the United States resulted in bipartisan political support for the proposal that the United States should host a meeting of all the American nations. Known as the **International American Conference**, this meeting was held in Washington from October 2, 1889, to April 19, 1890. The conference was marked more by a divergence than by a convergence of views. Nevertheless, the very fact that the conference had actually taken place provided a precedent for future meetings and also a means by which the United States could exercise its growing political and economic influence over the Latin American nations.

The idea for a follow-up meeting was made in 1899 on the initiative of President **William McKinley**. The Second Pan-American Conference met in Mexico City in 1901. Regular meetings were then scheduled, resulting in conferences at Rio de Janeiro in 1906 and Buenos Aires in 1910. A notable feature of the conferences held during the 1920s at Santiago de Chile in 1923 and Havana in 1928 was a mood of confrontation in which the U.S. delegation was severely criticized for their government's policy of unilateral military intervention, especially in the Central American–Caribbean region. The hostility against the United States was so marked at the Havana meeting that fears were expressed that the Pan-American Conference System could no longer continue.

Relations between the United States and the Latin American nations, however, were greatly improved by the adoption of the **Good Neighbor Policy** during the 1930s. This resulted in the holding of the 1933 conference at Montevideo on schedule. A Special Pan-American Conference for the Maintenance of Peace was convened in 1936 and was attended by President **Franklin D. Roosevelt**. Subsequent conferences held at Lima in 1938, Panama in 1939, Havana in 1940, Rio de Janeiro in 1942, and Mexico City in 1945 were valuable in facilitating hemispheric cooperation to resist the ideological and military threat to the hemisphere posed by **Germany** and Italy both before and during **World War II**.

At the Bogotá conference in 1948, the creation of the **Organization of American States (OAS)** established not only a permanent administrative headquarters but also a regular system of "inter-American" meetings designed to replace the Pan-American Conference System. The idea of holding meetings involving all the heads of state and their senior advisers was revived during the 1990s after the success of the First Summit of the Americas, which was held in Miami, Florida, in 1994. *See also* ARMED INTERVENTIONS.

PAN-AMERICAN UNION (PAU). The permanent organ of the inter-American system. The sole tangible achievement of the **International American Conference** held in Washington in 1889–1890 was the establishment of a Commercial Bureau to be located in Washington for an initial period of 10 years. The agreement to set up the bureau was signed on April 14, 1890, a date that has since been observed annually as "Pan-American Day." The Commercial Bureau was soon renamed the **Bureau of the American Republics**. Under its first director, **William E. Curtis**, the Bureau mainly answered inquiries from businessmen and published a series of bulletins and handbooks giving information on Latin American commercial conditions. Despite the modest nature of these activities, the bureau struggled in its early years to attract adequate funding from subscriptions drawn from the member governments.

At the Fourth Pan-American Conference held at Buenos Aires in 1910, a resolution was passed considerably expanding the functions of the bureau to include political and cultural activities and renaming it the "Pan-American Union." It would be housed in a large new building in Washington whose cost was met mostly by a generous donation from the American philanthropist **Andrew Carnegie**. At the Bogotá Pan-American Conference in 1948, a new inter-American institution was created in which the Pan-American Union became the permanent secretariat and headquarters of the **Organization of American States (OAS)**. *See also* PAN-AMERICANISM; ROWE, LEO S. (1871–1946).

PAN-AMERICANISM. Term describing a movement seeking to promote inter-American unity and cooperation. The idea of the peoples of the **Western Hemisphere** uniting together to affirm their separate identity from Europe has a long history and found expression notably in the **Congress of Panama** (1826) and President **James Monroe**'s 1823 message. More specifically, the term "Pan-Americanism" emerged during the 1880s to denote a policy seeking to establish an informal political alliance and commercial union of all the American republics under the leadership of the United States. In 1888, the U.S. Congress passed an act authorizing the president to invite Latin American governments to an **International American Conference** to be held in the nation's capital. The conference met from October 2, 1889, to April 19, 1890, and was more usually described in the American press as the "Pan-American Conference" instead of the official title of "International American Conference."

The economic benefits of increased inter-American contact were not disputed, but ironically Pan-Americanism contributed to making Latin Americans more aware that their historical roots were different from those of the United States. The Argentine delegate, **Roque Sáenz Peña**, reminded Latin Americans at the International American Conference that they should not forget their links with Europe. The concept of Pan-Americanism, however, continued into the 20th century and found expression in the **Pan-American Conference System**. The sense of a common Pan-American identity was also highly visible during the two world wars. On the other hand, disharmony also existed. Latin Americans admired the political, economic, and military achievements of the United States, but they also felt alienated by American military intervention in the Central American–Caribbean region. Far from promoting common Pan-American objectives, they frequently complained that the aim of the United States was to achieve political control and economic domination of the **Western Hemisphere**. *See also* ARMED INTERVENTIONS; BOLÍVAR, SIMÓN (1783–1830); BLAINE, JAMES G. (1830–1893); WESTERN HEMISPHERE.

PARAGUAY. A country in South America bordered by **Bolivia** and **Brazil** to the north and Argentina to the south. Geographically remote and isolated for much of its history, Paraguay declared its independence from Spain in 1811. Diplomatic relations between the United States and Paraguay were officially established in 1853. American diplomacy, however, has generally neglected Paraguay and has regarded the country as lacking in political and commercial significance. On a few occasions, such as the **War of the Triple Alliance** (1865–1870) and the **Chaco War** (1932–1935), U.S. officials have been involved in diplomatic efforts to bring about a peace settlement. In marked contrast to similar peace efforts in Central America and the Caribbean, U.S. diplomacy conspicuously avoided taking a leading role and accepted that the South American powers bordering Paraguay should exercise the most influence.

PARIS PEACE CONFERENCE (1919–1920). International conference, also known as the Versailles Conference, to discuss the ending of **World War I** and the peace settlement. The United States was represented at the peace conference by President **Woodrow Wilson** who as the leader of one of the "Big Four" great powers exercised an important role in the proceedings. Celebrated for his "Fourteen Points," Wilson took a close and active involvement in discussions to reshape Europe and avoid future war. He showed, however, little interest in Latin American concerns.

The Latin American nations that had declared war on or severed relations with **Germany** participated by right in the conference. However, they found themselves relegated to a very subordinate role in the proceedings. They all welcomed the proposal to create a new world organization to be known as the **League of Nations**, seeing this as not only an affirmation of their belief in the equality of nation states but also an opportunity to offset the preeminent political influence of the United States in the **Western Hemisphere**.

PAZ ESTENSSORO, VÍCTOR (1907–2001). Bolivian political leader and three-time president from 1952 to 1956, 1960 to 1964, and 1985 to 1989. Trained as a lawyer and economist, Paz was one of the founders of the left-wing **National Revolutionary Movement (MNR)** in 1941. Forced into political exile in **Argentina** in 1946, he returned to **Bolivia** in 1952 after the MNR seized political power in a violent uprising. As president, Paz pursued a revolutionary policy that included major land reform and the nationalization of the foreign-owned tin companies. By offering financial compensation to the American companies, however, Paz avoided conflict with the U.S. government. In fact, the **Dwight Eisenhower** administration agreed to continue programs of U.S. financial aid, including substantial purchases of Bolivian tin.

Paz stood down from the presidency in 1956 because the Bolivian Constitution stated that serving presidents were ineligible for consecutive terms of office. Paz won the next presidential election in 1960 and secured a revision of the Constitution to permit his reelection in 1964. Growing political and economic crisis, however, resulted in a military coup in November 1964. After a period of exile in **Peru**, Paz returned to Bolivia in 1971. At the age of 77, he won the presidential election in 1985. A feature of his presidency in terms of diplomatic relations was his stated desire to cooperate with the United States in interdicting the movement of illegal narcotics and engaging in joint paramilitary operations to destroy the cultivation of cocaine at its source in rural areas of Bolivia. As a result, among South American countries, Bolivia was the leading recipient of U.S. financial aid. *See also* NARCOTICS TRAFFICKING.

PEACE CORPS. A U.S. agency designed to aid developing countries. During his campaign for the presidency in 1960, **John F. Kennedy** spoke of devising a means of sending young Americans overseas to assist economic development in the Third World. In doing so, they would be acting as personal ambassadors for their country. Early in his administration in March 1961, Kennedy secured congressional funding to create the Peace Corps. The aim of the agency was to attract volunteers who would serve for two years on developmental projects in Africa, Asia, and Latin America.

By the end of 1961, 750 volunteers had been assigned to programs in countries all over the world, including **Brazil**, **Chile**, and **Colom-**

bia in Latin America. The Peace Corps subsequently continued to attract thousands of volunteers, and its activities were extended to cover most Latin American countries. Although part of Kennedy's strategy to "win the minds" of the people of the Third World in the battle against the forces of international communism in the **Cold War**, the young volunteers representing the Peace Corps attracted more praise than criticism in their host countries. Their personal efforts in aiding economic and social development and in trying to learn about and adapt to local conditions gave the Peace Corps a positive image in Latin America and helped to counter anti-American sentiment. *See also* AGENCY FOR INTERNATIONAL DEVELOPMENT (AID).

PEDRO II, EMPEROR OF BRAZIL (1825–1891). Emperor of **Brazil** from 1840 to 1889. On reaching the official age of majority in 1840, Pedro became the second emperor of Brazil and ruled until 1889. Although he had relatively little contact with the United States, Pedro acquired a positive image among Americans. During the American Civil War (1861–1865), he had privately sympathized with the cause of the Union. He was also rare among Latin American leaders of the 19th century in actually making a personal visit to the United States. Although he was received at the White House by President **Ulysses S. Grant**, Pedro's visit in 1876 was not for political reasons but to attend the Centennial Exhibition at Philadelphia and indulge his passion for discovery and scientific knowledge. At Philadelphia, Americans were intrigued and impressed by the tall, fair-complexioned, blue-eyed Brazilian who could speak and understand English and preferred to dress in a plain black suit. The U.S. press affectionately called him "the Yankee Emperor." Pedro was overthrown in a military coup on November 15, 1889, and left Brazil for exile in **France**. Americans enthusiastically welcomed the creation of the Brazilian republic, but official diplomatic recognition by the United States was delayed until January 1890 by a desire to soften the blow for the former but still much-admired Brazilian emperor.

PERÓN, JUAN DOMINGO (1895–1974). Argentine political leader and president from 1946 to 1955 and 1972 to 1974. Perón was one of the junior army officers who seized political power in **Argentina** in 1943. As secretary of labor and social welfare, he cultivated close links with labor unions and industrial workers who were popularly know as "descamisados" (the shirtless). After his arrest and imprisonment in 1945, mass demonstrations of descamisados in Buenos Aires forced the ruling generals to release Perón and allow him to be a candidate for the presidency in 1946. Regarding Perón as a fascist and sympathizer of the Nazis, the United States sought unsuccessfully to prevent his election. Two weeks before the election, the **State Department** released a document known as the "Blue Book" detailing Perón's wartime collusion with the Nazis. But the action was condemned as blatant interference in Argentine domestic affairs. It only provoked nationalist and anti-American sentiment and contributed to Perón's electoral victory.

As president, Perón pursued a nationalistic foreign policy that stressed Argentina's political and economic independence from foreign influence, including that of the United States. In effect, he echoed the sentiments of several previous Argentine political leaders in criticizing the American capitalist system. Perón also challenged the political preeminence of the United States in the **Western Hemisphere** by his attempt to persuade Latin American nations to follow Argentina's policy of adopting what he described as the "third position" between capitalism and communism. After securing reelection in 1951, increasing economic difficulties led to Perón seeking loans from the United States and adopting a more conciliatory foreign policy. He was overthrown in a military coup in 1955 and went into exile in **Spain**. Perón returned to Argentina in 1972 and served as president until his death in 1974. *See also* BRADEN, SPRUILLE (1894–1978).

PERSHING, JOHN J. (1860–1948). American general. A career army officer, Pershing served in the **Spanish-American War** (1898) and had experience of fighting insurgents in the Philippines. In March 1916, he was given command of 6,000 American troops and instructed by President **Woodrow Wilson** to go into northern Mexico to pursue and capture the Mexican revolutionary leader **Francisco "Pancho" Villa**. The action was in retaliation for an earlier armed incursion by Villa across the border into Columbus, New Mexico. In January 1917, after almost a year of fruitless pursuit that had taken him 400 miles into Mexican territory, Pershing gave up his attempt to apprehend Villa.

Pershing later gained distinction as the commander of the American Expeditionary Force that fought in France during **World War I**. After the war, he carried out various tasks for the U.S. government, including acting as a U.S. commissioner to organize a plebiscite to resolve the **Tacna-Arica dispute** between Chile and Peru.

PERU. A country facing the Pacific Ocean on the west coast of South America. Historically, American diplomacy has had little direct contact with Peru. The notable exception was during the **War of the Pacific** (1879–1884) and the resulting **Tacna-Arica dispute** over possession of Tacna and Arica. In the war, Peru suffered a number of military reverses, culminating in the Chilean occupation of Lima in January 1881. The conclusion of peace terms proved difficult because of **Chile**'s insistence on the cession of the southern Peruvian provinces of Tacna and Arica. The United States became diplomatically involved in moves to end the war because Secretary of State **James G. Blaine** suspected that **Great Britain** was secretly supporting Chile to gain special favors for British business interests. Peru was delighted when Blaine declared his opposition to the cession of any territory and sought to put diplomatic pressure on Chile to make concessions to Peru by proposing the holding of a Pan-American peace conference in Washington to discuss peace terms. Blaine's initiative, however, was repudiated by his successor, **Frederick Frelinghuysen**. In the process, Peru was diplomatically isolated. A peace settlement was eventually concluded in 1883 between the Chileans and the Peruvians without the mediation of or even consultation with the United States. Peru secured the withdrawal of Chilean troops but at the price of ceding Tacna and Arica to Chile.

Peru subsequently contested Chile's control of the provinces and argued that the cession had been intended to be a temporary arrangement. Unsuccessful attempts were regularly made by Peruvian diplomats in Washington to persuade the United States to intervene on Peru's behalf. In 1922, both countries accepted President **Warren Harding**'s offer of good offices. The result was a conference in Washington at which it was agreed to hold a plebiscite under U.S. supervision. In attempting to organize a plebiscite, American diplomats were frustrated by local objections. Like the War of the Pacific, American diplomatic involvement essentially proved to be a divisive factor and consequently an obstacle to reaching a peace settlement. In April 1929, after the conclusion of direct negotiations between themselves, the Chilean and Peruvian governments announced a settlement in which Chile retained Arica but returned Tacna to Peru.

During the 1960s, relations between the United States and Peru were strained by growing criticism over the extent of the control exercised over Peru's oil fields by the U.S.-owned International Petroleum Company (IPC). The decision of President **Belaúnde Terry** to reach a financial arrangement that did involve the payment of back taxes contributed to his overthrow in a military coup in 1968. The new military government headed by President **Juan Velasco Alvarado** nationalized IPC on the ground that the company had made excessive profits over many decades and owed $600 million in back taxes to the Peruvian state. Velasco resisted U.S. diplomatic pressure by successfully appealing to neighboring South American governments for support. He also pursued an independent foreign policy that resulted in the negotiation of a financial loan from the **Soviet Union**. In addition, he granted official recognition to communist China in 1971 and renewed diplomatic relations with **Cuba** in 1972. American officials, however, did not believe that Peru would become "another Cuba" or that Velasco was as dangerous a geopolitical threat as Chilean President **Salvador Allende** because it was known that the military government was strongly anticommunist. Despite making initial protests against Velasco's action and the withdrawal of programs of financial assistance, the U.S. government proved willing to accept a compromise settlement in 1974 that provided IPC with an agreed amount of financial compensation. *See also* GARCÍA PÉREZ, ALÁN (1949–).

PEURIFOY, JOHN E. (1907–1955). American diplomat. While ambassador to Greece from 1950 to 1953, Peurifoy openly demonstrated the abrasive anticommunist style that was often a feature of American diplomacy during the early years of the **Cold War**. In October 1953, he was appointed ambassador to **Guatemala** as part of the **Dwight Eisenhower** administration's policy of exerting diplomatic pressure on Guatemalan President **Jacobo Arbenz** to remove alleged communists from his inner circle of advisers. After a lengthy private meeting with Arbenz in December 1953, Peurifoy informed the **State Department** that their suspicions of Arbenz's procommunist ideological leanings were entirely justified. The information strengthened the determination of the Eisenhower administration to remove Arbenz from office. When this was achieved by **Operation PBSUCCESS** in June 1954, Peurifoy played an important and forceful role in ensuring that the senior Guatemalan military accepted the pro-American colonel **Castillo Armas** as the new president of Guatemala.

PINOCHET UGARTE, AUGUSTO (1915–). Chilean general and president from 1973 to 1990. A career army officer, Pinochet rose to become commander in chief of the Chilean army in 1973. He was a leading member of the military junta that organized a coup that overthrew the government of President **Salvador Allende** on September 11, 1973. Pinochet quickly established his ascendancy in the junta and became president in June 1970, a position that he held until 1990. Claiming that the nation was threatened by terrorism and communist insurgency, the Pinochet regime pursued a policy of systematic political repression that resulted in the arrest, torture, execution, and "disappearance" of thousands of Chileans who were identified as opponents and critics of the regime. At the same time, he reversed the socialist policies of Allende and openly lauded the free-enterprise capitalist ideas of the United States, especially those associated with economists trained at the University of Chicago and popularly referred to as "the boys from Chicago." The resulting improvement in the economy was attributed to the implementation of these ideas and contributed to a rise in support for Pinochet from the Chilean middle classes.

In the United States, the **Richard Nixon** administration was very pleased with the overthrow of Allende and regarded the event as an important victory for the West in the **Cold War** with the **Soviet Union**. President Richard Nixon and Secretary of State **Henry Kissinger**, therefore, welcomed the new military government and gave diplomatic and financial support while carefully avoiding making public comments on its increasingly repressive and authoritarian nature. American critics of Pinochet claimed that the Nixon administration had been directly involved in organizing the 1973 coup, a suspicion that was investigated by the **Church Committee** but has never been fully substantiated. The image in the United States of Pinochet, however, was steadily damaged by public revelations of his regime's excessive brutality in the immediate aftermath of the 1973 coup and also the death in suspicious circumstances of a Chilean political exile, **Orlando Letelier**, in Washington in 1976.

After Pinochet left presidential office in 1990, he continued to be a politically controversial and divisive figure both in Chile and overseas. In October 1998, he visited **Great Britain** for medical treatment and was arrested on a warrant from a Spanish judge that he be extradited to Spain to face charges of torturing Spanish nationals who had been resident in Chile at the time of the 1973 coup. In March 2000, Pinochet was eventually released for medical reasons and allowed to leave Britain and return to Chile. *See also* DIRTY WAR.

PLATT AMENDMENT (1901). A provision giving the United States a right to intervene in Cuban domestic affairs. In order to maintain political stability in **Cuba** in the aftermath of the **Spanish-American War** (1898) and at the instigation of Secretary of War **Elihu Root**, the U.S. Senate passed an amendment sponsored by Senator Orville H. Platt of Connecticut in February 1901 assigning the U.S. government the right of intervention to maintain political stability in Cuba and thereby preserve Cuban independence. The amendment was subsequently approved by a narrow vote of the Cuban Constitutional Convention and subsequently incorporated into the Cuban Constitution.

The right of intervention under the Platt Amendment was exercised first by President **Theodore Roosevelt** when he dispatched U.S. troops to Cuba in 1906. Although the Platt Amendment specifically applied to Cuba, Latin American critics of U.S. policy condemned "Plattismo" as a symbol of Yankee arrogance and oppression with direct links to the **Roosevelt Corollary** to the **Monroe Doctrine** and **dollar diplomacy**. The amendment was eventually abrogated in 1934 as part of **Franklin D. Roosevelt**'s **Good Neighbor Policy**. *See also* ARMED INTERVENTIONS.

POINSETT, JOEL ROBERTS (1779–1851). American diplomat. Poinsett served as special agent to **Chile** and Buenos Aires from 1811 to 1815. In 1822, he was sent to **Mexico** by President **James Monroe** to report on the political stability of the empire established by

Augustín de Iturbide. In 1825, Poinsett was appointed as the first U.S. minister to Mexico. Poinsett was active in promoting American political and commercial influence and regarded **Great Britain** as a major rival. However, his direct involvement in internal Mexican politics provoked local anti-American feeling and resulted in his recall to the United States in 1829. Poinsett's attitude of superiority and forceful behavior was a characteristic style that many American diplomats serving in Latin America adopted during the 19th century. Instead of cultivating friendly relations, it served to stimulate Latin American resentment toward the United States.

POLK, JAMES K. (1795–1849). American political leader and president from 1845 to 1849. Born in North Carolina, Polk moved to Tennessee, where he became a lawyer and Democratic congressman from 1825 to 1839. Elected president in 1844, he was intent on expanding the territory of the United States to include **Texas**, Oregon, and California. In his Annual Message to Congress on December 2, 1845, he warned European powers not to establish future colonies in what he called the "North American continent." In so doing, Polk not only affirmed the idea of America's **Manifest Destiny** but also drew public attention to the similar statement of the separation of the New World from the Old World made by President **James Monroe** in 1823. Polk's territorial ambitions also contributed to political tension with **Mexico** and eventually war in 1846. The resulting American military victory secured considerable territorial gains for the United States. In 1848, Polk revived public interest once more in the **Monroe Doctrine** when he sent a Special Message to the U.S. Congress stating that the United States would oppose the transfer of **Yucatán** to a European power.

PREBISCH, RAÚL (1901–1985). Argentine economist. As a leading economist and executive secretary from 1948 to 1963 of the **United Nations Economic Commission for Latin America (UNECLA or ECLA)**, Prebisch studied and expounded theories of economic development. He argued that the capitalist system had encouraged Latin American economies to stress exports of primary products while importing relatively more expensive machinery and capital goods. While this had been greatly to the economic benefit of First World countries such as the United States, the result for Third World countries such as those in Latin America had been unbalanced economic growth and an unhealthy state of dependency on the world economy. While Prebisch was a strong advocate of the adoption of economic plans designed to promote import substitution and restrict imports, he also recommended policies to encourage Latin American economic cooperation and integration. Critics of U.S. policy toward Latin America used his ideas to explain and condemn what they regarded as the inherently exploitative nature of U.S. imperialism. After leaving ECLA in 1963, Prebisch became head of the UN Conference on Trade and Development.

PUNTA DEL ESTE CONFERENCE (1961). Inter-American conference to discuss program of economic development. Acting on President **John F. Kennedy**'s initiative for an **Alliance for Progress**, a conference of hemispheric leaders met in August 1961 at Punta del Este, **Uruguay**, to discuss the proposal in more detail. Although the United States had only very recently attempted to overthrow the Cuban government by supporting a covert military operation at the **Bay of Pigs**, **Cuba** agreed to send a delegation headed by **Ernesto "Che" Guevara**. The conference resulted in the Charter of Punta del Este, which stated the aims of the alliance as the promotion of economic and social development leading to the achievement of self-sustaining growth. To help reach these goals, the United States agreed to a commitment to provide all the nations of Latin America, though excluding Cuba, the substantial sum of $20 billion in aid over a period of 10 years.

– Q –

QUADROS, JANIO (1917–1992). Brazilian political leader and president in 1961. A former mayor of the city of São Paulo and state governor, Quadros was elected president in 1960 as a political outsider dedicated to providing honest and efficient government. Contemporaries drew similarities between the political platforms offered by Quadros and that of **John F. Kennedy**, who also won a presidential victory in 1960. As president, Quadros announced radical changes in his country's foreign policy with a new stress on cultivating close economic and cultural links with the nations of the Third World, especially the newly independent African countries. Moreover, in what was interpreted as a calculated move away from **Brazil**'s traditional policy of close political alignment with the United States, he expressed sympathy for the revolutionary regime that had been recently established in **Cuba** by **Fidel Castro**. Despite diplomatic pressure from the Kennedy administration, Quadros refused to support American policies to isolate Cuba. Quadros suddenly resigned on August 25, 1961, and provoked a political crisis over his succession. A compromise was effected in which Vice President **João Goulart** became president. Despite his brief tenure of office from January to August 1961 and his controversial decision to resign presidential office, Quadros was widely respected in Latin America for having sought to pursue an independent foreign policy.

– R –

REAGAN, RONALD (1911–2004). American political leader and president from 1981 to 1989. Born in Illinois, Reagan moved to California, where he became a well-known Hollywood film star before entering politics and winning election as governor of California in 1966. He won the Republican presidential nomination in 1980 and went on to win the presidential election and to secure reelection in 1984. As president, Reagan exerted a considerable personal impact on **Cold War** politics. He took office in 1981 deeply distrustful of communism and holding strong views about America's duty to act as the leader of the "free world." In what came to be known as the **Reagan Doctrine**, he pledged support for those fighting for liberation against the tyranny of communism. The implementation of the doctrine aroused considerable controversy, especially the policy of giving covert support to the **Contras** in **Nicaragua**. Critics, both in the United States and in Latin America, argued that Reagan's policies were too confrontational. Some Latin American leaders independently sought a diplomatic solution to the **Central American crisis** in the form of the **Arias Peace Plan** and gained Reagan's assent only when his political standing in the United States was seriously undermined by the aftermath of the **Iran-Contra affair**.

Reagan was determined to defeat perceived communist expansion as he demonstrated by his dispatch of U.S. troops to overthrow the Marxist government of Grenada in 1983. During his presidency, the United States recaptured the sense of national self-confidence and international purpose that had been severely undermined by the traumatic experiences of the Vietnam War and the Watergate political scandal. Indeed, his supporters later claimed that it was his strong and farsighted leadership that was primarily responsible for bringing about the collapse of the **Soviet Union** and ending the Cold War. *See also* CONTADORA GROUP; SANDINISTAS; SHULTZ, GEORGE P. (1920–).

REAGAN DOCTRINE. A popular term used to describe the anticommunist policy of the **Ronald Reagan** administration (1981–1989). Speeches expressing hostility to communism and criticism of the Soviet Union were principal features of Ronald Reagan's presidency. In 1985, he publicly praised the activities of "freedom fighters" who were seeking to overturn pro-Soviet regimes in the Third World, especially in Afghanistan and **Nicaragua**. The president's positive assertion of the universality of Western democracy and moral values were historically in keeping with the ideas of the **American Revolution** and became popularly known as the "Reagan Doctrine."

Reagan, however, was mindful of the military and political lessons of the Vietnam War and avoided the direct deployment of American troops overseas as had occurred in Vietnam. Instead, he preferred "low-intensity conflict" that involved mainly the **Central Intelligence Agency (CIA)** in covertly equipping and training anticommunist forces such as the **Contras** in Central America. *See also* KIRKPATRICK, JEANE (1926–); SANTA FE REPORT (1980).

RECIPROCAL TRADE AGREEMENTS. Economic policy favored by the United States. During the late 19th century, there was frequent discussion in the United States of how to expand trade with Latin America. One idea was the negotiation of reciprocal trade agreements with individual Latin American nations. Reciprocity, however, normally entailed a mutual reduction in tariff duties and traditionally met with opposition in the U.S. Congress, where powerful political and business interests favored the policy of tariff protection for American manufacturers. A political compromise was effected in

1890 when Republican leaders in Congress responded to requests from President **Benjamin Harrison** and Secretary of State **James G. Blaine** and included a reciprocity amendment in the McKinley Tariff Bill, which became law on October 1, 1890. The amendment empowered the president to negotiate reciprocal commercial agreements with foreign nations by executive action and without requiring ratification by the U.S. Senate. In return for admission to an American list of goods free of import duty, countries would reciprocate by removing duties on their imports from the United States.

A treaty with **Brazil** was negotiated in early 1891, and similar arrangements followed with **Spain** (for **Cuba**), the Dominican Republic, **Guatemala**, **Honduras**, **El Salvador**, **Costa Rica**, **Nicaragua**, and **Great Britain** (for the British West Indies). The network of treaties never extended very far beyond the Caribbean and Central American countries, whose trade was already mostly with the United States. No treaties were concluded with either **Mexico** or any of the nations of Spanish South America, which stood to gain relatively little from admission to the limited American free list. The treaties were also in force for only a brief period of time because of the defeat of Harrison by **Grover Cleveland** in the 1892 presidential election. The Cleveland administration duly reversed the policy of tariff protection, including commercial reciprocity. Consequently, all the treaties were terminated by the passage of the Wilson Tariff Act in August 1894. Latin American complaints over the unilateral nature of the action were simply ignored.

The policy of reciprocity was revived during the 1930s at the time of the **Great Depression**. As one of several measures designed to stimulate domestic economic recovery, the U.S. Congress passed the Reciprocal Trade Agreements Act in June 1934. The 1934 Act was similar to the 1890 McKinley Tariff in authorizing the executive power to negotiate bilateral reciprocal trade agreements leading to mutual tariff reductions on imports. The policy was aimed mostly at the Latin American nations, which were also in the depths of economic depression and were known to be keen to conclude agreements to expand trade with the United States. The first treaty was signed with **Cuba** in August 1934. By 1939, the United States had concluded bilateral reciprocity arrangements with a total of 11 Latin American countries. The policy was successful not only in increasing

U.S. exports but also in making the countries signing the agreements more economically dependent than ever on the American market for their export growth. *See also* FOSTER, JOHN W. (1836–1917); HULL, CORDELL (1871–1955).

RIO BRANCO, BARON DO (1845–1912). Brazilian diplomat and foreign minister from 1902 to 1912. A career diplomat, the Baron do Rio Branco came to prominence during the 1890s because of his expertise on territorial claims, which he demonstrated in successful representations for his country in arbitration cases against Argentina in 1893 and France in 1898. In 1902, he was promoted to minister of foreign affairs and remained at this post until his death in February 1912. In marked contrast to many Spanish-American diplomats, Rio Branco regarded the United States as a benevolent guardian and even gave tacit approval to the **Roosevelt Corollary** that justified U.S. intervention to punish Latin American wrongdoing. Far from being a danger, he considered that the rising military power of the United States was a force for hemispheric peace because it promoted stability and served as a restraint on European aggression as exemplified by the **Venezuela Incident** (1902–1903). While still desiring friendly diplomatic relations with Europe, Rio Branco worked with the Brazilian ambassador in Washington, **Joaquim Nabuco**, to align Brazil's foreign policy as closely as possible to that pursued by the United States. The policy, known as the strategy of "approximation," achieved its most visible success in the choice of Rio de Janeiro to host the Third Pan-American Conference in 1906 and the decision of Secretary of State **Elihu Root** to attend the meeting. Claiming the support of the United States, Rio Branco asserted Brazil's claim to leadership of the southern continent. This inevitably heightened rivalry and tension between Brazil and **Argentina**. However, when Rio Branco looked to Washington for diplomatic support against Argentina, it was not forthcoming. The United States wished to appear evenhanded and was not willing to show any special favoritism to Brazil. Although Rio Branco was disappointed with the results of the policy of approximation, he was credited with establishing the tradition in Brazilian diplomacy of seeking close relations with the United States, often referred to as "the unwritten alliance."

RIO TREATY (1947). A collective security agreement also known as the Rio Pact and formally titled the **Inter-American Treaty of Reciprocal Assistance**. At the 1945 **Chapultepec Conference**, it was agreed that hemispheric relations should be strengthened by establishing a formal military alliance after the end of **World War II**. In 1947 at the Pan-American Conference held in Rio de Janeiro, the Inter-American Treaty of Reciprocal Assistance was approved by the United States and 20 Latin American countries. The treaty established a regional system of collective security that became popularly known as the Rio Treaty or Rio Pact. Article 3 of the treaty followed the **Declaration of Havana** (1940) and also served as a model for the 1949 North Atlantic Treaty Organization in declaring that an external attack against any member state would be considered as an attack against all the signatories to the treaty.

In the case of the Rio Treaty, however, a response to an external attack was not automatic and required the convening of a meeting of foreign ministers and a two-thirds majority vote in favor of retaliatory action. In effect, this was an important safeguard for the Latin American countries because it put in place a consultative procedure that was meant to constrain the United States from undertaking unilateral armed intervention. Nevertheless, the military role of the United States was acknowledged as crucial. Although the treaty was a pact rather than an alliance, it represented a commitment given by the United States to take primary responsibility for military action to defend the **Western Hemisphere** from external attack. It thereby demonstrated that the Latin American countries recognized the vital importance of military collaboration with the United States for their own national security. The treaty was formally invoked by the United States on several occasions, notably during the **Cuban Missile Crisis** in 1962 and after the September 11 terrorist attacks in 2001.

RÍOS MONTT, JOSÉ EFRAÍN (1926–). Guatemalan general and president from 1982 to 1983. A career military officer, Ríos Montt studied at the **School of the Americas** in **Panama** and throughout his military and political career adopted a staunch anticommunist attitude that was reinforced by his born-again evangelical Christianity.

In March 1982, he led a military coup in which he overthrew the government and assumed the presidency. Proclaiming war on communism, Ríos Montt launched a ruthless military campaign in the countryside that killed thousands of Guatemalan peasants and made many more thousands homeless. In August 1983, Ríos Montt was forced out of office by a military coup.

During his period as president, Ríos Montt was given economic and military assistance by the **Ronald Reagan** administration, which regarded him as an important ally in its struggle to defeat the communist guerrillas in Central America. Despite charges of having abused human rights to the extent of committing genocide against the Indian population, Ríos Montt remained active in Guatemalan politics. He was elected to the Guatemalan Congress and attempted to run for president in national elections on several occasions. *See also* CENTRAL AMERICAN CRISIS; GUATEMALA.

RIVADAVIA, BERNARDINO (1780–1845). Argentine political leader and president of Argentina from 1826 to 1827. While he stressed the importance of Argentina developing friendly political and commercial relations with **Great Britain**, Rivadavia was unusual among Latin American leaders in also showing awareness of the potential hemispheric importance of the United States. He publicly praised **Monroe**'s message to Congress in 1823 and ordered translations to be made and sent to the neighboring governments of **Chile**, **Peru**, and **Colombia**. *See also* MONROE DOCTRINE.

ROCKEFELLER, NELSON A. (1908–1979). American political leader, philanthropist, and vice president from 1974 to 1977. As a young man Nelson Rockefeller developed a personal and lifelong interest in Latin America. During the 1930s, he studied the Spanish language and made several visits to the region. At the start of **World War II**, he urged President **Franklin D. Roosevelt** to formulate programs of economic aid to Latin America in order to alleviate poverty and counter the spread of Nazi influence in the region. This resulted in the establishment of the Office of Inter-American Affairs in 1940, renamed the **Office of the Coordinator of Inter-American Affairs (OCIAA)** in 1941. Rockefeller held the post of coordinator from 1941 until December 1944. Under his direction, the OCIAA not only disseminated information and promoted cultural activities but also instituted important aid programs in agriculture, transportation, and public health. From December 1944 to August 1945, Rockefeller served as assistant secretary of state for American republic affairs. After 1945, he held several important political offices, including governor of New York from 1959 to 1973 and vice president in the Ford administration from 1974 to 1977. Rockefeller also continued to serve in official and unofficial capacities as an expert adviser on Latin American affairs to a number of Republican presidents, including **Richard Nixon**, who appointed him to head a commission that visited Latin America, and prepared a major report in 1969 on U.S. policy toward the region. *See also* ROCKEFELLER REPORT (1969).

ROCKEFELLER REPORT (1969). A U.S. report on relations with Latin America. In 1968, the former governor of New York, **Nelson Rockefeller**, was selected by President-elect **Richard Nixon** to head a commission to visit Latin America and give recommendations for future directions in U.S. policy toward the region. The Rockefeller Report, which was published in 1969, advocated that the United States should give special attention to Latin America, especially in the provision of increased economic and military aid. The Nixon administration, however, gave little priority to Latin American affairs. It took little notice of the report and preferred instead to concentrate its foreign policy on improving relations with the Soviet Union and extricating the United States from the Vietnam War.

RODÓ, JOSÉ ENRIQUE (1871–1917). Uruguayan writer. The victory by the United States in the **Spanish-American War** (1898) signified the final removal of Spanish imperial power from the New World. As a result, Latin American nations suddenly felt isolated and vulnerable to the growing military and economic power and also the cultural influence of the Anglo-Saxon United States. The Latin American predicament was eloquently expressed by Rodó whose influential work *Ariel* was published in 1900. Echoing the warnings made earlier by the Cuban poet and patriot **José Martí**, Rodó likened the United States to "Caliban" a character taken from Shakespeare's play *The Tempest* and representing a monster that was respected for its great energy and strength but feared for its insensitivity and seemingly insatiable appetite for material expansion.

ROMERO, MATÍAS (1837–1898). Mexican diplomat. Romero was a lawyer who became a close friend of **Benito Juárez** and joined the Mexican ministry of foreign affairs in 1855. From 1859 to 1867, he represented **Mexico** in Washington first as secretary of legation and then as chargé d'affaires. He was especially successful in cultivating a good working relationship with Secretary of State **William H. Seward**. In 1867, Romero returned to Mexico to become secretary of the treasury, a post that he held until 1872 and then again from 1876 to 1880 and from 1892 to 1893. In accordance with President **Porfirio Díaz**'s policy of developing the Mexican economy, Romero welcomed foreign investment, especially from the United States. During this period, he continued to cultivate close contacts with American political and business leaders, notably ex-President **Ulysses S. Grant**, with whom he collaborated in railroad investments. Romero was also involved in several special diplomatic missions to the United States, including the negotiation of a commercial treaty (1882), and as a delegate to the **International American Conference** (1889–1890). In 1893, Romero was once again appointed Mexican minister to Washington, and in 1898, when relations were raised to ambassadorial rank, he became Mexico's first ambassador to the United States and the first Latin American diplomat to be accorded that status.

ROOSEVELT, FRANKLIN D. (1882–1945). American political leader and president from 1933 to 1945. Born in New York and representing the Democratic branch of the Roosevelt family, Franklin D. Roosevelt served as assistant secretary of the navy from 1913 to 1919 in the **Woodrow Wilson** administration and as governor of New York from 1928 to 1932. As president from 1933 to 1945, Roosevelt was admired for his personal magnetism and political shrewdness. In domestic policy, he launched the New Deal to combat the massive economic and social problems caused by the **Great Depression** of the 1930s. In foreign policy, Roosevelt followed the ideas of Woodrow Wilson and believed that the United States should pursue a more active role in world affairs. Seeking to improve the image of the United States in Latin America, he basically continued the conciliatory policy of his predecessor, **Herbert Hoover**, although it now acquired a new name as result of a sentence taken from Roosevelt's inaugural address as president of March 4, 1933, in which he referred to "the policy of the good neighbor."

Roosevelt's decision to send warships to **Cuba** and to interfere openly in Cuban political affairs during the first year of his presidency appeared more reminiscent of the **Big Stick** policy of his cousin, **Theodore Roosevelt**, than the concept of the "good neighbor." But Roosevelt soon redeemed his personal image in 1934 by publicly disavowing the policy of armed intervention in the affairs of sovereign states and by agreeing to abrogate the **Platt Amendment** (1901), which had given the United States a constitutional right to intervene in Cuba. Moreover, the president's personal attendance at the Special Pan-American Conference for the Maintenance of Peace held in Buenos Aires in December 1936 was greatly appreciated by Latin Americans as a sincere gesture of his friendly feeling and consideration.

The marked improvement in inter-American relations brought about by Roosevelt and the **Good Neighbor Policy** resulted in greater Latin American willingness to cooperate with the United States in fighting the fascist threat posed by **Germany** and Italy both before and during **World War II**. While Roosevelt valued the military and especially the economic contribution made by the Latin American allies to the prosecution of the war effort, his priorities were winning the European and Pacific military campaigns. As the war came to its close, Roosevelt gave little attention to Latin American issues and concentrated on establishing the **United Nations Organization (UN)** to promote and guarantee peace and prosperity not just for the **Western Hemisphere** but for all nations in the postwar world. Roosevelt died on April 12, 1945, only a few weeks before the end of the war in Europe. *See also* DECLARATION OF PANAMA (1939); HULL, CORDELL (1871–1955); LEND-LEASE; OFFICE OF THE COORDINATOR OF INTER-AMERICAN AFFAIRS (OCIAA); VARGAS, GETÚLIO (1883–1954).

ROOSEVELT, THEODORE (1858–1919). American political leader and president from 1901 to 1909. Born in New York, Theodore Roosevelt represented the Republican branch of the Roosevelt family. In 1898, he gave up his post as assistant secretary of the navy in the

William McKinley administration to volunteer for service with the "Rough Riders" in the **Spanish-American War** (1898). A popular war hero, Roosevelt was chosen as governor of New York in 1898. Elected vice president in 1900, he became president on the assassination of William McKinley in 1901. As president, he advocated a characteristically robust foreign policy that was popular and much applauded in the United States but aroused considerable alarm and fear in Latin America. For example, in order to prevent a repetition of European gunboat diplomacy that had occurred in the **Venezuela Incident** (1902–1903), Roosevelt declared in 1904 that the United States would intervene to ensure that Latin American governments did not refuse to meet their financial obligations to overseas creditors. This policy became known as the **Roosevelt Corollary** to the **Monroe Doctrine** or the policy of the **Big Stick**. The first example was the sending of American marines to restore order in the Dominican Republic in 1905.

A major aim of Roosevelt was to start construction of an isthmian canal, which he viewed as a means of not only stimulating U.S. trade but also promoting world civilization. He was angered by the refusal of the Colombian Senate to ratify the **Hay-Herrán Treaty** in 1903 and privately let it be known that he would welcome the creation of an independent **Panama**. Roosevelt gained notoriety in Latin America for his speedy recognition of the new Panamanian republic and also later for a speech delivered in 1911 in which he boasted that he had "taken" the **Panama Canal Zone** in 1903. While most Americans approved his action and believed that it brought peace, prosperity, and security to the Caribbean–Central American region, deep resentment against the United States was stirred among Latin Americans over what was regarded as Roosevelt's insensitive attitude and expansionist designs. *See also* BUNAU-VARILLA, PHILIPPE (1859–1940); DOLLAR DIPLOMACY; DRAGO DOCTRINE; HAY, JOHN (1838–1905); PANAMA CANAL.

ROOSEVELT COROLLARY. Presidential statement concerning the **Monroe Doctrine**. President **Theodore Roosevelt** was alarmed by the example of gunboat diplomacy employed by the European powers in the **Venezuela Incident** (1902–1903). In his Annual Message to the U.S. Congress on December 6, 1904, he declared that, according to the Monroe Doctrine, the United States had a duty to ensure order in the **Western Hemisphere** and that his government would act unilaterally if necessary to achieve this. Roosevelt was referring to the particular threat of external intervention posed by the nations of the Old World, but **Great Britain** and the European powers were not displeased by his statement. In fact, they welcomed what became known as the "Roosevelt Corollary" to the Monroe Doctrine or the policy of the **Big Stick** because it meant that the United States would act as a self-appointed policeman to ensure that Latin American countries, especially those located in the Caribbean and Central America, acted responsibly and, most important, continued to meet their financial obligations to foreign investors. The first example of this policy was Roosevelt's decision to send U.S. marines and financial supervisors to restore order in the Dominican Republic in 1905. Most subsequent interventions involved countries in the Caribbean, but marines were sent to **Nicaragua** on the Central American mainland in 1912. *See also* DOLLAR DIPLOMACY; DRAGO DOCTRINE.

ROOT, ELIHU (1845–1937). American diplomat and secretary of state from 1905 to 1909. Born in New York, Root was a successful corporate lawyer who joined the **William McKinley** administration in 1899 and served as secretary of war from 1899 to 1904. At the war department, he was closely involved in supervising affairs in **Cuba** and Puerto Rico and was regarded as the instigator of the **Platt Amendment** (1901). This interest in Latin American affairs was maintained after he was appointed secretary of state in 1905. In fact, Root showed a particular desire to change the negative image of the United States that was held by many Latin Americans. He stressed the importance of good manners and of cultivating friendly personal relations and urged officials at the **State Department** to show Latin American officials more personal attention and consideration than they had experienced in the past. Root set an example by establishing cordial relations with Latin American diplomats, especially Brazilian Ambassador **Joaquim Nabuco**. Also important was his decision to attend the Third Pan-American Conference at Rio de Janeiro in 1906, an action that was regarded as significant because it represented the first time that a serving secretary of state had actually left the United States on a diplomatic mission.

During his visit to Latin America, Root took the opportunity to deliver speeches underscoring the peaceful motives of American foreign policy toward the region. Root's attempts at reassurance, however, were undermined by his government's unilateral declaration of the **Roosevelt Corollary** to the **Monroe Doctrine** and its frequently aggressive interventionist policy in the Central American–Caribbean region. After leaving the State Department, he served as Republican senator for New York from 1909 to 1915. Root's many activities on behalf of the U.S. government and especially his work to promote international arbitration brought him considerable personal distinction including the award of the Nobel Peace Prize in 1912. *See also* DOLLAR DIPLOMACY.

ROWE, LEO S. (1871–1946). Born in Iowa and educated at the University of Pennsylvania, Rowe became a college professor and was elected president of the American Academy of Political and Social Science in 1902. A strong advocate of developing closer relations with Latin America, he was appointed to several inter-American commissions and briefly served in the **State Department** as chief of the Latin American Division. In 1920, he became director general of the **Pan-American Union (PAU)** and held this post until his death in 1946. While he was critical of U.S. **armed intervention** in Latin American affairs, Rowe believed that Latin America greatly benefited not only from trade with the United States but also from contact with American political and cultural ideas. Rowe's tenure of office at the Pan-American Union was for such a long period that, for his contemporaries, he came to personify **Pan-Americanism**.

RUSK, DEAN (1909–1994). American diplomat and secretary of state from 1961 to 1969. Born in Georgia, Rusk served in the U.S. Army during **World War II**. After the war, he held various posts in the Department of Defense and the **State Department**, including assistant secretary of state for Far Eastern affairs from 1950 to 1952. In 1961, he was appointed secretary of state in the **John F. Kennedy** administration. Rusk proved to be a capable diplomat and loyal servant to both President Kennedy and his successor, President **Lyndon Johnson**. He was consistent in recommending that the West stand firm against communist aggression. Rusk supported the **Bay of Pigs** operation intended to overthrow **Fidel Castro** in 1961 and, at first, favored a vigorous U.S. military response in the **Cuban Missile Crisis** (1962). With the notable exception of Cuba, however, he showed relatively little personal interest in Latin American affairs. At the end of the Johnson presidency in 1969, Rusk left the State Department and became a professor of international law at the University of Georgia.

RUSSIA. A Eurasian country. During the early 19th century, imperial Russia briefly posed a theoretical threat to the security of the **Western Hemisphere** as the leader of the **Holy Alliance** of European monarchs and also because of its claim over territory on the Pacific coastline of the North American continent extending from Alaska to Bodega Bay, located just north of San Francisco in California. Although not specifically addressed to Russia, the Annual Message to Congress delivered by President **James Monroe** on December 2, 1823, warned against European military intervention and the colonization of territory in the New World. Russian diplomats rejected Monroe's arguments but chose not to make them an issue of either public or private correspondence. This reflected the fact that their country had negligible political and commercial interests in Latin America and showed minimal diplomatic interest in the region throughout the 19th century.

– S –

SÁENZ PEÑA, ROQUE (1851–1914). Argentine political leader and president from 1910 to 1914. Along with his fellow Argentine delegate, Manuel Quintana, Roque Sáenz Peña was conspicuous in presenting an outspoken attitude during the **International American Conference** (1889–1890). Showing a proud and independent spirit that has often characterized Argentine diplomacy toward the United States, both delegates were critical of what they claimed were American attempts to control the proceedings and restrict debate on contentious issues. Far from endorsing U.S. desires for a New World isolated from the Old World, Sáenz Peña pointed out the vital importance of past, present, and future links with Europe not only for the benefit of **Argentina** but for the whole of Latin America. He eloquently challenged the U.S.

view of **Pan-Americanism** when he countered the popular slogan of "America for the Americans" with the plea of "Let America be for humanity." From 1910 until his death in 1914, Sáenz Peña was president of Argentina. *See also* WESTERN HEMISPHERE.

SALINAS DE GORTARI, CARLOS (1948–). Mexican political leader and president from 1988 to 1994. Despite a long history of awkward and unfriendly relations with its northern neighbor, President Carlos Salinas believed that economic contacts with the United States should be expanded because that country was **Mexico**'s single most important trading partner and supplier of capital investment. In 1990, he proposed the negotiation of a commercial arrangement between Mexico and the United States on the lines of the **Canada**–U.S. Free Trade Agreement of 1989. President **George H. W. Bush** welcomed the proposal and began discussions that generated considerable political controversy and opposition in the United States but eventually resulted in the signing of the **North American Free Trade Agreement (NAFTA)** in 1992.

SANDINISTA NATIONAL LIBERATION FRONT (FSLN). *See* SANDINISTAS.

SANDINISTAS. The popular name generally given to the **Sandinista National Liberation Front** (Frente Sandinista de Liberación Nacional [FSLN]), which ruled **Nicaragua** from 1979 to 1990. The FSLN was established in 1961 and took the name "Sandinista" from **Augusto César Sandino**, a celebrated Nicaraguan nationalist and anti-American hero of the 1920s and 1930s. The Sandinistas fought a guerrilla campaign against the authoritarian rule of **Anastasio Somoza** and eventually took power in 1979. The proclaimed intention of the Sandinistas to implement radical political and economic changes in Nicaragua based on the model of the **Cuban Revolution** aroused the hostility of the United States. Moreover, friendly relations were openly cultivated with **Cuba** and the **Soviet Union**, leading the **Ronald Reagan** administration to fear that a communist beachhead was being established in Nicaragua that, if unchecked, would lead to neighboring pro-American regimes falling like dominoes throughout the region. Consequently, a policy of destabilizing the Sandinista government was pursued. This included a combination of economic pressure and the financing of an army of Nicaraguan exiles known as the **Contras** to promote internal disorder. The Contras made little military impact on the Sandinistas, who not only remained politically popular but also maintained effective control of the national army. During the late 1980s, however, economic conditions considerably deteriorated so that the Sandinistas eventually lost political power after being defeated in national elections held in 1990. *See also* CHAMORRO, VIOLETA BARRIOS DE (1929–); CENTRAL AMERICAN CRISIS; ORTEGA SAAVEDRA, DANIEL (1945–).

SANDINO, AUGUSTO CÉSAR (1895–1934). Nicaraguan national hero. The dispatch of U.S. marines to **Nicaragua** by the **Calvin Coolidge** administration in 1926 and the decision to reinforce those forces in 1927 provoked local guerrilla resistance that was organized by the Nicaraguan political leader, Augusto César Sandino. Denouncing the U.S. marines as foreign invaders and barbarians, Sandino's cause acquired the proportions of the epic battle between Ariel and Caliban as depicted by **José Enrique Rodó**. While American officials condemned him as a bandit and a communist, Sandino took on the image of a national hero in Nicaragua and became a symbolic figure throughout Latin America for those critical of the American policy of military intervention.

So long as Sandino eluded capture and remained at large, the United States felt it necessary to maintain a sizable, expensive, and politically controversial military presence in Nicaragua. In 1929, the number of U.S. marines reached 5,000. The military burden was gradually reduced by training local Nicaraguan forces to form a National Guard (Gardia Nacional). American marines were eventually withdrawn from Nicaragua in January 1932. Sandino subsequently negotiated peace terms with the Nicaraguan government but was murdered in February 1934 on the orders of the commander of the National Guard, **Anastasio Somoza García**. Sandino's memory was revered in Nicaragua, and in 1961 his name was adopted in the title of the newly formed **Sandinista National Liberation Front** (Frente Sandinista de Liberación Nacional [FSLN]), which would go on to assume political power in Nicaragua in 1979.

SANTA ANNA, ANTONIO LÓPEZ DE (1794–1876). Mexican general and dictator of **Mexico**. From 1823 on, Santa Anna was involved in a succession of military coups. His imposition of a personal dictatorship on Mexico in 1834 provoked protest and rebellion, including the proclamation of the **Texas** Revolution in November 1835. Santa Anna marched north with the aim of crushing the rebellion. He acquired a reputation for brutality in the United States as a result of his victory over the Texans at the Alamo in San Antonio in March 1836. However, he was later defeated and captured by **Sam Houston** at the Battle of San Jacinto on April 21. In return for his release, Santa Anna agreed to the secession of Texas from the Mexican Union. Santa Anna once again led a Mexican army against American forces in 1846 during the **Mexican-American War** (1846–1848). He failed, however, to prevent the fall of the national capital to the Americans in September 1847.

SANTA FE REPORT (1980). Influential report on U.S. Latin American policy. The ideas underpinning the Latin American policy of **President Ronald Reagan** were considerably influenced by the views of the right-wing Council for Inter-American Security expressed in the "Report of the Committee of Santa Fe," which was published in 1980 during the presidential election year. The committee was comprised of L. Francis Bouchey, Roger Fontaine, David C. Jordan, Gordon Sumner Jr., and Lewis Tambs. The report noted the recent expansion of communism, especially throughout the Caribbean region, and argued that, in defense of its national security, the United States must challenge and reverse the advance of Soviet influence. This would be achieved by decisively rejecting the policies of accommodation associated with President **Jimmy Carter** and demonstrating instead a determination to confront and, where necessary, use U.S. military power to defeat the threat of international communism. The ideas were enthusiastically endorsed by officials in the Reagan administration and helped shape the policy that became known as the **Reagan Doctrine**. *See also* KIRKPATRICK, JEANE (1926–).

SARMIENTO, DOMINGO FAUSTINO (1811–1888). Argentine political leader, writer, and president from 1868 to 1874. As a political exile, Sarmiento traveled to Europe and made two visits to the United

States during the 1840s. In contrast to most Argentine political leaders, he openly admired the United States, its democratic system of government, and especially its educational achievements. When he became president in 1868, Sarmiento introduced into **Argentina** the progressive educational methods that he had personally experienced and praised while resident in New England. As a writer, Sarmiento's most famous work was *Facundo, o Civilización y Barbarie* (published in 1845 and later translated into English as *Life in the Argentine Republic in the Days of the Tyrants*).

SCHOOL OF THE AMERICAS. U.S. academy for military education. The School of the Americas was established by the United States in **Panama** in 1946 with the aim of providing military education for Latin American officers. In addition to developing professional skills and military efficiency, it was believed that training would help to promote democracy in the Western Hemisphere. Critics, however, regarded the school as a training ground for officers with political ambitions. The school acquired the nickname of the "School of Coups" because several of its former graduates, such as **Manuel Noriega** of Panama and **Ríos Montt** of Guatemala, were actively involved in organizing military coups. In addition, the school was viewed as a means by which the United States transmitted skills in counterinsurgency and in maintaining internal security that were employed by military government in suppressing human rights. The reputation of the school became so notorious that it was required to leave Panama under the provisions of the 1977 Panama Canal Treaty between the United States and Panama. In 1985, the school was relocated to Fort Benning, Georgia.

SCOTT, WINFIELD (1786–1866). American general. While most of the initial fighting in the **Mexican-American War** (1846–1848) took place in northern Mexico, a separate American army under Scott's command landed at and captured the port of **Veracruz** in March 1847. After a slow inland advance to Mexico City, the Mexican capital was stormed and occupied in September. An American army of around 10,000 troops defeated a Mexican force of 30,000 soldiers defending the city. It was an outstanding military success and a tribute to the tactical skill of General Scott.

SCRUGGS, WILLIAM L. (1836–1912). American diplomat. Born in Georgia, Scruggs held various diplomatic appointments in Latin America as minister to **Colombia** from 1873 to 1876 and 1882 to 1885 and to **Venezuela** from 1889 to 1892. Dismissed from the **State Department** on charges of bribery, Scruggs returned to the United States, where he acted as a lobbyist for the Venezuelan government to win American support in its long-standing boundary dispute with **Great Britain**. In October 1894, Scruggs published a pamphlet titled "British Aggressions in Venezuela or the **Monroe Doctrine** on Trial." The allegation that Britain had secret designs on seizing Venezuelan territory and thereby would be violating the Monroe Doctrine was a masterstroke that stimulated considerable U.S. interest in the dispute. The result was a diplomatic dispatch from Secretary of State **Richard Olney** to the British Foreign Office in July 1895 stating that the issue should be submitted to binding arbitration. In effect, Scruggs had been instrumental in transforming a remote and little-known boundary dispute into first a domestic political issue and then into an international crisis. *See also* CLEVELAND, GROVER (1837–1908); OLNEY MEMORANDUM (1895); VENEZUELA BOUNDARY DISPUTE (1895).

SEWARD, WILLIAM H. (1801–1872). American political leader and secretary of state from 1861 to 1869. Seward was a lawyer who represented New York in the U.S. Senate from 1849 to 1861, first as a Whig and then as a Republican. As secretary of state from 1861 to 1869, Seward supported the territorial expansion of the United States and was instrumental in negotiating the purchase of Alaska from imperial **Russia** in 1867. Seward also showed a close interest in the question of an isthmian canal. He notably abandoned the idea of an international canal expressed in the 1850 **Clayton-Bulwer Treaty** and favored instead an "American" canal, whose construction, operation, and ownership would be determined largely by the views of the U.S. government. A treaty to secure for the U.S. government the rights to build a canal in the isthmian region of **Panama** was negotiated with **Colombia** in 1869 just as Seward left office. The treaty, however, was not brought to a vote for ratification in the U.S. Senate. The policy of securing an "American" canal was pursued by Seward's successors and eventually resulted in the construction of the **Panama Canal**. *See also* WAR OF THE TRIPLE ALLIANCE (1865–1870).

SHULTZ, GEORGE P. (1920–). American economist, diplomat, and secretary of state from 1982 to 1989. A professor of industrial relations at the University of Chicago, Shultz served in the **Richard Nixon** administration as secretary of labor from 1969 to 1970 and secretary of the treasury from 1972 to 1974. After a period of working as president of the Bechtel Corporation, he returned to public office in 1982 when he was appointed secretary of state in the **Ronald Reagan** administration. Like President Reagan, Shultz was strongly anticommunist and endorsed the policy of supporting anti-Soviet movements in the Third World. He was particularly critical of the **Sandinistas** in **Nicaragua** and backed the policy of seeking to destabilize their regime with economic sanctions and covert military operations. In global politics, however, Shultz, favored diplomacy rather than confrontation with the **Soviet Union** and worked with Reagan to secure important arms control agreements. *See also* COLD WAR.

SOMOZA DEBAYLE, ANASTASIO (1925–1980). Nicaraguan political leader and president. The second son of **Anastasio Somoza García**, Somoza was appointed head of the National Guard in 1947. He was elected president in 1967 but acted like a dictator. Although disliked by the **Jimmy Carter** administration for his repressive rule, Somoza was supported in Washington by the well-funded "**Nicaragua** lobby," which dutifully argued that he was a staunch anticommunist and a long-standing friend of the United States. A combination of persistent American diplomatic pressure and a series of military defeats against the **Sandinistas** persuaded Somoza to resign and leave **Nicaragua** in July 1979. After a brief residence in Miami, Somoza chose to go into exile in **Paraguay**, where he was assassinated in 1980.

SOMOZA GARCÍA, ANASTASIO (1896–1956). Nicaraguan political leader and president. As commander of the National Guard, Somoza gave orders for the murder of **Augusto Sandino** in 1934. In 1936, he seized political power in a military coup and became president in 1937, a position he held continuously until his assassination in 1956. Although Somoza imposed what amounted to a brutal dictatorship in **Nicaragua**, he was able to cultivate friendly relations with the United States. In 1939, he visited Washington and was met at Union Station by President **Franklin D. Roosevelt** and later went to tea at the White House. In return for American financial and military aid, Somoza proved most cooperative in assisting the United States during **World War II** and later in supporting policies of anticommunism during the **Cold War**, notably providing military bases for the **Central Intelligence Agency (CIA)** to organize covert operations against Guatemalan President **Jacobo Arbenz** in 1954. *See also* FIGUERES FERRER, JOSÉ (1906–1990).

SOUTH ATLANTIC WAR (1982). A conflict between **Great Britain** and **Argentina** also known as the Falklands War. In April 1982, Argentina launched an unexpected military invasion of the **Falkland Islands** and seized possession of territory that had been under the colonial control of Great Britain since 1833. Great Britain sent a military task force of more than 100 ships to retake the islands, the first armed intervention by a European power in the **Western Hemisphere** since the **Venezuela Incident** (1902–1903).

Although it voted in favor of the British-sponsored **United Nations (UN)** Security Council Resolution 502 condemning Argentine aggression and calling for Argentine withdrawal from the islands, the **Ronald Reagan** administration initially adopted an evenhanded approach and offered mediation to secure a peaceful end of the crisis. Secretary of State **Alexander Haig** engaged in frantic and highly visible shuttle diplomacy between Washington, London, and Buenos Aires, but his claim to be evenhanded could not disguise the fact that the Reagan administration sympathized with Great Britain by being openly critical of Argentine aggression. This was made apparent when the United States imposed economic sanctions on Argentina. The British task force was also secretly supplied with U.S. military equipment and valuable intelligence information on the location of enemy forces. The Argentine invasion force was defeated in June, and Great Britain successfully recaptured the islands.

The South Atlantic War illustrated the predisposition of the United States during the **Cold War** to look at events everywhere in an East–West perspective and to attach much greater importance to aiding its European allies than its Latin American neighbors. While Latin American governments were opposed in principle to Argentina's employment of armed force to resolve a territorial dispute, they were alarmed by American support for what was essentially regarded as a reassertion of British colonialism in the region. They were also disturbed by the lack of consideration given to a Peruvian attempt at mediation and the evident ineffectiveness of the inter-American system in dealing with a regional dispute involving armed conflict with an external power. By stating that Security Council Resolution 502 calling for Argentine withdrawal should be implemented, the United States demonstrated an unaccustomed preference for action by the United Nations rather than the **Organization of American States (OAS)**. *See also* BELAÚNDE TERRY, FERNANDO (1912–2002).

SOVIET UNION. The superpower rival of the United States during the **Cold War**. During the Cold War, American officials constantly stressed the seriousness of the threat that the Soviet Union posed to the security of all the nations in the **Western Hemisphere**. In reality, the Soviet Union (and earlier imperial **Russia**) was a geographically remote power that had a history of minimal political and economic contact with Latin America. Only **Argentina**, **Mexico**, and **Uruguay** maintained official diplomatic relations with Moscow during the 1950s. Although the Soviet Union successfully established a beachhead in **Cuba** during the 1960s, the alarmist American predictions of a rapid and relentless Soviet advance throughout the Central American–Caribbean region proved to be incorrect. As demonstrated by the 1962 **Cuban Missile Crisis**, the Soviet Union did not want to fight a war over Cuba and recognized the Western Hemisphere as a well-established U.S. sphere of influence. Furthermore, it was evident that communism was regarded as an alien ideology by the strongly Catholic societies of Latin America.

Much to the relief of American officials, the Cuban example of armed struggle and enacting a socialist revolution was not successfully copied elsewhere in the hemisphere during the 1960s. Indeed, the failure of Cuba's attempts to "export revolution" to the mainland was most vividly illustrated by the capture and death of **Ernesto "Che" Guevara** in **Bolivia** in 1967. The communist threat revived when **Salvador Allende** became president of **Chile** in 1970 and also during the 1980s in the **Central American crisis**, but the involvement of the Soviet Union in terms of active political support and military and economic aid for guerrilla movements steadily diminished as the Cold War came to an end in 1991. Indeed, the sudden and severe curtailment of financial subsidies for Cuba contrasted markedly with the simultaneous desire to increase commercial links with the United States, a policy that was continued by the Russian Federation, which replaced the Soviet Union in 1991.

SPAIN. A European power. Spain's dramatic loss of its colonial empire and decline as an "American" power throughout the 19th century considerably assisted the rise of the United States to a position of political and military preeminence in the **Western Hemisphere**. Early in the 19th century, the **James Monroe** administration took advantage of Spain's economic difficulties to negotiate the **Adams-Onís Treaty** (1819) and acquire possession of Florida. By achieving victory in the **Spanish-American War** (1898), the United States finally brought an end to Spain's last colonial possessions in the New World by taking possession of Cuba and Puerto Rico. For the people of Spain, the war was regarded as "a disaster" and a humiliation for the Spanish race. Latin Americans shared the sense of humiliation and recognized that Spain's ejection from Cuba would lead to the development of the Central American and Caribbean region as an American sphere of influence. This mood was eloquently conveyed in the writings of **José Enrique Rodó** and **Rubén Darío**.

SPANISH-AMERICAN WAR (1898). A war between the United States and **Spain**. An armed revolt broke out in February 1895 inspired by the Cuban poet and patriot **José Martí** with the aim of achieving freedom for **Cuba** from Spain. A brutal colonial war ensued during which the United States proclaimed a policy of neutrality. In April 1898, President **William McKinley** informed the U.S. Congress that American military intervention was necessary to compel Spain to give up Cuba and bring peace to the island and its people. War between the United States and Spain officially began on April 21, 1898. Just over three months later, on August 12, the fighting was declared at an end. For Americans, it was called a "splendid little war." In fact, the American victories extended beyond Cuba to include Spain's other colonies of Puerto Rico, Guam, and the Philippines.

Going to war against Spain required the projection of American military power, both army and navy, beyond the continental borders of the United States. The subsequent victory not only demonstrated the impressive military power of the United States but also advanced the development of the Caribbean as an "American lake," a sphere of influence that U.S. presidents in the 20th century sought to insulate from foreign interference while seeking to dominate politically, militarily, and economically.

Although Latin American governments were generally critical of Spanish political repression in Cuba and adopted policies of neutrality, once American military intervention occurred, there was considerable private sympathy with Spain rather than the United States. Part of the reason was the long-standing tradition of regarding the United States as an expansionist and aggressive Anglo-Saxon power with particular designs on acquiring territory in the Central American–Caribbean region. Fear and distrust of the "Yankees" was the theme of *Ariel*, the influential work written by **José Enrique Rodó** and published in 1900. But not all Latin American opinion was hostile to the United States. **Brazil**, for example, adopted a conspicuously friendly and helpful attitude. Two warships were sold to the American navy, while ships of the U.S. fleet were allowed to take on fuel and refit in Brazilian ports during the war. Nevertheless, the initial denial of home rule to Cuba and Puerto Rico and the establishment instead of interim American military governments in those islands served only to confirm and harden anti-American sentiment in Latin America. This attitude was reinforced when Cuba became independent only after accepting the humiliating **Platt Amendment** (1901), which gave the United States a legal right of intervention in Cuban affairs. *See also* ARMED INTERVENTIONS; HAY, JOHN (1838–1905).

STATE DEPARTMENT. Department of the U.S. government responsible for the conduct of foreign affairs. The official in charge of the Latin American policy of the United States is the secretary of state. Diplomatic instructions in his name are dispatched from the State Department in Washington to the various American diplomats resident throughout the capitals and leading cities of the individual Latin American nations. For most of the 19th century, the United States was represented by diplomats with the rank of a minister. Latin

American postings were not generally regarded as attractive. They lacked the prestige of Europe and were relatively low paid. In 1898, relations with **Mexico** were upgraded to ambassadorial rank, and this status was gradually extended to other countries throughout the 20th century.

American officials serving in Latin America generally lacked diplomatic experience. They also lacked security of tenure because diplomatic appointments were an essential part of the spoils system and were regarded as a reward for political services. Moreover, the selection by the president of his secretary of state was heavily influenced by party politics and not diplomatic considerations. Few secretaries of state possessed diplomatic experience, let alone any personal interest or acquaintance with Latin American affairs.

Expertise was provided by the career officials at the State Department who staffed the Diplomatic Bureau in Washington. During the 20th century, political factors still remained a determining factor in the choice of the secretary of state. The State Department, however, became much more professional in terms of recruitment and training of its personnel. In 1909, the Diplomatic Bureau was organized into sections with administrative responsibility for particular geographical areas of the world. This resulted in the formation of a separate Latin American Division. During **World War II**, Latin American policy was also conducted by the Office of Inter-American Affairs, which was created in August 1940 and renamed in July 1941 the **Office of Coordinator of Inter-American Affairs (OCIAA)**. The Office of Inter-American Affairs was abolished after the end of the war in 1946. Meanwhile, in December 1944, the Bureau of American Republic Affairs had been created with an assistant secretary of state at its head. This was renamed the Bureau of Inter-American Affairs in 1949.

STIMSON, HENRY L. (1867–1950). American diplomat and secretary of state from 1929 to 1933. Born in New York City, Stimson became a lawyer and joined the Republican Party. He served as secretary of war in the **William H. Taft** administration. In 1927, Stimson was sent by President **Calvin Coolidge** to bring order between the conflicting factions in **Nicaragua** and arrange for elections to be held. Appointed secretary of state in 1929, he worked with President

Herbert Hoover to improve U.S. relations with Latin America and initiate what became later known as the **Good Neighbor Policy** during the presidency of **Franklin D. Roosevelt**. Seeking to bring a peaceful settlement of the **Chaco War** between **Bolivia** and **Paraguay** in 1932, Stimson secured agreement from all the Latin American governments, with the exception of Bolivia and Paraguay, to the "Stimson Doctrine," stating that territory acquired by force would not be recognized. Stimson left office in 1933. After a period of retirement, he returned to government service at a period of international crisis and served as secretary of war in the **Franklin D. Roosevelt** administration from 1940 to 1945.

SUMMITS OF THE AMERICAS. A series of meetings of heads of state of the nations of the **Western Hemisphere**. The first Summit of the Americas was held in Miami, Florida, in December 1994 and was attended by 34 heads of state, including President **Bill Clinton**. The summit was similar to the **Pan-American Conference System** in providing a forum for high-level discussion of current hemispheric issues ranging from the promotion of democracy to proposals for economic integration and the protection of the environment. Further summits to exchange ideas and discuss the progress made in achieving mutual political, economic, and social goals were held at Santiago de Chile in April 1998; at Quebec City, **Canada**, in April 2001; and at Mar del Plata, **Argentina**, in November 2005. *See also* FREE TRADE AREA OF THE AMERICAS (FTAA); TRADE.

SURINAME. The smallest independent country in South America bordered by Guyana to the west and by French Guiana to the east. Formerly known as Dutch Guiana, Suriname was a colony of Holland until achieving independence in 1975.

– T –

TACNA-ARICA DISPUTE. A territorial dispute between **Chile** and **Peru**. As a result of its military defeat in the **War of the Pacific** (1879–1884), Peru ceded its southern provinces of Tacna and Arica to Chile. Claiming that the cession was intended to be temporary,

Peru subsequently contested Chile's control of the provinces and demanded that a plebiscite be held to decide the issue. Chile refused. The impasse was eventually broken by American diplomacy. In 1922, both countries accepted President **Warren Harding**'s offer of good offices and agreed to attend a conference in Washington. The delegates agreed that the question should be settled by holding a plebiscite under U.S. supervision. A number of American officials, including General **John J. Pershing**, attempted to organize a plebiscite but were frustrated by Chilean and Peruvian objections. Finally, in April 1929, a satisfactory settlement was reached between the two governments in which Chile retained Arica but returned Tacna to Peru.

TAFT, WILLIAM H. (1857–1930). American political leader and president from 1905 to 1909. Born in Cincinnati, Ohio, Taft pursued a legal career and served as solicitor general in the **Benjamin Harrison** administration. His administrative skills led to appointment as governor of the Philippines from 1901 to 1904 and secretary of war from 1904 to 1908. Regarded as a protégé of President **Theodore Roosevelt**, Taft was nominated by the Republicans as their presidential candidate in 1908. It was during the Taft administration that **dollar diplomacy** became the proclaimed aim of U.S. foreign policy. This approach reflected the desire to support an American economy that was eager to take advantage of the growing commercial opportunities in Latin America and especially in the Middle America–Caribbean region. Taft was also prepared to enforce the **Roosevelt Corollary** as a means of assisting the maintenance of public order and thereby protecting endangered American economic interests. This was demonstrated by the dispatch of U.S. marines to **Nicaragua** in 1912. Taft was defeated in the 1912 presidential election and later became chief justice of the U.S. Supreme Court from 1921 to 1930. *See also* KNOX, PHILANDER C.

TAYLOR, ZACHARY (1784–1850). American general and president from 1849 to 1850. Born in Virginia and raised on the Kentucky frontier, Taylor became a career army officer who fought with distinction in the War of 1812 and later in campaigns against the Native American Indians. Ordered by President **James K. Polk** in 1846 to take command of U.S. forces stationed at the Rio Grande in Texas, Taylor became involved in a battle with Mexican troops that began the **Mexican-American War** (1846–1848). His military victories at Palo Alto and Buena Vista brought him national attention and popularity that led to his nomination by the Whigs in 1848 as their presidential candidate. His period as president was short lived and brought to an abrupt end by an attack of cholera in July 1850, but in terms of U.S. relations with Latin America, his administration was notable for securing the negotiation of the **Clayton-Bulwer Treaty** (1850).

TEXAS. A territory originally part of **Mexico** that was incorporated into the United States in 1845. During the 1820s, the frontier province of Texas in northern Mexico experienced steady encroachment by Americans, known as "Anglos," mostly taking the form of peaceful settlement under the leadership of Stephen Austin. The Anglo settlers formed successful agricultural communities and soon outnumbered the local Mexicans. Joining in the internal political struggle that was taking place in Mexico against the centralizing policy of the dictator **Antonio López de Santa Anna**, the Anglos proclaimed the Texas Revolution in November 1835. Their aim was outright secession from the Mexican Union. Despite an initial defeat at the Alamo in San Antonio in March 1836, the Anglos defiantly proclaimed the independent republic of Texas. On April 21, they achieved a notable military success at San Jacinto under the command of **Sam Houston**. Santa Anna was captured. In return for his release, he agreed to the secession of Texas from the Mexican Union. The new nation was officially recognized by the United States on March 3, 1837, and later by **Great Britain** and **France** but not by Mexico. Fearful of counterattack by Mexican forces and conscious of the difficulty of preserving their independent status as "the lone star republic," the Texans desired annexation to the United States.

During the 1840s, the issue of annexing Texas to the United States became fused with the powerful movement of people westward across the North American continent that was popularly known as **Manifest Destiny**. When Texas was eventually incorporated into the United States by a joint resolution passed by the U.S. Congress in March 1845, the Mexican government protested and refused to recognize the Rio Grande River as marking its new border with the

United States. Continued friction between Mexico and the United States resulted in the **Mexican-American War** (1846–1848), which ended in defeat for Mexico. The **Treaty of Guadalupe Hidalgo** in 1848 confirmed the Rio Grande River as the border between Mexico and the United States.

TORRES, MANUEL (1762–1822). Colombian diplomat. The first official act in which the United States conferred diplomatic recognition on the new governments of Latin America took place on June 19, 1822, when Secretary of State **John Quincy Adams** presented Manuel Torres to President **James Monroe** as chargé d'affaires from the Republic of Colombia. Torres was chosen because he had been resident in the United States since 1797 and was the only accredited Latin American diplomat currently serving in Washington.

TORRIJOS HERRERA, OMAR (1929–1981). Panamanian political leader and chief of government. An army officer, Torrijos took part in a military coup that overthrew President Arnulfo Arias in 1968. In the following year, Torrijos promoted himself to the rank of general and assumed personal control of the government with the title of "maximum chief," a position that he held until 1978. The major diplomatic achievement during his period of government was to bring international attention to focus on **Panama**'s desire for a revision of its canal arrangements with the United States. A special meeting of the **United Nations (UN)** Security Council was held in Panama City in March 1973 at which Torrijos delivered a well-received speech asserting that the United States had established a colony in the **Panama Canal Zone** and that this state of affairs was unacceptable in an age of decolonization. A resolution was overwhelmingly passed calling for a renegotiation of the 1903 **Hay-Bunau-Varilla Treaty** between the United States and Panama. The issue proved to be politically contentious in the United States, where critics described Torrijos as a dictator and not a democratically elected leader. However, the diplomatic strategy pursued by Torrijos proved successful. New **Panama Canal Treaties** were eventually signed and ratified in 1977–1978 providing for the transfer to Panama on December 31, 1999, of sole control of the canal. Torrijos died in a plane crash on August 1, 1981. *See also* CARTER, JIMMY (1924–); LINOWITZ REPORT (1976); PANAMA CANAL.

TRADE. Commercial exchange between the United States and the Latin American nations. The United States and the nations of Latin America have historically shown a desire for overseas commerce and the development of hemispheric economic relations. During the colonial period, the American colonists established a profitable local trade with the Spanish-American colonies in the Caribbean. Trade, however, mostly took the form of smuggling because of the determination of **Spain** to maintain the policy of mercantilism that sought to prevent foreigners from trading with its American empire.

The achievement of Latin American independence at the beginning of the 19th century marked the end of the Spanish mercantilist system so that the whole of the region was opened for the first time to contact with the world economy. A modest trade was developed between the United States and the new Latin American states based mainly on the export of foodstuffs and the import of raw materials. This pattern of trade continued for most of the 19th century and reflected the fact that the United States was an agrarian economy and very similar to the economies of the Latin America countries. By contrast, **Great Britain** was the "workshop of the world" and was able to supply what the new nations needed: cheap manufactured goods in large quantities and capital for economic and political purposes. American merchants competed with the British, but they compared badly in terms of the range of goods, shipping, and credit facilities that they offered.

American political constraints also frustrated the development of closer commercial relations with Latin America. This was particularly exemplified by the support in the U.S. Congress for a high protective tariff on imports into the United States and its reluctance to vote financial subsidies for American shipping lines to establish improved communications with Latin America. Changes occurred at the end of the 19th century when the emergence of the United States as an industrial economy with growing surplus capital combined with the ideas of **Pan-Americanism** to produce a policy of seeking closer economic relations with Latin America. Bipartisan political activity was reflected in the holding of the **International American Conference** (1889–1890) in Washington. With the notable exception of the Middle America–Caribbean region, American merchants made only relatively limited progress in South America because European nations, especially Britain, **France**, and **Germany**, were well established there and continued to be the leaders in foreign trade and capital **investment**.

A significant change in trading patterns occurred as a result of **World War I** (1914–1918). The serious economic dislocation to trade with Europe caused by the war provided a signal opportunity for the extension of the commercial influence of the United States throughout Latin America. This was particularly evident in South America, where American exports tripled and by 1920 amounted to more than 40 percent of all South American imports. Commercial advance was continued during the 1920s and was underscored by the emergence of a new pattern of trade in which the United States was preeminent. Whereas Britain's commercial dominance in Latin America had been based largely on the export of coal and textiles, the countries in the region now looked to the United States to supply the new products of the 20th century, such as automobiles, films, radio and telephone communications, petroleum products, and electrical goods.

During the 1930s, inter-American trade was adversely affected by the **Great Depression**. From 1929 to 1933, American exports to Latin America fell by more than 75 percent, while imports declined by more than 60 percent. Beginning with **Cuba** in August 1934, the United States concluded bilateral reciprocity arrangements with 11 Latin American countries by 1939. Trade was also expanded by the creation of the **Export-Import Bank (EXIM)** in February 1934. Although its share of the Latin American export trade actually declined during the 1930s, the United States remained the largest single market for Latin American goods, especially **oil** and commodities, such as copper and tin.

World War II (1939–1945) was similar to the previous world war in providing a major boost to hemispheric economic activity. Once again, Latin American countries were highly valued by Washington as suppliers of strategic raw materials and commodities. Moreover, the United States compensated for the drastic decline of the region's prewar trade with Europe by purchasing large quantities of Latin American agricultural produce. The fact that World War II had severely damaged the economies of Western Europe meant that the economic preeminence of the United States in the **Western Hemisphere**

remained unchallenged by foreign rivals until well into the 1960s. American exports to Latin America, however, began a period of relative decline during the 1970s because of the revival of the Western European economies, especially Germany, and the rise of Japan as one of the world's leading economic powers.

The remarkable growth of the American economy during the 1990s has reestablished the United States as the leading economic power in the Western Hemisphere. For most Latin American countries, the United States is still the largest single market for their exports and the main supplier of not only manufactured and capital goods but also access to capital investment and technological innovation. In response to the emergence of the globalization of economic activity and the appearance of powerful international trading blocs such as the European Union, there has been increasing interest in promoting hemispheric trade integration. A significant development has been the agreement of the United States along with **Canada** and **Mexico** to conclude the **North American Free Trade Agreement (NAFTA)** in 1992, which was ratified by the U.S. Congress in 1993. NAFTA was generally regarded as the first step in a process toward what would become a hemispheric free trade area. The idea of hemispheric commercial union, however, was raised at the International American Conference in 1889–1890 and has traditionally provoked divisive political debate.

Discussions toward establishing a **Free Trade Area of the Americas (FTAA)** have taken place at the series of summit meetings of heads of state in Miami (1994), Santiago de Chile (1998), Quebec City (2001), and Mar del Plata (2005). While there has been general support in principle for the concept of the FTAA, concern has been expressed, notably by President **Hugo Chávez** of Venezuela, that it will only increase the economic influence and preeminence of the United States. This view was reinforced by massive public protests and demonstrations that have been a feature of each summit since the meeting at Quebec City in 2001. *See also* DOLLAR DIPLOMACY; FORD MOTOR COMPANY; RECIPROCAL TRADE AGREEMENTS; SUMMITS OF THE AMERICAS; UNITED NATIONS ECONOMIC COMMISSION FOR LATIN AMERICA (UNECLA or ECLA).

TREATY OF GUADALUPE HIDALGO (1848). A treaty between the United States and **Mexico**. The signing of the Treaty of Guadalupe Hidalgo in February 1848 marked the official ending of the Mexican-American War (1846–1848). In the treaty, a vanquished Mexico accepted the Rio Grande River as its border with Texas and also ceded to the United States a vast portion of territory extending from the modern state of New Mexico to California. In return, the United States paid $15 million for what was equivalent to half the territory of the Mexican nation in 1848. Additional land was gained later by the **Gadsden Purchase** in 1853.

TRUMAN, HARRY (1884–1972). American political leader and president from 1945 to 1953. Born in Missouri, Truman joined the Democratic Party and served in the U.S. Senate from 1935 to 1944. Elected to the vice presidency in 1944, he succeeded to the presidency on **Franklin D. Roosevelt**'s death in April 1945. Truman had little experience of foreign affairs, but he loathed communism and believed that the **Soviet Union** was bent on world conquest and had to be resisted. In March 1947, he announced the Truman Doctrine and embarked on a policy of extending massive American economic aid to Western Europe in the form of the **Marshall Plan**. Although he attended the Pan-American Conference held at Rio de Janeiro in September 1947, Truman showed little personal interest in Latin American affairs. Despite his offer of a "Point Four" program of technical assistance in 1949, Latin American governments complained that there was no counterpart of the Marshall Plan for Latin America and that they had been allocated an inferior status to Western Europe. Consequently, Truman's request for a modest Latin American military contribution to the forces of the **United Nations (UN)** engaged in the **Korean War** (1950–1953) met with a very disappointing response. *See also* VARGAS, GETÚLIO (1883–1954); COLD WAR.

– U –

UNITED FRUIT COMPANY (UFCO). A large American corporation with extensive business interests in Central America. Established in Boston in 1899 as a merger between the Boston Fruit Company and the business interests of the entrepreneur **Minor C. Keith**, UFCO was involved primarily in the cultivation and export of bananas and owned large plantations in Central America, especially in **Guatemala**, where it was popularly and unflatteringly known as "the Octopus." In 1952, as part of the **Guatemalan Revolution**, President **Jacobo Arbenz** sought to implement schemes of radical agrarian reform based on the expropriation of uncultivated land of which UFCO owned large amounts. While the Guatemalan government offered UFCO $1 million in compensation, the American company declared that this was derisory because the market value of the land in question was at least $16 million. The dispute, however, had ramifications far beyond Guatemala because American diplomats suspected that the agrarian reform measure was being instigated by local communists. Moreover, UFCO mounted a skillful lobbying exercise in the United States, which not only effectively presented the case that the company was suffering excessively harsh and unfair treatment in Guatemala but also, more important, convinced officials in the **Dwight Eisenhower** administration that Arbenz was being influenced if not manipulated by communists.

The economic interests of UFCO were a secondary consideration as American officials became more concerned over the real prospect that a Soviet satellite state was about to be created in Central America. This led to the organization and implementation of the covert operation known as **Operation PBSUCCESS**, which brought about Arbenz's resignation in 1954. The new pro-American government of President **Castillo Armas** reversed the policies of agrarian reform and satisfactorily renegotiated UFCO's financial contracts. While UFCO regained its virtual monopoly of banana production, the company's negative image was enhanced throughout the region, where it continued to be denounced by left-wing critics as the supreme symbol of ruthless and exploitative American imperialism. The UFCO ceased to exist in name in 1970 when it was involved in a corporate restructuring in which it became part of United Brands Company. *See also* FIGUERES FERRER, JOSÉ (1906–1990).

UNITED NATIONS ECONOMIC COMMISSION FOR LATIN AMERICA (UNECLA or ECLA). Latin American regional organization also known in Spanish as Comisión Economica para América

Latina. The ECLA was established in 1948 as a subagency of the **United Nations (UN)** to encourage economic cooperation among its member states. These included not only the Latin American nations but also the United States, **Canada**, and leading European nations, such as **France**, **Great Britain**, the Netherlands, Portugal, and **Spain**, which had colonial possessions in the **Western Hemisphere**. With its headquarters in Santiago de Chile and under the direction of the Argentine economist **Raúl Prebisch**, who served as its first executive secretary from 1948 to 1963, ECLA published influential studies expounding theories of economic development and proposed strategies to promote growth with particular reference to Latin America.

ECLA's argument that the capitalist system had imposed an unhealthy state of economic dependency on the Third World aroused considerable controversy among economists and politicians. In effect, ECLA became an active pressure group working within the United Nations but outside the **Organization of American States (OAS)**. American officials were generally critical of ECLA's ideas and preferred to pursue programs that originated in Washington, such as the **Alliance for Progress**, as the best way to promote the economic development of Latin America. In 1984, in response to the admission of the new Caribbean states as members, ECLA was retitled the Economic Commission for Latin America and the Caribbean. *See also* FREE TRADE AREA OF THE AMERICAS (FTAA).

UNITED NATIONS ORGANIZATION (UN). An international organization designed to promote world peace and security. The United Nations was created in 1945 to replace the **League of Nations**. All the nations of the **Western Hemisphere** became members. As one of the five great powers, the United States was made a permanent member of the Security Council with the power of veto. In 1948, the **Organization of American States (OAS)** was created in accordance with Articles 52 to 54 of the UN Charter, which allowed member states to enter into separate regional organizations to deal with their local security problems. This meant that regional disputes would be settled by the OAS. In some instances, individual Latin American countries have preferred to appeal directly to the UN and bypass the

OAS, which has been seen as too much under the control of the United States. This occurred in 1954 when **Guatemala** complained of aggression from **Honduras** and **Nicaragua** and in 1961 when **Cuba** condemned the United States for causing the invasion at the **Bay of Pigs** in 1961. Direct UN diplomatic involvement took place during the 1980s as part of attempts to reach diplomatic settlements of the **South Atlantic War** and the **Central American crisis**.

The founders of the UN had envisaged the creation of an instrument to preserve world peace. But the conflict of interests between the great powers ensured that the United Nations was effectively deprived of real economic and military power for as long as the **Cold War** existed. It became therefore primarily a platform for the expression of political propaganda and an institution to distribute economic and cultural welfare. This latter function had important implications for Latin America because a separate agency known as the **United Nations Economic Commission for Latin America (UNECLA or ECLA)** was created in 1948 to encourage economic cooperation and integration among the Latin American countries. A prominent influence on ECLA was the Argentine economist **Raúl Prebisch**, who argued that the structure of the world economy and its domination by the United States was fundamentally disadvantageous to Latin America. Most governments, however, still recognized the importance of securing financial assistance from the United States to promote trade and economic development. This resulted in major schemes such as the **Alliance for Progress** that were separate from programs of economic aid that were administered by the United Nations. *See also* LAW OF THE SEA.

URUGUAY. A country in southern South America bordered by **Argentina** and **Brazil**. Uruguay became an independent nation in 1828 and established official diplomatic relations with the United States in 1834. Regarded for most of its history as the most politically stable and socially cohesive country in South America, Uruguay has had slight diplomatic and commercial significance for the United States. During the 19th century, Uruguay followed Argentina in developing a close economic relationship with **Great Britain**. In fact, it was not until 1870 that the U.S. minister to Uruguay first took up his official residence in Montevideo.

– V –

VANCE, CYRUS (1917–2002). American lawyer, diplomat, and secretary of state from 1977 to 1980. Educated at Yale University, Vance became a lawyer and served in the Defense Department during the **Lyndon Johnson** administration. He supported the presidential candidacy of **Jimmy Carter** in 1976 and shared the latter's foreign policy views on giving more attention to Latin American affairs and stressing the international observance of human rights. Appointed secretary of state by Carter, Vance strongly advocated the return of the **Panama Canal** to **Panama**. He also endorsed the placing of restrictions on arms sales to those military governments in Latin America that were guilty of violating human rights. In 1980, Vance resigned as secretary of state after disagreeing with Carter's decision to approve a covert military operation to rescue American hostages trapped in the U.S. embassy in Teheran, Iran. *See also* LINOWITZ REPORT (1976); PANAMA CANAL TREATIES (1977).

VARGAS, GETÚLIO (1883–1954). Brazilian political leader and president from 1930 to 1945 and 1951 to 1954. After assuming political power in a military coup in 1930, Vargas served as president until 1945 and from 1951 to 1954. Although outwardly regarded as a fascist sympathizer during the 1930s, Vargas consistently stressed the importance of maintaining a close diplomatic relationship with the United States. He sought to establish a friendly personal rapport with President **Franklin D. Roosevelt** by praising the idea of the **Good Neighbor Policy**. Roosevelt responded in November 1936 by making a point of stopping off in Rio de Janeiro en route to the Pan-American Conference in Buenos Aires and lavishing praise on Vargas for his successful adoption of social welfare policies in Brazil.

Despite seeking increased trade with **Germany** during the 1930s, Vargas carefully avoided becoming identified with the international ambitions of Nazi Germany and continued his country's traditional policy of seeking friendly diplomatic relations with the United States. After the United States joined the world war in December 1941, Brazil severed diplomatic relations with Germany in January 1942 and formally entered the war on August 22, 1942. The policy of close cooperation with the United States resulted in Brazil being rewarded with a massive amount of **lend-lease** aid amounting to 70 percent of the total lend-lease aid given by the United States to the whole of Latin America during **World War II**. A Brazilian military expeditionary force (Força Expeditionária Brasileira) was also equipped, transported, and supplied by the U.S. government and placed under American military commanders in the Italian campaign in 1945. A high point of Brazil's regional and international status was underlined by the meeting between the Vargas and Roosevelt in Natal in northeastern Brazil in January 1943.

Vargas was compelled to resign as president in 1945. In 1951, however, he won the next presidential election. His administration was dominated by domestic crisis leading to his suicide in 1954. In terms of foreign policy, Vargas found that Brazil no longer enjoyed the wartime position of a favored ally of the United States. In fact, he joined other Latin American leaders in criticizing the United States for being too preoccupied with European affairs and for neglecting to help those nations, such as Brazil, that had been loyal allies during World War II. As a show of displeasure, Vargas refused American requests to commit troops to the **Korean War** (1950–1953).

VELASCO ALVARADO, JUAN (1910–1977). Peruvian general and president from 1968 to 1975. A career army officer, Velasco became a general and commander in chief of the Peruvian army. In 1968, he led a coup that overthrew President **Belaúnde Terry**. One of the principal reasons for the coup had been Belaúnde's controversial decision not to nationalize but to reach a financial arrangement with the U.S.-owned International Petroleum Company (IPC). In **Peru**, IPC had long been unpopular and was regarded as a symbol of oppressive American imperialism. The new military government headed by Velasco nationalized IPC on the ground that the company had made excessive profits and owed $600 million in back taxes. Velasco successfully secured diplomatic support for his action from other South American governments. He also pursued an independent foreign policy that resulted in the negotiation of a financial loan from the **Soviet Union**, Peruvian recognition of communist China in 1971, and the renewal of diplomatic relations with **Cuba** in 1972. At the same time, Velasco introduced a program of radical agrarian reform that sought a major improvement in the living standards of Peruvian agricultural workers.

Shortly after Velasco came to power, **Salvador Allende** was elected president of Chile in 1970. American officials, however, did not regard Velasco as posing the same geopolitical threat that Allende represented. Nor did they believe that the agrarian reform program meant that Peru would become "another Cuba" because it was known that the military government was strongly anticommunist. Despite making initial protests against Velasco's policy of nationalization and threatening retaliatory economic measures, the U.S. government proved willing to accept a compromise financial settlement in 1974 that provided IPC with an agreed amount of compensation. After 1972, Velasco was in ill health. Moreover, his authority and popularity was diminished by rising inflation and growing unemployment, which brought increasing discontent and resulted in his replacement by another military figure as president in 1975.

VENEZUELA. A country in northern South America bordered by **Colombia** and **Brazil** to the south and by **Guyana** to the east. As part of Gran Colombia, Venezuela established official diplomatic relations with the United States in 1823. During the 19th century, the single most important issue in diplomatic relations between the United States and Venezuela was the **Venezuelan Boundary Dispute**. Ever since the 1840s, Venezuela had been in diplomatic conflict with **Great Britain** over the exact location of its eastern border with the British colony of British Guiana (now known as Guyana). Venezuelan governments appealed to the United States for diplomatic support but received a negative response. In 1895, however, President **Grover Cleveland** was persuaded that the British were secretly seeking to take possession of Venezuelan territory in defiance of the **Monroe Doctrine**. Consequently, he demanded that the dispute be submitted to binding arbitration. After initial reluctance, the British government agreed to Cleveland's proposal for arbitration. For the United States, the episode represented an important historic victory in that the Monroe Doctrine was vindicated and American political preeminence in the **Western Hemisphere** was finally recognized by Great Britain. Arguably, however, Venezuela lost rather than gained by American diplomatic intervention. Cleveland never consulted the Venezuelan government over his policy, and the arbitration procedure was basically imposed on Venezuela. That country's sense of grievance was further increased when the arbitration award in 1899 granted Britain most of the disputed territory.

Venezuela was also instrumental in contributing to the further development of the Monroe Doctrine in the **Venezuela Incident** (1902–1903). The incident arose from Venezuela's refusal to service its foreign debt and the subsequent decision by Great Britain, **Germany**, and Italy to send a squadron of gunboats to impose a punitive naval blockade of the main Venezuelan ports in December 1902. The blockade was lifted in February 1903 after all parties to the dispute agreed to seek arbitration at The Hague Court of Permanent Arbitration. The ruling of The Hague Court on February 22, 1904, found in favor of the case made by the European powers and thereby appeared to vindicate their resort to gunboat diplomacy. In order to prevent a repetition of the Venezuela Incident, President **Theodore Roosevelt** declared that the United States would intervene in cases where Latin American governments refused to be accountable for their financial obligations to foreign investors. This policy became known as the **Roosevelt Corollary** to the Monroe Doctrine or the policy of the **Big Stick**.

Venezuela once again briefly attracted the attention of U.S. diplomats in May 1958 during Vice President **Richard Nixon**'s goodwill tour of Latin America. Nixon's visit had started peacefully in Buenos Aires. In Lima, however, he was confronted by student riots. The most violent scenes occurred in Caracas, where his life was endangered when a howling mob attacked his motorcade. The **Dwight Eisenhower** administration was startled by the depth of anti-American hostility that had been so visibly displayed. President Eisenhower and his successor, **John F. Kennedy**, sought to improve relations with Venezuela by cultivating President **Rómulo Betancourt**. The Venezuelan president was regarded by the Kennedy administration as a key Latin American figure in helping to achieve the successful implementation of the **Alliance for Progress**. American officials also welcomed Betancourt's antipathy toward **Fidel Castro** and the **Cuban Revolution** and valued his support for the policy of seeking to isolate Cuba both politically and economically.

By contrast, recent U.S. relations with President **Hugo Chávez** have been considerably more difficult and strained. Elected president in 1998, Chávez has openly acknowledged his admiration of Fidel

Castro. In foreign affairs, he has been openly critical of the United States and has claimed to be following the ideas of the Venezuelan hero **Simón Bolívar** in urging Latin American countries to unite against American imperialism, which he argues has inflicted a state of damaging "neocolonialism" on Latin America and its people. *See also* CASTRO, CIPRIANO (1858–1924); DRAGO DOCTRINE; OIL; SCRUGGS, WILLIAM L. (1836–1912).

VENEZUELA BOUNDARY DISPUTE (1895). Diplomatic crisis between the United States and **Great Britain**. Since the 1840s, the governments of **Venezuela** and Great Britain had engaged in diplomatic correspondence over the exact location of the boundary in the remote and virtually inaccessible jungle region separating Venezuela and the British colony of British Guiana (now known as **Guyana**). Venezuelan governments frequently looked to the United States for diplomatic support against Great Britain. They received, however, little more than polite expressions of sympathy.

The likelihood of American diplomatic intervention in the dispute began to look much more probable in 1895 when the administration of President **Grover Cleveland** was persuaded to the view that Britain was violating the **Monroe Doctrine** by deviously seeking to acquire territory at Venezuela's expense. On July 20, 1895, Secretary of State **Richard Olney** dispatched a diplomatic note, known as the **Olney Memorandum**, to the British Foreign Office demanding that Britain agree to submit the boundary dispute to arbitration. The implication was that the United States, solely by reason of its geographical position, possessed an inherent right to intervene in diplomatic questions relating to the **Western Hemisphere** even if it was not a party to the dispute. The British government rejected Olney's demand. President Cleveland responded by sending a Special Message to the U.S. Congress on December 17, 1895, affirming the principles of the Monroe Doctrine and requesting congressional funds to set up an American commission to investigate and decide the boundary dispute. The message was interpreted in the British and American press as a virtual ultimatum to accept arbitration, which, if rejected, would pose the possibility of the United States and Britain having no alternative but to go to war.

The war scare was short lived. The British government agreed to Cleveland's proposal for arbitration and thereby acknowledged the right of the United States to intervene in the boundary dispute. For the United States, the episode represented an important historic victory. The Monroe Doctrine was vindicated, and American political preeminence in the Western Hemisphere was finally recognized by Great Britain. Ironically, this outcome only aroused apprehension in Latin America. The United States claimed to be acting selflessly on behalf of its Latin American sisters in defeating European imperialism, but the apparent altruism was exercised in a characteristically unilateral and arrogant matter. Neither Cleveland nor Olney consulted the Venezuelan government over their policy, and the arbitration procedure was basically forced on Venezuela. That country's sense of grievance was further heightened when the award of the arbitration commission in 1899 granted Great Britain most of the disputed territory. *See also* SCRUGGS, WILLIAM L. (1836–1912).

VENEZUELA INCIDENT (1902–1903). Example of gunboat diplomacy employed by European powers against **Venezuela**. The refusal of Venezuela to compensate foreigners for losses incurred as a result of civil disorder and also to service its foreign debt resulted in December 1902 in **Great Britain**, **Germany**, and Italy sending a squadron of gunboats to impose a punitive naval blockade of the main Venezuelan ports. The blockade was lifted in February 1903 after all parties to the dispute agreed to seek arbitration at The Hague Court of Permanent Arbitration. Germany had initially declined to go to arbitration. President **Theodore Roosevelt** later claimed that he had secretly threatened American naval intervention and that this explained Germany's change of attitude. In fact, the European powers needed little persuasion because it was evident that the blockade by itself was unlikely to secure payment of their claims. Moreover, so long as the blockade continued, it was both politically unpopular at home and economically damaging to their interests.

The ruling of The Hague Court on February 22, 1904, found in favor of the European powers and appeared therefore to vindicate the resort to gunboat diplomacy. In order to preempt European action and thereby prevent a repetition of the Venezuela Incident, Roosevelt declared that the United States would be prepared to intervene militarily in cases where Latin American governments misbehaved and refused to service their financial obligations to foreign creditors. This policy became known as the **Roosevelt Corollary** to the **Monroe Doctrine** or the policy of the **Big Stick**. *See also* CASTRO, CIPRIANO (1858–1924); DRAGO DOCTRINE.

VERACRUZ. A city and port in **Mexico**. As the major Mexican seaport on the Gulf of Mexico, Veracruz was a target that was vulnerable to external naval attack from foreign naval powers. On two occasions during the 19th century, it provided an example of "gunboat diplomacy" in which European governments employed military force in an attempt to secure redress for grievances allegedly suffered by their nationals resident in Mexico. In 1838, French troops briefly occupied Veracruz. In 1862, the port was the scene of British, French, and Spanish naval intervention that subsequently resulted in the **French Intervention** (1862–1867). During the 20th century, the major foreign military intervention took place in April 1914 when President **Woodrow Wilson**, as part of his strategy to remove Mexican President **Victoriano Huerta** from office, ordered U.S. marines to occupy the port. In the fighting that followed, 19 Americans and more than 200 Mexicans were killed. The timely diplomatic mediation of the **ABC** powers prevented the fighting from escalating into a full-scale war between Mexico and the United States. Huerta later resigned, and American troops were withdrawn from Veracruz by November 1914. *See also* ARMED INTERVENTIONS.

VILLA, FRANCISCO "PANCHO" (1878–1923). Mexican general. The **Mexican Revolution** beginning in 1910 was characterized by violent struggle among the various revolutionary factions in **Mexico**. One of the foremost military leaders was Francisco "Pancho" Villa. Operating in northern Mexico close to the border with the United States, Villa made an armed raid into New Mexico in March 1916 during which a number of American civilians were killed. The incursion represented the sole invasion of the continental United States by a foreign army during the 20th century.

President **Woodrow Wilson** ordered General **John J. Pershing** to pursue Villa into Mexico. After almost a year of futile pursuit, Pershing gave up his attempt to capture Villa. Wilson was ostensibly seeking to maintain order along the U.S.–Mexican border and to promote democracy in Mexico, but his aggressive policy only further antagonized Mexican nationalism and anti-American opinion. At the same time, Pershing's pursuit served to reinforce Villa's image as a Mexican folk hero who was successfully embarrassing the Americans. Villa fell victim to the violence of Mexican revolutionary politics when he was assassinated in 1923.

– W –

WALKER, WILLIAM (1824–1860). A prominent American **filibuster**. Originally from Tennessee, Walker became a journalist in California. After organizing an unsuccessful filibuster in 1853 to Baja California in **Mexico**, he looked for economic opportunity farther to the south in Central America. In 1855, he arrived in **Nicaragua** with just over 50 men. This small group evolved into an "army" of 2,000 that took advantage of internal political conflicts to establish a government in which Walker ruled as a dictator. Exaggerated reports of Walker's exploits attracted considerable public attention in the United States, where he became something of a popular hero, especially in the South. In the North, however, he was known as a supporter of slavery and regarded as more of an adventurer. Walker astutely called himself "the gray-eyed man of destiny," a reference to the oral traditions of the Indians in Nicaragua that predicted that at some time in the future they would be liberated from Spanish oppression by "the gray-eyed man." Sharing the racist attitudes of many of his countrymen, however, Walker believed in white superiority and had little sympathy for the local Indians, whom he regarded as an inferior race.

The ambitious plans of American filibusters such as Walker to establish permanent control over the countries and peoples of the Central American region had little substance in political reality. Despite assuming the title of president of Nicaragua, Walker's actual authority did not extend very far beyond his immediate headquarters. With financial and military support from the government of neighboring **Costa Rica**, the political factions in Nicaragua joined together to form an army to expel the foreign intruders. Walker was forced to flee from Nicaragua in 1857 and return to the United States. Undaunted, he continued his filibustering activities until they came to an end in 1860 when he was captured and executed by a firing squad in **Honduras**.

WALTERS, VERNON (1917–2002). American army general and diplomat. A gifted linguist, Walters often acted as interpreter for several American presidents and secretaries of state in their meetings with Latin American leaders. During **World War II**, he served as a liaison army officer and interpreter for the Brazilian Expeditionary Force that fought under U.S. command in the Italian campaign. In the process he made a number of personal contacts with Brazilian officers, some of whom went on to hold senior commands in the Brazilian military. In 1962 at a time of growing political crisis in **Brazil**, Walters was appointed as U.S. defense attaché. The relationship between the U.S. embassy and the senior Brazilian military was so cordial that Walters was secretly given prior information of the date of the military coup that overthrew President **João Goulart** in April 1964. Supporters of the ex-president charged that Walters, along with Ambassador **Lincoln Gordon**, had been active participants in the planning of the coup. This was strongly denied by Ambassador Gordon.

After his service in Brazil, Walters was subsequently involved in numerous diplomatic missions, many conducted in secrecy and on behalf of the **Central Intelligence Agency (CIA)**. During the **Ronald Reagan** administration, his knowledge of Latin America and his personal acquaintance with its leaders was particularly valuable in assisting Secretary of State **Alexander Haig** in efforts to mediate the conflict between **Great Britain** and **Argentina** over the **Falkland Islands** in 1982. Walters later served as ambassador to the **United Nations (UN)** from 1985 to 1988 and as ambassador to West **Germany** from 1989 to 1991.

WAR OF THE PACIFIC (1879–1884). A war fought by **Bolivia** and **Peru** against **Chile**. The War of the Pacific originated as a local dispute between Bolivia and Chile over the amount of nitrate export taxes levied by the Bolivian authorities on Chilean merchants. Fighting broke out in February 1879, and Peru joined Bolivia's side against Chile in March 1879. The story that followed was one of slow but steady Chilean military success culminating in the invasion of Peru and the occupation of Lima by Chilean forces in January 1881. But Chile lacked the financial resources to maintain a prolonged military presence on Peruvian territory. Nevertheless, peace terms proved elusive, and a diplomatic impasse ensued over Chilean demands for the cession of the southern Peruvian provinces of Tacna and Arica. The United States had no direct interest in the conflict but became diplomatically involved in moves to end the war because Secretary of State **James G. Blaine** suspected that **Great Britain** was secretly providing financial and military support for Chile in order to gain special favors for British business interests. Blaine wanted Chile to accept a financial indemnity in return for giving up its demand for the cession of Peruvian territory. He sought to put diplomatic pressure on Chile by proposing the holding of a Pan-American peace conference in Washington to discuss peace terms.

A peace settlement known as the Treaty of Ancón was eventually arranged in 1883 between the Chileans and the Peruvians without the mediation of or even consultation with the United States or the great European powers. Peru secured the withdrawal of Chilean troops but at the price of ceding Tacna and Arica to Chile. A truce known as the Treaty of Valparaíso was signed between Chile and Bolivia in April 1884 and brought the war to a formal end. The outcome illustrated the independence of action that Chile had enjoyed and maintained ever since the beginning of the war. By contrast, Blaine's diplomatic interference appeared ill considered and insensitive. Moreover, a legacy of bitterness was provoked between the United States and Chile that was to affect their relations for some years. *See also* BALTIMORE AFFAIR (1891); FRELINGHUYSEN, FREDERICK T. (1817–1885); TACNA-ARICA DISPUTE.

WAR OF THE TRIPLE ALLIANCE (1865–1870). Military conflict also known as the "Paraguayan War" between **Argentina**, **Brazil**, and **Uruguay** against **Paraguay**. Territorial rivalry between Paraguay and Brazil resulted in the outbreak of military conflict in 1865 in which the "Triple Alliance" of Argentina, Brazil, and Uruguay invaded Paraguay. A war of attrition ensued during which

Paraguay suffered military defeat, occupation, and economic devastation. The United States chose not to pursue an active diplomatic role during the conflict. Like his predecessor **John Quincy Adams** during the **wars for Latin American independence**, Secretary of State **William H. Seward** wished to avoid diplomatic entanglements in South America. Conscious that there was little likelihood of either diplomatic or military intervention by the European powers in the conflict, he believed that the United States should not interfere unless formally requested to do so by the belligerents. His decision demonstrated that American political leaders considered that South America was a geographically remote region of much less geopolitical significance to the United States than **Mexico** and the countries of Central America and the Caribbean.

WARS FOR LATIN AMERICAN INDEPENDENCE (1808–1826). Conflicts occurring in Latin America for independence from **Spain**. The outbreak of the wars for independence brought Latin American affairs to the notice of the people of the United States and represented a virtual "discovery" by Americans of their southern neighbors. In 1808, the French emperor **Napoleon Bonaparte** unilaterally declared his brother, Joseph, as the king of Spain. The action provoked rebellion in Spain that subsequently spread to the Spanish-American empire and resulted in movements for economic and political independence.

While the agents of the Spanish-American insurgents were allowed to purchase ships and supplies in the United States and to have access to American ports, the U.S. government maintained an official policy of neutrality and stressed its desire to maintain friendly relations with Spain. The policy of neutrality advanced American national self-interest because it brought a number of benefits. For example, the need of the European powers for money to finance their wars persuaded Napoleon to sell the **Louisiana** Territory to the United States in 1803. Similar financial necessity compelled Spain to consider the sale of Spanish Florida and set in train a process that resulted in the negotiation of the **Adams-Onís Treaty** (1819). The desire to conclude the treaty was an influential reason for a continuation of the policy of American neutrality in that, until formal ratification of the treaty was finally secured in 1821, the United States delayed recognizing the independence of the new Latin American republics.

This apparently self-serving approach was noticed and caused resentment in South America.

President **James Monroe** eventually conferred diplomatic recognition on the new governments starting on June 19, 1822, when he received the chargé d'affaires from the Republic of **Colombia** at the White House. By the end of his administration in 1825, Monroe had recognized the independence of **Mexico**, the Federation of Central America, Colombia, **Chile**, **Argentina**, and **Brazil**. The timing of American action ahead of that of **Great Britain** was both politically and commercially motivated in that the United States hoped to gain special political and commercial advantages in the new states. In addition, there was a desire to support and promote the spread of liberty and republicanism even though both Mexico and Brazil were still monarchies when diplomatic recognition was first conferred. Nevertheless, Latin American suspicions of U.S. motives persisted because of Monroe's past record of caution and his decision not to recognize any change in the governments of **Peru** or **Cuba** so long as Spanish forces in those colonies remained undefeated. *See also* ADAMS, JOHN QUINCY (1767–1848); BOLÍVAR, SIMÓN (1783–1830); MIRANDA, FRANCISCO DE (1750–1816); JEFFERSON, THOMAS (1743–1826).

WESTERN HEMISPHERE. A geographical term. Western Hemisphere has been commonly used in the United States by politicians, diplomats, and writers as a convenient term to describe the Americas and includes the nations of North, Central, and South America and the Caribbean. The concept of a separate Western Hemisphere has historical significance because it provided the rationale for the enunciation and development of the **Monroe Doctrine**, which declared that the New World of the Americas was geographically distinct and had different political interests from the nations of the Old World of Europe. The idea of protecting the Western Hemisphere from external danger was also used to justify U.S. political and military leadership during **World War II** and the Cold War.

The concept of a separate Western Hemisphere met resistance in Latin America. In his invitations to the **Panama Congress** (1826), **Simón Bolívar** initially envisaged a union of Latin American nations that excluded the United States. The validity of the idea of separation from Europe was later challenged at the **International American Conference** (1889–1890) by the Argentine diplomat **Roque Sáenz Peña**, who stressed the vital importance of past, present, and future links with Europe for the whole of Latin America. He also queried whether the popular contemporary slogan of "America for the Americans" signified not a relationship of equal nations but a hemisphere dominated by the "North Americans." *See also* CHÁVEZ, HUGO (1954–).

WILSON, WOODROW (1856–1924). American political leader and president from 1913 to 1921. Born in Virginia, Wilson became a professor of government and president of Princeton University from 1902 to 1910. Advocating progressive reform, he was elected Democratic governor of New Jersey in 1910 and president in 1912. As president, Wilson saw his priority as the achievement of his reform program known as the "New Freedom." In terms of foreign affairs, he publicly declared his intention of cultivating a new relationship with Latin America that was firmly based on reason and trust. This was made apparent in his celebrated speech known as the **Mobile Address**. Wilson's idealistic rhetoric conflicted, however, with the more pragmatic considerations of American national self-interest as exemplified by his decisions to intervene with military force in Caribbean republics such as Haiti and the Dominican Republic. He also became directly involved in Mexican affairs. Wilson was alarmed by the disorder and violence arising from the **Mexican Revolution**. He condemned the assassination of **Francisco Madero** in 1913 and refused to recognize the new military government established by General **Victoriano Huerta**. Unable to force Huerta's voluntary resignation, Wilson sent U.S. marines to occupy the port of **Veracruz** in April 1914. But Wilson's meddling in Mexican domestic politics proved to be a miscalculation. The potential escalation of the conflict at Veracruz into a full-scale war between **Mexico** and the United States was avoided by the timely diplomatic intervention of the three leading Latin American nations—**Argentina**, **Brazil**, and **Chile** (the **ABC**).

Although Huerta resigned in July 1914, this failed to bring an end to the violent struggle among the various revolutionary factions in Mexico. With the qualified permission of the Mexican government, Wilson ordered another military intervention when American troops under the command of General **John J. Pershing** pursued the Mexican leader **Pancho Villa** into northern Mexico in 1916–1917. Wilson was ostensibly seeking to maintain order along the U.S.–Mexican border and to aid the establishment of democracy in Mexico, but his forceful actions led to an increase in anti-American feeling.

By taking the United States into **World War I** in 1917 and working so visibly for world peace at the Versailles Peace Conference, Wilson became popularly acclaimed throughout the world as a great statesman. But Latin American opinion remained ambivalent. Only eight Latin American nations responded to his call to join the war against **Germany**, while seven chose to remain neutral. Wilson's high moral principles and political idealism evoked respect and admiration, but his reputation could not escape being tarnished by his record of frequent military interventions in Mexico, Central America, and the Caribbean. *See also* DOLLAR DIPLOMACY; PARIS PEACE CONFERENCE (1919–1920); ZIMMERMANN TELEGRAM (1917).

WORLD BANK. *See* INTERNATIONAL BANK FOR RECONSTRUCTION AND DEVELOPMENT (IBRD).

WORLD WAR I (1914–1918). A world war involving the active military participation of the United States and eight Latin American nations. When war broke out in Europe in August 1914, the United States and the Latin American nations regarded the conflict as a European issue and sought to avoid any direct military involvement. President **Woodrow Wilson** declared that the United States would adopt a policy of strict neutrality. While Wilson publicly championed the defense of neutral rights during time of war, he proved unwilling to provide the positive leadership that would facilitate the formulation of a common hemispheric policy. In practice, he took little account of Latin American views and left those nations to evolve their own separate policies of neutrality toward the war. The period of neutrality from 1914 to 1917 was therefore marked largely by diplomatic indecision and confusion.

The Wilson administration, however, showed a very keen interest in promoting closer economic links with Latin America. Indeed, the serious economic dislocation caused by the war provided a signal and historic opportunity for the extension of U.S. commercial influence throughout Latin America and especially in South America at the expense of its European competitors. Less than two months after the passage of its congressional appropriation, the Pan-American Financial Conference speedily assembled at Washington in May 1915. The meeting was welcomed by Latin American governments and was attended by business executives as well as diplomats and finance ministers.

Diplomatic events took a dramatic turn in January 1917 when **Germany** announced its intention of enforcing unrestricted submarine warfare in the war zone that it had established around the British Isles. A number of neutral merchant ships were subsequently sunk by German submarines. Wilson concluded that conflict could not be avoided. On April 6, the U.S. Congress adopted his recommendation and declared war on Germany. Although the decision had not involved prior consultation with the Latin American governments, Wilson hoped they would support his action by joining the war against Germany because they were similarly affected by the submarine threat. However, only eight nations joined the Allied side, seven of which were Central American–Caribbean states already strongly under American influence—**Costa Rica**, **Cuba**, **Guatemala**, Haiti, **Honduras**, **Nicaragua**, and **Panama**. Brazil was the only South American country to declare war on Germany. The fact that important countries such as **Argentina**, **Chile**, **Mexico**, and **Colombia** remained neutral throughout the war showed not only that there were strong doubts in Latin America over Wilson's policy but also that the memory of recent conflicts with Washington on a variety of issues still rankled.

In contrast to the United States, the Latin American countries that joined the war did not provide a material military contribution to the actual fighting that subsequently achieved the defeat of Germany in 1918. The Wilson administration valued the Latin American countries for the symbolic support that their decision showed for the principle of neutral rights and for their economic cooperation, especially the provision of important strategic raw materials and minerals. However, all the Latin American nations that had declared war on or severed relations with Germany participated by right in the Peace Conference that was held at Versailles, Paris, in 1919. *See also* ABC; DOLLAR DIPLOMACY; MOBILE ADDRESS (1913); PARIS PEACE CONFERENCE (1919–1920); ZIMMERMANN TELEGRAM (1917).

WORLD WAR II (1939–1945). A world war involving the military participation of the United States and the Latin American nations. In September 1939, the governments of the United States and the Latin American nations responded to the outbreak of war in Europe with declarations of neutrality. A meeting of foreign ministers assembled at Panama City in September 1939 and declared a neutrality or "safety" zone around the coastline of the **Western Hemisphere**. Insulation from the war proved impossible as German military success in 1940 dramatically altered the military balance in Europe. Growing sympathy for the plight of **Great Britain** and especially the desire of President **Franklin D. Roosevelt** to help that country against **Germany** meant that the concept of the neutrality zone effectively became redundant. A particular concern of the Roosevelt administration was that Germany might convert the French and Dutch colonies in the Caribbean into bases for offensive military aggression in the Western Hemisphere. In response to this threat, the Havana Conference of foreign ministers in July 1940 approved an American proposal that the transfer of existing European colonies to a nonhemispheric power would not be recognized.

The United States formally entered the war in December 1941 as a result of the Japanese surprise attack at Pearl Harbor. A Pan-American conference of foreign ministers to discuss measures of common hemispheric defense was immediately scheduled for Rio de Janeiro in January 1942. Just prior to the meeting at Rio, nine Central American and Caribbean countries joined the United States in declaring war against Japan and then a few days later taking the same action against Germany and Italy. In contrast to their attitudes during **World War I** and in what was gratifyingly regarded by U.S. officials as a vindication of the success of the **Good Neighbor Policy**, the South American nations also affirmed their support for the United States by breaking off relations with the Axis powers. Shortly afterward, **Mexico** declared war in May and was followed by **Brazil** in August. The notable exceptions were **Argentina** and **Chile**. Chile eventually severed relations in January 1943 and joined the war in February 1945. In March 1945, at a time when the Axis powers faced imminent military defeat, Argentina finally declared war on Germany and Japan.

The United States took the lead in organizing the practical measures for hemispheric defense during World War II. In 1942, an **Inter-American Defense Board (IADB)** was established in Washington to direct military preparations and strategy. Just like World War I, little was required in the way of a Latin American contribution to actual military operations in World War II. In fact, only Mexico and Brazil actually sent combat troops overseas. Mexico dispatched an air force squadron to the Philippines, while a Brazilian infantry division fought under American command in Italy. Several thousand Latin Americans, mostly from Mexico, joined the U.S. armed forces as volunteers.

While the wartime policy of close cooperation bordered on virtual subordination to the United States, it contained distinct material benefits. In a similar fashion to World War I, the Latin American countries were highly valued as suppliers of strategic raw materials, especially oil, tin, manganese, and copper. The United States also compensated for the drastic decline of the region's prewar trade with Europe by purchasing large quantities of agricultural produce, including sugar, coffee, tobacco, and fruit. While the resulting economic benefits were considerable for the Latin American economies, traditional links with Europe were greatly reduced so that they became noticeably more dependent on the United States not only as their biggest single market for exports but also as a source of continuing capital investment for economic development.

The United States concluded numerous bilateral agreements in the form of treaties, **lend-lease** arrangements, and the dispatch of military and economic commissions that were specifically intended to boost the production and extraction of strategic raw materials. Although some support was given for public works programs, these were mainly designed with the specific purpose of aiding the war effort, such as the large air and naval bases, especially in Brazil, Mexico, and **Ecuador**. At the same time, American military missions concentrated on developing programs to help modernize military and police forces in terms of their training and equipment. A visible result was the closer association and identification between Latin American military officers and their counterparts in the United States. Many Latin American junior officers received training at U.S. military academies where they developed close professional and personal associations with their American teachers and colleagues.

The fact that the large majority of Latin American countries willingly joined the United States in World War II illustrated the success of the Good Neighbor Policy and especially Roosevelt's effective presentation of that policy. The 1940 Havana meeting of foreign ministers represented the high point of inter-American cooperation and also American diplomatic interest in Latin America because it occurred at a time when American officials were placing great value on the countries of the region as a source of vital raw materials, military bases, and symbolic diplomatic support against the Axis powers. However, once the United States actually entered the war in December 1941, American diplomatic interest shifted sharply to Europe and Asia, while Latin America was moved to the periphery. Roosevelt was particularly eager to attend conferences with British and Soviet leaders. Conversely, the Roosevelt administration discouraged the holding of Pan-American meetings of consultation and policymaking during wartime. Such meetings had become a frequent feature of the prewar period but were now regarded by U.S. officials as unnecessary and a diversion of diplomatic resources. It was only toward the end of the war that they agreed to schedule a Special Pan-American Conference on the Problems of War and Peace at the Chapultepec Palace in Mexico City from February 21 to March 8, 1945. *See also* BLACK LIST; CHAPULTEPEC CONFERENCE (1945); DECLARATION OF HAVANA (1940); DECLARATION OF PANAMA (1939); FEDERAL BUREAU OF INVESTIGATION (FBI); VARGAS, GETÚLIO (1883–1954).

– Y –

YANKEE. Descriptive term. The nickname "Yankee" was a term originally applied and often in a pejorative sense to English settlers in the New England colonies. Along with "gringo," the term was later used by Latin Americans to describe the people of the United States in general and to emphasize perceived racial and cultural differences.

YUCATÁN. A province of **Mexico**. In 1847–1848, serious racial conflict between Creoles and Indians, known as the "Caste War," erupted in Yucatán. The local creole authorities pleaded for foreign military assistance. Supporters of the **All-Mexico Movement** argued that the

United States should respond by annexing the province. In 1848, the U.S. Congress debated the issue but decided against the annexation of such a remote territory. President **James K. Polk** was concerned more about the possibility that either **Great Britain** or **Spain** might use the civil disturbances in Yucatán as a justification for military intervention. Alluding to **President James Monroe**'s Message in 1823, he sent a Special Message to the U.S. Congress declaring that the United States would oppose the transfer of Yucatán to a European power. In fact, neither Great Britain nor Spain contemplated military involvement in the civil war. Nevertheless, Polk's Message was historically significant because it revived public interest in the 1823 Message and thereby contributed to the development of the **Monroe Doctrine**.

– Z –

ZIMMERMANN TELEGRAM (1917). German diplomatic document relating to **World War I**. In 1917, a secret telegram from the German foreign minister, Arthur Zimmermann, to the German minister in **Mexico** was intercepted by British intelligence officials and leaked to the American government for publication. In the telegram, Zimmermann instructed the minister to promise the Mexican government the restitution of territory lost as a result of the **Mexican-American War** (1846–1848) should Mexico join **Germany** in a war against the United States. In fact, Mexico had no intention of entering into a military alliance with Germany, but the public revelation that secret discussions had actually taken place was embarrassing to both the German and the Mexican governments and contributed to the decision of the United States to go to war against Germany in April 1917. In addition, the telegram illustrated the awkward state of relations existing between President **Woodrow Wilson** and the Mexican government during the period of the **Mexican Revolution** and also the ill feeling against the United States that still endured in Mexico as a result of the country's defeat and humiliating loss of national territory in the Mexican-American War. *See also* CARRANZA, VENUSTIANO (1859–1920); WORLD WAR I (1914–1918).

Appendix A: U.S. Presidents and Secretaries of State, 1789–2006

President	Secretary of State

George Washington
1789–1797
	Thomas Jefferson
	    March 1790–December 1793
	Edmund Randolph
	    January 1794–August 1795
	Timothy Pickering
	    December 1795–March 1797

John Adams
1797–1801
	Timothy Pickering
	    March 1797–May 1800
	John Marshall
	    June 1800–February 1801

Thomas Jefferson 1801–1809	James Madison May 1801–March 1809

James Madison
1809–1817
	Robert Smith
	    March 1809–April 1811
	James Monroe
	    April 1811–September 1814
	    February 1815–March 1817

James Monroe 1817–1825	John Quincy Adams September 1817–March 1825
John Quincy Adams 1825–1829	Henry Clay March 1825–March 1829

Andrew Jackson
1829–1837
	Martin Van Buren
	    March 1829–March 1831
	Edward Livingston
	    May 1831–May 1833
	Louis McLane
	    May 1833–June 1834

(continued)

President	Secretary of State
	John Forsyth July 1834–March 1837
Martin Van Buren 1837–1841	John Forsyth March 1837–March 1841
William Henry Harrison 1841	Daniel Webster March 1841
John Tyler 1841–1845	Daniel Webster April 1841–May 1843 Abel P. Upshur July 1843–February 1844 John C. Calhoun April 1844–March 1845
James K. Polk 1845–1849	James Buchanan March 1845–March 1849
Zachary Taylor 1849–1850	John M. Clayton March 1849–July 1850
Millard Fillmore 1850–1853	Daniel Webster July 1850–October 1852 Edward Everett November 1852–March 1853
Franklin Pierce 1853–1857	William L. Marcy March 1853–March 1857
James Buchanan 1857–1861	Lewis Cass March 1857–December 1860 Jeremiah S. Black December 1860–March 1861
Abraham Lincoln 1861–1865	William H. Seward March 1861–April 1865
Andrew Johnson 1865–1869	William H. Seward April 1865–March 1869
Ulysses S. Grant 1869–1877	Elihu B. Washburne March 1869

President	Secretary of State
	Hamilton Fish March 1869–March 1877
Rutherford B. Hayes 1887–1881	William M. Evarts March 1877–March 1881
James A. Garfield 1881	James G. Blaine March 1881–December 1881
Chester A. Arthur 1881–1885	Frederick T. Frelinghuysen December 1881–March 1885
Grover Cleveland 1885–1889	Thomas F. Bayard March 1885–March 1889
Benjamin Harrison 1889–1893	James G. Blaine March 1889–June 1892
Grover Cleveland 1893–1897	Walter Q. Gresham March 1893–May 1895 Richard Olney June 1895–March 1897
William McKinley 1897–1901	John Sherman March 1897–April 1898 William R. Day April 1898–September 1898 John Hay September 1898–September 1901
Theodore Roosevelt 1901–1909	John Hay September 1901–July 1905 Elihu Root July 1905–January 1909 Robert Bacon January 1909–March 1909
William H. Taft 1909–1913	Philander C. Knox March 1909–March 1913
Woodrow Wilson 1913–1921	William Jennings Bryan March 1913–June 1915

(continued)

President	Secretary of State

	Robert Lansing
	    June 1915–February 1920
	Bainbridge Colby
	    March 1920–March 1921

Warren G. Harding 1921–1923	Charles Evans Hughes March 1921–March 1923

Calvin Coolidge
1923–1929
	Charles Evans Hughes
	    March 1923–March 1925
	Frank B. Kellogg
	    March 1925–March 1929

Herbert Hoover 1929–1933	Henry L. Stimson March 1929–March 1933

Franklin D. Roosevelt
1933–1945
	Cordell Hull
	    March 1933–November 1944
	Edward R. Stettinius Jr.
	    December 1944–June 1945

Harry Truman
1945–1953
	James F. Byrnes
	    July 1945–January 1947
	George C. Marshall
	    January 1947–January 1949
	Dean Acheson
	    January 1949–January 1953

Dwight Eisenhower
1953–1961
	John Foster Dulles
	    January 1953–April 1959
	Christian A. Herter
	    April 1959–January 1961

John F. Kennedy 1961–1963	Dean Rusk January 1961–November 1963
Lyndon Johnson 1963–1969	Dean Rusk November 1963–January 1969

Richard Nixon
1969–1974
	William P. Rogers
	    January 1969–September 1973
	Henry A. Kissinger
	    September 1973–August 1974

President	Secretary of State
Gerald Ford 1974–1977	Henry A. Kissinger August 1974–January 1977
Jimmy Carter 1977–1981	Cyrus Vance January 1977–April 1980 Edmund Muskie May 1980–January 1981
Ronald Reagan 1981–1989	Alexander M. Haig Jr. January 1981–July 1982 George P. Shultz July 1982–January 1989
George H. W. Bush 1989–1993	James A. Baker III January 1989–August 1992 Lawrence S. Eagleburger (served as acting secretary of state) December 1992–January 1993
William J. Clinton 1993–2001	Warren M. Christopher January 1993–January 1997 Madeleine Albright January 1997–January 2001
George W. Bush 2001–	Colin L. Powell January 2001–January 2005 Condoleezza Rice January 2005–

Appendix B: Extracts from Selected Presidential Statements on United States–Latin American Policy

NO. 1. PRESIDENT JAMES MONROE, ANNUAL MESSAGE TO CONGRESS, DECEMBER 2, 1823[1]

In the wars of the European powers in matters relating to themselves we have never taken any part, nor does it comport with our policy so to do. It is only when our rights are invaded or seriously menaced that we resent injuries or make preparation for our defense. With the movements in this hemisphere we are, of necessity, more immediately connected, and by causes which must be obvious to all enlightened and impartial observers. The political system of the allied powers is essentially different in this respect from that of America. This difference proceeds from that which exists in their respective governments. And to the defense of our own, which has been achieved by the loss of so much blood and treasure, and matured by the wisdom of these most enlightened citizens, and under which we have enjoyed unexampled felicity, this whole nation is devoted. We owe, it therefore, to candor, and to the amicable relations existing between the United States and those powers, to declare that we should consider any attempt on their part to extend their system to any portion of this hemisphere as dangerous to our peace and safety. With the existing colonies or dependencies of any European power we have not interfered and shall not interfere. But with the governments who have declared their independence and maintained it, and whose independence we have, on great consideration and on just principles, acknowledged, we could not view any interposition for the purpose of oppressing them, or controlling in any other manner their destiny, by any European power, in any other light than as the manifestation of an unfriendly disposition toward the United States. In the war between these new governments and Spain we declared out neutrality at the time of their recognition, and to this we have adhered and shall continue to adhere, provided no change shall occur which, in the judgment of the competent authorities of this Government, shall make a corresponding change on the part of the United States indispensable to their security.

NO. 2. RUTHERFORD B. HAYES, SPECIAL MESSAGE TO CONGRESS, MARCH 8, 1880[2]

The policy of this country is a canal under American control. The United States cannot consent to the surrender of this control to any European power, or to any combination of European powers. If existing treaties between the United States and other nations, or if the rights of sovereignty or property of other nations stand in the way of this policy—a contingency which is not apprehended—suitable steps should be taken by just and liberal negotiations to promote and establish the American policy on this subject, consistently with the rights of the nations to be affected by it.

The capital invested by corporations or citizens of other countries in such an enterprise must, in a great degree, look for protection to one or more of the great powers of the world. No European power can intervene for such protection without adopting measures on this continent which the United States would deem wholly inadmissible. If the protection of the United States is relied upon, the United States must exercise such control as will enable this country to protect its national interests and maintain the rights of those whose private capital is embarked in the work.

An interoceanic canal across the American Isthmus will essentially change the geographical relations between the Atlantic and Pacific coasts of the United States, and between the United States and the rest of the world. It will be the great ocean thoroughfare between our Atlantic and our Pacific shores, and virtually a part of the coast line of the United States. Our merely commercial interest in it is greater than that of all other countries, while its relations to our power and prosperity as a nation, to our means of defense, our unity, peace, and safety, are matters of paramount concern to the people of the United States. No other great power would, under similar circumstances fail to assert a rightful control over a work so closely and vitally affecting its interest and welfare.

Without urging further the grounds of my opinion, I repeat, in conclusion, that it is the right and the duty of the United States to assert and maintain such supervision and authority over any interoceanic canal across the isthmus that connects North and South America as will protect our national interests. This I am quite sure will be found not only compatible with, but promotive of, the widest and most permanent advantage to commerce and civilization.

NO. 3. THEODORE ROOSEVELT, ANNUAL MESSAGE TO CONGRESS, DECEMBER 6, 1904[3]

It is not true that the United States feels any land hunger or entertains any projects as regards the other nations of the Western Hemisphere save such as are for their welfare. All that this country desires is to see the neighboring countries stable, orderly, and prosperous. Any country whose people conduct themselves well can count upon our hearty friendship. If a nation shows that it knows how to act with reasonable efficiency and decency in social and political matters, if it keeps order and pays its obligations, it need fear no interference from the United States. Chronic wrongdoing, or an impotence which results in a general loosening of the ties of civilized society, may in America, as elsewhere, ultimately require intervention by some civilized nation, and in the Western Hemisphere the adherence of the United States to the Monroe Doctrine may force the United Sates, however reluctantly, in flagrant cases of such wrongdoing or impotence, to the exercise of an international police power. If every country washed by the Caribbean Sea would show the progress in stable and just civilization which with the aid of Platt amendment Cuba has shown since our troops left the island, and which so many of the republics in both Americas are constantly and brilliantly showing, all question of interference by this Nation with their affairs would be at end. Our interests and those of our southern neighbors are in reality identical. They have great natural riches, and if within their borders the reign of law and justice obtains, prosperity is sure to come to them. While they thus obey the primary laws of civilized society they may rest assured that they will be treated by us in a spirit of cordial and helpful sympathy. We would interfere with them only in the last resort, and then only if it became evident that their inability or unwillingness to do justice at home and abroad had violated the rights of the United States or had invited foreign aggression to the detriment of the entire body of American nations. It is a mere truism to say that every nation, whether in America or anywhere else, which desires to maintain its freedom, its independence, must ultimately realize that the right of such independence can not be separated from the responsibility of making good use of it.

NO. 4. PRESIDENT WOODROW WILSON, "THE MOBILE ADDRESS," OCTOBER 26, 1913[4]

The future, ladies and gentlemen, is going to be very different for this hemisphere from the past. These States lying to the south of us, which have always been our neighbors, will now be drawn closer to us by innumerable ties, and I hoe, chief of all, by the tie of a common understanding of each other. Interest does not tie nations together; it sometimes separates them. But sympathy and understanding does untie them, and I believe that by the new route that is just about to be opened, while we physically cut two continents asunder, we spiritually unite them. It is a spiritual union which we see . . .

We must prove ourselves their friends, and champions upon terms of equality and honor. You cannot be friends upon any other terms than upon the terms of equality. We must show ourselves friends by comprehending their interest whether it squares with our own interest or not. It is a very perilous thing to determine the foreign policy of a nation in the terms of material interest. It not only is unfair to those with whom you are dealing, but it is degrading as regards your own actions.

Comprehension must be the soil in which shall grow all the fruits of friendship, and there is a reason and a compulsion lying behind all this which is dearer than anything else to the thoughtful men of America. I mean the development of constitutional liberty in the world. Human rights, national integrity, and opportunity as against material interests — that, ladies and gentlemen, is the issue which we now have to fact. I want to take this occasion to say that the United States will never again seek one additional foot of territory by conquest. She will devote herself to showing that she knows how to make honorable and fruitful use of the territory she has, and she must regard it as one of the duties of friendship to see that from no quarter are material interests made superior to human liberty and national opportunity. I say this, not with a single thought that anyone will gainsay it, but merely to fix in our consciousness what our real relationship with the rest of America is. It is the relationship of a family of mankind devoted to the development of true constitutional liberty. We know that that is the soil out of which the best enterprise springs. We know that this is a cause which we are making in common with our neighbors, because we have had to make it for ourselves.

NO. 5. PRESIDENT FRANKLIN D. ROOSEVELT, SPEECH ON "PAN AMERICAN DAY," APRIL 12, 1933[5]

I rejoice at this opportunity to participate in the celebration of "Pan American Day" and to extend on behalf of the people of the United States a fraternal greeting to our sister American Republics. The celebration of "Pan American Day" in this building, dedicated to international good-will and cooperation, exemplifies a unity of thought and purpose among the peoples of this hemisphere. It is a manifestation of the common ideal of mutual helpfulness, sympathetic understanding and spiritual solidarity.

There is inspiration in the thought that on this day the attention of the citizens of the twenty-one Republics of America is focused on the common ties—historical, cultural, economic, and the social—which bind them to one another. Common ideals and a community of interest, together with a spirit of cooperation, have led to the realization that the well-being of one Nation depends in large measure upon the well-being of its neighbors. It is upon these foundations that Pan Americanism has been built.

This celebration commemorates a movement based upon the policy of fraternal cooperation. In my Inaugural Address I stated that I would "dedicate this Nation to the policy of the good neighbor—the neighbor who resolutely respects himself and, because he does so, respects the rights of others—the neighbor who respects his obligations and respects the sanctity of his agreements in and with a world of neighbors." Never before has the significance of the words "good neighbor" been so manifest in international relations. Never have the need and benefit of neighborly cooperation in every form of human activity been so evident as they are today.

NO. 6. PRESIDENT JOHN F. KENNEDY, SPEECH ON "THE ALLIANCE FOR PROGRESS," MARCH 13, 1961[6]

One hundred and thirty-nine years ago this week the United States, stirred by the heroic struggle of its fellow Americans, urged the independence and recognition of the new Latin American Republics. It was then, at the dawn of freedom throughout this hemisphere, that Bolívar spoke of his desire to see the Americas fashioned into the greatest region in the world, "greatest," he said, "not so much by virtue of her area and her wealth, as by her freedom and her glory."

Never in the long history of our hemisphere, has this dream been nearer to fulfillment, and never has it been in greater danger. The genius of our scientists has given us the tools to bring abundance to our land, strength to our industry, and knowledge to our people. For the first time we have the capacity to strike off the remaining bonds of poverty and ignorance—to free our people for the spiritual and intellectual fulfillment which has always been the goal of our civilization . . .

Throughout Latin America—a continent rich in resources and in the spiritual and cultural achievements of its people—millions of men and women suffer the daily degradations of hunger and poverty. They lack decent shelter or protection from disease. Their children are deprived of the education or the jobs which are the gateway to a better life. And each day the problems grow more urgent. Population growth is outpacing economic growth, low living standards are even further endangered, and discontent—the discontent of a people who know that abundance and the tools of progress are at last within their reach—that discontent is growing. In the words of José Figueres, "once dormant peoples are struggling upward toward the sun, toward a better life."

If we are to meet a problem so staggering in its dimensions, our approach must itself be equally bold, an approach consistent with the majestic concept of Operation Pan America. Therefore I have called on all people of the hemisphere to join in a new Alliance for Progress—*Alianza para Progreso*—a vast co-operative effort, unparalleled in magnitude and nobility of purpose, to satisfy the basic needs of the American people for homes, work and land. Health and schools—*techo, trabajo y tierra, salud y escuela.*

NO. 7. PRESIDENT RONALD REAGAN, SPEECH ON "U.S. INTERESTS IN CENTRAL AMERICA," MAY 9, 1984[7]

The defense policy of the United States is based on a simple premise: we do not start wars. We will never be the aggressor. We maintain our strength in order to deter and defend against aggression—to preserve freedom and peace. We help our friends defend themselves.

Central America is a region of great importance to the United States. And it is so close—San Salvador is closer to Houston, Texas, than Houston is to Washington, D.C. Central America is America; it's at our doorstep. And it has become the stage for a bold attempt by the Soviet Union, Cuba, and Nicaragua to install communism by force throughout the hemisphere . . .

As the National Bipartisan Commission on Central America, chaired by Henry Kissinger, agreed, if we do nothing or if we continue to provide too little help, our choice will be a communist Central America with additional communist military bases on the mainland of this hemisphere and communist subversion spreading southward and northward. This communist subversion poses the threat that 100 million people from Panama to the open border on our south could come under the control of pro-Soviet regimes.

If we come to our senses too late, when our vital interests are even more directly threatened, and after a lack of American support causes our friends to lose the ability to defend themselves, then the risks to our security and our way of life will be infinitely greater . . .

We can and must help Central America. It's in our national interest to do so; and, morally, it's the only right thing to do. But, helping means doing *enough*—enough to protect our security and enough to protect the lives of our neighbors so that they may live in peace and democracy without the threat of communist aggression and subversion . . .

We Americans should be proud of what we're trying to do in Central America, and proud of what, together with our friends, we can do in Central America, to support democracy, human rights, and economic growth, while preserving peace so close to home. Let us show the world that we want no hostile, communist colonies here in the Americas: South, Central, or North.

NOTES

1. Cited in Dexter Perkins, *The Monroe Doctrine, 1823–1826* (Cambridge, Mass.: Harvard University Press, 1927), 83–84.

2. Cited in Committee on Foreign Relations, U.S. Senate, *Background Documents Relating to the Panama Canal* (Washington, D.C.: U.S. Government Printing Office, 1977), 51.

3. Cited in Henry S. Commager, ed., *Documents of American History*, vol. 2 (New York: Appleton-Century-Crofts, 1968), 33–34.

4. 63rd Congress, 1st session, Senate Document no. 226, "Address of Woodrow Wilson delivered before the Southern Commercial Congress held at Mobile, Alabama, October 27, 1913" (Washington, D.C.: U.S. Government Printing Office, 1913).

5. Cited in John Edwin Fagg, *Pan Americanism* (Malabar, Fla.: Krieger, 1982), 163–64.

6. Cited in Department of State Bulletin, April 3, 1961.

7. Cited in Robert H. Holden and Eric Zolov, eds., *Latin America and the United States* (New York: Oxford University Press, 2000), 295–96.

Bibliography

CONTENTS

I.	Introduction	251
II.	Documents and Documentary Collections	258
III.	Reference Works	259
IV.	General Surveys	260
V.	Bilateral Relations	260
VI.	Special Studies	262
VII.	From Colonies to Independent Nations	263
VIII.	Diplomatic Detachment	264
IX.	Pan-Americanism	266
X.	Dollar Diplomacy	267
XI.	Good Neighbors	270
XII.	Cold War Diplomacy	271
XIII.	Transition to a New Century	274

I. INTRODUCTION

There are a large number of general overviews of the history of diplomatic relations between the United States and Latin America. Most are designed to serve as college textbooks for courses in U.S. diplomatic history. Among the most recent are Joseph Smith, *The United States and Latin America: A History of American Diplomacy*; Kyle Longley, *In the Eagle's Shadow: The United States and Latin America*; and Peter H. Smith, *Talons of the Eagle: Dynamics of U.S.-Latin American Relations*. For examples of old-fashioned traditional diplomatic history emphasizing the preeminent role of the United States in the Western Hemisphere, see Samuel Flagg Bemis, *The Latin American Policy of the United States: An Historical Interpretation*, and J. Lloyd Mecham, *A*

Survey of United States-Latin American Relations. A broader more conceptual approach to hemispheric relations is evident in Lester D. Langley, *America and the Americas: The United States in the Western Hemisphere*, and in Don M. Coerver and Linda B. Hall, *Tangled Destinies: Latin America and the United States*. Arthur P. Whitaker, *The Western Hemisphere Idea: Its Rise and Decline*, is a brief but scholarly examination of the history of the idea of a separate Western Hemisphere. On inter-American diplomatic relations in the 20th century, see Lester D. Langley, *The Americas in the Modern Age*, and Mark T. Gilderhus, *The Second Century: U.S.-Latin American Relations since 1889*. Alan McPherson, *Intimate Ties, Bitter Struggles: The United States and Latin America since 1945*, is a concise analysis of recent trends. For critical interpretations of U.S. policy by European scholars, see Gordon Connell-Smith, *The United States and Latin America: An Historical Analysis of Inter-American Relations*, and Frank Niess, *Hemisphere to Itself: A History of U.S.-Latin American Relations*. Specialist studies by Latin American historians on diplomatic relations with the United States are rare. Two notable exceptions are Moniz Bandeira, *Presença dos Estados Unidos no Brasil*, and Luis G. Zorilla, *Historia de las relaciones entre México y lost Estados Unidos de América 1800–1958*. For contemporary Spani American views, see John T. Reid, *Spanish American Images of the United States, 1790–1960*. J. C. M. Ogelslby, *Gringos from the Far North: Essays in the History of Canadian-Latin American Relations, 1866–1968*, provides a Canadian perspective.

Harold Molineu, *U.S. Policy toward Latin America: From Regionalism to Globalism*, is a perceptive analysis by a political scientist. For studies of U.S. diplomatic relations with individual Latin American countries, see the volumes in the excellent series "America and the Americas" edited by Lester D. Langley and published by the University of Georgia Press. Instructive surveys of the international relations system of the Western Hemisphere are G. Pope Atkins, *Latin America in the International Political System*, and Peter Calvert, *The International Politics of Latin America*. An investigation of the cultural aspects of the relationship between the United States and its neighbors is the theme of the essays in Gilbert M. Joseph, Catherine C. LeGrand, and Ricardo D. Salvatore, eds., *Close Encounters of Empire: Writing the Cultural History of U.S.-Latin American Relations*.

An interesting overview of the period in which the Latin American countries won their independence from Europe is Lester D. Langley, *The Americas in the Age of Revolution, 1750–1850*. Arthur P. Whitaker, *The United States and the Independence of Latin America, 1800–1830*, is rather dated, but it is still the most informative study on the actual diplomatic developments. There is also an excellent introduction and valuable diplomatic material in Charles K. Webster, ed., *Britain and the Independence of Latin America, 1812–1830. Select Documents from the Foreign Office Archives* (2 vols.). For a full discussion of the Adams-Onís Treaty, see Philip C. Brooks, *Diplomacy and the Borderlands: The Adams-Onís Treaty of 1819*. The standard work on the origins of the Monroe Doctrine remains Dexter Perkins, *The Monroe Doctrine, 1823–1826*. On its later evolution, see Gretchen Murphy, *Hemispheric Imaginings: The Monroe Doctrine and Narratives of U.S. Empire*, and the essays in Donald M. Dozer, ed., *The Monroe Doctrine: Its Modern Significance*. Ron Seckinger, *The Brazilian Monarchy and the South American Republics, 1822–1831: Diplomacy and State Building*, is an excellent analysis of the balance of power in South America during the early years of the independence period.

On diplomatic relations between the United States and Latin America during the first half of the 19th century, see John J. Johnson, *A Hemisphere Apart: The Foundations of United States Policy toward Latin America*, and the chapters dealing with individual Latin American countries in T. Ray Shurbutt, ed., *United States-Latin American Relations, 1800–1850*. An excellent study on the emergence of Texas is David J. Weber, *The Mexican Frontier, 1821–1846: The American Southwest under Mexico*. On diplomatic aspects of the Texas Question, see David M. Pletcher, *The Diplomacy of Annexation: Texas, Oregon, and the Mexican War*. American racist attitudes are examined in Reginald Horsman, *Race and Manifest Destiny: The Origins of American Racial Anglo-Saxonism*. On Manifest Destiny, see Frederick Merk, *Manifest Destiny and Mission: A Reinterpretation*. Readable accounts of the activities of the filibusters are Charles H. Brown, *Agents of Manifest Destiny: The Lives and Times of the Filibusters*, and Joseph A. Stout, *Schemers and Dreamers: Filibustering in Mexico, 1848–1921*. For this topic, see also Robert E. May, *Manifest Destiny's Underworld: Filibustering in Antebellum America*.

American diplomatic relations with individual countries during the second half of the 19th century are expertly covered in Thomas M. Leonard, ed., *United States-Latin American Relations, 1850–1930: Establishing a Relationship*. On James G. Blaine and his policies toward Latin America, see David Healy, *James G. Blaine and Latin America*. The foreign policy of the Garfield and Arthur administrations is expertly analyzed in David M. Pletcher, *The Awkward Years: American Foreign Relations under Garfield and Arthur*. The important theme of rivalry between the United States and Great Britain is examined in Joseph Smith, *Illusions of Conflict: Anglo-American Diplomacy toward Latin America, 1865–1896*. The most influential study stressing the importance of economic factors on American expansion is Walter LaFeber, *The New Empire: An Interpretation of American Expansion, 1860–1898*. David M. Pletcher, *The Diplomacy of Trade and Investment: American Economic Expansion in the Hemisphere, 1865–1900*, is a balanced work that places more emphasis on the importance of political issues. A perceptive study is Robert L. Beisner, *From the Old Diplomacy to the New, 1865–1900*, which is still one of the best overviews of American foreign policy at the end of the 19th century. On the relationship between Argentina and the United States, see Thomas F. McGann, *Argentina, the United States, and the Inter-American System, 1880–1914*. John A. S. Grenville and George B. Young, *Politics, Strategy, and American Diplomacy: Studies in Foreign Policy, 1873–1917*, is an excellent study of the diplomacy of the Venezuelan Boundary Dispute. On the wider diplomatic context of the Spanish-American War, see Ernest R. May, *Imperial Democracy: The Emergence of America as a Great Power*.

On dollar diplomacy and the Caribbean region at the beginning of the 20th century, see the overviews by Dana G. Munro, *Intervention and Dollar Diplomacy in the Caribbean, 1900–1921*, and David Healey, *Drive to Hegemony: The United States in the Caribbean, 1898–1917*. For this topic, see also Lester D. Langley and Thomas Schoonover, *The Banana Men: American Mercenaries and Entrepreneurs in Central America, 1880–1930*, and the two pioneering studies by Emily S. Rosenberg, *Spreading the American Dream: American Economic and Cultural Expansion, 1890–1945* and *Financial Missionaries to the World: The Politics and Culture of Dollar Diplomacy, 1900–1930*. On Theodore Roosevelt's Latin American diplomacy, see Richard H. Collin, *Theodore*

Roosevelt's Caribbean: The Panama Canal, the Monroe Doctrine and the Latin American Context. On the diplomacy of the canal, see the detailed study by John Major, *Prize Possession: The United States and the Panama Canal, 1903–1979*, and the interpretive overview Walter LaFeber, *The Panama Canal: The Crisis in Historical Perspective*. Michel Gobat, *Confronting the American Dream: Nicaragua under U.S. Imperial Rule*, is a well-researched account of American policy toward and influence on Nicaragua. On the policy of "approximation" between Brazil and the United States, see Joseph Smith, *Unequal Giants, Diplomatic Relations between the United States and Brazil, 1889–1930*. Wilson's attitude and policy toward Latin America is explored in Mark T. Gilderhus, *Pan American Visions: Woodrow Wilson in the Western Hemisphere*. Tensions with Mexico are highlighted in Robert E. Quirk, *An Affair of Honor: Woodrow Wilson and the Occupation of Veracruz*, and Joseph A. Stout, *Border Conflict: Villistas, Carrancistas, and the Punitive Expedition, 1915–1920*. Percy A. Martin, *Latin America and the War*, is a dated but still very informative study of the various policies adopted by the Latin American nations toward World War I. For an overview of the diplomatic context stressing the role of the United States, see Emily S. Rosenberg, *World War I and the Growth of United States Predominance in Latin America*. On diplomatic relations after World War I, see Kenneth J. Grieb, *The Latin American Policy of Warren G. Harding*, and Joseph S. Tulchin, *The Aftermath of War: World War I and U.S. Policy toward Latin America*.

On the formulation of the Good Neighbor Policy during the 1930s, see Alexander DeConde, *Herbert Hoover's Latin American Policy*, and Bryce Wood, *The Making of the Good Neighbor Policy*. For a perceptive analysis of U.S. economic policies during the years of the Great Depression, see Dick Steward, *Trade and Hemisphere: The Good Neighbor Policy and Reciprocal Trade*. Another valuable study also stressing the significance of economic factors is David Green, *The Containment of Latin America: A History of the Myths and Realities of the Good Neighbor Policy*. For the general diplomatic background to World War II, see R. A. Humphreys, *Latin America and the Second World War* (2 vols.). Informative studies of U.S. wartime relations with individual countries are Frank D. McCann, *The Brazilian-American Alliance, 1937–1945*, and Michael J. Francis, *The Limits of Hegemony: United States Relations with Argentina and Chile during World War II*.

For readable accounts of U.S. policy toward Latin America after World War II, see Bryce Wood, *The Dismantling of the Good Neighbor Policy*, and Gaddis Smith, *The Last Years of the Monroe Doctrine, 1945–1993*. The creation of the Rio Pact and the Organization of American States are carefully examined in J. Lloyd Mecham, *The United States and Inter-American Security, 1889–1960*. The alleged influence of big business on U.S. policy toward Guatemala is critically described in Stephen C. Schlesinger and Stephen Kinzer, *Bitter Fruit: The Untold Story of the American Coup in Guatemala*. Richard H. Immerman, *The CIA in Guatemala: The Foreign Policy of Intervention*, is a scholarly examination of the policy of the Eisenhower administration, while Piero Gleijeses, *Shattered Hope: The Guatemala Revolution and the United States, 1944–1954*, provides a comprehensive study that includes copious evidence from Guatemalan archival and oral sources. An excellent examination of Eisenhower's policies toward Latin America is Stephen G. Rabe, *Eisenhower and Latin America: The Foreign Policy of Anti-Communism*. See also, by the same author, *The Most Dangerous Area in the World: John F. Kennedy Confronts Communist Revolution in Latin America*, for an insightful study of the personal concern that Kennedy showed toward developments in the region. Alan McPherson, *Yankee No! Anti-Americanism in U.S.-Latin American Relations*, conveys very well the tense atmosphere that was often a feature of inter-American diplomatic relations during the Kennedy and Johnson years. Early assessments of the Alliance for Progress are Jerome Levinson and Juan de Onís, *The Alliance That Lost Its Way: A Critical Report on the Alliance for Progress*, and William D. Rogers, *The Twilight Struggle: The Alliance for Progress and the Politics of Development in Latin America*. Informative accounts of U.S. diplomatic relations with Brazil are W. Michael Weis, *Cold Warriors and Coups d'Etat: Brazilian-American Relations, 1945–1964*, and Phyllis R. Parker, *Brazil and the Quiet Intervention, 1964*. Seymour M. Hersh, *Kissinger: The Price of Power*, is severely critical of U.S. policy toward Salvador Allende. For a balanced scholarly approach of the Nixon administration's relations with Chile, see Paul Sigmund, *The Overthrow of Allende and the Politics of Chile, 1964–1976*. Several distinguished American scholars have contributed articles in the collections edited by John D. Martz, *United States Policy in Latin America: A Quarter Century of Crisis and Challenge, 1961–1986*, and, in a volume covering the

1980s, *United States Policy in Latin America: A Decade of Crisis and Challenge*. Abraham F. Lowenthal, *Partners in Conflict: The United States and Latin America*, is an excellent assessment of the state of inter-American relations during the early 1980s. The controversial issue of human rights is carefully examined in Lars Schoultz, *Human Rights and the United States Policy toward Latin America*. However, Martha K. Huggins, *Political Policing: The United States and Latin America*, reveals the dangers of developing too close an involvement in training Latin American police forces. William J. Jorden, *Panama Odyssey*, presents a diplomat's account of the negotiations leading to the Panama Canal Treaties. A readable and detailed account of U.S. diplomacy toward the Central American crisis that includes coverage of the policies of both the Carter and Reagan administrations is William M. LeoGrande, *Our Own Backyard: The United States in Central America, 1977–1992*. A perceptive study of U.S. policy toward Nicaragua by a diplomatic insider is Robert A. Pastor, *Condemned to Repetition: The United States and Nicaragua*. For further reading on Reagan's Latin American policy, see Thomas Carothers, *In the Name of Democracy: U.S. Policy toward Latin America in the Reagan Years*. Jack Child, *The Central American Peace Process, 1983–1991: Sheathing Swords, Building Confidence*, discusses the diplomatic efforts of the Latin American leaders to mediate the Central American crisis. Margaret Scranton, *The Noriega Years: U.S.-Panamanian Relations, 1981–1990*, examines the difficulties faced by the Reagan and George H. W. Bush administrations in dealing with the Panamanian dictator. The complex history of diplomatic negotiations leading to the signing of the North American Free Trade Agreement (NAFTA) is informatively recounted in Maxwell Cameron and Brian Tomlin, *The Making of NAFTA: How the Deal Was Done*. An excellent study of U.S. policy and the problem of illegal narcotics is William O. Walker, *Drug Control in the Americas*.

Selected U.S. diplomatic correspondence with individual Latin American countries has been published since 1862 in the U.S. Department of State, *Papers Relating to the Foreign Relations of the United States*. The volumes covering relations with the nations of the Western Hemisphere during the 1960s can be accessed at the website of the Office of the Historian, www.state.gov/www/about_state/history/frus .html. Official government documents relating to U.S. policy on controversial issues during the Cold War, such as the 1954 Guatemala coup and the overthrow of Salvador Allende in Chile, can be accessed at the National Security Archive maintained by George Washington University at www.gwu.edu/~nsarchiv. The International History Department of the London School of Economics has recently created a very useful guide to international diplomatic archives that includes the United States and several Latin America countries: www.archivesmadeeasy .org. For information on the history and current activities of the Organization of American States, see www.oas.org, and for the Free Trade Area of the Americas, see www.ftaa-alca.org.

II. DOCUMENTS AND DOCUMENTARY COLLECTIONS

Bacon, Robert, and James Brown Scott, eds. *Latin America and the United States: Addresses by Elihu Root.* Cambridge, Mass.: Harvard University Press, 1917.

Free Trade Area of the Americas. www.ftaa-alca.org.

Gantenbein, James W., ed. *The Evolution of Our Latin-American Policy: A Documentary Record.* New York: Octagon, 1950.

Garrison, George P., ed. *Diplomatic Correspondence of the Republic of Texas.* 3 vols. Washington, D.C.: U.S. Government Printing Office, 1908–1911.

Holden, Robert H., and Eric Zolov, eds. *Latin America and the United States: A Documentary History.* New York: Oxford University Press, 2000.

International History Department, London School of Economics. www .archivesmadeeasy.org.

Manning, William R. *Diplomatic Correspondence of the United States concerning the Independence of the Latin-American Nations.* 3 vols. New York: Oxford University Press, 1925.

National Security Archive, George Washington University. www.gwu.edu/ ~nsarchiv.

Organization of American States. www.oas.org.

Richardson, James D., ed. *A Compilation of the Messages and Papers of the Presidents, 1789–1897.* 10 vols. Washington, D.C.: U.S. Government Printing Office, 1896–1899.

Scott, James Brown, ed. *The International Conferences of American States, 1889–1928.* New York. Oxford University Press, 1931.

———, ed. *The International Conferences of American States, 1889–1928: First Supplement, 1933–1940.* Washington, D.C.: Carnegie Endowment for International Peace, 1940.

Ulibarri, George S., and John P. Harrison. *Guide to Materials on Latin America in the National Archives of the United States*. Washington, D.C.: National Archives and Records Service, 1974.

U.S. Department of State. *Papers Relating to the Foreign Relations of the United States*. Washington, D.C.: U.S. Government Printing Office, 1962–.

U.S. Department of State, Office of the Historian. www.state.gov/www/about_state/history/frus.html.

U.S. Senate, Committee on Foreign Relations, Select Committee to Study Government Operations with Respect to Intelligence Activities. *Covert Action in Chile, 1963–1973*. Washington, D.C.: U.S. Government Printing Office, 1975.

Webster, Charles K., ed. *Britain and the Independence of Latin America, 1812–1830. Select Documents from the Foreign Office Archives*. 2 vols. London: Oxford University Press, 1938.

III. REFERENCE WORKS

Atkins, G. Pope, ed. *Encyclopedia of the Inter-American System*. Westport, Conn.: Greenwood Press, 1997.

Beisner, Robert L., ed. *American Foreign Relations since 1600: A Guide to the Literature*. Santa Barbara, Calif.: ABC-CLIO, 2003.

Berner, Brad. *Historical Dictionary of the Spanish-American War*. Lanham, Md.: Scarecrow Press, 1998.

Blume, Kenneth J. *Historical Dictionary of U.S. Diplomacy from the Civil War until World War I*. Lanham, Md.: Scarecrow Press, 2005.

Clark, Paul C., and Edward H. Moseley. *Historical Dictionary of the U.S.-Mexican War*. Lanham, Md.: Scarecrow Press, 1997.

Dent, David W. *The Legacy of the Monroe Doctrine: A Reference Guide to U.S. Involvement in Latin America and the Caribbean*. Westport, Conn.: Greenwood Press, 1999.

Sheinen, David. *The Organization of American States*. New Brunswick, N.J.: Transaction Publishers, 1996.

Smith, Joseph, and Simon Davis. *Historical Dictionary of the Cold War*. Lanham, Md.: Scarecrow Press, 2000.

Trask, David F., Michael C. Meyer, and Roger R. Trask, eds. *A Bibliography of United States-Latin American Relations since 1810*. Lincoln: University of Nebraska Press, 1968.

Tutorow, Norman E., ed. *The Mexican-American War: An Annotated Bibliography*. Westport, Conn.: Greenwood Press, 1981.

Wilson, Larman C., and David W. Dent. *Historical Dictionary of Inter-American Organizations*. Lanham, Md.: Scarecrow Press, 1997.

IV. GENERAL SURVEYS

Bemis, Samuel Flagg. *The Latin American Policy of the United States: An Historical Interpretation*. New York: Norton, 1971.

Coerver, Don M., and Linda B. Hall. *Tangled Destinies: Latin America and the United States*. Albuquerque: University of New Mexico Press, 1999.

Connell-Smith, Gordon. *The United States and Latin America: An Historical Analysis of Inter-American Relations*. London: Heinemann, 1974.

Gil, Federico G. *Latin American-United States Relations*. New York: Harcourt Brace Jovanovich, 1971.

Gilderhus, Mark. *The Second Century: U.S.-Latin American Relations since 1889*. Wilmington, Del.: Scholarly Resources, 2000.

Langley, Lester D. *America and the Americas: The United States in the Western Hemisphere*. Athens: University of Georgia Press, 1989.

———. *The Americas in the Modern Age*. New Haven, Conn.: Yale University Press, 2003.

Longley, Kyle. *In the Eagle's Shadow: The United States and Latin America*. Wheeling, Ill.: Harlan Davidson, 2002.

Lieuwen, Edwin. *U.S. Policy in Latin America: A Short History*. New York: Praeger, 1965.

Mecham, J. Lloyd. *A Survey of United States-Latin American Relations*. Boston: Houghton Mifflin, 1965.

Molineu, Harold. *U.S. Policy toward Latin America: From Regionalism to Globalism*. Boulder, Colo.: Westview, 1986.

Niess, Frank. *Hemisphere To Itself: A History of U.S.-Latin American Relations*. London: Zed Press, 1990.

Perkins, Dexter. *Hands Off: A History of the Monroe Doctrine*. Boston: Little, Brown, 1941.

Schoultz, Lars. *Beneath the United States: A History of U.S. Policy toward Latin America*. Cambridge, Mass.: Harvard University Press, 1998.

Smith, Peter H. *Talons of the Eagle: Dynamics of U.S.-Latin American Relations*. New York: Oxford University Press, 1996.

V. BILATERAL RELATIONS

Bandeira, Moniz. *Presença dos Estados Unidos no Brasil*. Rio de Janeiro: Editora Civilizacão Brasileira, 1973.

Clayton, Lawrence A. *Peru and the United States: The Condor and the Eagle*. Athens: University of Georgia Press, 1999.

Coatsworth, John H. *Central America and the United States: The Clients and the Colossus*. New York: Twayne, 1994.

Conniff, Michael L. *Panama and the United States: The Forced Alliance*. Athens: University of Georgia Press, 1992.

Ewell, Judith. *Venezuela and the United States: From Monroe's Hemisphere to Petroleum's Empire*. Athens: University of Georgia Press, 1996.

Findling, John E. *Close Neighbors, Distant Friends: United States-Central American Relations*. New York: Greenwood Press, 1987.

Hill, Lawrence F. *Diplomatic Relations between the United States and Brazil*. Durham, N.C.: Duke University Press, 1932.

Hirst, Mônica. *The United States and Brazil: A Long Road of Unmet Expectations*. New York: Routledge, 2005.

LaFeber, Walter. *Inevitable Revolutions: The United States in Central America*. New York: Norton, 1983.

Lehman, Kenneth D. *Bolivia and the United States: A Limited Partnership*. Athens: University of Georgia Press, 1999.

Leonard, Thomas M. *Central America and the United States: The Search for Stability*. Athens: University of Georgia Press, 1991.

———. *Panama, the Canal and the United States: A Guide to Issues and References*. Claremont, Calif.: Regina Books, 1993.

Muñoz, Heraldo, and Carlos Portales. *Elusive Friendship: A Survey of U.S.-Chilean Relations*. Boulder, Colo.: Lynne Rienner, 1991.

Ogelslby, J. C. M. *Gringos from the Far North: Essays in the History of Canadian-Latin American Relations, 1866–1968* Toronto: Macmillan, 1976.

Parks, E. Taylor. *Colombia and the United States, 1765–1934*. Durham, N.C.: Duke University Press, 1935.

Pérez, Louis A., Jr. *Cuba and the United States: Ties of Singular Intimacy*. Athens: University of Georgia Press, 1990.

Peterson, Harold F. *Argentina and the United States, 1810–1960*. Albany: State University of New York Press, 1964.

Pike, Frederick B. *Chile and the United States, 1880–1962: The Emergence of Chile's Social Crisis and the Challenge to United States Diplomacy*. Notre Dame, Ind.: University of Notre Dame Press, 1963.

———. *The United States and the Andean Republics: Peru, Bolivia, and Ecuador*. Cambridge, Mass.: Harvard University Press, 1977.

Raat, W. Dirk. *Mexico and the United States: Ambivalent Vistas*. Athens: University of Georgia Press, 1996.

Randall, Stephen J. *Colombia and the United States: Hegemony and Independence*. Athens: University of Georgia Press, 1992.

Sater, William F. *Chile and the United States: Empires in Conflict*. Athens: University of Georgia Press, 1990.

Schmitt, Karl M. *Mexico and the United States, 1821–1973: Conflict and Coexistence*. New York: Wiley, 1974.

Tulchin, Joseph S. *Argentina and the United States: A Conflicted Relationship.* Boston: Twayne, 1990.

Vázquez, Josefina Zoraida, and Lorenzo Meyer. *The United States and Mexico.* Chicago: University of Chicago Press, 1985.

Wesson, Robert. *The United States and Brazil: Limits of Influence.* New York: Praeger, 1981.

Whitaker, Arthur P. *The United States and the Southern Cone: Argentina, Chile, and Uruguay.* Cambridge, Mass.: Harvard University Press, 1976.

Zorilla, Luis G. *Historia de las relaciones entre México y los Estados Unidos de América 1800–1954.* Mexico City: Editorial Porrúa, 1965.

VI. SPECIAL STUDIES

Aguilar, Alonso. *Pan-Americanism from Monroe to the Present: A View from the Other Side.* New York: Monthly Review Press. 1965.

Atkins, G. Pope. *Latin America in the International Political System.* Boulder, Colo.: Westview, 1989.

Bailey, Norman A. *Latin America in World Politics.* New York: Walker, 1967.

Berger, Mark T. *Under Northern Eyes: Latin American Studies and U.S. Hegemony in the Americas, 1898–1900.* Bloomington: Indiana University Press, 1995.

Bulmer-Thomas, Victor. *The Economic History of Latin America since Independence.* Cambridge: Cambridge University Press, 1994.

Calvert, Peter. *The International Politics of Latin America.* New York: St. Martin's Press, 1994.

Connell-Smith, Gordon. *The Inter-American System.* Oxford: Oxford University Press, 1966.

Cotler, Julio, and Richard R. Fagen, eds. *Latin America and the United States: The Changing Political Realities.* Stanford, Calif.: Stanford University Press, 1974.

Dozer, Donald Marquand. *The Monroe Doctrine: Its Modern Significance.* New York: Knopf, 1965.

Fagg, John Edwin. *Pan Americanism.* Malabar, Fla.: Krieger, 1982.

Grabendorff , Wolf, and Riordan Roett, eds. *Latin America, Western Europe and the U.S.: Reevaluating the Atlantic Triangle.* New York: Praeger, 1985.

Hart, John M. *Empire and Revolution: The Americans in Mexico since the Civil War.* Berkeley: University of California Press, 2002.

Humphrey, John P. *The Inter-American System: A Canadian View.* Toronto: Macmillan, 1942.

Hunt, Michael H. *Ideology and U.S. Foreign Policy.* New Haven, Conn.: Yale University Press, 1987.

Inman, Samuel Guy, ed. *Inter-American Conferences, 1826–1954: History and Problems*. Washington, D.C.: University Press, 1965.

Johnson, John J. *Latin America in Caricature*. Austin: University of Texas Press, 1980.

Joseph, Gilbert M., Catherine C. LeGrand, and Ricardo D. Salvatore, eds. *Close Encounters of Empire: Writing the Cultural History of U.S.-Latin American Relations*. Durham, N.C.: Duke University Press, 1998.

Kane, William E. *Civil Strife in Latin America: A Legal History of U.S. Involvement*. Baltimore: Johns Hopkins University Press, 1972.

Kenworthy, Eldon. *America/Américas: Myth in the Making of U.S. Policy toward Latin America*. University Park: Pennsylvania State University Press, 1995.

LaFeber, Walter. *The Panama Canal: The Crisis in Historical Perspective*. New York: Oxford University Press, 1989.

Logan, John A. *No Transfer: An American Security Principle*. New Haven, Conn.: Yale University Press, 1961.

McCullough, David. *The Path between the Seas: The Creation of the Panama Canal, 1870–1914*. New York: Simon and Schuster, 1977.

Mecham, J. Lloyd. *The United States and Inter-American Security, 1889–1960*. Austin: University of Texas Press, 1961.

Murphy, Gretchen. *Hemispheric Imaginings: The Monroe Doctrine and Narratives of U.S. Empire*. Durham, N.C.: Duke University Press, 2005.

O'Brien, Thomas F. *The Century of U.S. Capitalism in Latin America*. Albuquerque: University of New Mexico Press, 1999.

Park, James William. *Latin American Underdevelopment: A History of Perspectives in the United States, 1870–1965*. Baton Rouge: Louisiana State University Press, 1995.

Pike, Fredrick B. *The United States and Latin America: Myths and Stereotypes of Civilization and Nature*. Austin: University of Texas Press, 1992.

Reid, John T. *Spanish American Images of the United States, 1790–1960*. Gainesville: University Press of Florida, 1977.

Sheinin, David, ed. *Beyond the Ideal: Pan Americanism in Inter-American Affairs*. Westport, Conn.: Praeger, 2000.

Thomas, A. V., and A. J. Thomas. *The Organization of American States*. Dallas: Southern Methodist University Press, 1963.

VII. FROM COLONIES TO INDEPENDENT NATIONS

Bernstein, Harry. *Origins of Inter-American Interest,1700–1812*. Philadelphia: University of Pennsylvania Press, 1945.

Brooks, Philip C. *Diplomacy and the Borderlands: The Adams-Onís Treaty of 1819*. Berkeley: University of California Press, 1939.

Cady, John F. *Foreign Intervention in the Rio de la Plata, 1838–1850*. Philadelphia: University of Pennsylvania Press, 1929.

Chávez, Thomas E. *Spain and the Independence of the United States: An Intrinsic Gift*. Albuquerque: University of New Mexico Press, 2002.

Griffin, Charles C. *The United States and the Disruption of the Spanish Empire, 1810–1822*. New York: Columbia University Press, 1937.

Hilton, Stanley E. "The United States and Brazilian Independence." In *From Colony to Nation*. Edited by A. J. R. Russell-Wood. Baltimore: Johns Hopkins University Press, 1975, 109–29.

Horsman, Reginald. *The Diplomacy of the New Republic, 1776–1815*. Arlington Heights, Ill.: Harlan Davidson, 1985.

Johnson, John J. *A Hemisphere Apart: The Foundations of United States Policy toward Latin America*. Baltimore: Johns Hopkins University Press, 1990.

Langley, Lester D. *The Americas in the Age of Revolution, 1750–1850*. New Haven, Conn.: Yale University Press, 1996.

Liss, Peggy K. *Atlantic Empires: The Network of Trade and Revolution, 1713–1826*. Baltimore: Johns Hopkins University Press, 1983.

Lynch, John. *The Spanish-American Revolutions, 1808–1826*. London: Norton, 1973.

May, Ernest R. *The Making of the Monroe Doctrine*. Cambridge, Mass.: Harvard University Press, 1975.

Perkins, Dexter. *The Monroe Doctrine, 1823–1826*. Cambridge, Mass.: Harvard University Press, 1927.

Rippy, J. Fred. *Rivalry of the United States and Great Britain over Latin America (1808–1830)*. Baltimore: Johns Hopkins University Press, 1929.

Shurbutt, T. Ray, ed. *United States-Latin American Relations, 1800–1850*. Tuscaloosa: University of Alabama Press, 1991.

Weeks, William Earl. *John Quincy Adams and American Global Empire*. Lexington: University Press of Kentucky, 1992.

Whitaker, Arthur P. *The United States and the Independence of Latin America, 1800–1830*. Baltimore: Johns Hopkins University Press, 1941.

———. *The Western Hemisphere Idea: Its Rise and Decline*. Ithaca, N.Y.: Cornell University Press.

VIII. DIPLOMATIC DETACHMENT

Bauer, K. Jack. *The Mexican War, 1846–1848*. Lincoln: University of Nebraska Press, 1974.

Bosch García, Carlos. *Historia de las relaciones entre Mexico y los Estados Unidos, 1819–1848*. Mexico City: Escuela Nacional de Ciencias Políticas y Sociales, 1961.

Brown, Charles H. *Agents of Manifest Destiny: The Lives and Times of the Filibusters*. Chapel Hill: University of North Carolina Press, 1980.

Goebel, Julius. *The Struggle for the Falkland Islands: A Study in Legal and Diplomatic History*. New Haven, Conn.: Yale University Press, 1927.

Greenberg, Amy S. *Manifest Manhood and the Antebellum American Empire*. New York: Cambridge University Press, 2005.

Horsman, Reginald. *Race and Manifest Destiny: The Origins of American Racial Anglo-Saxonism*. Cambridge, Mass.: Harvard University Press, 1981.

Lockey, Joseph B. *Pan-Americanism: Its Beginnings*. New York: Macmillan, 1920.

May, Robert E. *Manifest Destiny's Underworld: Filibustering in Antebellum America*. Chapel Hill: University of North Carolina Press, 2002.

———. *The Southern Dream of a Caribbean Empire, 1854–1861*. Baton Rouge: Louisiana State University Press, 1973.

Merk, Frederick. *Manifest Destiny and Mission in American History: A Reinterpretation*. New York, Vintage, 1966.

Paolino, Ernest N. *The Foundations of the American Empire: William Henry Seward and U.S. Foreign Policy*. Ithaca, N.Y.: Cornell University Press, 1973.

Perkins, Dexter. *The Monroe Doctrine, 1826–1867*. Baltimore: Johns Hopkins University Press, 1933.

———. *The Monroe Doctrine, 1867–1907*. Baltimore: Johns Hopkins University Press, 1937.

Pletcher, David M. *The Diplomacy of Annexation: Texas, Oregon, and the Mexican War*. Columbia: University of Missouri Press, 1973.

Rodríguez, Mario. *A Palmerstonian Diplomat in Central America: Frederick A. Chatfield, Esq*. Tucson: University of Arizona Press, 1964.

Schoonover, Thomas D. *Dollars over Dominion: The Triumph of Liberalism in Mexican-United States Relations, 1861–1867*. Baton Rouge: Louisiana State University Press, 1978.

Seckinger, Ron. *The Brazilian Monarchy and the South American Republics, 1822–1831: Diplomacy and State Building*. Baton Rouge: Louisiana State University Press, 1984.

Stout, Joseph A. *Schemers and Dreamers: Filibustering in Mexico, 1848–1921*. Fort Worth: Texas Christian University Press, 2002.

Weber, David J. *The Mexican Frontier, 1821–1846: The American Southwest under Mexico*. Albuquerque: University of New Mexico Press, 1982.

Weinberg, Albert K. *Manifest Destiny: A Study of Nationalist Expansion in American History*. Baltimore: Johns Hopkins University Press, 1935.

IX. PAN-AMERICANISM

Beisner, Robert L. *From the Old Diplomacy to the New, 1865–1900*. Arlington Heights, Ill.: Harlan Davidson, 1986.

Burr, Robert N. *By Reason or Force: Chile and the Balancing of Power in Latin America, 1830–1905*. Berkeley: University of California Press, 1967.

Campbell, Charles S. *The Transformation of American Foreign Relations, 1865–1900*. New York: Harper and Row, 1976.

Foner, Philip S. *The Spanish-Cuban-American War and the Birth of American Imperialism*. 2 vols. New York: Monthly Review Press, 1972.

Goldberg, Joyce S. *The Baltimore Affair*. Lincoln: University of Nebraska Press, 1986.

Grenville, J. A. S., and George B. Young. *Politics, Strategy, and American Diplomacy: Studies in Foreign Policy, 1873–1917*. New Haven, Conn.: Yale University Press, 1966.

Healy, David. *James G. Blaine and Latin America*. Columbia: University of Missouri Press, 2001.

LaFeber, Walter. *The New Empire: An Interpretation of American Expansion, 1860–1898*. Ithaca, N.Y.: Cornell University Press, 1963.

Leonard, Thomas M., ed. *United States-Latin American Relations, 1850–1903: Establishing a Relationship*. Tuscaloosa: University of Alabama Press, 1999.

McCullough, David. *The Path between the Seas: The Creation of the Panama Canal, 1876–1914*. New York: Simon and Schuster, 1977.

McGann, Thomas F. *Argentina, the United States, and the Inter-American System, 1880–1914*. Cambridge, Mass.: Harvard University Press, 1957.

May, Ernest R. *Imperial Democracy: The Emergence of America as a Great Power*. New York: Harcourt Brace and World, 1961.

Millington, Herbert. *American Diplomacy and the War of the Pacific*. New York: Columbia University Press, 1948.

Offner, John L. *An Unwanted War: The Diplomacy of the United States and Spain over Cuba, 1895–1898*. Chapel Hill: University of North Carolina Press, 1992.

Parks, E. Taylor. *Colombia and the United States, 1765–1934*. Durham, N.C.: Duke University Press, 1935.

Pérez, Louis A., Jr. *The War of 1898: The United States and Cuba in History and Historiography*. Chapel Hill: University of North Carolina Press, 1998.

Perkins, Dexter. *The Monroe Doctrine, 1867–1907*. Baltimore: Johns Hopkins University Press, 1937.

Pletcher, David M. *The Awkward Years: American Foreign Relations under Garfield and Arthur*. Columbia: University of Missouri Press, 1962.

———. *The Diplomacy of Trade and Investment: American Economic Expansion in the Hemisphere, 1865–1900*. Columbia: University of Missouri Press, 1998.

Schoonover, Thomas D. *The United States in Central America, 1860–1911: Episodes of Social Imperialism and Imperial Rivalry in the World System.* Durham, N.C.: Duke University Press, 1991.

Smith, Joseph. *Illusions of Conflict: Anglo-American Diplomacy toward Latin America, 1865–1896.* Pittsburgh: University of Pittsburgh Press, 1979.

———. *The Spanish-American War: Conflict in the Caribbean and the Pacific, 1895–1902.* New York: Longman, 1994.

Topik, Steven C. *Trade and Gunboats: The United States and Brazil in the Age of Empire.* Stanford, Calif.: Stanford University Press, 1996.

Trask, David F. *The War with Spain in 1898.* New York: Macmillan, 1981.

X. DOLLAR DIPLOMACY

Albert, Bill. *South America and the First World War: The Impact of the War on Brazil, Argentina, Peru, and Chile.* Cambridge: Cambridge University Press, 1988.

Britton, John A. *Revolution and Ideology: Images of the Mexican Revolution in the United States.* Lexington: University Press of Kentucky, 1995.

Bunau-Varilla, Philippe. *Panama: The Creation, Destruction, and Resurrection.* New York: McBride, Nast and Co., 1914.

Burns, E. Bradford. *The Unwritten Alliance: Rio Branco and Brazilian-American Relations.* New York: Columbia University Press, 1966.

Callcott, Wilfrid H. *The Caribbean Policy of the United States, 1910–1920.* Baltimore: Johns Hopkins University Press, 1942.

Carreras, Charles. *United States Economic Penetration of Venezuela and Its Effects on Diplomacy, 1895–1906.* New York: Garland, 1987.

Clendenen, Clarence C. *The United States and Pancho Villa: A Study in Unconventional Diplomacy.* Ithaca, N.Y.: Cornell University Press, 1961.

Collin, Richard H. *Theodore Roosevelt's Caribbean: The Panama Canal, the Monroe Doctrine, and the Latin American Context.* Baton Rouge: Louisiana State University Press, 1990.

Dosal, Paul J. *Doing Business with the Dictators: A Political History of United Fruit in Guatemala, 1899–1944.* Wilmington, Del.: Scholarly Resources, 1993.

Drake, Paul W. *The Money Doctor in the Andes: The Kemmerer Missions, 1923–1933.* Durham, N.C.: Duke University Press, 1989.

———, ed. *Money Doctors, Foreign Debts, and Economic Reforms in Latin America from the 1890s to the Present.* Wilmington, Del.: Scholarly Resources, 1994.

Durán, Esperanza. *Guerra y revolución: Las grandes potencias y México, 1914–1918.* Mexico City: El Colegio de México, 1985.

Gardner, Lloyd C. *Economic Aspects of New Deal Diplomacy*. Madison: University of Wisconsin Press, 1964.

Gilderhus, Mark T. *Pan American Visions: Woodrow Wilson in the Western Hemisphere, 1913–1921*. Tucson: University of Arizona Press, 1986.

Gobat, Michel. *Confronting the American Dream: Nicaragua under U.S. Imperial Rule*. Durham, N.C.: Duke University Press, 2006.

Grieb, Kenneth J. *The Latin American Policy of Warren G. Harding*. Fort Worth: Texas Christian University Press, 1976.

———. *The United States and Huerta*. Lincoln: University of Nebraska Press, 1969.

Hall, Linda B., and Don M. Coerver. *Revolution on the Border: The United States and Mexico, 1910–1920*. Albuquerque: University of New Mexico Press, 1988.

Haring, Clarence H. *South America Looks at the United States*. New York: Macmillan, 1929.

Healy, David. *Drive to Hegemony: The United States in the Caribbean, 1898–1917*. Madison: University of Wisconsin Press, 1988.

Hood, Miriam. *Gunboat Diplomacy, 1895–1905: Great Power Pressure in Venezuela*. London: George Allen & Unwin, 1975.

Hughes, Charles E. *Our Relations to the Nations of the Western Hemisphere*. Princeton, N.J.: Princeton University Press, 1928.

Kamman, William. *A Search for Stability: United States Diplomacy toward Nicaragua, 1925–1933*. Notre Dame, Ind.: University of Notre Dame Press, 1968.

Katz, Friedrich. *The Secret War in Mexico: Europe, the United States, and the Mexican Revolution*. Chicago: University of Chicago Press, 1981.

Kelchner, Warren H. *Latin American Relations with the League of Nations*. Boston: World Peace Foundation, 1929.

Lael, Richard L. *Arrogant Diplomacy: U.S. Policy toward Colombia, 1903–1922*. Wilmington, Del.: Scholarly Resources, 1987.

Langley, Lester D. *The Banana Wars: United States Intervention in the Caribbean, 1898–1934*. Lexington: University Press of Kentucky, 1985.

Langley, Lester D., and Thomas D. Schoonover. *The Banana Men: American Mercenaries and Entrepreneurs in Central America, 1880–1930*. Lexington: University Press of Kentucky, 1995.

Macaulay, Neill. *The Sandino Affair*. Chicago: Quadrangle Books, 1967.

Major, John. *Prize Possession: The United States and the Panama Canal, 1903–1979*. Cambridge: Cambridge University Press, 1993.

Martin, Percy A. *Latin America and the War*. Baltimore: Johns Hopkins University Press, 1925.

Meyer, Lorenzo. *Mexico and the United States in the Oil Controversy, 1917–1942*. Austin: University of Texas Press, 1972.

Miner, Dwight C. *The Fight for the Panama Route: The Story of the Spooner Act and the Hay-Herrán Treaty.* New York: Columbia University Press, 1940.

Munro, Dana G. *Intervention and Dollar Diplomacy in the Caribbean, 1900–1921.* Princeton, N.J.: Princeton University Press, 1964.

———. *The United States and the Caribbean Republics, 1921–1933.* Princeton, N.J.: Princeton University Press, 1974.

Nearing, Scott, and Joseph Freeman. *Dollar Diplomacy: A Study in American Imperialism.* New York: Viking, 1925.

O'Brien, Thomas F. *The Revolutionary Mission: American Enterprise in Latin America, 1900–1945.* New York: Cambridge University Press, 1996.

Pérez, Louis A., Jr. *Cuba under the Platt Amendment, 1902–1934.* Pittsburgh: University of Pittsburgh Press, 1986.

Perkins, Whitney T. *Constraint of Empire: The United States and Caribbean Interventions.* Westport, Conn.: Greenwood Press, 1981.

Quirk, Robert E. *An Affair of Honor: Woodrow Wilson and the Occupation of Veracruz.* New York: Norton, 1967.

Rosenberg, Emily S. *Spreading the American Dream: American Economic and Cultural Expansion, 1890–1945.* New York: Hill and Wang, 1982.

———. *Financial Missionaries to the World: The Politics and Culture of Dollar Diplomacy, 1900–1930.* Cambridge, Mass.: Harvard University Press, 1999.

Scholes, Walter V., and Marie V. Scholes. *The Foreign Policies of the Taft Administration.* Columbia: University of Missouri Press, 1970.

Sharbach, Sarah E. *Stereotypes of Latin America, Press Images, and U.S. Foreign Policy, 1920–1933.* New York: Garland, 1993.

Sheinin, David. *Searching for Authority: Pan Americanism, Diplomacy and Politics in United States-Argentine Relations, 1910–1930.* New Orleans: University Press of the South, 1998.

Smith, Joseph. *Unequal Giants: Diplomatic Relations between the United States and Brazil, 1889–1930.* Pittsburgh: Pittsburgh University Press, 1991.

Smith, Robert Freeman. *The United States and Revolutionary Nationalism in Mexico, 1916–1932.* Chicago: University of Chicago Press, 1972.

Stout, Joseph A. *Border Conflict: Villistas, Carrancistas, and the Punitive Expedition, 1915–1920.* Fort Worth: Texas Christian University Press, 1999.

Tulchin, Joseph S. *The Aftermath of War: World War I and U.S. Policy toward Latin America.* New York: New York University Press, 1971.

Ulloa, Berta. *La revolución intervenida: Relaciones diplomáticas entre México y Estados Unidos, 1910–1914.* Mexico City: El Colegio de Mexico, 1976.

Wilson, Joe F. *The United States, Chile and Peru in the Tacna and Arica Plebiscite.* Washington, D.C.: University Press of America, 1979.

XI. GOOD NEIGHBORS

Adams, Frederick C. *Economic Diplomacy: The Export-Import Bank and American Foreign Policy, 1934–1939.* Columbia: University of Missouri Press, 1976.

Beals, Carleton, Bryce Oliver, Herschel Brickell, and Samuel Guy Inman. *What the South Americans Think of Us: A Symposium.* New York, McBride, 1945.

DeConde, Alexander. *Herbert Hoover's Latin-American Policy.* Stanford, Calif.: Stanford University Press, 1951.

Delpar, Helen. *Enormous Vogue of Things Mexican: Cultural Relations between the United States and Mexico, 1920–1935.* Tuscaloosa: University of Alabama Press, 1992.

Francis, Michael J. *The Limits of Hegemony: United States Relations with Argentina and Chile during World War II.* Notre Dame, Ind.: University of Notre Dame Press, 1977.

Frank, Gary. *Struggle for Hegemony in South America: Argentina, Brazil, and the United States during the Second World War.* Coral Gables, Fla.: Center for Advanced International Studies, University of Miami, 1979.

Friedman, Max Paul. *Nazis and Good Neighbors: The United States Campaign against the Germans of Latin America in World War II.* Cambridge: Cambridge University Press, 2003.

Frye, Alton. *Nazi Germany and the American Hemisphere, 1933–1941.* New Haven, Conn.: Yale University Press, 1967.

Gardner, Lloyd C. *Economic Aspects of New Deal Diplomacy.* Madison: University of Wisconsin Press, 1964.

Gellman, Irwin F. *Good Neighbor Diplomacy: United States Policies in Latin America, 1933–1945.* Baltimore: Johns Hopkins University Press, 1979.

Green, David. *The Containment of Latin America: A History of the Myths and Realities of the Good Neighbor Policy.* Chicago: Quadrangle Books, 1971.

Guerrant, Edward O. *Roosevelt's Good Neighbor Policy.* Albuquerque: University of New Mexico Press, 1950.

Hilton, Stanley E. *Brazil and the Great Powers, 1930–1939: The Politics of Trade Rivalry.* Austin: University of Texas Press, 1975.

Humphreys, R. A. *Latin America and the Second World War.* 2 vols. London: Athlone Press, 1981–1982.

McCann, Frank D., Jr. *The Brazilian-American Alliance, 1937–1945.* Princeton, N.J.: Princeton University Press, 1974.

O'Brien, Thomas F. *The Revolutionary Mission: American Enterprise in Latin America, 1900–1945.* Cambridge: Cambridge University Press, 1996.

Pike, Fredrick B. *FDR's Good Neighbor Policy: Sixty Years of Generally Gentle Chaos.* Austin: University of Texas Press, 1995.

Ramírez Necochea, Hernán. *Los Estados Unidos y América Latina, 1930–1965.* Santiago de Chile: Editora Austral, 1965.

Schmitz, David F. *Thank God They're on Our Side: The United States and Right-Wing Dictatorships, 1921–1965.* Chapel Hill: University of North Carolina Press, 1999.

Steward, Dick. *Trade and Hemisphere: The Good Neighbor Policy and Reciprocal Trade.* Columbia: University of Missouri Press, 1975.

Wood, Bryce. *The Making of the Good Neighbor Policy.* New York: Norton, 1967.

——. *The United States and Latin American Wars, 1932–1942.* New York: Columbia University Press, 1966.

XII. COLD WAR DIPLOMACY

Bailey, Samuel L. *The United States and the Development of South America, 1945–1975.* New York: New Viewpoints, 1976.

Benjamin, Jules R. *The United States and the Origins of the Cuban Revolution: An Empire of Liberty in an Age of National Liberation.* Princeton, N.J.: Princeton University Press, 1990.

Black, Jan Knippers. *United States Penetration of Brazil.* Philadelphia: University of Pennsylvania Press, 1977.

Blasier, Cole. *The Giant's Rival: The USSR and Latin America.* Pittsburgh: University of Pittsburgh Press, 1983.

——. *The Hovering Giant: U.S. Responses to Revolutionary Change in Latin America.* Pittsburgh: University of Pittsburgh Press, 1976.

Burr, Robert N. *Our Troubled Hemisphere.* Washington, D.C.: Brookings Institution, 1967.

Child, John. *Unequal Alliance: The Inter-American Military System, 1938–1978.* Boulder, Colo.: Westview, 1980.

Cobbs, Elizabeth E. *The Rich Neighbor Policy: Rockefeller and Kaiser in Brazil.* New Haven, Conn.: Yale University Press, 1992.

Commission on United States-Latin American Relations. *The Americas in a Changing World.* New York: Quadrangle Books, 1975.

——. *The United States and Latin America: Next Steps.* New York: Center for Inter-American Relations, 1976.

Cottam, Martha L. *Images and Intervention: U.S. Policies in Latin America.* Pittsburgh: University of Pittsburgh Press, 1994.

Cullather, Nick. *Secret History: The CIA's Classified Account of its Operations in Guatemala, 1952–1954.* Stanford, Calif.: Stanford University Press, 1999.

Davis, Nathaniel. *The Last Two Years of Salvador Allende.* Ithaca, N.Y.: Cornell University Press, 1985.

Davis, Sonny B. *A Brotherhood of Arms: Brazil-United States Military Relations, 1945–1977*. Niwot: University Press of Colorado, 1994.

Eisenhower, Milton. *The Wine Is Bitter: The United States and Latin America*. Garden City, N.Y.: Doubleday, 1963.

Gambone, Michael D. *Capturing the Revolution: The United States, Central America, and Nicaragua, 1961–1972*. Westport, Conn.: Praeger, 2001.

———. *Eisenhower, Somoza, and the Cold War in Nicaragua, 1953–1961*. Westport, Conn.: Praeger, 1997.

Gleijeses, Piero. *The Dominican Crisis: The 1965 Constitutionalist Revolt and American Intervention*. Baltimore: Johns Hopkins University Press, 1978.

———. *Shattered Hope: The Guatemalan Revolution and the United States, 1944–1954*. Princeton, N.J.: Princeton University Press, 1991.

Haines, Gerald K. *The Americanization of Brazil: A Study of U.S. Cold War Diplomacy in the Third World, 1945–1954*. Wilmington, Del.: Scholarly Resources, 1989.

Hersh, Seymour M. *Kissinger: The Price of Power. Henry Kissinger in the White House*. London: Faber & Faber, 1983.

Higgins, Trumbull. *The Perfect Failure: Kennedy, Eisenhower, and the CIA at the Bay of Pigs*. New York: Norton, 1987.

Huggins, Martha K. *Political Policing: The United States and Latin America*. Durham, N.C.: Duke University Press, 1998.

Immerman, Richard H. *The CIA in Guatemala: The Foreign Policy of Intervention*. Austin: University of Texas Press, 1982.

Jorden, William J. *Panama Odyssey*. Austin: University of Texas Press, 1984.

Langley, Lester D. *Mexico and the United States: The Fragile Relationship*. Boston: Twane.

Leacock, Ruth. *Requiem for Revolution: The United States and Brazil, 1961–1969*. Kent, Ohio: Kent State University Press, 1990.

Levinson, Jerome, and Juan de Onís. *The Alliance That Lost Its Way: A Critical Report on the Alliance for Progress*. Chicago: Quadrangle Books, 1970.

Longley, Kyle. *The Sparrow and the Hawk: Costa Rica and the United States during the Rise of José Figueres*. Tuscaloosa: University of Alabama Press, 1997.

Lowenthal, Abraham F. *The Dominican Intervention*. Cambridge, Mass.: Harvard University Press, 1972.

———, ed. *Exporting Democracy: The United States and Latin America: Themes and Issues*. Baltimore: Johns Hopkins University Press, 1991.

McPherson, Alan. *Intimate Ties, Bitter Struggles: The United States and Latin America since 1945*. Washington, D.C.: Potomac Books, 2006.

———. *Yankee No! Anti-Americanism in U.S.-Latin American Relations*. Cambridge, Mass.: Harvard University Press, 2003.

Martz, John D. *Communist Infiltration in Guatemala*. New York: Vintage Press, 1956.

———, ed. *United States Policy in Latin America: A Quarter Century of Crisis and Challenge, 1961–1986* Lincoln: University of Nebraska Press, 1988.

Miller, Nicola. *Soviet Relations with Latin America, 1959–1987*. New York: Cambridge University Press, 1989.

Muñoz, Heraldo, ed. *Las políticas exteriores latinoamericana frente a la crisis*. Buenos Aires: Grupo Editor Latinoamericano, 1985.

Newfarmer, Richard, ed. *From Gunboats to Diplomacy: New U.S. Policies for Latin America*. Baltimore: Johns Hopkins University Press, 1984.

Niblo, Stephen R. *War, Diplomacy, and Development: The United States and Mexico, 1938–1954*. Wilmington, Del.: Scholarly Resources, 1995.

Parker, Phyllis R. *Brazil and the Quiet Intervention, 1964*. Austin: University of Texas Press, 1979.

Paterson, Thomas G. *Contesting Castro: The United States and the Triumph of the Cuban Revolution*. New York: Oxford University Press, 1994.

Prados, John. *Presidents' Secret Wars: CIA and Pentagon Covert Operations since World War II*. New York: William Morrow, 1986.

Quirk, Robert E. *Fidel Castro*. New York: Norton, 1993.

Rabe, Stephen G. *Eisenhower and Latin America: The Foreign Policy of Anti-communism*. Chapel Hill: University of North Carolina Press, 1988.

———. *The Most Dangerous Area in the World: John F. Kennedy Confronts Communist Revolution in Latin America*. Chapel Hill: University of North Carolina Press, 1999.

———. *U.S. Intervention in British Guiana: A Cold War Story*. Chapel Hill: University of North Carolina Press, 2005.

Rivas, Darlene. *Missionary Capitalist: Nelson Rockefeller in Venezuela*. Chapel Hill: University of North Carolina Press, 2002.

Rockefeller, Nelson A. *The Rockefeller Report on the Americas*. Chicago: Quadrangle Books, 1969.

Rogers, William D. *The Twilight Struggle: The Alliance for Progress and the Politics of Development in Latin America*. New York: Random House, 1967.

Schlesinger, Arthur M., Jr. *A Thousand Days: John F. Kennedy in the White House*. Boston: Houghton Mifflin, 1965.

Schlesinger, Stephen, and Stephen Kinzer. *Bitter Fruit: The Untold Story of the American Coup in Guatemala*. Garden City, N.Y.: Doubleday, 1982.

Schneider, Ronald M. *Communism in Guatemala, 1944–1954*. New York: Praeger, 1958.

Schoultz, Lars. *Human Rights and the United States Policy toward Latin America*. Princeton, N.J.: Princeton University Press, 1981.

———. *National Security and United States Policy toward Latin America*. Princeton, N.J.: Princeton University Press, 1987.

Sigmund, Paul E. *The Overthrow of Allende and the Politics of Chile, 1964–1976.* Pittsburgh: University of Pittsburgh Press, 1977.

Slater, Jerome. *The OAS and United States Foreign Policy.* Columbus: Ohio State University Press, 1967.

Smith, Gaddis. *The Last Years of the Monroe Doctrine, 1945–1993.* New York: Hill and Wang, 1994.

Streeter, Stephen M. *Managing the Counterrevolution: The United States and Guatemala, 1954–1961.* Athens: Ohio University Center for International Studies, 2000.

Weis, W. Michael. *Cold Warriors and Coups d'état: Brazilian-American Relations, 1945–1964* Albuquerque: University of New Mexico Press, 1993.

Wood, Bryce. *The Dismantling of the Good Neighbor Policy.* Austin: University of Texas Press, 1985.

XIII. TRANSITION TO A NEW CENTURY

Arnson, Cynthia J. *Crossroads: Congress, the President, and Central America, 1976–1993.* University Park: Pennsylvania State University Press, 1993.

Bagley, Bruce M., ed. *Contadora and the Diplomacy of Peace in Central America.* 2 vols. Boulder, Colo.: Westview, 1987.

Bandeira, Moniz. *As relações perigosas: Brasil-Estados Unidos (De Collor a Lula, 1990–2004).* Rio de Janeiro: Civilizacão Brasileira, 2004.

Carothers, Thomas. *In the Name of Democracy: U.S. Policy toward Latin America in the Reagan Years.* Berkeley: University of California Press, 1991.

Child, Jack. *The Central American Peace Process, 1983–1991: Sheathing Swords, Building Confidence.* Boulder, Colo.: Lynne Rienner, 1992.

Committee of Santa Fe. *A New Inter-American Policy for the Eighties.* Washington, D.C.: Council for Inter-American Security, 1980.

Grayson, George W. *The North American Free Trade Agreement: Regional Community and the New World Order.* Lanham, Md.: University Press of America, 1995.

Haig, Alexander M., Jr. *Caveat: Realism, Reagan, and Foreign Policy.* New York: Macmillan, 1984.

Jorden, William J. *Panama Odyssey.* Austin: University of Texas Press, 1984.

LeoGrande, William M. *Our Own Backward: The United States in Central America, 1977–1992.* Chapel Hill: University of North Carolina Press, 1998.

Lorey, David E. *The U.S.-Mexican Border in the Twentieth Century: A History of Economic and Social Transformation.* Wilmington, Del.: Scholarly Resources, 1999.

Lowenthal, Abraham. *Partners In Conflict: The United States and Latin America.* Baltimore: Johns Hopkins University Press, 1987.

Martz, John D., ed. *United States Policy in Latin America: A Decade of Crisis and Challenge* Lincoln: University of Nebraska Press, 1995.

Menjivar, Cecilia, and Nestor Rodriguez, eds. *When States Kill: Latin America, the U.S. and the Technologies of Terror.* Austin: University of Texas Press, 2005.

Middlebrook, Kevin, and Carlos Rico, eds. *The United States and Latin America in the 1980s: Contending Perspectives in a Decade of Crisis.* Pittsburgh: University of Pittsburgh Press, 1986.

Newfarmer, Richard S., ed. *From Gunboats to Diplomacy: New U.S. Policies for Latin America.* Baltimore: Johns Hopkins University Press, 1984.

Pastor, Robert A. *Whirlpool: U.S. Foreign Policy toward Latin America and the Caribbean.* Princeton, N.J.: Princeton University Press, 1992.

Ryan, David. *U.S.-Sandinista Diplomatic Relations: Voice of Intolerance.* New York: St. Martin's Press, 1995.

Schoultz, Lars. *Human Rights and United States Policy toward Latin America.* Princeton, N.J.: Princeton University Press, 1981.

Scranton, Margaret E. *The Noriega Years: U.S.-Panamanian Relations, 1981–1990.* Boulder, Colo.: Lynne Rienner, 1991.

Smith, Christian. *Resisting Reagan: The U.S. Central American Peace Movement.* Chicago: University of Chicago Press, 1996.

Solaun, Mauricio. *U.S. Intervention and Regime Change in Nicaragua.* Lincoln: University of Nebraska Press, 2005.

Walker, Thomas W., ed. *Reagan versus the Sandinistas: The Undeclared War on Nicaragua.* Boulder, Colo.: Westview, 1987.

Walker, William O. *Drug Control in the Americas.* Albuquerque: University of New Mexico Press, 1989.

About the Author

Joseph Smith (B.A., Durham University; Ph.D., London University) is a reader in American diplomatic history in the Department of History at Exeter University, England. An expert on American foreign relations, especially with Latin America, he has conducted archival research in Brazil, Argentina, and Chile. He is a fellow of the Royal Historical Society of Great Britain and a member of the Council of the Historical Association of Great Britain. He has written several books, including *A History of Brazil, 1500–2000* (2002), *The United States and Latin America: A History of American Diplomacy, 1776–2000* (2005), and, with Simon Davis, *Historical Dictionary of the Cold War* (Scarecrow, 2000) and *The A to Z of the Cold War* (Scarecrow, 2005). He has also been the editor for several years of *History*, the journal of the Historical Association of Great Britain.